WHAT CHINA AND INDIA ONCE WERE

What China and India Once Were

THE PASTS THAT MAY SHAPE
THE GLOBAL FUTURE

EDITED BY

Sheldon Pollock and Benjamin Elman

Columbia University Press
New York

Columbia University Press
Publishers Since 1893
New York   Chichester, West Sussex
cup.columbia.edu
Copyright © 2018 Columbia University Press

All rights reserved
Library of Congress Cataloging-in-Publication Data
Names: Pollock, Sheldon I., editor. | Elman, Benjamin A., 1946- editor.
Title: What China and India once were : the pasts that may shape the global future /
edited by Sheldon Pollock and Benjamin Elman.
Description: New York : Columbia University Press, [2018] | Includes bibliographical
references and index.
Identifiers: LCCN 2018006946 (print) | LCCN 2018022232 (ebook) |
ISBN 9780231545624 (electronic) | ISBN 9780231184700 (cloth)
Subjects: LCSH: India—History. | China—History. | India—Social life and customs. |
China—Social life and customs.
Classification: LCC DS421 (ebook) | LCC DS421 .W43 2018 (print) | DDC 951—dc23
LC record available at https://lccn.loc.gov/2018006946

Cover design: Guerrilla Design
Cover images: Top: A Literary Gathering at Hsi Yuann in the eleventh century
(colour litho), Chou Ying (fl.1550) (after) / Bibliotheque des Arts Decoratifs,
Paris, France / Archives Charmet / Bridgeman Images
Bottom: Courtesy of The David Collection, Copenhagen, (20.6-D28-1994-Foedsel-i-et-palads).
Photograph by Pernille Klemp.

Contents

Preface vii
Maps ix

Introduction
Benjamin Elman and Sheldon Pollock 1

PART I

I   Life and Energy
Sumit Guha and Kenneth Pomeranz 27

II   Conquest, Rulership, and the State
Pamela Crossley and Richard M. Eaton 63

III   Gender Systems: The Exotic Asian and Other Fallacies
Beverly Bossler and Ruby Lal 93

PART II

IV   Relating the Past: Writing (and Rewriting) History
Cynthia Brokaw and Allison Busch 127

V Sorting Out Babel: Literature and Its Changing Languages
   Stephen Owen and Sheldon Pollock 165

PART III

VI Big Science: Classicism and Conquest
    Benjamin Elman and Christopher Minkowski 199

VII Pilgrims in Search of Religion
     Zvi Ben-Dor Benite and Richard H. Davis 232

VIII Art and Vision: Varieties of World Making
      Molly Aitken and Eugene Wang 265

Afterword: The Act of Comparing (Both Sides, Now)
Dipesh Chakrabarty and Haun Saussy 310

Chronology 343
Chinese and Indian Terms 345
List of Contributors 347
Index 349

Preface and Acknowledgments

What China and India Once Were was from the first conceived as a book for the general educated reader. We have accordingly avoided the narrower scholarly controversies and dense footnoting that mark academic writing, and have tried as far as possible to eliminate the even denser jargon that often mars it. We have provided brief suggestions for further reading at the end of each chapter where interested readers can find up-to-date guidance for pursuing particular questions; maps (general maps of China and India in the early modern era, and bearing the names of places cited in the chapters; and political maps illustrating Qing and Mughal expansion); a timeline of all kingdoms, dynasties, and the like referred to in the text; and a brief glossary of technical terms.

The editors are deeply grateful to the Andrew W. Mellon Foundation for the Distinguished Achievement Award that each of us received and that permitted us to imagine this project in the first place and bring it to fruition.

At Princeton, we thank the Princeton Institute for International and Regional Studies for its support of the East Asia Research Cluster. Additional support came from the Princeton East Asian Studies Department and Program; the David A. Gardner '69 Magic Project Grants in the Princeton Humanities Council; the Davis Center in the Princeton History Department; and the Princeton–EAS Mellon Project coordinators Kathleen Amon and Jenny Chao-Hui Liu. Jessica Rechtschaffer of Columbia's Middle

Eastern, South Asian, and African Studies Department provided essential assistance in the administration of the Mellon award.

Daniel Barish, formerly of the Princeton history department and now teaching at Baylor University, served as rapporteur at our gatherings. Quinn Clark of the Columbia religion department helped assemble our maps and other ancillary materials.

Jennifer Crewe, director of Columbia University Press, has been a strong supporter of our initiative and graciously welcomed the proposal when we submitted it to the Press. Leslie Kriesel provided outstanding editorial guidance just about from the beginning of the project to the very end. Lisa Moore offered important help as development editor. Thomas Trautmann and a second (anonymous) reviewer for the Press helped us improve the overall structure of the book. To all of them we express our deep appreciation.

Benjamin Elman, Princeton
Sheldon Pollock, Columbia

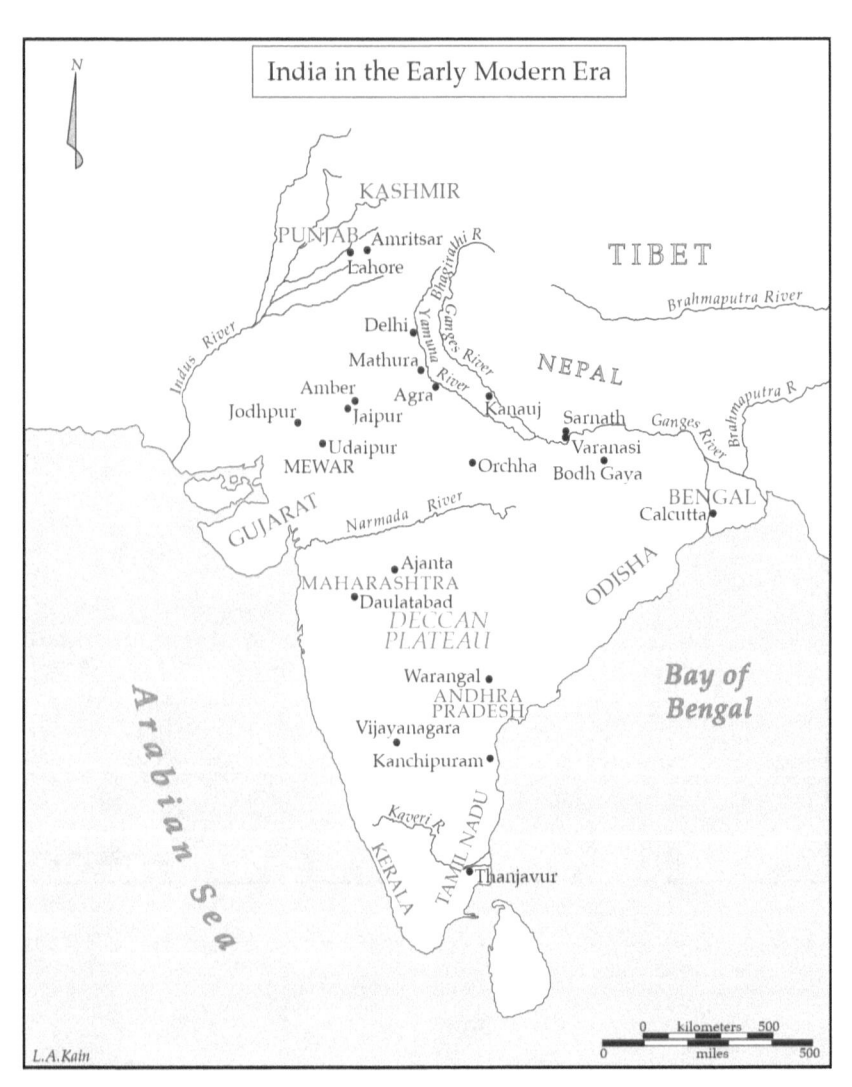

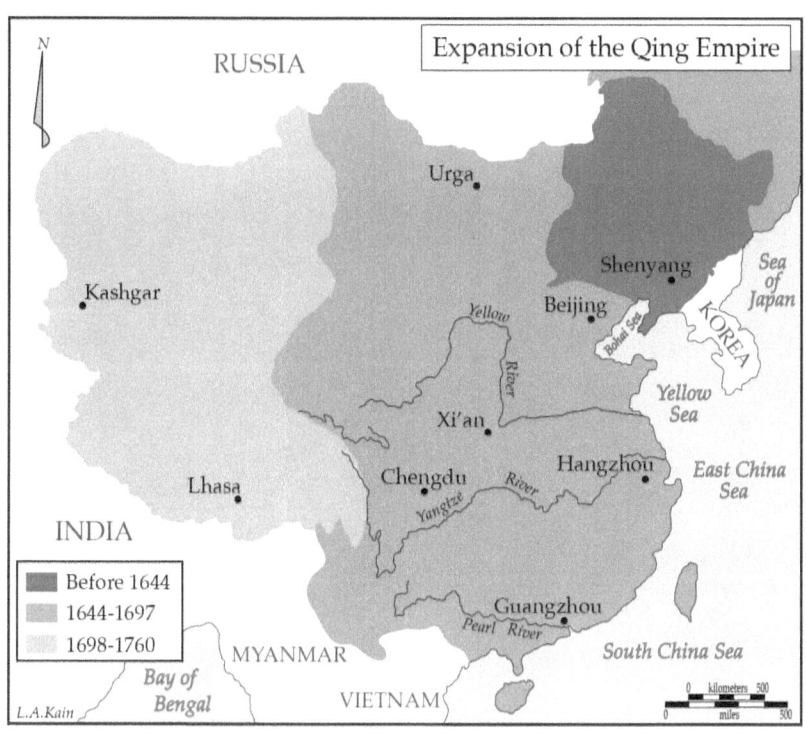

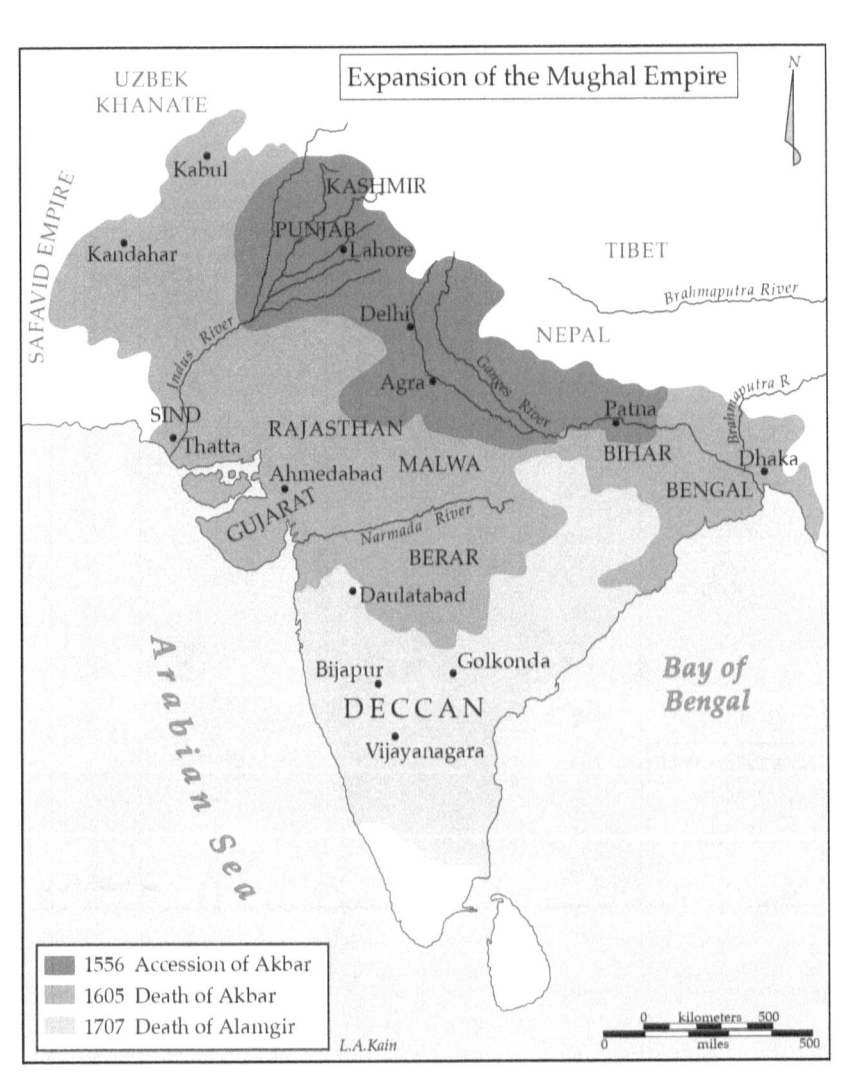

WHAT CHINA AND INDIA ONCE WERE

Introduction

BENJAMIN ELMAN AND SHELDON POLLOCK

Open a recent newspaper and you are likely to read about some incident of Hindu–Muslim violence in India. You are also likely to have read that such incidents happen because Hindus and Muslims have hated each other for centuries. Or you may have learned that, on the contrary, these tensions are the result of the divide-and-rule strategy used by the British during the colonial period, or the mobilizing tactics of contemporary nationalist political parties. In the same way, many observers who reflect on the prevalence of Chinese manufactured goods on our store shelves would think that China has always had abundant and obedient, cheap labor, or that it has always learned from the West, has now adopted capitalism and industrial technology, and is beating us at our own game. People similarly assume that the many successful students from China and India enrolled in U.S. universities are either showing traditional reverence for education or just taking advantage of the opportunities our society offers, as immigrants have always done. The fabulous weddings and dowries of Indian brides and the lavish funerals of Chinese elites are either traditional expressions (of female subordination in the one case and ancestor worship in the other) or demonstrations of how Western consumerism has penetrated every aspect of Eastern life.

In all these cases, the stories are actually much messier than these facile accounts suggest. On the one hand, we are not encountering unchangeable and typically burdensome essences inherited from the hoary past. Yet, on the other, not everything that really matters is a creation of the modern period and the transformative powers the West has exerted. On both sides we find truisms that are seriously misleading. Knowing something about the pasts of China and India can give us a better sense of which features have or have not been perpetuated. And thereby a better understanding of the present—not a definitive but a more textured and dynamic understanding—becomes possible, along with better practices. In addition, seeking knowledge of these pasts across the wide spectrum of activities and identities that made traditional life no less complex, if differently complex, than modern life is one way to increase the depth of that knowledge. And last, knowing them comparatively helps ensure that China and India recover their individuality and specificity, and do not fall victim to this or that large, equally facile explanatory account that usually winds up homogenizing all past societies ("Oriental despotism" in the nineteenth century, for example, and "modernization theory" in the twentieth).

These three ways of knowing frame the three aims of this book: (1) to explore the nature of Asian pasts so as to get a better grasp of Asian presents; (2) to establish a domain of inquiry broad enough to investigate both these sets of issues with some hope of adequacy; and (3) to directly compare non-European countries.

While all three objectives have presented challenges to the contributors of this book, there are some basic areas where we achieved clear consensus. While the past is not inevitably prologue, the present cannot come to exist or be understood without it. Making sense of its shaping influence across a wide arena of traditional life allows us to better understand its durability into the present. Understanding its particularities through comparison enables us to better grasp how contingent the present really is—to realize, in other words, that it is the product of enduring forces that might easily have worked out differently, and that may well do so in the future.

Why China and India?

The 2015 United Nations Climate Change Summit offered compelling evidence of what so many other global indicators, from stock market shifts to security threats to trends in popular culture, have long suggested to attentive observers: China and India have become decisive players in determining the world's future. The commitment to cut carbon emissions that these two countries made will affect the fate of the planet in more fundamental ways than the actions of any other nation except the United States. And indeed, with the U.S. withdrawal from the accords in June 2017 and new evidence that both China and India appear to be on track to beat the targets they set in the UN agreement, it may even ensure the world has a future.

That the influence of China and India is on the rise is not news, of course. Their entry onto the world stage has been on the radar of politicians, business leaders, scholars, journalists, and others for several decades. And a substantial body of literature has been produced during this period testifying to the varied reactions—now welcoming, now anxious, almost always surprised if not bemused—to this historic development. What has not often been realized, let alone seriously examined, is the fact that this "entry" is actually a re-entry. Such an examination would need to ask what the two nations were like during the period of their first global domination some five or six centuries ago; how those older ways of life may have shaped their presents; and, perhaps most intriguingly, what comparison between the two can help us learn about each.

One simple explanation why these questions have not been systematically explored is that doing so is no easy task. The meaning of the past for the present, as just noted, is a general problem that haunts, or should haunt, every historian. Even the truth that there is no single "past" anywhere, let alone a past that works in a direct way on the present, often goes unacknowledged. Nobel Prize winner Amartya Sen, for example, recently asked "Why is China ahead of India?" He pinpoints contemporary India's low overall quality of education, poor health care, and skewed energy provision, among other subsidies, in saying that contemporary India has "failed to learn" the East Asian lesson. But are things that simple? Is any role in this "failure" to be assigned to, say, India's deep history of inequality? The 20 percent of India's population classified as untouchable/tribal has been part of the structure of Indian society for a long time, while evidence for some sort of meritocratic processes via civil examinations is available for China long before the modern era. Can we provide any good explanation for their present without reference to their past?

In addition, comparison between the two regions has never been the norm in scholarship. The deficit can in part be explained by the fact that, to be convincing, comparison requires a level playing field—we must compare comparables—and careful consideration about how to level it reveals some hard conceptual puzzles, not only in the comparison between China and India but equally in the comparison of the two with the West. During the period roughly from 1250 to 1600, for example, China and India (along with Persia) were the global leaders in mathematical astronomy. Their complex calendrical systems were models for the Pax Mongolica centered on the Yuan dynasty (1280–1368) in Beijing and the Ilkhanate in Tabriz, as well as, later, Mughal India. Yet, Western scholars have routinely associated early modern discoveries in astronomy and mathematics with the "rise of the West" after the "age of Copernicus," 1500–1700. Such deep-seated preconceptions about the world can derail comparison even before it can begin.

Thus, our comparative historical aspirations are at once confronted by several hard, overarching questions. It is a challenge to understand not only how the pasts of China and India relate to their presents but also how to compare them directly with each other without the disrupting presence of Western standards and received views. And there are three additional problems: What do the terms "China" and "India" actually refer to, and how did these referents became the conceptually unified entities they are—whatever those entities (regions? civilizations? nations?) may be? Which parts of their millennial pasts count as relevant to their relationship to the present? How is direct comparison of non-Western traditions supposed even to start if we deprive ourselves of the supposedly stable categories—"state," "literature," "art," "religion," and the like—that the Western lexicon automatically would seem to provide?

What Is "China" and What Is "India"?

The countries, nations, regions, or civilizations—depending on how we define these apparently simple but actually complex terms—that we now identify by the names China and India have long and complicated histories. Any particular definition of either China or India is going to appear, to sharp historical eyes, to be dubious generalization, a freeze-frame, as it were, of a continuously running film of development and change. Yet, even while we acknowledge continuous change, certain constants of internal practices and external assessments still allow us to make use of these categories with the same cautious confidence with which we employ the equally messy "Europe" (or, messier, "West").

"China": The Central Kingdom?

The China that resides in the minds of most of us as a coherent object of study is the "Central Kingdom"—the literal translation of *Zhongguo*, the Chinese name for "China"—an idea dating back to the idealized early empires of Qin and Han, circa 200 BCE to 200 CE. Of these two, the Han has been by far the most influential. It was long-lived; it committed legitimate governments in traditional China to public veneration of Confucius (551–479 BCE) and his ostensible social, ethical, and political ideals; and it bequeathed the name of the identity of the majority of the "Han" Chinese population today. Our imaginary view of unbroken Chinese unity is largely based on a formulaic rendering of Han history and culture. The righteousness of social hierarchy, the power of standardized language and ritual, and the social justice of a society that privileges agriculture and marginalizes commerce and technology have all become features of a distinct "China" that is neither entirely repudiated nor entirely justified by the richness of history.

Whereas "China" is not some confection of early modern lore but has a deeper, if ultimately elusive, conceptual history, we question a starting point that predetermines an idealized classical world asserting itself effortlessly in the hearts and minds of Han Chinese and their culturally diverse neighbors. For half its history, today's geographic China has been divided among states of Han Chinese and of Turkic, Mongolian, Tibetan, and Manchurian origin, all of which contributed to the economic and cultural development of what we recognize as China, yielding an unstable political environment of contending Han Chinese insiders and non-Han outsiders. The last dynasty, the Qing (1644–1912), rose from Manchurian roots to create a complex, cosmopolitan culture and expansive political boundaries that are the direct sources of modern China's world stature.

"India": A Not So New Nation

Independence in 1947 brought cataclysmic partition to the country that the British ruled for more than a century as "India," creating Pakistan in the west and, in 1971, Bangladesh in the east. (Ceylon, later renamed Sri Lanka, attained independence in 1948.) The entrance of India and the rest into the post–World War II world order at the same time led some observers, deceived by the apparent timelessness of their own nations, to think of India as a new one. (E. M. Forster wrote, with mock incredulity, in 1924: "India a nation! What an apotheosis! . . . Waddling in at this hour of the world to take her seat!") But the idea of India, some sort of idea, is far older. Ancient Sanskrit geographies describe a "Clime of the Bharatas" (Bharatavarsha) that, while shading into fantasy around the edges, marks off a familiar South Asian space.

Greeks as early as Herodotus spoke of an *indikē* (*chōrē*), an "Indian" place or land (referring to the lands east of the Indus River); the Chinese Buddhist pilgrim Xuanzang (603–664) named it Indu; Arab traders and military adventurers some centuries later took to calling it Al-Hind (again referencing the Indus) and later Hindustan, the "Place of the Indians." Recognizable Indian forms of political organization and religious belief no doubt spread far from the South Asian landmass in the first millennium, creating the so-called Indianized states of Southeast Asia (including Thailand, Cambodia, and southern Vietnam) and carrying Buddhism as far west as Iran and into Central Asia, and, along with Hinduism, as far east as Java and Bali. Yet the Indian subcontinent itself was subject to imperial processes, such as those of the Mauryas (322–187 BCE), the Kushans (c. 30–230), the Guptas (320–550), and the Mughal (1526–1857), that largely hewed to its geographical boundaries and, in some measure at least, imposed or sought to impose integrating structures of rule across a population dramatically varied in languages, customs, and beliefs.

If Indian cultural practices and products spread far and wide, with Sanskrit poetry being written by Cambodian princes in Angkor in the tenth century and Indo-Persian poetry circulating as far as Istanbul in the seventeenth, the generative core was known to be a geocultural space largely coterminous with today's South Asia. Indeed, even though the phrase "South Asia" is a recent coinage, the region itself possesses some sort of coherence—an unfamiliar, prenational sort of coherence—that is far older.

Accordingly, when, the contributors to this book refer to "Chinese" or "Indian" art or literature or science, they do so with a lively awareness that, while the categories are certainly labile and are marked far more by diversity than by homogeneity, their referent is a recognizable and analytically meaningful one.

What Parts of Their Pasts Matter?

Ongoing archeological research in both regions takes human habitation and, to some degree, recognizable cultural patterns back to at least the third millennium BCE. It would take another book to explore the processes of unification and consolidation of the two regions and their long-term continuity as early agrarian, literate societies. Instead, our intention here has been to concentrate on what scholars now call, not without some hesitation, the "early modern" period, generally taken to comprise the three or four centuries before 1800. We admittedly lose sight of some important features by foreshortening our gaze. But what we lose in terms of scope we gain, we think, in terms of comprehensiveness.

That said, there is by no means universal agreement about the precise boundaries of this early modern period for either of the two regions, let alone that those boundaries are the same for both. The end point of the early modern is largely unproblematic, for around 1800 many processes were set in motion, especially in global commerce and industrialization, that would constitute the sharpest break with the past in the historical record of both countries and set them on a path toward ever greater convergence with the modern West.

In China, the Opium War (1839–42) epitomized the British empire's triumph over China via the shibboleth of "free" commerce, whereby English opium merchants traded for Chinese tea and thereby reversed the flow of Chinese silver back to India and Great Britain. The Manchu empire ended with the Republican revolution of 1911; Japan took advantage of China's reversal of fortune to invade and make China part of the Japanese empire by 1937. Final independence came with the establishment of the People's Republic of China in 1949. In India, 1800 marks the start in earnest of British colonialism, which would gain momentum through the century: Thanjavur (Tanjore, in south India) was taken by Lord Wellesley in 1776; Varanasi in the north was ceded to the British in 1803; in the west, the Peshwas of Maharashtra were defeated in the course of the following decade (1817–1818). The Indian Rebellion of 1857 led to the nation's formal incorporation into the British empire a year later, where it would remain until gaining independence in 1947.

What causes difficulty, then, is not the chronological end point of our study, which is well known, but the starting point we have chosen—"three or four centuries before 1800"—and the conceptual coherence of the "early modernity" that underlies that choice. While many enduring features of the two regions long antedate even these older eras (and some contributors to the book begin their stories centuries earlier), it was during the early modern period that distinctive form was given to many patterns of polity, society, and culture that persisted until the coming of Western modernity. That said, the early modern era more strictly conceived (c. 1500–1800) has historical salience in both spheres, as recent scholarship has been increasingly able to demonstrate. It is characterized by important transformations that mark a new era while at the same time underscoring the durability of older civilizational features. The two regions saw comparable dramatic changes in trade, as they participated in what for the first time became a truly global system; in demography, with the tripling of China's population and the doubling of India's; in state formation, where large-scale imperial formations were consolidated; in urbanization, monetization, and elsewhere.

Early Modernity in the Ming-Qing Era

The Ming-Qing dynastic rule that marks the beginnings of the early modern period in China produced social, demographic, and economic pressures that placed new demands on the Qing dynasty (1644–1911) that the rulers, now Manchus, and government scholar-officials, still Han Chinese, had never faced before. These pressures include the just-mentioned rise, steep and unprecedented, in general population from about 1500 to 1700 (proportionally paralleling the rates of global population increase), despite severe episodes of prolonged disorder connected to the late Ming rural uprisings that made the Qing invasion possible; the recovery and dramatic expansion of the systems of internal transportation; an increase of arable land and efficiency in agricultural production, making possible larger urban populations and greater commercial specialization in the countryside; the displacement of much of the traditional elite (largely due to the Qing conquest) and promotion of a new ruling caste; greater engagement with regional and global societies through trade, travel, strategic rivalry, and conscious cultural relativity.

This latter infiltration refers to acknowledgment of European achievement in science, technology, architecture; legalization of Christian freedom to proselytize (before the middle eighteenth century), dissemination of

American "New World" and African crops, and attendant changes in foodways; customization of Chinese products to meet the specifications of foreign brokers; acceptance of innovative institutions of credit, security, and legal administration in response to growing commercial engagement with Korea, Britain, and France in particular; creation of a recognizably diplomatic treaty relationship with Russia. In addition, ancient ideals drawn from earlier times were already deemed unsatisfactory. Many Han literati realized that the institutions enshrined in the imperial system were not inviolate. To "accord with the new times" became the slogan of a generation of statecraft (*jingshi*) scholars who during the early nineteenth century sought pragmatic solutions to the myriad organizational and logistical breakdowns that seemed to come all at once. The Opium War and anti-Manchu Taiping Rebellion (1850–1864) exacerbated such tensions. With hindsight, we know that Qing China, like Mughal India, was also on the eve of a confrontation with Western imperialism, which would unleash revolutionary forces at all levels of society.

Early Modernity in the Mughal Era

In India, a similar political transformation occurred with the founding of the Mughal Empire in 1526. Although the Delhi sultans had nourished an ideal of limitless political space, it was the Mughals who—like their Qing, Ottoman, Spanish, and Habsburg contemporaries—actually achieved the characteristically early modern institution of a large-scale "universal" empire. Proud of their descent from Timur (r. 1370–1405), founder of the Timurid Empire (1307–1526) in Central Asia and Persia, the Mughals emulated their famous ancestor, just as Timur himself had patterned his career of universal world conquest on the remarkable achievement of Chinggis Khan (1162–1227; r. 1206–1227). Regarding statecraft, scientific surveys of a country's resources and products, together with an increased use of skilled bureaucrats, were hallmarks of early modern states everywhere. And in India, it was the Mughals who first established standard units of measurement and maintained offices of meticulous record keepers and auditors, departing from the more haphazard methods of earlier regimes. Meanwhile, professional Hindu banking and clerical castes became prominent in their sprawling bureaucratic machine. By the end of the sixteenth century, their revenue and judicial administrations also exhibited an obsessive preoccupation with order, the efficient management of time, and a spirit of rational self-control—all of them characteristics of early modernity.

Mughal India's early modern character, like China's, is also seen in its integration with an expanding global economy. Within just fifty years of the empire's launching, the descendants of Babur (r. 1526–1530), founder of the Mughal dynasty, had conquered the wealthy and commercially vibrant coastal province of Gujarat, and soon Bengal as well. Despite their roots in land-locked, seminomadic Inner Asia, the Mughals thereby joined a global network of maritime trafficking and commerce, with far-reaching consequences. Expanded cash crops (tea, coffee, opium, sugar, tobacco) and new food crops (potatoes, maize, chilies, tomatoes, etc.) transformed India's patterns of production and consumption, while the diffusion of gunpowder and cannon technology helped the Mughals consolidate their power across the flat Indo-Gangetic plain. Perhaps most important, by the early 1600s, Dutch and English trading companies had begun carrying vast quantities of New World silver to Mughal seaports in Gujarat and Bengal. Because India possessed hardly any silver mines of her own, minting this imported metal into coinage significantly monetized the Mughal economy, which in turn enhanced merchant wealth, eroded social barriers, and intensified land use, since mobile cash helped marshal labor to transform dense tracts of jungle into arable fields for cultivating food crops.

The Mughals also created the context for new and dynamic circulation, innovation, and experimentation in many areas of society, including the intellectual and artistic spheres. Mughal cultural life evinces a fascinating blend of Persian and more local styles. Emperor Akbar (1556–1605) is famous for his commitment to translating Sanskrit classics into Persian. He and his son Jahangir (r. 1605–1627) organized philosophical and religious debates at court and were avidly interested in Indian thought. The official political ethos of the day was "peace for all" (*sulh-i kull*), a guarantee that people of different religious backgrounds would be protected by the state. Persian literati and adventurers from around the globe found a congenial home in the cosmopolitan centers of the empire. Mughal painting offers an especially eloquent example of the new sensibilities. Here the world was embodied more tangibly than in any earlier Indian art form. Master painters in imperial ateliers studied European imagery and adopted techniques according to their own needs. Intuitive perspective and other methods, along with the extensive study of nature and individuation, made for a naturalism that diverged from the Persian tradition from which it had directly descended, as well as from earlier Indic idealism.

Comparing the pasts of China and India is not, however, merely a question of finding parallels that qualify them for the title of "early modern." What we now consider early modern in European terms may have roots in the trading and textual worlds of East and South Asia. But before we consider what to compare, we need to ask why compare at all, and how.

The Logic of Comparison

Many scholars, especially in the last few decades, have sought to avoid comparison for various reasons, prominent among them the troubling historical origins, in colonial science, of "comparativism," or the systematic method of comparing. More recent times have seen a new interest in capturing what we might call processes of mutuality, where actual interactions of two cases produced exchanges and influences. This sort of "connected history" (sometimes called contingent, entangled, or crossed history) is usually offered as a corrective or even replacement for comparative study. While we acknowledge and try as far as possible to avoid the prejudices of colonial comparison, we have also avoided the connective history approach. China and India have interacted for two or more millennia in every domain from to art to literature, religion, and science, not to speak of the more concrete exchanges of trade and diplomacy, so much so that to try to separate these phenomena is to tear apart a real and densely woven fabric. But what we seek to capture here is not those connections and the ensuing emergence of particular material or cultural phenomena—their embryology, so to speak—but rather the nature of those phenomena when fully achieved—their physiology.

We are accordingly concerned less with whether or not Chinese painting influenced Indian painting or Indian literature Chinese literature. To know that the Chinese or Indians borrowed this or that cultural element from the other and preserved or changed them only adds to the basic problem of comparison, and does not fundamentally reconstitute it. What interests us is what the Chinese and the Indians did with a given political, social, or cultural form, not where those forms may have originated. One chapter, on science, does occasionally explore connection in addition to comparison, but that procedure is dictated by the peculiar nature of the object of study: no boundary whether regional or civilizational, in the past or today, can bar the movement of science. While traditions of learning in the two worlds developed along their own lines, their history is in considerable part a history of how the learned classes and their patrons responded to the availability of new knowledge from elsewhere. This "elsewhere" in the early modern period was Central Asia, from which both China and India imported new astronomical knowledge.

If comparison is the paramount method of this book, we need to explain what it means, or what we believe it means, to think comparatively. From one rather abstract Western viewpoint going back to Immanuel Kant in the late eighteenth century and Georg Friedrich Hegel in the early nineteenth, it is clear that humans cannot *not* think comparatively, that comparison is fundamental to knowledge. The identity of any given thing is established by implicit comparison with what it is not. A person cannot be tall or beautiful or rich except by comparison with less fortunate others. Comparativism, however, as a formalized mode of systematic thought, is by no means fundamental or even in fact all that old. It is largely unknown in the world before the rise of early modern Europe and seems to have taken on a particular urgency as European colonialism encountered and sought to master, through systematic knowledge, many of those perceived, comparatively, as less fortunate others.

A crucial aspect of the colonial sort of comparativism is the defining status given to the European "standard" (the *secundum comparatum*, to use the technical term of Western rhetoric, to which *biaozhun* in Chinese and *upamāna* in Indic correspond), and the assertion that everything compared with it (the *primum comparandum*, Chinese *mofang*, "model to be emulated," Indic *upameya*, "thing-to-be-compared") was not just different but deviant and even deficient. This is most evident in the works of Hegel, some of whose stereotypes of China and India are taken up for study in several chapters in this book. Western–non-Western comparison, from Hegel until very recently, would typically and without hesitation—and usually without self-awareness—incorporate this basic aspect of inequality.

This history makes the direct comparison of non-Western entities here—we might call it cosmopolitan comparison—not only novel but also necessary. Such comparison, decentered from the West, hardly escapes all of the epistemological traps of the colonial sort. One obvious danger is—to use an overused term that nonetheless captures a real problem—the essentialization of our objects of study. We have already alluded to worries about the "China" or "India" that we are comparing when, for example, we compare "Chinese painting" and "Indian painting," where at every point illegitimate generalization would seem to lurk. Yet in the many collective discussions among our contributors, all of them sensitive to the threat of essentialization, the coherence and analytical purchase of those geocultural terms were never called into question. All of us clearly believed, without feeling compelled to say so, that larger categories of life than the individual actor do exist and could be studied, and to do so carried no real threat of essentializing misrepresentation.

To be sure, these configurations of political, social, and cultural existence may now bear names in English cited earlier—"region," "area," "civilization," "nation," indeed "China" and "India"—that we may wish to contest whenever they are, as they often are, unhistorically treated. One might even argue that in the very selection of our cases a sort of "civilizationism," or the illegitimate generalization of a particular as a whole, is being smuggled in through the back door. What, after all, is the reason for choosing items for comparison if the one is not somehow marked as Chinese and the other as Indian, and to what do those descriptors in the end refer, if not some civilization, empire, nation, country, area?

For one thing, we saw that "China" and "India" are not modern constructs but old spaces created by long-lasting political, social, and cultural forces. We can affirm this while acknowledging that these spaces shifted over time in their boundedness—indeed, they were split by real internal division: just consider the many north/south divergences in both China and India, resulting from real, long-term processes of representation, circulation, language, governance, aesthetic taste, ideas of ultimate concern, and so on. For another, quite aside from our shared sensitivity to the historical processes that underlie collectivizing titles such as "China" and "India," none of the book's contributors ever hesitated to affirm that our different efforts were adding to some whole, that understanding any part—language or historiography or religion or ecology—required understanding it in relation to the other parts.

Even more challenging than addressing the problem of essentialization is making sense of the nature of the knowledge produced by the comparisons explored in this book, and what, if anything distinguishes them from standard comparative research. The goals of standard comparative research are generally held to be fourfold: heuristic, descriptive, analytical, and (let us call it) estranging. Heuristic comparison aims toward generating new questions and problems: we ask whether something that occurred in case A might also have occurred in case B. With descriptive comparison, we aim to clarify case A by contrasting it with case B, something that alone enables us to identify case A's particularity. In this sense, as Kant and Hegel saw, comparison is a basic part of thinking. With analytical comparison, we seek to answer causal questions, to discover robust tendencies, to test hypotheses. The fourth aim is to introduce a certain distance from the paradigmatic nature of the comparatum (for example, the Homeric epic, which for Hegel was the standard of comparison for all epics everywhere), unsettling its self-evident nature, so that it becomes just one case among other possibilities, and hence "estranged."

Much of the comparative work done in the humanities today seems to be largely descriptive; much done in the social sciences, analytical; the heuristic is less explicitly cultivated, and the estranging is less often made an actual theme of inquiry. Many of these aims are evident in this book, but our dominant concern, whether implicitly or explicitly, has been with estrangement, if of a special kind. Not only does our sort of cosmopolitan comparison require that we actively try to bracket the Western objects—paintings, poems, power formations, whatever—that have functioned as the standards, in order to gain as undistorted a view as possible of the non-Western objects of comparison. But it also leaves us with objects that wind up estranging—sometimes profoundly estranging—each other.

The Knowledge Derived from Historical Comparison

What new knowledge, then, has this procedure actually enabled us to produce in the following chapters? We have found three different kinds. The first two concern categories and disciplines and turn out to be supplemental, not central, to our concerns. The third, which we can call simply the production of *difference*—the outcome of the estrangement just mentioned—has proven to be the heart of the matter. (Our chapter review follows these categories, and accordingly does not need to recapitulate their actual order in the book as presented in the table of contents.)

It is hardly surprising, first of all, that cosmopolitan comparison should explode our received conceptual categories for understanding the larger world, given that those categories originated in Western historical experience.

But this occurred so frequently in the course of our project that it seems to have been intensified by the act of comparison itself. A useful example is "religion." Confusion about what was and was not religion in China and India can be widely observed among the first European travelers, most prominently the Jesuits in China. The great diversity of spiritual practices in both regions was unlike anything they had previously encountered. For these visitors, "religion" was something that was supposed to have "clear doctrines, founding texts, and ecclesiastical institutions," as Zvi Ben-Dor Benite and Richard Davis put it in chapter 7.

A kind of comparative thinking was clearly operating here (the earliest works of European comparativism, in the first half of the eighteenth century, were in fact comparative religion), in which the European standard was deeply buried and never questioned. It brought not just definition and classification but differentiation and separation, with serious historical consequences in both worlds. In addition to having to confront (as most of the chapters do) long-standing popular and historiographical misconceptions of China and India—in the case of religion, "rational China" and "spiritual India" are always lurking in the background—Ben-Dor Benite and Davis show how cosmopolitan comparison enables us to see especially clearly how the new category produced the new totalities now called "Confucianism" and "Hinduism," and, equally important, prompted modern observers to misunderstand much that, historically, was never differentiated and separated to begin with.

It was equally predictable, to move to the second sort of new knowledge, that the degree of uniformity or variation across the two regions that has emerged from the kind of big comparison engaged in here—across diverse objects of study—should depend on the object of analysis, largely in relation to the degree of structure, process, or agency that characterizes it. But again, it has proven particularly important to confirm such uniformity/variation in two non-Western sites.

Deeper, structural determinations seem to have been at issue in producing uniform inequalities in gender relations, for example, in China and India, as Beverly Bossler and Ruby Lal show in chapter 3. The prominence and consequences of patrilocal residence (women always moved to the home of their husband's family); the correlation between status and control (the higher the status of women, the more stringent their confinement in China, the stricter the ban on widow remarriage in India); the control of women's bodies (foot binding in China, widow burning in India);

ingrained popular conceptions of the place of women in society; and, not least, the difficulty of using sources predominantly produced by men to grasp the real issues of concern to women—all these phenomena seem to be constant across the two regions, and to be largely unaffected by cultural particularity. Comparable too, in a more counterintuitive way, is the dynamism of gender relations: far from being fixed and abstract constructs imposed on men and women, they involved active negotiations among historical individuals. Even apparently restrictive gender regimes provided emotional rewards and allowed for autonomy of action in both places; individuals worked creatively within, or in defiance of, inherited prescriptions and constraints to construct meaningful lives. Comparison here serves not only to disrupt common stereotypes and deepen the understanding of Chinese and Indian societies but also to demonstrate the fluidity and historical contingency at the heart of the concepts of "gender" and "comparison" themselves.

Other structural determinants were at issue in producing comparable consequences in ecological and to some degree economic history. The process of energy harvesting, for example, followed similar patterns in both regions. As chapter 1 by Sumit Guha and Kenneth Pomeranz argues, China and India were both low energy-use societies, typically adapting to low energy supplies rather than boosting efforts to increase them—even when in the early modern period population tripled in China and doubled in India—and almost entirely restricted to the year's production of biomass. In other words, both regions were content to tolerate extraordinary levels of poverty.

Structures could obviously vary in the two regions, however, and produce different outcomes. The introduction of New World crops had highly disruptive consequences in overpopulated China and fewer in India, where tastes and patterns of consumption ensured continuity. Importantly, varying cultural factors had ecological consequences too. India preserved most of its original animal population into the early modern era, in particular its "charismatic megafauna," above all elephants, for which religious attitudes were responsible to a considerable degree (not all people ravage their environment as far as resource extraction permits). In China, most large animals became extremely rare, and the elephant vanished entirely. "While China's ecology had been engineered to support impressive numbers of one large mammal and its companions (e.g., hogs), this had been done by pushing almost all other large mammals to the margins."

The category of estrangement made possible by non-Western comparison, to turn to our third sort, will be of greater interest to the general reader than how comparison has caused us to rethink received categories like "religion" or to discover stable patterns of structural constraint. But it is also less straightforward to characterize in terms of knowledge. We can describe it as emerging from the mutual illumination of objects of analysis that can now be seen to be equally different: neither deficient nor deviant in the light of some standard regarded as perfect, and often radically different from one another. Comparison unencumbered by misapprehensions about the essential nature of things—what a poem or a painting or a power formation like empire really, invariantly, is—allows us to better capture the specificity of a given case, which can be seen only against the backdrop of a comparative partner.

Consider once again the problem of religion (chapter 7), and in particular the history of Buddhism. Buddhism in China had long been marked by a judgment of foreignness. Adherents of the pre-Buddhist religion known as Daoism sought not only to demonstrate their chronological priority to Buddhism but even to prove that Daoism was its source (most dramatically by promulgating legends of Laozi's travels to India and even his fathering the Buddha). By the mid-ninth century Buddhists came under direct attack and were suppressed by the Tang state in what is often referred to as the "Great Anti-Buddhist Persecution," entailing the destruction of temples and monasteries, the confiscation of property, and the exiling of monks.

Indian polities, by contrast, evince over centuries almost complete indifference to the regulation of religious communities (though not to patronizing them, sometimes unequally). Although Buddhism was the object of vigorous philosophical critique for a millennium or more beginning almost from the time of its founder (though never on the grounds of temporal priority), it continued to receive royal patronage in many regions, especially in the northeast (today's West Bengal and Bangladesh), well into the thirteenth century, before it faded under the joint pressures of external attacks by Central Asian power seekers and internal splits and assimilation to local religious forms.

Analogous to the nature and degree of religious management on the part of the polity is the highly differentiated status of historical memory, which emerges clearly in chapter 5 by Cynthia Brokaw and Allison Busch. However complicated it is to make sense of historical discourse in India—poetry, not prose, was the vehicle of history, and the exemplary, not the factual, was its substance—every polity was concerned to define its place in historical memory in one way or another; the inscriptional record provides abundant evidence of this. Yet never did this concern remotely attain the political centrality visible in premodern China, where every imperial court from the seventh century onward had a History Office—and where things could get very serious very quickly.

When, for example, it came to the attention of the Kangxi emperor (r. 1662–1722), the second leader of the new Manchu dynasty, that a Chinese scholar had completed a history sympathetic to the antecedent Ming dynasty, "he had the text destroyed; its editor's corpse exhumed and burned; the family members of all the scholars who had participated in the work either executed or enslaved; the printers and purchasers of the work executed, together with any officials who had known of its publication and not reported it to the throne. A total of seventy people were put to death, and many others exiled." India saw nothing remotely similar; the closest case known to us is the reluctance on the part the chief of Akbar's translation bureau (c. 1600) to publish his *History of Akbar* in the emperor's lifetime, lest criticism of the ruler's religious reforms provoke his displeasure.

The capacity of comparison to produce deeply instructive differentiation is illustrated in chapter 4 on literature by Stephen Owen and Sheldon Pollock. Chinese lyric poems, like those of Du Fu (712–770), are usually located securely in time and place. Indian lyrics, like those of Amaru (sixth century? or seventh? or eighth?) seem as if they could have been written at almost any time or place in the vast world of Sanskrit. In both cases, these effects were intentionally sought, in conformity with radically different aesthetic standards. In China, poetry could not be understood without a detailed historical apparatus identifying the poet and when and where he wrote. In India, poetry could not be understood with a historical apparatus, since the poem was meant precisely to capture what exists beyond historical particularity. In China, Du Fu's poems were read in the same script, that of Chinese characters, everywhere the culture extended, but everywhere the language was spoken differently. In India, Sanskrit, the language of Amaru's poems, was spoken everywhere more or less similarly, but it was read everywhere in as many as twenty different scripts. In China, the unity of the written language, despite its several demotic versions, produced a unified literary culture. In India, that unity, to the degree it exists, emerged out of a shared pool of narratives, motifs, allusions, and expressive techniques.

Few of these features of literary culture could manifest themselves, certainly not so dramatically, unless the Chinese and Indian cases were brought into comparison. And they could not have emerged as pure, mutually estranging differences, rather than deficiencies, unless compared directly with each other, intentionally distanced from the normative standard of Europe. Many of the same arguments can be made in the realm of art.

In the course of the second millennium in both China and India, landscape painting took a central place in visual culture. Molly Aitken and Eugene Wang in chapter 8 show that there was no single or essential "Asian" tradition of art, as the early twentieth-century pan-Asianist discourse on "haze" in painting tried to suggest. In China, landscape painting became a "self-sufficient" genre, but in a way that never occurred in India. The human element, for example, was largely irrelevant, whereas an unpeopled landscape was of no interest to the Indian artist. In China, landscape painting increasingly became the pursuit of literary elites who inhabited a wide range of social locations; in India, painting was always an artisanal practice, conducted at court, in which the artisan seems usually to have been indifferent to or sometimes even ignorant of the text (when there was a text) that he was illustrating.

Calligraphy was central to Chinese painting and entirely inconsequential in non-Islamicate India, the text often being just scrawled at the top of the picture. The Chinese landscape was an object of intellectual engagement and empiricist scrutiny, and yet haze was a core aesthetic value. The Indian landscape was an object of emotion and imagination, and yet clarity was a core aesthetic value. The relentless secularity of the one contrasts with the relentless spiritualization of the other, a polarity further reinforced by the stunning contrast between the cerebral, plain ink and spare surface in China and the sensual, richly colored and opulent surface in India.

Equally distinctive, if more foundational, is the character of the state in the early modern period, as chapter 2 by Pamela Crossley and Richard Eaton demonstrates. Both regions experienced what to today's historical eye appear to be strikingly comparable moments of political rupture, when power was seized by outsiders: in China, the beginning of the Qing conquest with the capture of Beijing by the Manchu Prince Dorgon in 1644; in India, the victory of the Central Asian Turk Babur over Ibrahim Lodi in the first Battle of Panipat near Delhi in 1526 and the subsequent founding of the Mughal sultanate. But both the responses to these developments and the subsequent character of the regimes differed dramatically. Chinese intellectuals regarded the conquest by what they viewed as a barbarian people who could never in their view legitimately rule China as a profound humiliation that demanded analysis and explanation of what had gone wrong. (Scholars concluded that political autonomy had been lost because the true meaning of the classics had been lost.) In India, there is much evidence that local actors regarded Mughal overlordship as largely continuous with preceding forms of polity, and far less evidence that they saw it as a fundamental and unbridgeable break (which is not to say there was no resistance).

The sorts of governance that evolved in the two cases were equally divergent. Both had to find accommodation with local cultures not fully their own, and to synthesize multiple modalities of rule. But the styles of synthesis differed greatly. In the Qing we find comingling, with the parts preserved in combination; in the Mughal world we find mixture, with the parts disappearing in combination. To speak as some scholars do of an organic "composite" culture of Mughals may be something of an overstatement, but it still stands in contrast to the studied conglomeration of the Qing, who "ostensibly uttered simultaneous messages in three [official] languages, governed on the basis of three codes of legitimacy, and occupied the moral center of three civilizations simultaneously."

With regard to the social world broadly viewed, there is a notable distinction in the area of social advancement. Although in China elite families could perpetuate their standing over generations by the careful management of wealth, official status was not legally hereditary, and "rags to riches and back" in five generations was proverbial (as noted in chapter 3); in India, the place of the social group in the status hierarchy may have been movable a notch or two up or down the scale, but that place was always inherited. And the same contrast can be seen in the systems of recruitment and advancement in the two empires.

In the Chinese civil examination system during the Song and Ming, as Benjamin Elman and Christopher Minkowski remark in chapter 6, examinations were for the first time held in the provinces, prefectures, and counties and hence open to local people, not just court and capital elites. "The examination system produced millions of literates who, after repeated failures [only 5 percent succeeded], became doctors, Buddhist priests, pettifoggers, teachers, notaries, merchants, and lineage managers, not to mention astronomers, mathematicians, printers, and publishers." By contrast, in the Indian *mansabdari* system (a graded hierarchy of officers appointed directly by the emperor), *mansabs*, or ranks, were only available to the nobility and gentry, and further strengthened it; elite status was therefore constantly being reproduced. Something consequential and long-term seems to have been manifesting itself in the two instances: a constant stimulation, however unintended it may have been, of meritocratic advancement in China; an uninterrupted reproduction of hereditary privilege in India.

With respect to territorial ambitions, very old limits of political geography seem to have constrained the Mughals, whereas the horizons of Qing expansionism at times appear limitless. In the most remarkable contrast of all we can juxtapose the fragmentation of power in the Indian case to the centralization—or at least the aspiration to centralization—in the case of China. Of a piece with this is the ideological control exercised by the Qing and the ideological laxity of the Mughals. In the Mughal world there is nothing comparable to the Chinese state's reclaiming of power, over the course of the eighteenth century, through what Crossley describes as "a torrent of literary inquisitions, prosecutions for corruption and factionalism, and a rewriting of seventeenth-century history aimed at discrediting some of the leading lineages of the civil government." But the most eloquent evidence of this contrast is also in some ways the simplest: the treatment of the calendar.

There are deep commonalities in the structures of production of systematic knowledge in China and India, such as the dominance of high languages with their transregional communicative capacity, the embeddedness of scientific specializations in kinship networks, the systematized nature of the world of learning, created in the Chinese case by the examination system and in India by an ancient system of Vedic learning, and, later, of Perso-Arabic classical culture. But how profound the contrast is between the role of the state in China in the social organization of knowledge and the "delegative and pluralistic forms" in India becomes clear in chapter 6 by Elman and Minkowski. In China, "the state declared a monopoly" on the subjects of astronomy and the calendar system, since calendrical uniformity across the empire was a core feature of the dynasty's political legitimacy and statecraft. For the Indians, divergent dating systems were always available. Even today, we find a wide range of traditional calendars still current, "and calendar makers working in different traditions can decide that a major festival like Diwali should be celebrated on different days, or even in different months." Not only did China and India live in different temporalities, but India itself did.

We have so far explained why China and India have been chosen for this experiment in comparative history; what those terms refer to; what parts of their history are of interest to us here, and why; and the challenges especially when comparing two non-Western worlds directly, and the kinds of knowledge this can produce. What we have yet to explain is why we have chosen the themes we did, how these themes interrelate, and what has been left out.

The big comparison engaged in here has no built-in boundaries. Academic knowledge today begins in disciplinary sites, and that is where we began: with economy and ecology; government; gender, language, and literature; history, religion, science, and art. We could easily have added more such disciplinary topics: law, philosophy, music, and so on. To some degree our choices were entirely opportunistic: familiarity with people open to or actually working on China-India comparison, or already linked, by some elective affinity, with a colleague in the neighboring region. We do not doubt that the subjects chosen are core aspects of polity, society, and culture; at the same time we acknowledge that being necessary is not the same thing as being sufficient—even while recognizing that in the end no possible grouping of topics can be sufficient. We were also hostage, if happily so, to the topics that contributors were actually interested in exploring, rather than what they felt, from some preconceived Humean notion of the "national characters" of China and India, should be explored. So in the Chinese case there is more on literati learning and less on neo-Confucianism than might be expected, for example; in the Indian, less on caste, although aspects of both are touched on in the various chapters.

Two other features of the nature of discipline-based knowledge presented in this book merit brief comment. First, while the volume is self-evidently multidisciplinary, it was never our intention to conduct an experiment in interdisciplinarity. Individuals within their area may have come to the project already "inter," but that was entirely incidental. Second, and more unfortunately, but also perhaps inevitably, topics that fall into no particular disciplinary catchment area have been treated less directly than a far more open-ended (and better financed) research project might have achieved.

Consider just the nature of archives, a topic fundamental to almost all the subjects treated here. Our contributors were constantly acknowledging the copiousness of the Chinese documentary sources and the relative poverty of the Indian. What accounts for such a striking disparity? One might argue that, as was the case in Absolutist Europe during the seventeenth century, where stunning amounts of data on the citizenry were collected and stored by anxious regimes (even despite periodic deficiencies in the availability of paper in revolutionary Paris, for example), the centralized Chinese state had an apparently insatiable appetite for information about its subjects. Nothing of the sort was felt in India until perhaps the eve of colonial rule (the quasi-absolutist Peshwa dynasty in late-eighteenth-century Maharashtra assembled an unusually large and detailed archive of social and political information). Just consider the fact that, from among the thousands of scholar families in seventeenth-century Varanasi, the capital of Hindu intellectual life, not a single personal document—diary, letter, or the like—survives, while tens of thousands of literary, philosophical, and religious manuscripts do (which rules out the environmental explanation).

Think also of the history of conceptual change, such questions as why the impact of the Jesuits was so great in China and so minor in India. Here is a problem even more complex than that of the archive, one whose ramifications to other aspects of the two societies are potentially large. Are such issues in any way related to other questions of technology? Why, for example, did China take to printing so eagerly and so early, and India actively reject it; why was paper so important in China whereas in India, indigenous materials for writing, birch bark and palm leaf, maintained their currency long after paper was introduced? Why—and here we overstate the case, but only a little—did it turn out that China today makes hardware and India software?

If we have not been able to directly address such themes in this book, we hope at least to have offered some pointers toward how they may be further developed. On the serious comparison of these two complex worlds, the implications of their differences, and the extent of the continuation of those differences into the present, ours is merely the first word, and most certainly not the last.

Further Reading

Asher, Catherine B. and Cynthia Talbot. *India Before Europe.* Cambridge: Cambridge University Press, 2006.

Das, Satayajit. *The Age of Stagnation.* Amherst, NY: Prometheus Press, 2015.

Elman, Benjamin. *On Their Own Terms: Science in China, 1550–1900.* Cambridge, MA: Harvard University Press, 2005.

Felski, Rita and Susan Stanford Friedman. *Comparison: Theories, Approaches, Uses.* Baltimore: Johns Hopkins University Press, 2013.

Keschnick, John and Meir Shahar, eds. *India in the Chinese Imagination: Myth, Religion, and Thought.* Philadelphia: University of Pennsylvania Press, 2016.

Kocka, Jürgen. "Comparison and Beyond." *History and Theory* 42 (2003): 39–44.

Lightman, Bernard, Gordon McOuat, and Larry Stewart, eds. *The Circulation of Knowledge Between Britain, India, and China.* Leiden: E. J. Brill, 2013.

Mutschler, F.-H. and A. Mittag, eds. *Conceiving the Empire: China and Rome Compared.* Oxford: Oxford University Press, 2008.

Pollock, Sheldon. *The Language of the Gods in the World of Men: Sanskrit, Culture, and Power in Premodern India.* Berkeley and London: University of California Press, 2006.

——. "Conundrums of Comparison." *KNOW* 1, no. 2 (2017): 273–294.

Scheidel, W., ed. *Rome and China: Comparative Perspectives on Ancient World Empires.* Oxford: Oxford University Press, 2009.

Sen, Tansen. *India, China, and the World: A Connected History.* Lanham, MD: Rowman and Littlefield, 2017.

Van der Veer, Peter. *The Modern Spirit of Asia: The Spiritual and the Secular in China and India.* Princeton, NJ: Princeton University Press, 2013.

PART ONE

CHAPTER I

Life and Energy

SUMIT GUHA AND KENNETH POMERANZ

All beings accumulate and expend energy, some rapidly, others slowly. Long-lived human societies develop durable and complex ways to do this. Markets and the associated institution of money represent one way of controlling energy flows and turning them to the ends of the powerful. The modern epoch has been marked by its increasing reach back in time via the energy resources embodied in fossil fuels; it may be dated, economically and ecologically speaking, from the successful union of fossil fuel and Watt's steam engine at the end of the eighteenth century. Petroleum was added a century later; natural gas in the twentieth century. Thus stores of solar energy fossilized as much as 400 million years ago were mobilized for modern consumption in an era that began roughly 200 years ago. This is what fueled the European demographic and economic explosion that has overrun much of the world in recent centuries. The chronological reach of contemporary lifestyles is enormous, and we have re-created atmospheric conditions (CO_2 levels) that last existed three million years ago.

India and China have lately become major participants in this alarming race to plunder the energy resources embodied in fossil fuels. However, the predominance of agriculture despite major handicraft exports (like silk in China and cotton textiles in India) was even more marked four centuries ago than today.

Beginning in the seventeenth century, China became a major exporter of glazed chinaware and expanded its exports of tea (an industrially processed leaf) beyond the Eastern and Central Asian markets it had served for centuries. India supplied cotton fabrics to much of the world and enlarged its export of an old dyestuff to which the country lent its name: indigo. The principal Chinese exports were a little more energy-intensive than the Indian ones—a difference that has become very marked in recent times. However, both regions were energy-sparing economies by today's standards. The Indian subcontinent's energy consumption was largely from the current year's production, with a small fraction of old-growth timber. China's was not much different. Their complex societies and empires relied largely on solar energy via photosynthesis (and plant materials and animal waste) as a renewable and sustainable source of fuel.

This frugal agro-ecological system lay at the heart of the light impact of China's and India's massive populations. A bewildering range of local environments in both China and India were often connected to each other by trade, migration, resource extraction by elites, and the movement of sediment by rivers. By the beginning of the nineteenth century, both regions had developed numerous and elaborate structures—physical and organizational, local and supralocal, private and public—that allowed more humans to mobilize more energy to sustain more activities, and to multiply the plants and animals they favored (such as rice, wheat, cotton, oxen, horses, pigs) while others (elephants, tigers, various sorts of vegetation) were forced to retreat.

Water and Food

Agriculture is essentially the diversion of plant materials into forms favored by humans. Most of the plants at the foundation of Old World agriculture are annuals that are killed or damaged if soil moisture is outside a tolerable range during key periods. Yet the Asian monsoon pattern concentrates rainfall in a few months of the year, with a dry season intervening. In the warmer lands of Southern and Eastern Asia, water availability is *the* major constraint on plant biomass (food and nonfood) production. It certainly has been the most important constraint on Indian agriculture from the earliest times. Great famines were almost always consequences of monsoon failures. The population that the land could support varied with its total rainfall; as late as 1975, one could explain almost half the variation in population density between Indian states by the variation in summer rainfall between them. When the Mughal emperor Babur (r. 1526–30) came to north India from the arid lands of Inner Asia, he was struck by the ability of farmers to manage rain-fed crops: "the agriculture and orchards have absolutely no need for water. Fall crops are watered by the monsoon rains, and strangely the spring crops come even if there is no rain." In parts of Punjab and northern India, he however noted the use of the "Persian wheel" lifting a chain of buckets as well as the simpler, large leather container being used to draw water from wells for irrigation.

The combination of a dryer climate and a larger animal population resulted in a somewhat smaller human population working a larger area of land in India than China; this pattern persists today, with approximately 1.3 billion people in each region being fed from circa 450 million acres of arable land in the four countries of subcontinental India and 270 million acres in the People's Republic. If we were to move back to 1800, we would have far fewer people—about 190 million and roughly 300 million respectively—but also smaller areas under crops, especially in India.

For much of the Indian subcontinent, this relatively dry climate and a heavy dependence on rain-fed agriculture meant that farmers relied on the extensive tillage of comparatively low-yielding plants whose seeds had to be put in the ground during the narrow windows afforded by the capricious monsoon. Rapid and extensive tillage then required animal power, which explains the large stock of oxen that was a ubiquitous feature of Indian farming for centuries and remain an important resource today. Oxen were vital even where moisture was provided by wells or other water sources, as a pair of oxen would generate the power of perhaps twenty men while digesting foods unusable by humans. Finally, even in the smallholding rice paddies usually located in heavy rainfall or gravity-flow irrigated lands, the work of plowing and puddling needed to make the land fit for transplanting was usually done by oxen or buffaloes.

While working within these broad constraints, farmers were extraordinarily perceptive and industrious in using every little feature of soil and terrain to raise plants and animals. A sixteenth-century traveler, starting from the Sulaiman Mountains in the eastern Afghan borderlands, would have found ancient water-harvesting schemes that captured the runoff from often distant snow banks to irrigate patches of land in suitable sites. In the mountains of Baluchistan (Pakistan), little trickles of runoff from rocky expanses of arid desert could nonetheless feed a few acres of millet or barley, even where average annual rainfall was a bare four or five inches and summer temperatures reached 120 °F. But the main users of these lands were pastoral nomads who grazed camels, goats, and a few sheep. Arid lands also formed much of the center and south of the great valley created by the Indus and its tributaries. Changing river courses often left seasonal channels, and by early modern times a network of diversion canals was built in the Indus basin that harnessed the seasonal fluctuation of river levels and the many abandoned distributaries of that river system. This created seasonally inundated fields. The Mughal emperors (who flourished 1556–1700) added several longer canals in north India. In 1900, around three million acres of land was regularly sown in the lower Indus; five-sixths of that area was irrigated in some way. Over immense areas this meant that even villages did not exist: instead small communities clustered around a well or other water source. Seasonal inundation (where fields were flooded, then drained) left subsoil water to be drawn up by various-animal powered devices, including a large leather bucket drawn out by ox power and the Persian wheel. Intermediate uncultivated lands were used by herdsmen with animals ranging from goats to camels. In the winter months the local herds were supplemented by nomad caravans that came down from Inner Asia, carrying goods back and forth. All herdsmen bought and sold (as well as stole) animals along the way and historically helped replace stock depleted by widespread animal diseases or the fodder shortages of famine years. Thomas Coats, a close observer of rural life, wrote in 1819 that because the very existence of the farmer depended on his cattle he nursed them with extreme care, but if the monsoon came late, cattle became emaciated and disease broke out, "which reduces the cultivators to beggary." Specialized traders also brought a key military resource: the horse, not as a work animal but as an instrument of war and symbol of power.

The arid to semiarid region of the Indian subcontinent stretches from the eastern borders of Afghanistan almost down to the tip of the southern peninsula. Away from the alluvial plains and the sand deserts of the middle and lower Indus basin, more undulating terrain and impermeable rock foundations allowed the building of embankments to form reservoirs. This usually supported pockets of rice paddy but also the cultivation of other crops such as sugarcane, specialized tree crops, and vegetables. But rain-fed millets, oil seeds, and cotton covered most agricultural land. A new spurt in water harvesting began in southern India during the fifteenth century. Great cities like Vijayanagara, built in semidesert areas, needed careful water management. Narrow valleys were closed to capture runoff and rice was grown below the dam. The narrow valleys of western India offered other opportunities. Here small dams diverted hill torrents into channels that followed the upper slopes and released water onto more level ground. Much-prized grapes and sugarcane were grown this way. But archeologists are discovering that the builders frequently miscalculated. Dams failed and reservoirs silted up occasionally, just as in the vast water-control projects of the Ming and Qing periods. Derelict water works bred malarial mosquitoes—a deadly barrier to reclamation.

Water drawn from relatively stable river flows in the extreme south allowed huge tracts of rice paddies that—especially in the Kaveri delta—approached East Asian levels of intensive land use. However, the eastern third of the subcontinent gets much more rain than its western side and maintained a stable and productive rain-fed agriculture. In the 1620s, a Dutch merchant described how much of the food consumed in the great imperial cities of Agra and Delhi was transported from the east, up the rivers Ganga and Yamuna.

This was before much of the great delta lying east of the Bhagirathi (or Hugli) River was reclaimed by rice farmers. That area came under intensive agriculture many centuries after the Yangzi and even the Pearl river systems. Parts of its southeastern extension were still being reclaimed from salt flat and swamp around World War I when this frontier region enjoyed the highest farm wages in India, with tens of thousands traveling from north India to what is now Bangladesh during the busy season. Its population rose from less than 20 million in 1800 to 50 million by 1920. The opening of this and the neighboring Irrawaddy delta rice-paddy frontier contributed to a massive spurt in India's population during a period when violent unrest, invasions, famine, and catastrophic deforestation, drought, and flooding (c. 1850–1950) checked China's growth.

Pre-1800 China did more than India to divert energy through large-scale structures for water control. Large dikes contained flooding on major rivers, despite enormous seasonal differences in water flow and very high rates of upstream erosion. High levels of siltation were a long standing problem on northern rivers, which cut through easily eroded and long-deforested plateaus of light, easily eroded loess soil; on many southern waterways, greatly increasing erosion resulted from the widespread clearance of hillside forests after about 1550. The clearing of highland forests in this period was greatly accelerated by the worldwide food revolution created by the European conquest of the Americas and the subsequent spread of American potatoes, corn, and other crops that would grow at high altitudes. Large irrigation projects manipulated surface water, affecting perhaps 30 percent of cultivated land in the late eighteenth century, with much higher percentages in the southern and eastern provinces.

The government played a major role in a few of the largest water control projects, and many small projects were built by families; however, the vast majority of irrigation systems were the work of cooperative organizations spanning one or more villages. Local magistrates might play some role in these irrigation systems, but it rarely went beyond loose oversight. These groups tended to be relatively informal, though many were institutionalized around temples, villages, or corporate lineages; leadership was sometimes inherited, sometimes elected, and sometimes by election or co-optation. The state played a role in some very large-scale projects—e.g., building a sea wall, and repairing the large outer dikes along the Yangzi after they had been badly damaged during the wars that replaced the Ming with the Qing empire in the seventeenth century—but for the most part, southern and central China managed their own water control. One important exception was the Grand Canal, originally constructed in the sixth century. The Grand Canal became, and remains, the world's longest canal at roughly 1,000 miles. In its fourteenth-to-nineteenth century configuration, it linked the Lower Yangzi, economic core of the empire, with the capital in Beijing. The Grand Canal sustained Beijing, which was perched on a semiarid northern plain that did not yield enough surplus to feed such a large city. While southern taxes paid for the canal, it was mostly northerners who benefited, and the hydraulic system was managed by a central bureaucracy, assisted by provincial governors appointed from Beijing.

Both locally and centrally managed water control infrastructure continued to expand, but the rate slowed considerably as many regions approached the limits of what was practical with existing technology. By the mid-eighteenth century, the resources needed to maintain existing water projects vastly exceeded those going into new construction, as one would expect in a mature system. Despite growing maintenance expenditures, ecological pressures caused by population and economic growth increasingly outstripped the government's capacity to fulfill its role in environmental stabilization, and so threatened to overwhelm inherited structures for managing nature more generally. Southern communities suffered from a weakening state, but as long as peace prevailed, they could usually sustain the necessary environmental management. Other regions were much more vulnerable to weakening state efforts.

In northern China—defined loosely as provinces entirely north of the Yangzi River, south of Mongolia and the Manchurian plain, and east of Xinjiang—most agriculture depended on rainfall, because there simply was very little surface water to exploit. Today this region has about 30 percent of China's population and over 40 percent of its agricultural acreage, but only 7 percent of its surface water, putting per capita supplies at about 5–7 percent of the global average. Subsurface water is more abundant, but much of it lay too far below the surface for affordable use before twentieth-century power-driven pumping equipment was available. Small wells were common but often inadequate for irrigation.

Deeper and larger wells were most common where agriculture was relatively commercialized (e.g., in tobacco and cotton areas near the Grand Canal in Shandong) or where significant trade routes passed through an area, generating mercantile wealth that could be mobilized to support wells (as was also common in parts of Central and West Asia), increasing local food production. But much of north and northwest China fit neither of these descriptions. During a series of eighteenth- and nineteenth-century campaigns, the Qing government sought to fill these gaps by encouraging and subsidizing hundreds of thousands of deeper wells in places that did not have them. Rough estimates, based on very incomplete data, suggest that such efforts may have raised grain yields enough to feed about three million people annually during the eighteenth century. But these campaigns were episodic, and reliable, adequate irrigation remained exceptional in northern China. The economist Dwight Perkins, relying on J. L. Buck's 1930s data, estimated that only one northern province (Henan, at 14 percent), had more than 8 percent of its farmland irrigated at the dynasty's end; the figure was probably higher before China's strife-filled nineteenth century, but not dramatically so. On the whole, then, this was a rainfall-fed agricultural regime, in an area that (with some exceptions) averages 20–30 inches of rain per year.

North China lies outside the Asian monsoon zone (which reaches only as far as southeastern China), but like in those areas, its precipitation is heavily concentrated in a short period of time. Sixty-four percent of Beijing's annual rainfall comes in July and August; 85 percent in June through September. (By contrast, London, Paris, and Berlin get no more precipitation than Beijing, but it is very evenly spread through the year; no month accounts for more than 10 percent of Paris's precipitation, 11 percent of London's, or 13 percent of Berlin's.) Consequently, north China's water is often not available when needed or in excess when not needed, unless humans undertake to store and manipulate it. North and northwest China also have some of the world's largest year-to-year fluctuations in rainfall and surface water availability: it is not unusual for the Yellow River's flow in a heavy year to exceed that in an ordinary year by five or even ten times.

However, north China's loess soil holds abundant nutrients and has an excellent structure for moving moisture between the surface and lower levels; the region gets adequate sunshine for agriculture. Thus, if water supplies are adequate, it can produce high agricultural yields. Per-acre yields in the late eighteenth century were slightly below English levels (the highest in Europe) for a given season's crop; they were significantly higher over a cycle of several seasons, since intense manuring practices and soil characteristics reduced the need for leaving fields fallow for a time to replenish the soil, and so allowed for more crops in a given number of years than could be grown in England. Historically, those high yields have been accompanied by dense rural populations, so that surpluses were generally small; at the same time, the region has usually been host to large numbers of soldiers (patrolling the boundaries between states based in China and those based in Inner Asia) and to China's capital (always one of the world's biggest cities). Under the circumstances, even modest output fluctuations could potentially create subsistence crises; thus, even though irrigation in this region was limited, it was quite important (as was flood control). Under the Qing in the late seventeenth and eighteenth centuries, the state was particularly vigorous about managing north China water—creating a large, specialized agency to manage the Yellow River waterway. This enabled the Qing to increase the importation of grain from the south—employing a long-standing system where "tribute grain" was rendered to the state as part of an economic system that also included land and other taxes. This grain was mostly used to feed the population of Beijing, though a substantial portion reached other people in north China too. The Qing increased these imports to unprecedented levels (enough to feed perhaps two million people per year), attempted to turn marshy areas south of Beijing into rice paddies, and initiated campaigns to encourage deep wells. But all these projects proved difficult to sustain, especially as budgetary pressures caused by dramatic population growth and stagnant tax revenue intensified in the late eighteenth century.

A worldwide food revolution also transformed Asian agriculture. A global trade network provided many new plants. Indian and Chinese cuisine rapidly added the easily raised red chili plant to supplement costly black pepper. Tobacco became a necessity even to the very poor. The potato—a New World tuber—spread into select highland habitats to supplement grain in local diets. Maize provided both food and fodder in moister, hilly terrain and ripened sooner than other crops. It was also well suited to hoe agriculture in upland soils. Though Indian farmers already had several grains that could occupy that niche, maize dramatically changed China's farming and is doing so to this day. In recent years, India produced 103 million tons of milled rice while China produced 145 million; but India only produced 23 million tons of maize against China's 216 million. This, as we shall see, dramatically changed the regional distribution of China's population and allowed commercial agriculture, logging, and forest-based occupations such as paper- and charcoal-making and hunting to reach deep into the rugged southwestern mountains bordering Tibet and Burma, as well as the Han River highlands in China's west and northwest.

Forest, Savanna, and Domesticated Animals

We have so far focused on crop production because it produced most of what humans ate and wore. But it is necessary also to look at other important parts of the ecology of agriculture: particularly the use of animals, fertilizer, and what we can tell about changes in land use and quality. Cultivated fields drew much from the untilled lands that surrounded them, especially in India. The most important element was undoubtedly fodder for work and (in India) milk animals. This reduced their competition for the concentrated foods that supported the human population (though working animals needed supplements of potentially human food as well as byproducts like bran and oil cake). A study of five Indian villages in a dry deciduous monsoon climate found that 80 to 95 percent of cattle feed came from woodlands around the villages, with the rest deriving from crop residues. Some of this forest biomass then returned to the hearth as dung cakes needed for cooking. But in this still forested area it was usually supplemented by firewood. Only in places where firewood became excessively expensive did dung cakes become the major fuel. It is likely that both sources of heat energy were also used in the early modern era. A gradual move to complete dependence on dung and finally to fossil fuels began later. Brushwood and reeds served many other purposes. Particular crafts drew on woodland resources, with particular types of reed, for example, being essential for weavers and the secretion of the lac insect forming the basis of bangle production and dyes. Even thorn bushes served for fuel and fencing against stray animals and wild beasts.

Beyond soil moisture, plants draw macronutrients, notably nitrogen and potassium compounds, from the soil. These minerals are depleted when crops are harvested for human use, and natural sources such as nitrogen-fixing bacteria and lightning cannot replace them. Dense human populations could not afford to allow fields to replenish the soil nutrients by leaving them untilled for some seasons and had to devise strategies to sustain yields. The problem was reduced in rural India where purity taboos ensured (and often still ensure) that humans relieved themselves *al fresco* in the fields. So human populations usually returned a fair amount of nitrogen to the land directly. Much biomass was also consumed by the large domestic animal population. Bovines consumed materials unavailable to human digestion, substantially accelerating nutrient recycling. A good deal was directly returned to fields and pastures. Some was gathered for fertilizer. Residual energy in animal dung was also turned to account by the universal practice of making dung cakes for fuel. A classic study of cattle in Singur subdivision, West Bengal, evaluated the animals in terms of gross energetic efficiency, or the ratio of output to input in calorie terms. This was calculated to range from a minimum of 10 to a maximum of 20 percent of lifetime calories ingested, most of which were from straw and crop residue indigestible by humans. By contrast, the live weight of even a range-fed steer in the United States at the time was 4 percent of calories ingested, but only half of that biomass was processed into food.

Returning to the sixteenth century, oxen either carried packs or drew carts to move commodities and military supplies from place to place. Early European visitors often remarked that the role of horses in their own societies was taken by oxen in India. Fast-trotting bullocks drew fashionable carts. Oxen turned oil mills and drew water from wells. Huge trains of pack oxen accompanied armies and trading caravans. The French traveler Tavernier wrote, "it is an astonishing sight to behold caravans numbering 10,000 or 12,000 oxen together, for the transport of rice, corn, and salt . . . carrying rice to where only corn grows, and corn to where only rice grows, and salt to the places where there is none."

A wide variety of breeds had developed to fit different ecological niches and functions. After some experiments, the early British-Indian army replaced gun horses with oxen and harnessed horses only for actual combat. Crop residues such as straw, husk, and oil cake were important sources of animal feed: working animals could not expect to survive on the limited herbage and grazing time available to them. This meant that relatively low-yielding, long-stemmed crops still provided valuable fodder, and even a crop that gave disappointing amounts of grain was valuable because the stalks sustained the plow cattle needed to plant again next year. (Modern high-yielding cultivated grain crops achieve much of their grain yield by shortening stems and directing energy to the seeds.)

China's domestic animal situation was rather different from India's. From the Yangzi Valley southward, the dominant draft and transport animals were oxen and water buffalo; farther north, they were donkeys, mules, and the occasional horse, plus camels on the edge of the steppe. The dominant meat animal was the pig, except on the steppe and in western areas with large Muslim populations. (In both those places sheep predominated, with smaller numbers of cattle.) While the work animals were largely fed with various grasses, Chinese hogs (unlike Indian cattle) got their nutrition from the farm itself. Forest and savanna were thus less important here as complements to arable land.

Beyond this, we know surprisingly little about domestic animals until farm surveys begin appearing in the twentieth century. Dwight Perkins has hypothesized that the number of hogs per person probably changed very little over the very long haul from the thirteenth century to the early twentieth (when it was about 1:9), but he admits that this is very speculative; one could also interpret the limited evidence as suggesting a gentle decline over time in hogs per person. Either way, this was a diet with little meat, even compared to many equally poor or poorer populations elsewhere; fish, poultry, eggs, and bean curd provided much more protein. Those sources were plentiful enough that average protein supplies were perfectly adequate; but individual consumption would have varied enormously, and significant numbers of people were undoubtedly malnourished.

Hogs in particular were a vital fertilizer source, but relatively few animals were used for labor, as fodder crops competed with food and fiber crops for land. (Hogs, by contrast, mostly ate chaff, garbage, and so on.) Work animals were scarce in the south, where farms were small, deep plowing was rarely needed, and numerous waterways made animals less essential for transportation than in the north (and in most of India). In the particularly crowded Lower Yangzi, some Qing-era documents discuss labor animals that were jointly owned by up to four families. Such practices may have existed before the records we have of them; on the other hand, the appearance of such documents may reflect increased numbers of farmers who tilled too little land to justify owning an ox or buffalo themselves. Increased sharing might thus have meant that the amount of animal labor used per acre remained steady while the number of animals per acre and, *a fortiori*, per person declined.

The direct consequences of this scenario for humans were not bad. With the number of people—and perhaps hogs—roughly tripling between 1500 and 1800, while cultivated acreage only doubled, fertilizer input per acre would have grown significantly. After 1500, bean cake—a dried and compressed "cake" of beans—supplemented hog manure as a significant source of fertilizer, and the use of bean cake as fertilizer spread farther once significant imports from Manchuria began circa 1683. Even without the enormous boost provided by that imported bean cake, any loss of fertilizer from having fewer labor animals should have been no problem. And while less animal labor meant more human labor—as did increases in cropping intensity—this was being spread across more humans. While farmers of course worked hard—burning over 4,000 calories per day at peak season, by one estimate—agriculture was less of a year-round occupation in China than in other parts of the eighteenth-century world, and underemployment arguably a bigger problem than overwork. For women in particular—especially in the Yangzi Valley—the agricultural labor year almost certainly became shorter. What increased was the time devoted to handicrafts—above all textiles, to which we will turn later.

Chinese farmers, as we have seen, were less dependent than Indian ones on complementary inputs from grasslands and forests, and had less forest to rely on. Yet the day-to-day situation in the late eighteenth century generally remained quite manageable.

Parts of the Chang-Huai-Huang-Hai plain—which stretches along China's coast from roughly 40 degrees north (near Beijing) to 29 degrees (a bit south of the Yangzi) and inland for anywhere from 150 to several hundred miles—have been intensively farmed for millennia, and much of it became deforested centuries ago. Empirewide, however, the situation was different. Ling Daxie, who has used historical documents and modern surveys and statistics to research forest dynamics in China, has estimated that in 1700 about 26 percent of the Qing empire was forest. But if we subtract sparsely populated Tibet, Xinjiang, Qinghai, and Outer Mongolia, the figure rises to 37 percent.

By far the largest forests were in the humid south and in mountainous areas. The Lower Yangzi and north and northwest China, by contrast, were probably no more than 10 percent forest. (Ling's estimate is even lower.) In those areas, trees tended to be scattered thinly, with many behind the walls of courtyard houses or in small groves near a temple, burial place, or other significant spot; most were close enough to people's homes that it was worth the labor to collect even small bits of wood, leaves, and so on. Together with the use of crop residues, this seems to have created adequate fuel supplies for domestic needs.

To be sure, heat energy was comparatively expensive in most of eastern China, especially relative to human labor. One scholar has estimated that wood accounted for only 8 percent of energy used by humans in China, versus roughly 50 percent in Europe; another has provided data suggesting that charcoal was more than 20 times as expensive, relative to food calories, in Guangzhou as in London, circa 1700. Such numbers are necessarily very imprecise, but they do give a sense of the degree to which high population density and sparse forests shaped the energy environment in some parts of the country. Clearly it was unlikely that the use of heat energy would expand under these circumstances; however, it does not appear that fuel was in critically short supply for traditional uses in 1700, or probably even in 1800. It was, as we will see, wild animals and future humans who were disadvantaged by the loss of tree cover.

The highland boom in agriculture that had been spurred by the introduction of plants native to the Americas stimulated growth but had far-reaching consequences. Deforestation made room for new crops, intensified cropping patterns, and population growth but also led to soil erosion and flooding. In addition, another problem emerged when forests were cleared from the gentler hills of subtropical Guangdong, mostly in the late eighteenth and nineteenth centuries: the rapid loss of soil fertility. In those areas, as in many parts of the tropics, the underlying soils were poor, and fertility depended on the rapid recycling of nutrients from leaves that fell to the forest floor. When that cycle was interrupted—often to grow sweet potatoes for food—soils rapidly became impoverished, and tough savanna grasses, largely useless to humans, took over. Thus, losing some indirect benefits of forests—whether the ability of tree roots to hold soil in place or of fallen leaves to enrich poor soils—posed more serious problems for the eighteenth-century Chinese than any loss of such directly consumable forest goods as fuel, fodder, or lumber. More generally, both China and India were adapting to population growth in ways that allowed them to maintain, or perhaps even slightly improve, basic levels of subsistence while remaining at low levels of per capita energy use; but both were also generating environmental stresses that had serious consequences for other species and would eventually have serious consequences for humans as well.

Political Ecology

Beyond land form and soil moisture, another structuring force shaped the human geography of both countries: the dynamic of political power. Much of the Indian subcontinent was dry enough (outside the monsoon season) for Inner Asian cavalry to range over it. Indeed, the autumn festival marking the first major harvest (*kharif*) was from ancient times the beginning of the campaign season. When Babur, the latest in a series of Inner Asian empire builders, came to India in the 1500s he observed that north Indian villages and towns could be set up and deserted easily:

> Large cities in which people have lived for years, if they are going to be abandoned, can be left in a day, even half a day, so that no sign or trace remains. If they have a mind to build a city, there is no necessity for digging irrigation canals or building dams.... There is no limit to the [number of] people. A group gets together, makes a pond, or digs a well. There is no making of houses or raising of walls. They simply make huts from the plentiful straw and innumerable trees, and instantly a village or city is born.

Grazing and woodcutting around settlements would lead to the selection of thorny vegetation. Abandoned land quickly developed thickets of thorn bush that in turn served as refuges for escaping peasants. Babur also noted that the plains contained "forests of thorny trees in which the people of those districts hole up and obstinately refuse to pay tribute." Their capacity to resist was increased by the gradual diffusion of firearms. Simple matchlock muskets spread after 1600. While untrained peasants could not withstand cavalry in the open field, they could deter and harass troops from thickets or behind mud walls. Cavalrymen usually owned their horses and were reluctant to risk losing them to random gunshot. The worldwide adoption of gunpowder weapons led to a boom in Indian nitrate production and export. Potassium and sodium nitrate was extracted by a specialized caste from village sites well saturated with human and animal urine. Bengal "saltpetre" was the cheapest in the world, and the East India Company ran a thriving trade in this compound.

The presence of refuges and ease of migration and resettlement served to soften the impact of periodic heavy blows dealt by man and nature, summed up in the pithy phrase "*asmani wa sultani*" (literally "from the kings and from the heavens"). This had two effects. One was on what might be called the political ecology of India. A present-day historian of early modern Asia, Jos Gommans, has persuasively argued that pastoralism, trade, and horse-based warfare were intimately present in the everyday life of dry-zone India from about 1200. Peripatetic rulers used a repertoire of pack oxen convoys, dromedaries, and sheep to sustain horse-centered militiamen. The pronounced seasonality of the monsoon also meant that the ecological dry zone advanced and receded with the seasons. It might be used peaceably for itinerant caravans or shepherds, but also to forcibly impose rule and extract tribute from village harvests by marauding horsemen. The horse could not compete with the ox for draft purposes, but even rustic rebels could find a few on occasion.

By contrast, warfare visited Chinese farmers far less often, though some regions did suffer from endemic banditry; the Manchus would prove to be the last northern invaders to reach the Chinese heartland, even for raids, until the twentieth-century Japanese. When large-scale violence did hit Chinese villages, it came in the form of occasional rebellions; these were overwhelmingly dependent on foot soldiers, though the largest ones obtained ships and artillery. Cavalry was a significant factor only on the steppe frontiers, and even there forces from China proper had a chronic disadvantage in mounts until the conquest of Xinjiang in the 1750s. By contrast, the Inner Asian advantage in "heavy" horses was offset by Indian horsemen in the sixteenth century. They bred smaller but hardier horses and deployed swarms of light cavalry to delay, harass, and wear down more powerful forces such as those of the Mughals. So the horse had a more widespread presence in India than in most of China.

Political authorities were not merely predators. They could also serve to promote productivity beyond the simple provision of security from other marauders. Ever-vital water resources depended on coordinated labor beyond the capacity of household groups or even villages. That coordination was often provided by superior lords who maintained legitimate armed followings, lived in fortresses, and both shared in and defied central authority. In the Indus basin they regularly conscripted labor to clear canals or rebuild embankments to impound or exclude water. In other regions complex systems by which waterways fed and drained a succession of village reservoirs were coordinated by large landowners or by assemblies of dominant gentry. Sometimes, especially in southern India, great temples were dominant landowners and worked through village corporations to manage land and water as efficiently as possible. Similar irrigation systems (*aharpain*) existed on the dryer hill fringes of eastern India and were supervised by large landowners. The massive seasonal rise of the lower Indus River usually spilled into secondary channels. Big landowners there annually conscripted their tenants to clear channels and manage an inundation irrigation system. Winter crops were raised on the residual moisture. Even smaller irrigation systems often depended on the delegation of coercive power. Much of the undulating plateau of southern India is underlain by hard rock, and harvesting seasonal run-off is the major water resource. Villages often formed around small reservoirs. Local potentates oversaw necessary maintenance projects and overhauled existing works. Finally, of course there were large projects undertaken by imperial powers. As previously mentioned, the great south Indian empire of Vijayanagara (c. 1350–1600) built great cities on the dry central plateau that needed complex irrigation systems to sustain them. But archaeologists have pointed out that these were not invariably successful and a number were left incomplete or abandoned after breaches or other setbacks. In the north, the Mughal emperors initiated new projects, including several canals that drew water into the arid lands between the Indus and Ganges river systems. The British administration enlarged and extended all of the above and constructed an elaborate network of reservoirs, barrages, and canals across South Asia.

But the superstructures of imperial states made considerable demands on the ecosystem even as they directly or indirectly increased agrarian productivity. Monumental architecture in India often involved massive stone buildings that needed huge amounts of skilled labor supplemented by unskilled labor from conscripted peasants. Earlier Indian stone buildings had used little mortar, fitting carved stones together through patient labor. Rubble masonry cores, slaked lime cement, and plaster came into extensive use from the thirteenth century. So did enormous quantities of brick. All these drew on wood fuel from regional forests. Many buildings additionally needed large timbers for key elements. The maritime traffic in the Indian Ocean after 1500 also increased the demand for good naval timber such as teak. Teak forests in suitable locations began to be preserved as state monopolies by the 1700s.

Governments in both countries had considerable long-run effects on the state of the environment. Apart from occasional demands for large timber, there was the recurring need for firewood, and also for fodder to feed the numerous elephants, bullocks, and horses that transported great households, not to mention the cavalry chargers that maintained that greatness. These might sometimes be supported by seizing the peasants' stores.

Marathi archival documents studied by Sumit Guha bring out how inequalities of power affected the control of ecological resources: the small needs of local villagers and townspeople could be met through free public lands, but these areas were enclosed for private use when the gentry appeared on the scene. Such closures might be temporary or might become permanent; in that case, the lands would become the private or government "meadows" often found in the records. Many of these formed the core of colonial forest reserves in the nineteenth century.

In China too, of course, both the state and other power holders sometimes appropriated resources from rural communities, and at other times placed resources off-limits to preferred economic uses. Yet in general, such actions seem to have been less ecologically significant than in India. Considerable amounts of wood were taken for palace building in the immediate aftermath of the Qing overthrow of the Ming dynasty in the seventeenth century, but this demand did not persist. Likewise, the new government initially expropriated quite a bit of land near Beijing for the support of its horses. However, on an empirewide scale this was a pinprick, and much of this land drifted back into agricultural use over the succeeding decades as Manchu soldiers increasingly sought additional income to supplement declining stipends. Hunting was popular among the Manchu and Mongol elite, and some hunting grounds (again, mostly near Beijing) were therefore kept off-limits to other uses; but the larger Qing elite (mostly composed of Han Chinese) was thoroughly civilianized, largely indifferent to both hunting and horsemanship, and so—both for better and for worse—unlikely to care much about preserving large blocks of either forest or pasture. Temples, monasteries, and schools were more important landowners and occasionally significant as stewards of forests, but not on the scale that they were in Europe. The graveyards of powerful lineages were probably more significant, especially in parts of south China. But these lands were often on hillsides that had not been attractive to farmers anyway until American plants arrived. However, once these plants were available and an enlarged population was looking for places to use them, it was not unusual for even supposedly inviolate grave lands to be either occupied by squatters or leased out by cash-hungry kinsmen.

Probably the most important way resources were kept off-limits was not through such local exclusions but instead by the state restricting migration to frontiers where it feared instability. The Ming had tried, unsuccessfully, to freeze mobility entirely; the Qing tolerated and sometimes encouraged migrants, but forbade them from entering certain areas. Millions of people moved to these places anyway, and some of the places about which the state was concerned were semiarid regions that probably would have attracted few people anyway. But in the cases of Manchuria, Taiwan, and perhaps Inner Mongolia, Qing prohibitions almost certainly slowed the pace of settlement. Probably just over a million north Chinese settled in Manchuria around 1644–1850, but eight million more settled there in the 50 years after the state began encouraging such settlement in 1895. While they lasted, these restrictions exacerbated population pressure in areas that would otherwise have sent more migrants, but it is hard to know how much.

The Chinese state did, of course, tax people, but in general these burdens were relatively light in both absolute and comparative terms. Land tax quotas, which accounted for two thirds of Qing revenue, were frozen in 1713; though some other taxes did increase a bit, state income grew only slowly (declining in per capita terms) until major new commercial taxes were created after 1853. Eighteenth-century government revenues have been estimated at about 4 percent of total agricultural output (perhaps 3 percent of GDP). A few places—notably the Yangzi delta—were taxed more heavily (15 percent of agricultural yields at the most) and tax collectors often collected more than ever made it to state coffers. In-kind requisitions (e.g., straw and stone for dike repair, fodder for post-station horses) could sometimes be heavy, but these were occasional, not chronic problems. In general, tax burdens were not a big drain on rural communities, in part because military expenditures were comparatively low. The army was significantly smaller in 1800 than it had been in 1040, while the population had more than tripled, and various expedients were used to make supporting it less expensive. In short, the Qing rulers kept warfare far from most peasants, and did so at a very tolerable cost. Especially after about 1850, the state's increasing inability to maintain ecologically important services—such as north China flood control and the transport of southern tribute grain—or even to provide basic law and order, especially in the highlands, burdened people far more than its extractions did.

The Differing Fates of Charismatic Megafauna

All human societies have chosen totemic animals, as anthropologist Claude Lévi-Strauss famously said, because "they are good to think with," even as humans have destroyed both species and their habitats. India retained a significant number of its original animals from 1200 to the early 1800s. These included the last surviving population of the Asian lion; a larger population of tigers, cheetahs, and other felines; and most of Asia's rhinoceroses. Additionally, it had large populations of both domesticated and wild elephants. All of these survive today, with the exception of the cheetah, which became extinct in the twentieth century. Still, the population of India in the early seventeenth century would have been about 120 million spread over approximately one and a half million square miles. The ranges of some animals had shrunk significantly since early historic times. The lion ranged almost to the Yamuna River and only shrank back into the Gujarat peninsula as a result of colonial trophy hunting after 1800. Interestingly, Gujarat had a much higher density of humans and domesticated herbivores than regions of West Asia where the lion became extinct.

Hunting was a kingly sport and charismatic beasts (so-called because of their compelling grace and beauty) were often its targets. Animal parts entered the pharmacopeia of both India and China. On the other hand, royal hunting reserves also served as wildlife refuges—and indeed, many national parks in today's India derive from such reserved lands. But the equilibrium was clearly moving against animals, especially those dangerous to humans. Still, human populations seem to have been exceptionally tolerant. The English official Thomas Marshall wrote from Gujarat in 1820:

> A Koonbee [farmer] would as soon and does in point of fact, much sooner kill a man than the deer which is eating up his crop before

his eyes. There is something very benign, perhaps almost sublime in the answer which has often been given me . . ."God gave the land and its fruits for these animals as well as for us. . . . All our efforts would not sensibly diminish the numbers of these animals; why then should we teach ourselves to be cruel to no purpose?"

This also brings up the fact that many wild species in southern Asia could survive as commensals to man. Elsewhere, however, dry-season hunts for deer or hares and the like were village pursuits. But in general hunting animals was the prerogative of kings or the duty of specialized castes.

So the Gujarat lion was reserved to the rulers of the petty state of Junagadh and fed largely on the cattle that grazed in woodlands where it was preserved. It was largely destroyed outside such areas in the mid-nineteenth century when colonial officials with their new rifles diverted themselves with trophy hunting. The tiger is nocturnal and solitary in its habits and does not inhabit open woodlands preferred by lions. Large tiger populations survived into the early twentieth century over the wetter two-thirds of the Indian subcontinent. They were widely hunted because of their predation on domestic cattle and occasionally on humans. But enough woodland and prey existed for tens of thousands of tigers until at least 1850. The Asian elephant was only domesticated in India and, like the horse, largely used for war and show. But unlike horses or lions, it breeds too slowly to be easily raised in captivity and has to be trapped and tamed from wild populations. Wild elephants needed large tracts of woodland savanna to sustain themselves, and the growth of human farming populations encroached on that resource. But elephants were protected by kings and also by the religious awe in which they were held. Much Buddhist iconography had associated the Buddha with the bull elephant, and Hindus across the region still invoke the elephant-headed Ganesha at the start of any enterprise. A scientist studying this has written that the risks to an elephant from a trigger-happy farmer are obviously different from the risks with one who worships an elephant's footprint in his field. Over the elephant's distributional range in two continents, the reaction of local communities to elephant depredation varies from vicious retaliation to resigned tolerance.

Still, habitat destruction meant that by 1600 wild elephants were no longer found in the dryer Western part of the subcontinent and becoming scarce in the Gangetic plains. Really large tuskers began to be imported from Sri Lanka. In the mid-eighteenth century, Brahmendra Swami, a Hindu holy man on the southwest coast, was caught trying to smuggle an elephant sent by the Sultan of Mysore to a Muslim potentate on the west coast. (The animal was confiscated and the intended recipient, believing himself betrayed, ravaged the Swami's well-endowed ascetic retreat.)

In China, as we have seen, forests and grasslands were smaller in area than in India, and resistance to their conversion into arable fields was generally weak; and while having many small clumps of trees might have met most human needs, large wild animals need big blocks of uninterrupted forest (or for some beasts, savanna). Consequently, large wild animals had become extremely rare in China's eastern lowlands; and as deforestation of the highlands accelerated circa 1680–1850, many vanished there as well. Elephants, once plentiful in parts of the humid south, had been disappearing for centuries and were essentially gone by 1200. Tigers held out longer. The environmental historian Robert Marks has carefully traced mentions of tiger attacks on villages to determine when these predators could no longer find enough food while avoiding human contact. In Guangdong's most densely populated prefecture, the last recorded tiger attack was in 1690; in the next most densely populated, in 1723. Most other prefectures in both Guangdong and Guangxi record their last tiger attack in the second half of the eighteenth century, though a few mountainous parts of the province had incidents in the early 1800s. One traveler reported hearing of a tiger sighting in a mountainous part of Fujian as late as the 1920s, but this was extremely rare. Guangdong and Guangxi were still probably 50 percent forest in 1700 but experienced rapid population increase thereafter, and were only 5–10 percent forested in 1937. Probably the only places in China in which tigers remained plentiful were in parts of Manchuria and perhaps some mountain forests of Yunnan and Guizhou. Wolves survived in larger numbers, at least to judge by popular warnings about them (which are found in some heavily farmed areas even in the early twentieth century), but there is little doubt that they, too, were in retreat. The large wild animal most associated with China today—the panda—has long had a rather restricted range, mostly at elevations above 3,000 feet. With only slight exaggeration, one could say that while China's ecology had been engineered to support impressive numbers of one large mammal—the human—and its companions (e.g., hogs), this had been done by pushing almost all other large mammals to the margins.

Beyond Food, Fuel, and Fodder: Textiles and Other Manufactures

The earliest domestication of Old World cotton probably occurred in India. Cotton fabric was widely, almost exclusively, used across the subcontinent. The export of cotton textiles was well established by 1000 CE. It grew manyfold with the new global era that began with the Iberian voyages and intensified with the establishment of great state-sponsored trading enterprises after 1600. A large export sector grew up around it. The economic historian Om Prakash has used English and Dutch Company data to calculate that around 1700 some 45,000 to 50,000 looms in the Bengal region were producing fine fabrics for the export market and so employed about 300,000 persons. But he failed to adequately account for the workforce in spinning and preparatory work; if this is suitably revised, then the number would go up to about 900,000—mainly women engaged in hand ginning, combing, carding, and spinning. That would have been some 5 percent of the population of the region, so a significant part of the embodied food energy of local agriculture sailed away to other continents. But this was a labor-intensive exportable fabric.

Coarser cloth for domestic use needed less labor but used more cotton per unit area. Though the climate in many regions of India makes clothing a burden rather than a comfort (prudish visitors often misunderstood the functional choice of minimal covering as a mark of barbarism or poverty), the aggregate demand was considerable, the individual consumption was small. We may estimate consumption in an inland, cotton-growing region at about 2 pounds of fabric per person per year, or about 3–4 yards of cloth. Over a population of 200 million that would still use (at a guesstimate) the yield of over seven million acres of arable land and maybe 5 or 6 percent of the labor force, most of it in spinning and antecedent processes.

In return for this and other exports, the rest of the world returned enormous amounts of hard-won silver, mostly from Spanish America where massive amounts of silver had been discovered. An early English visitor commented: "India is rich in silver, for all nations bring coyne and carry away commodities for the same; and this coyne is buried in India and goeth not out." This was an old pattern in Indian trade, and initially India absorbed two to three times as much American silver (nearly 100 tons per annum) as Ming China (which until the mid-1600s was still importing a great deal of its silver from Japan). The Mughal empire that emerged in the 1550s was able to switch its currency base from copper and silver-copper alloy to pure silver. Given the often destructive methods of gold- and silver-mining—especially the use of mercury and more recently cyanide to separate bullion from ore -- this Asian demand imposed a considerable ecological load on the silver and gold-rich parts of the world.

Until roughly 1300, cotton was a marginal crop in most of China; fine clothing was made from silk and ordinary clothing from hemp or ramie. Over the next 500 years, cotton gradually became the dominant clothing fiber throughout the empire, though the others certainly did not disappear; even as late as 1914–18, China produced roughly 3.5 pounds per capita of ramie. Estimates of cotton production vary wildly; an informed guess of 1.5 billion pounds circa 1750 (between 6 and 7 pounds per capita) is at the high end and assumes little if any growth in total output (and thus a decline in per capita output) over the next 150 years. Large amounts of raw cotton were also imported from India in the late eighteenth and early nineteenth centuries. Most regions of China either imported raw cotton (as did much of the densely populated southeast, often exporting cane sugar in return) or imported the cloth itself (mostly from the Lower Yangzi, which was sometimes said to "clothe the empire"). However, regional self-sufficiency in low- and medium-quality textiles was becoming increasingly common over the course of the eighteenth century as interior regions engaged in a kind of import-substituting (handicraft) industrialization.

Cotton is notoriously hard on the soil, requiring frequent fallowing in much of the world. But this was not the case in the two most important cotton-growing regions of China: the Lower Yangzi and the North China Plain. In the Lower Yangzi, soil fertility was maintained through a very intensive fertilization regime, which mixed locally generated manures, nightsoil from a dense network of nearby towns, and imported soybean cakes (first from the Middle Yangzi provinces, and after circa 1683, from Manchuria). Sir George Staunton, visiting in 1793, remarked that "the collecting of compost for the land is, with them, an object of the greatest attention; in which business are employed old and young, incapable of any other kind of labor. They rummage every street, road, jakespot, river and canal."

A local source said more simply that one should "treasure nightsoil as if it were gold." With time, however, ecological balance shifted increasingly toward reliance on imported commercial fertilizer, which took far less labor to apply. (By the late eighteenth century, Manchurian bean cake, some of it produced by people defying the abovementioned Qing immigration restrictions, was also replenishing sugarcane fields in China's far south.) Since we see no sign of decreasing yields over time, it seems likely that these methods were sufficient to maintain soil quality. The picture for north China is less clear. Lower population densities than in the south meant less nightsoil; while work animals were somewhat more plentiful than in the south, their wastes would not have been enough to compensate. Soybean fertilizer was used here as well; however, locally grown beans were used. Most of the north China cotton country was too poor and too far from good water transport to import large amounts of Manchurian bean cake, but the extraordinary depth of the fertile loess layer may help explain the region's ability to maintain cotton yields, since quite a bit of nutrient-rich soil remained despite erosion.

Most of the labor in cotton cloth production came from farm families (though more specialized weavers produced most luxury fabrics). In the Yangzi Valley and farther south, this was overwhelmingly female labor: indeed, it became proverbial to say that "men farm and women weave," while the older saying "husband and wife work together" gradually became far less common. Average earnings per day appear to have been above what women could have earned in agriculture, though below male agricultural earnings; the virtuous widow, spurning suitors while raising children with the profits of her weaving, is a staple figure in Qing biography. In the north, with a shorter growing season and lower incomes per work day, both men and women wove and spun. Most cloth-producing households owned their own looms and spinning wheels and sold their goods in what appear to have been (by the sixteenth century) very competitive local markets. Large merchants were quite prominent in long-distance trade, with some developing informal trademarks and significant market power, but this was rarely the case in local markets, where harassment by local toughs was a more frequent "market imperfection." Historian Mark Elvin, who has found exceptionally low female life expectancies in a Lower Yangzi textile county generally considered to be quite prosperous, has speculated that the amount of textile work that farm women did (estimates for the 1700s vary from about 150–210 days per year), together with their other burdens, may have seriously impaired their health. Thus far, however, we have no data from elsewhere to confirm that textile centers in general had high female mortality rates, much less to confirm any particular explanation of such a phenomenon.

Yangzi delta textile exports were also important to inter-regional environmental balances. The delta had well over 1,000 residents per square mile by the 1770s, probably exceeded only by Japan's Kinai region. It imported large amounts of grain, raw cotton, sugar, timber, and bean cake, as well as small but ecologically significant numbers of oxen; interruptions of those imports during mid-seventeenth-century rebellions caused intense suffering. Exporting light manufactures, principally textiles, was thus crucial to both short-run food security and long-run environmental stability. Earnings from those exports were also recycled to stabilize other areas: the delta, which was taxed much more heavily than the rest of the empire, paid not only for most of its own public goods but also for certain key projects elsewhere, especially the northern parts of the Grand Canal and the huge dikes on the middle and lower Yellow River.

The outside world was probably less important to China's environment than to India's, though China certainly had a large impact on some external areas. Moreover, this statement must be immediately qualified, because if we were to use Ming borders rather than Qing ones—making Manchuria and Mongolia external to China—environmental exchanges with "the outside world" would become much more important. While it is true that the transformation of much of Manchuria and Inner Mongolia into farmland was a relatively slow process until about 1850, Chinese demand for products from pearls to furs to pine nuts was already changing the ecology of these areas by 1700.

China exported large amounts of both silk and cotton cloth, though less of the latter than India; quite a bit of porcelain; and some other goods, mostly light manufactures. Its imports tended to be products of the land—and especially of noncultivated land (i.e., land that was not used very intensively, which was a luxury China could less and less afford). The one important exception—silver—might be classed as either a mineral or a manufacture (since most was imported after being coined), but in environmental terms it was the mining that placed a great burden on the exporting countries.

Seventeenth- and eighteenth-century China was a significant importer of furs from land mammals in Siberia (and later North America) and sea mammals in the Pacific, reflecting in part the depletion of indigenous forest creatures. (The first Chinese visitor to New York identifiable by name arrived on Jacob Astor's ship *The Beaver*, which was returning from selling pelts in Canton.) Chinese luxury demand for sandalwood (and other aromatics), sea cucumbers, pearls, and other exotica was sufficient to have a very large impact on certain island ecosystems. Even more Latin American silver (though much less gold) flowed into China than into India after about 1600, until nineteenth-century opium imports and other shifts in trading patterns reversed the process and caused a silver drain. By the late eighteenth century, Guangdong province (surrounding the port of Canton) was importing significant amounts of land-intensive staples from overseas (principally rice from Siam and Vietnam and raw cotton from India). And even in the seventeenth century, the depletion of Shanxi forests, which had supplied much of China's ginseng, had had a major political impact; it caused huge amounts of the silver China imported to flow northeastward toward Manchuria and Korea, greatly facilitating the construction of the Qing state that eventually conquered China.

However, internal trade was both economically and ecologically far more important than exchanges with the outside. Foreign contacts had a very large environment impact on China through the adoption of potatoes, maize, tobacco, and other American crops, as already noted. However, precisely because Chinese farmers quickly domesticated these crops, the empire never imported these products on any significant scale, and their exotic origins quickly became as irrelevant as those of cotton or early ripening rice. Thus the significance of China's environmental exchanges with the outside world for China's own environment depends on what time frame we use to assess them. In the long run, movements of plants and knowledge transformed China, but at at any given moment prior to the late twentieth century, the flows of goods between China and the outside world were too small to have an environmental impact even remotely comparable to the goods and people moving back and forth within the empire. Indeed, China was in many ways an interdependent economic and ecological system by Qing times; Mark Elvin has even suggested that by late imperial times both internal trade and administratively directed resource flows were sufficiently large that "the only possible [environmental] equilibrium was an empire-wide one." To be sure, local circuits mattered much more on a daily basis than long-distance ones. Beyond the easily navigable rivers, extremely high transport costs greatly limited market integration. (Barriers to transportation were exacerbated by the relatively low numbers of draft animals and large mountain ranges.) State efforts to facilitate long-distance flows of environmentally sensitive goods sometimes yielded very impressive results while they remained a high priority, but that focus was rarely sustained beyond a few decades. Even at the peak of Qing effectiveness, moreover, some officials still felt that although long-distance trade could enhance social and ecological stability, encouraging these exchanges was a second-best alternative to an idealized world of local self-sufficiency.

Despite these official hesitations, long-distance internal trade increased in economic and ecological significance during the period known as the "high Qing" or "prosperous age" (1683–1795), when the Qing were at the height of their social, economic, and military power. The circuits linking the Lower Yangzi to its trading partners were the most significant, but there were other important exchanges of basic commodities: above all an enormous and still poorly studied long-distance timber trade, but also copper traded from the southwest frontier to the rest of the country, livestock from the steppe (mostly Inner Mongolia) to north China, and grain toward densely populated coastal areas of Guangdong and Fujian. The volumes of these exchanges seem to have increased from the sixteenth to at least the mid-to-late-eighteenth century, with a painful interruption during the civil wars of the middle seventeenth. As measured by the correlation of price movements in different localities, China's long-distance grain markets (the only ones for which we have adequate data) were among the best integrated in the world before railways. Some of these trade circuits were probably contracting by the late eighteenth century, as interior regions became more densely populated, had smaller surpluses of primary products to export, and began producing more of their own cloth; the massive civil wars of the mid-nineteenth century would then shake them profoundly. But some reasserted themselves afterward, and even those that did not (often losing out to international trade through the new treaty ports) had been crucial in their day.

Migrations, Voluntary and Involuntary

People moved long distances too. Chinese long-distance migration in our period was mostly a private and plebeian affair, though the government was sometimes important. Migration directed by the state, or by great families who moved semifree dependents with them, had been more important before circa 1600.

While some people—particularly elites and skilled craftsmen—moved up the urban hierarchy toward the most specialized and lucrative opportunities, most migrants moved the other way, toward less developed regions. Within that general pattern, we can distinguish three principal kinds of long-distance migration. By far the smallest—though often politically significant—migrations were state-directed movements toward contested frontiers. Most of the people involved were supposed to develop food production in the vicinity of frontier garrisons (principally in Xinjiang, in Yunnan, and in Sichuan, where they supported garrisons in Tibet), reducing dependence on supplies shipped from the interior. These migrations diminished after 1759, once the Qing had won their wars against Mongols based in Xinjiang. There were also coerced movements of exiled criminals to various frontiers, but except perhaps in late-eighteenth-century Xinjiang, these migrations were not sufficiently large or permanent enough to be ecologically important.

These streams of coerced migrants were, however, dwarfed by the streams of freely migrating people whom we have retrospectively labeled "Han" Chinese (though very few of them would have used that term before the mid-nineteenth century). We can designate three subcategories of free migrants, depending on the kinds of destinations they went to.

One group went to ethnic minority areas in Hunan, Sichuan, Yunnan, Guizhou, and Guangxi, mixing with local populations amidst varying degrees of symbiosis and conflict. Some of these migrants brought techniques for more intensive cultivation, forestry, or mining than the area's indigenous peoples had used; others used local resources in much the same way as earlier residents.

A second group went to valleys and plains that had been depopulated by civil war and plague in the mid-1600s. They had less need to either displace or come to terms with existing communities and were moving to places that had already been found suitable for Chinese-style agriculture. Thus, they generally fared the best of these migrant streams, with their communities proving both socially and ecologically sustainable.

A third group involved people going to highland areas, often adjacent to densely populated valleys, which had previously had very few inhabitants. For these areas, the spread of American cultivars that would grow where indigenous food crops would not—above all, maize and potatoes—beginning in the late sixteenth century was absolutely critical. However, the highlands were often opened for commercial activities, not subsistence farming; maize and potatoes made it possible to cheaply feed a highland labor force that catered to growing lowland demand for timber, bamboo, indigo, tea, medicinal herbs, iron and iron goods, and so on. Comments by local officials from the early 1820s give some sense of the scale these activities reached:

> An investigation revealed that there were more than 150,000 settlers in the mountains [of one county in southern Shaanxi], and also three large timber enterprises, ten or more sawyers' yards and several smithies. . . .
>
> In the mountains [also of southern Shaanxi] there is a living to be made in iron smelting, in logging, in the paperworks, or in processing mushrooms and edible fungi. One enterprise may employ several hundred men, the small ones several dozen. . . . A hundred li [33 miles] of forest can provide timber for two or three years. . . . A large enterprise may employ several thousand men . . . half of them are vagrants [i.e., poor migrants from elsewhere] and countless numbers depend on them for a living.

These migrations had the greatest environmental impact. Forests disappeared or were replaced by commercially preferred species (chiefly the fast-growing *cunninghamia* trees native to China and prized for their timber). The erosion and flooding caused by deforestation was discussed earlier in this chapter, and these migrations resulted in increased population density sustained by the cultivation of new crops (especially maize and potatoes). These crops failed to hold the soil as well as trees had, and soil washed down steep hillsides. Riverbeds rose and flooding increased. In the process some hillsides lost so much soil so fast that they became barren, forcing the immigrants to repeat the same process elsewhere. By roughly 1800, many local governments were trying (but usually failing) to stop or reverse this movement up the slopes, which local literati (who usually owned land in the valleys below) repeatedly lamented as the pursuit of "a moment's profit" at the expense of "harm to a hundred generations."

Sichuan included examples of all three kinds of destinations: minority areas, areas depopulated by disasters, and previously uninhabited highland zones. At least 8.5 million immigrants moved to Sichuan between 1660 and 1800, more than to any other province. The whole empire probably doubled that number during the same period. The government sometimes subsidized these migrations by giving grants of seed, oxen, tools, etc., and/or cheap credit, especially when people were repopulating lowlands deserted during the turmoil and epidemics of the Ming-Qing transition in the mid-seventeenth century. The Qing also encouraged frontier migrants indirectly by taxing much reclaimed land lightly or not at all. Nonetheless, the migrants organized their movements and their new communities themselves, often on kinship or native-place lines: the scale of organization could range from individuals to thousands of people arriving together to take over a particular highland area.

Indian migration looked rather different from China's, but like China's it was concentrated within its own subcontinent. Few inhabitants emigrated voluntarily. A handful maintained the seafaring traditions of the Indian Ocean. Ram Singh Malana, a sailor from western Gujarat, was shipwrecked in East Africa about 1750 and taken to Holland on a Dutch ship. He returned equipped with new skills in glassmaking and cannon founding, and rose to be an important adviser to the Maharao of Kutch, helping to design a palace with mirrored walls. Enough Indian merchants visited Southeast Asia for them to form a recognized ethnic group, the Kling (a name derived from the Kalinga, ancient name for today's Odisha). Khatri merchants from Punjab settled as far north as Moscow in the time of Czar Ivan IV (r. 1547–84). Other migrants did not go by their own volition: thousands of slaves from Southern Asia were traded overland to Inner Asia and by sea around the Indian Ocean, the latter especially to Portuguese and Dutch tropical enclaves, east and west. But relative to the population of the area, their numbers were small. Vastly greater numbers were usually on the move within the subcontinent itself. Jos Gommans has carefully delineated the range of environments and resources to be found in close proximity within India, with pockets of rich rice paddy reminiscent of the Yangzi delta interspersed among dry thorn scrub resembling Somalia, or rich fields of wheat and barley ending abruptly at the edge of sandy uplands sustaining only nomadic camel herders. And of course, there were extensive tracts of modified woodlands—lopped, grazed, and frequented by humans. Cultivable lands were still available and emigration, short- or long-term, was, as we have seen, the major recourse available to peasants beset by tax collectors or ruined by harvest failures. They moved to the lands of more accommodating lords who were ready to encourage them with better terms. John Malcolm recorded in 1820 that once peace was restored in central India, entire villages that had temporarily migrated west to Gujarat or become bandits lurking in the forests that covered their fields now "flocked to their roofless houses. Infant Potails [headmen] (the second and third in descent from the emigrator) were carried at the head of these parties ... and in a few days every thing [sic] was in progress, as if it had never been disturbed." (It was only in the later nineteenth century that cultivable land became scarce and migration en bloc was no longer a viable strategy.) Emigration was also a recourse after crop failures. In 1782–83 crop failure coincided with warfare and a famine of exceptional severity hit the middle Gangetic plain. Tens of thousands died and many more migrated in bands to the south, where harvests were reputedly better. Wanderers often perished by the wayside. But as soon as steady rains fell, these bands halted and began a journey back to their ancestral homes. Still, we find many reports of parents selling their children because they could no longer feed them. The Dutch company instructed its agents to buy slaves at times when famine made them cheap. Survival strategies might cushion the blows of man and nature, but they were never completely successful in mitigating their effects. As far as agricultural colonization was concerned, Indian farmers were often just filling in thinly settled areas rather than moving to virgin land. Permanent farming might replace slash and burn, or irrigated replace rain-fed tillage. Permanent rice paddy might, as in the Bengal delta, replace lightly used wetlands.

Space, Time, and Political-Ecological Decline

Eighteenth-century China had a stronger, more centralized state than India, which, as we have seen, played significant economic and ecological roles despite making relatively light claims on society's resources. It was able to do this partly by being selective about its interventions, stepping back in cases where other parties could handle things without much help or oversight. Yet there were some things only the state could do, and by the late eighteenth century it was having far more trouble doing them.

One set of state-managed resources was directed toward providing external security. During the first half of the Qing the state directed considerable resources toward frontiers of conquest, especially near the steppe. These areas were mostly nonarable, and so largely separate from the frontiers of settlement. The logistical challenges of campaigning in these areas were formidable, and the Qing managed them with unprecedented skill. From ancient times to the end of the Ming (1644), no large "Chinese" infantry force had been able to campaign on the northwest frontier for longer than 90 days; the Qing, however, could sustain 50,000 troops in the steppe for years at a time, and much larger forces for up to 150 days. This involved some local development (e.g., of military farms in northwestern oases), some hefty subsidies to merchants who supplied basic goods to strategic areas, large expenditures for road building in the northwest, and some dredging of rivers near the Yunnan frontier to facilitate shipping. By roughly the 1780s, however, these efforts were ebbing as the Qing administration began to deteriorate and the state's military capacity declined. This became a huge problem in the nineteenth century, as prolonged, often unsuccessful campaigns against both internal rebellions (most of which originated in frontier areas) and foreign invaders (especially seaborne ones from the West) took a huge toll in lives and resources.

Second, the state at its height had directed considerable resources toward areas such as north China, which were not frontiers but were ecologically and socioeconomically vulnerable. These stabilization efforts became increasingly challenging in the very late eighteenth and especially the nineteenth century. The Yellow River's enormous silt burden ineluctably raised its bed. It was not unusual then—and is not unusual now, even with modern dredging equipment—for the Yellow River's bed to be 10–15 yards (as much as 50 feet) above the land outside the dikes. Consequently, floods could only be prevented (and the Grand Canal, which crossed the river and used its water, could only be kept open) by building ever-higher dikes, and even this extremely expensive response could not do the job forever. Other kinds of environmental management also became more difficult as population increased, and the state's limited fiscal base (and a political culture in which low tax rates were an important part of legitimacy) eventually made herculean interventions unsustainable.

Third, as population grew and people innovated—for instance, by taking advantage of new crops to exploit previously unexploitable ecological niches—the state's regulatory capacity failed to keep pace. Chinese governments had never had tight control in many highland areas, but they had usually been able to live with that. Now it became an enormous problem, and after roughly 1780, records frequently mention frustrated magistrates who knew that highland settlement was causing lowland flooding but could do nothing about it—even in cases where the highland settlers were illegal squatters. (As one nineteenth-century gazetteer put it, "The local people do not dare to enter into altercations with [the highland squatters]; the officials do not dare to investigate them.")

In one sense, the political economy kept going as well as it did because there were so few barriers to moving either people or goods, and people adjusted rationally to the opportunities and pressures scattered across the landscape. But this dynamism amid a narrow ecological margin required very sophisticated counterbalancing of a sort that the Qing could no longer perform, and reliance on a big political structure meant intense pain when that structure weakened.

Although this ecological decline coincided with the political decline of China's particular institutions and trajectory, one could also adopt a more general phrasing, relevant to both societies. Between 1500 and 1800, both China and India came to be crisscrossed by more and more routes for moving people and goods. Some were local, some linked areas across these huge societies, and some connected to places still farther away. All were superimposed on natural circulations—of river water (and silt), monsoon winds, atmospheric and fixed nitrogen, and so on—seeking to direct them for the benefit of the actors involved. Some of the resulting movements generated greater environmental security (for humans) along with increased current prosperity; others intensified environmental vulnerability at one end or the other of the exchange. And the gains in employment, population, and (perhaps) per capita income resulting from these long-distance connections were vulnerable to all sorts of events, including the social and political results of the same environmental stresses that trade itself could either ease or exacerbate. For all the problems that these actions left unsolved, they unquestionably generated impressive growth, shaping landscapes to the advantage of millions of humans.

Arbitraging resources across time was another matter. In both China and India, this mostly involved either the present reducing the future's stock of resources (e.g., by deforesting China's highlands or depleting India's elephant populations) or people accumulating resource stocks to be drawn down in the relatively near future (e.g., by storing grain now for use in a few months, or feeding a young work animal for future use). The available technologies and socioeconomic conditions (e.g., interest rates) rarely favored long-term investment in building buffer stocks of environmental resources when decisions were guided by straightforward profit seeking; we see, for instance, only a few parallels to the commercially motivated reforestation projects in many parts of Japan by 1800. (Relatively successful and sustainable tree plantations did become more common in parts of southwestern China during the nineteenth century, but by that time a great deal of damage had been done, as discussed earlier.) In India rulers sometimes reserved teak forest for the durable timber it yielded; other woodlands and wetlands might be protected as hunting preserves. Ordinary peasants often protected small patches of woodland and particular species of bird or animal, often for religious reasons. But overall, there is little doubt that environmental resources were destructively "mined" as the number of humans grew through the centuries. Large-scale investment in future ecological stability under these circumstances was likely to require vigorous and farsighted government, which was only intermittently present and fragile even then, for social, political, and ecological reasons.

By the end of our period, then, both regions featured increasingly numerous and elaborate structures— physical and organizational, local and supralocal, private and public, and energized by multiple motives—that allowed more humans to mobilize more energy to sustain more activities, and to multiply the plants and animals they favored (rice, wheat, cotton, oxen, horses, pigs) while others (elephants, tigers, various sorts of vegetation) retreated. Additionally, both countries were important participants in the global exchanges energized by European conquest and settlement in the Americas. One of these, the arrival of the maize plant, had a more profound impact in China, while the initial torrent of silver led to the rise of important crafts in India before it generated a boom in Chinese silk, porcelain, and tea exports.

In some subregions, these structures made families and communities less vulnerable to short-term fluctuations in rainfall, temperature, and other natural variables than they had been in previous centuries. But the very multiplicity and complexity of these structures entailed other risks: state failure, trade disruptions, and so on. Meanwhile, the simple cumulative effect of increased numbers and many individually rational acts of resource exploitation added to the risks that needed to be offset by human creativity; these creative interventions were sometimes forthcoming, but in the end were not enough to keep the problems at bay indefinitely. The relative weights of specific resources, innovations, and risks naturally differed between India and China, but there were also basic resemblances between the clusters of issues present in each place, and natural limits to how much the internal relationships within these clusters could vary. In both countries, those issues continue to echo, even amid the very different technologies, politics, and problems of the present.

For Further Reading

China

Bello, David. *Across Forest, Steppe, and Mountain: Environment, Identity, and Empire in Qing China's Borderlands.* Cambridge: Cambridge University Press, 2016.

Brook, Timothy. *The Confusions of Pleasure: Commerce and Culture in Ming China.* Berkeley: University of California Press, 1998.

Elvin, Mark. *The Retreat of the Elephants: An Environmental History of China.* New Haven: Yale University Press.

Elvin, Mark and Liu Ts'ui-jung, eds. *Sediments of Time: Environment and Society in Chinese History.* Cambridge: Cambridge University Press, 1998.

Lee, James and Wang Feng. *One Quarter of Humanity: Malthusian Mythology and Chinese Realities.* Cambridge, MA: Harvard University Press, 1999.

Li Bozhong. *Agricultural Development in Jiangnan, 1620–1850.* New York: St. Martin's Press, 1998.

Marks, Robert. *China: Its Environment and History.* Lanham, MD: Rowman and Littlefield, 2012.

———. *Tigers, Rice, Silk and Silt: Environment and Economy in Late Imperial South China.* New York: Cambridge University Press.

Perdue, Peter. *Exhausting the Earth: State and Peasant in Hunan, 1500–1850.* Cambridge, MA: Council on East Asian Studies, Harvard University, 1987.

Pomeranz, Kenneth. *The Great Divergence: China, Europe, and the Making of a Modern World Economy.* Princeton, NJ: Princeton University Press, 2000.

Von Glahn, Richard. *An Economic History of China: From Antiquity to the Nineteenth Century.* Cambridge: Cambridge University Press, 2016.

India

Divyabhanusinh. *The End of a Trail: The Story of the Cheetah in India.* New Delhi: Banyan Books, 1995.

———. *The Story of Asia's Lions.* Revised and enlarged ed. Mumbai: Marg Publications, 2008.

Gadgil, Madhav R. and Ramachandra Guha. *This Fissured Land: An Ecological History of India.* Delhi: Oxford University Press, 1992.

Guha, Sumit. *Environment and Ethnicity in India, c. 1200–1991.* Cambridge: Cambridge University Press, 1999.

Kumar, Mayank. *Monsoon Ecologies: Irrigation, Agriculture and Settlement Patterns in Rajasthan During the Pre-Colonial Period.* Delhi: Manohar, 2013.

Rangarajan, Mahesh. *Fencing the Forest: Conservation and Ecological Change in India's Central Provinces, 1860–1914.* Delhi: Oxford University Press, 1996.

Rangarajan, Mahesh and K. Sivaramakrishnan, eds. *India's Environmental History. Volume I: From Ancient Times to the Colonial Period; Volume II: Colonialism, Modernity and the Nation.* Ranikhet: Permanent Black, 2012. These volumes reprint 33 important articles published in the last 40 years.

Saberwal, Vasant K. *Pastoral Politics: A Film on the Gaddi Herders of Himachal Pradesh.* DVD. New Delhi: CENDIT, 1998.

Saberwal, Vasant K., Mahesh Rangarajan, and Ashish Kothari. *People, Parks and Wildlife: Towards Coexistence.* Delhi: Orient Longman, 2001.

Sukumar, Raman. *Elephant Days and Nights: Ten Years with the Indian Elephant.* Delhi: Oxford University Press, 1994.

Thapar, Valmik. *The Land of the Tiger: A Natural History of the Indian Subcontinent.* Berkeley: University of California Press, 1997 [also a documentary film available as DVD].

Trautmann, Thomas. *Elephants and Kings: An Environmental History.* Chicago: University of Chicago Press, 2015.

CHAPTER II

Conquest, Rulership, and the State

PAMELA CROSSLEY AND RICHARD M. EATON

Like other continental empires of early modern Eurasia, the Mughal (1526–1858) in India and the Qing (1636–1912) in China were high and personal at the center and everywhere else thin on the ground. They also shared some inheritance from the Mongol empires of the thirteenth to fifteenth centuries (particularly the Yuan [1272–1368] in China and the Chaghatay khans of Central Asia), who supported a vigorous east-west trade network descended from the ancient Silk Road. In the ensuing centuries, the Timurid successors (1370–1507) of the Chaghatay khans led to the Mughal order in South Asia, and the founders of the Qing brought together several strands of Mongol political tradition to create their own state.

Both the Mughals, who emerged from the Timurid dynasty, and the Qing, who succeeded the Ming, were "conquest dynasties," that is, states established by outsiders who patronized the institutions and culture of the society they had conquered. As such, both the Mughals (Turco-Mongolian Muslims) and the Qing (Manchus) not only had the opportunity to incorporate political and cultural elements of the societies they ruled but also were required to do so in the interest of continued stability. Their fundamental tool for this incorporation was rulership as represented in ritual and law. Nevertheless, their methods of building ideologically plural rulerships were different, as were the effects upon the peoples they ruled.

This chapter explores first how conceptions of state power and governance in India had evolved prior to the sixteenth century, and then the ways that power and governance were articulated under the Mughals. In like manner, it examines the sources of Qing imperial ideologies, followed by an examination of how politics and governance under the Qing actually operated. Finally, by teasing out fundamental areas of convergence or divergence, this chapter provides a lens for investigating the ways that political power was imagined and articulated in early modern India and China.

India—Two Traditions of Kingship

One way of narrating the past millennium of Indian history and the role of state power in it would focus on the emergence and interplay of two distinct models of polity, elite culture, and society—one Sanskrit-based, the other Persian-based. Grounded in a transregional language and a body of literature that enjoyed immense prestige across a great expanse of territory—Sanskrit across the Indian subcontinent and Southeast Asia, and Persian across the Indian subcontinent and much of the Middle East—each model interacted in complex ways with the other, and also with local conceptions of power and authority rooted in village culture. Each model celebrated an ideology of a universal ruler, personified respectively by the maharaja and the sultan. Each articulated a blueprint for social and moral order by elaborating codes of conduct and a discourse of proper courtly comportment. And, unlike the British colonial use of religion as a lens for envisioning precolonial Indian history, each model transcended particular religions, even while serving as a vehicle for elaborating, critiquing, and transmitting them.

The Sanskritic model of kingship attained clear definition by the fourth century and persisted unrivaled for nearly a thousand years, furnishing a template for how new states emerged and asserted their claims to legitimate authority throughout South and even Southeast Asia. From around the early second millennium, this model began to be articulated in South Asian vernacular languages, displacing Sanskrit's former monopoly on political discourse. Then from the early thirteenth century a second transregional model of state and society—the Persianate—appeared, first in north India and soon thereafter in the south. Each had much to say about state building.

In the earlier, Sanskritic model, chiefs who managed to acquire control over strategic forts would appropriate the title of *raja* and claim descent from illustrious royal predecessors or mythological figures. They also performed—or were said to have performed—stunning deeds of conquest, including actual or ritualized conquests of neighboring kings (the *digvijaya*, or "conquest of the quarters"). Once in power in their own courts, these rulers sought to transform former or potential enemies into dependent vassals. They also patronized Brahman priests, built and maintained temples, bestowed royal titles on their vassals, and, in India's dryer regions, supported the construction of irrigation systems for enhancing the productive wealth of their respective domains. Crucially, they ascribed ritual sovereignty over their domains to a form of one of the great Hindu gods (usually Shiva or Vishnu), conceived of as their state's cosmic overlord, whose image was typically placed in an elaborately adorned royal temple located in the heart of the kingdom's capital. Viewing himself as a servant of his kingdom's patron deity, a king thus shared with the gods a common pool of symbols respecting power and authority. However, because they were professionally engaged in the shedding of blood—a deeply polluting substance in the Hindu universe—kings were ritually disqualified from interacting directly with the divine world, an activity that consequently fell to Brahman priests attached to royal courts.

The nexus of king, dynastic temple, and cosmic overlord carried important political implications. Unlike the mass of village temples—humble, ubiquitous, and apolitical structures—dynastic temples visually manifested a king's claim to rulership. They were sites of political establishment, renewal, or contestation, and thus vulnerable to attack by political enemies. Indeed, it was not unusual for victorious adversaries to desecrate royal temples by carrying off, as trophies, images associated with the sovereign power of a defeated king. In their own inscriptions, kings were most consistently represented not as pious, morally righteous, or godlike figures but as fierce warriors who, possessing awesome and overwhelming power, violently subjugated their foes.

By the eighth or ninth century, India's political universe had become crowded with little kings, bigger kings, and emperors—i.e., kings of kings. But it was also a world of constantly shifting political sands. Rulers had few permanent enemies or allies, since classical political theory recommended that, in conducting the business of warfare, enemies be not annihilated but rather co-opted and transformed into loyal subordinates. Once so transformed, yesterday's enemies could be put to use as allies against tomorrow's potential enemies. Indeed, by this logic territory itself was conceived of very much like a large chessboard on which kings maneuvered with allies and against rivals with a view to creating an idealized political space—or *mandala*—consisting of a series of concentric circles, with one's own capital and heartland occupying the center, surrounded by a second circle of one's allies and a third of one's enemies. Beyond that lay one's enemies' enemies, therefore potential allies. With this model in mind, kings endeavored to ally themselves with distant enemies of nearby enemies. With all of India's major dynastic houses playing by the same geostrategic rules, no single dynasty could achieve lasting dominance over large swaths of territory within India, much less over the subcontinent as a whole.

Toward the end of the twelfth century, a very different conception of interstate relations, kingship, and governance reached India when the northern half of the subcontinent—the Indo-Gangetic plain—was conquered by Persianized Turkish speakers who had reached the subcontinent from Central Asia and the Iranian plateau. Between the eighth and thirteenth centuries the caliph ("successor" to the Prophet Muhammad) in Baghdad theoretically ruled over the entire Muslim world, from Spain to eastern Afghanistan. But by the tenth century, his authority had shrunk to religious affairs only, while in the eastern, Persian-speaking half of the Muslim world leadership in worldly matters was seized by powerful confederations of ethnic Turks who had migrated southward into the Muslim world from Central Asia. The most successful of these converted the seminomadic traders into bands of armed followers, led by men who had taken the potent title and ideology of "sultan." By the twelfth century, as caliphal political authority continued to weaken, Persian theorists began to endow these sultans with all the majesty, might, and ceremony that had been associated with pre-Islamic Persian emperors. For during those same centuries, the modern Persian language had been crystallizing amid a general revival of memories of Persian history and culture before the Arab conquest (642). Like its Sanskritic predecessor, then, this Persianate model of worldly power was also sustained by a language and literature that was both prestigious and transregional.

A critical stage in the evolution of the sultan as an all-powerful political figure was reached in 1258 when Mongol armies destroyed Baghdad and abolished the office of the caliph of Islam. The elimination of this politically feeble but symbolically still-potent figure had the effect of elevating and confirming the place of sultans as supreme rulers in the Persianate world. Moreover, since their stature had evolved in culturally plural Central Asia—with its mixture of Christian, Buddhist, Jewish, Sunni, and Shi`i Muslim, as well as shamanistic and pagan Mongol traditions—sultans were understood as standing above and beyond all religious communities. Notably, the sovereign territory included within a sultanate—that is, a state ruled by a sultan—was in principle limitless, shaped by neither regional, nor ethnic, nor religious identities. This enabled sultanates to span vast swaths of land and to encompass communities of considerable ethnic diversity.

At the same time, the void in religious authority created by the abolition of the caliphate was filled by charismatic Sufi shaikhs—Muslim mystics or holy men popularly understood as spiritually powerful owing to their alleged nearness to the divine world. Thus emerged a de facto separation of religion and state in mainstream Persianate thought: political authority was appropriated by sultans, while religious authority was displaced onto a host of Sufi shaikhs and their tomb sites where, it was believed, a shaikh's spiritual power continued to abide after his physical death. Lacking religious authority or charisma of their own, many sultans took pains to patronize popular shaikhs or tombs of renowned Sufis by way of securing a firmer foothold with the masses, since such figures (or their tomb shrines) were revered by peoples of various faiths.

Merged Models of Political Authority

Between 1192 and 1206 Persianized Muslim Turks based in Afghanistan defeated the major dynastic houses then ruling over northern India and, in 1206, established the Delhi Sultanate (1206–1526), named after its capital city. From then until the advent of the British Raj in the late eighteenth century, the greater part of South Asia was ruled by dynasties that traced their historical origins to Central Asia or Persia and subscribed to Persianate ideals of a sultanate. In practice, however, the Persianate and Sanskritic models of political authority were never pure or mutually exclusive; nor were they immune from the expectations of their subject peoples, whose own political cultures tended to seep upward into these two transregional models of power and authority.

The result was hybridized patterns of political behavior. By the fourteenth century, some Hindu rulers, aspiring for the most powerful and widely known titles then available to them, began referring to themselves by the title *sultan*. They also incorporated into their ruling ideologies rites and norms of Persian kingship, such as the idea of justice as a fundamental principle of rulership, together with Persian architectural styles and sartorial customs, such as headgear and tunics. By the fifteenth century, vernacular languages had replaced Sanskrit as the principal medium of political discourse, and as this happened, these tongues readily assimilated Persian terms pertaining to power or governance. In both the Bengali and Telugu languages, for example, the ordinary words for fort, cannon, stirrup, and saddle are all Persian; the same is true for terms dealing with technologies of knowledge (pen, paper), architecture (bastion, dome), and other domains strongly influenced by Persianate culture, such as cuisine and dress. In a word, India's gradual incorporation into this expanding Persianate discourse of worldly power and statecraft was facilitated by a ruling ideology that had jettisoned the political authority of a caliph, focused on principles of universal sovereignty and justice, and accommodated itself to cultural diversity.

Conversely, and simultaneously, states in India established by immigrants or invaders from Central Asia freely assimilated political practices of the Rajputs, north India's indigenous ruling class since at least the tenth century. This is seen from the very beginning of Persianate rule in India. Having defeated an important Rajput maharaja in 1192, thereby gaining control of the north Indian plain, Sultan Mu'izz al-Din Ghuri (r. 1192–1206) immediately minted and put into circulation coins proclaiming his right to rule. On one of these he stamped an image of the goddess Lakshmi, imitating the coins issued by his defeated Rajput opponent. On the reverse side the sultan's name appeared, not in Persian script but in the locally familiar Nagari script, together with Sanskrit honorifics. The sultan also governed in the manner of a classical Indian maharaja, as a sort of over-king reigning over a circle of Indian princes who had been allowed to retain elements of their former sovereignty, and to whom he sent signet rings with his name carved in Sanskrit. In effect, India's first ruling sultan established a classical Indian *mandala*, or circle of sovereignty, with himself at its center.

By the early fourteenth century, Mu'izz al-Din's successors, the rulers of the Delhi Sultanate, leaned even more heavily on Sanskritic political culture and local understandings of political legitimacy. In 1326 Muhammad bin Tughluq (r. 1325–51), shortly after annexing a large part of the Indian peninsula to the Delhi Sultanate, restored a Shiva temple to ordinary worship. The inscription recording this act not only was engraved in Sanskrit but also styled the sultan according to classic Indian titles for a supreme emperor, *maharajadhiraja sri suratana*. The same ruler also adopted Indian political rituals relating to the sacred Ganges River. In 1327, after establishing the southern city of Daulatabad as the co-capital of his vast, all-India empire, he had Ganges River water carried a distance of forty days' journey from north India for his personal use. These actions would have recalled the events that occurred around 1022, when Maharaja Rajendra Chola I famously marched an army a thousand miles from the Tamil country in India's deep south up to Bengal, where he defeated local kings and then had pots of Ganges water carried back to his southern capital. By adopting such measures, rulers of India's Delhi Sultanate period, though rhetorically invested in Persianate norms of kingship, enacted political rituals fundamental to the authority of earlier Indian kings.

In their revenue and justice administrations—the proper business of any state, apart from making war—one sees how deeply Persianate states in India had come to rely on local traditions. In 1535 the sultan of Bijapur, who reigned over much of the western portion of the peninsula, announced that all official documents would thenceforth be kept not in Persian but in the local languages, Kannada and Marathi. He also placed Brahmans in key positions of his kingdom's revenue bureaucracy. Similar measures were taken in the sultanate of Golkonda (c. 1500–1687), in the eastern peninsula. It is revealing too that despite attempts of Persianate sultanates in peninsular India to introduce gold and silver currencies in accordance with Middle Eastern standards of weight, metallic content, and inscriptional programs, local bankers would accept only coinage that conformed to the region's pre-Persianate norms. In the fifteenth century, rulers of the Bahmani sultanate (1347–c. 1500) could not prevent bankers and money changers from melting down state-minted gold *dinars* and *tankas* and recoining them in a regionally familiar format—the *hon*. Indian bankers and merchants had been using this gold coin since it was established by the prestigious Chalukya dynasty, which had reigned over much of peninsular India between 973 and 1200. As late as the seventeenth century Persianate sultanates in this region, aware of the continued demand for coinage that conformed to Chalukya standards, began minting their own gold *hons*—albeit without Hindu images and Nagari script—and carrying out normal revenue functions in that currency.

In sum, while Indian courts of whatever historical origin drew on both Persianate and Sanskritic models of political authority, they also assimilated considerable local culture into their state institutions, ranging from vernacular languages used for their revenue administrations to local customs recognized in adjudicating disputes and coins minted in traditional formats. This much we know from court chronicles, inscriptions, coinage, and the accounts of foreign travelers. A trickier question is determining how local populations assessed their Turco-Persianate rulers, although tantalizing shreds of evidence do give clues. For example, in a 1276 Sanskrit inscription not patronized by the Delhi Sultanate or even known to its officers, a Brahman priest recorded the construction of a well near Delhi that had been financed by a petty Hindu landholder to benefit local villagers. Closely conforming to the format that Indian courts had been using for centuries, the inscription opens with a flowery panegyric to and genealogy of the current sovereign, Sultan Balban (r. 1265–87), together with the entire line of rulers, both Rajput and Turkish, who had reigned over north India in the preceding several centuries. The author evidently saw no sharp break, much less a civilizational rupture, between (the Sanskritic) Rajput and (the Persianate) Turkish rule in north India. In his view, one dynasty had simply succeeded another. With Balban identified not by his Persian title of *sultan* but by the Sanskrit honorific "Nayaka Sri Hammira," Turkish rule was smoothly accommodated within conventional Sanskrit tropes of powerful and worthy rulers. Indeed, Balban's realm was said to have enjoyed such stability and contentment that even Vishnu—the great god who appears periodically in various incarnations to rescue the world in times of distress—could sleep peacefully on an ocean of milk, without a care in the world. Already by the late thirteenth century the Persianate and Sanskritic discursive universes had begun to overlap each other.

The Mughal State in Operation

In 1526 Zahir al-Din Babur, a Central Asian prince whose lively memoir, the *Baburnama*, has made him one of the most vivid figures in Indian history, rode down from the mountains of Afghanistan to the wide Indo-Gangetic plain, swept away the last dynasty of Delhi sultans, and established the Mughal Empire (1526–1858). A proud descendant of the great Central Asian warlord Timur (a.k.a. "Tamerlane," r. 1370–1405), Babur sought to transplant Timurid political and aesthetic norms to north India. His descendants would go on to build the largest and most powerful state India would see before British imperialists occupied South Asia in the late eighteenth century. Although Babur (r. 1526–30) and his son Humayun (r. 1530–39, 1556) brought fresh infusions of Central Asian and Iranian military and administrative personnel to north India, for several decades the Mughal state differed little from the regime it had replaced.

But the Mughals' third dynast, Akbar (r. 1565–1605), profoundly altered the empire's character. Instead of endeavoring to defeat entrenched Rajput ruling houses and annex their territories, as the Delhi sultans had long sought to do, Akbar made them partners in the Mughal enterprise, enlisting leading Rajputs in a newly created cadre of ruling officials. The move was both politically astute and mutually advantageous. On their side, the Mughals obtained the services of India's finest cavalry, regular tribute payments, the right to regulate succession within Rajput houses, the circulation of Mughal coinage in Rajasthan (the Rajputs' ancestral homeland), safe passage through that region for merchants and pilgrims traveling to ports on the Arabian Sea, and an effective counterweight to a powerful Central Asian faction in the Mughal nobility. For their part, the Rajputs received high ranks in Akbar's newly crafted service-elite, guarantees of noninterference in their internal affairs, a wider arena of political and military action since they could now serve throughout the empire, and guarantees that they would not be pressured to convert to Islam. This last measure reconfirmed the classic Persianate ideal of the sultanate, which effectively separated religion and state.

Even more importantly, Akbar's policy transformed the Mughal state's character by thoroughly indigenizing its ruling culture, as Rajput styles of warfare crept into the ranks of the Mughal army, Rajput aesthetics infused imperial architecture, and Rajput princesses, who had been incorporated in the Mughal harem as part of Akbar's new policy, became the mothers of successive emperors. (Akbar's harem as a means of creating political alliances is discussed further in chapter 3 on gender systems.) All of this had the effect of gradually assimilating an originally Central Asian dynastic house to the norms of north Indian culture. Consider the *jharokha*, a small, elevated balcony that projected from palaces, where Rajput rulers traditionally sat and were viewed by members of the nobility or commoners. Although for Rajputs this had been a strictly political ritual, it resonated with the ordinary way in which Hindus interact with the divine world, since establishing mutual visual contact with the image of deities lies at the heart of Hindu devotion. Therefore, when Akbar introduced the tradition of *jharokha darshan*—i.e., "viewing" the *jharokha*—in his royal palace, he was drawing as much on Hindu religious practice as on Rajput political ceremony.

Akbar also developed sophisticated institutions for administering the empire's revenue and military systems. Needing a body of capable, talented men who could act as generals, governors, advisors, and administrators both in the provinces and at the imperial center, he created a new cadre of men known as *mansabdars*, or "holders of a *mansab*" (rank). A direct antecedent to the Indian civil service of British colonial and even modern times, the "*mansabdari* system" was a graded hierarchy of ranked officers appointed directly by the emperor. These were the great public figures in the sixteenth and seventeenth centuries, replacing the remnants of the Delhi Sultanate or its successors in every region where the empire expanded. The court closely monitored the *mansabdars*, increasing or decreasing their ranks according to their civil and/or military performance. Although Akbar recruited only several hundred *mansabdars* into his ruling elite, the total number grew to some eight thousand by the end of the seventeenth century. Yet even then the core of the ruling group remained at around five hundred. The highest-ranking *mansabdars* functioned as provincial governors, field generals, or central ministers, while middle-ranking *mansabdars* served as fort commanders or district or provincial officers. The lowest-ranking *mansabdars* held positions as office superintendents or keepers of arsenals.

In a measure that effectively merged the empire's revenue and military systems, *mansabdars* were given land assignments known as *jagirs*, the size and quality of which was carefully calculated to yield each *mansabdar* sufficient revenue to recruit, equip, train, and maintain a specified number of cavalry, available to the emperor on demand. Although the Delhi sultans had instituted a similar system, inherited from their Persianate political ancestors in Central Asia, Akbar's *mansabdari* system was far more sophisticated. Notably, Akbar instituted procedures intended to prevent *mansabdars* from acquiring independent power bases. In theory, a *mansabdar*'s position could not be inherited, and a new appointee had to pay a large security bond; upon his death, a *mansabdar*'s property reverted to the state. Most importantly, these men were regularly rotated through the empire's domains—a measure aimed at discouraging their acquiring a local political base that might divert their loyalty from the imperial center.

Since the extent of an emperor's patronage depended on the amount of land available to dispense in the form of revenue assignments, the Mughals had an inherent incentive to expand their sovereign territory. However, apart from just several decades when they governed parts of the Deccan plateau (the heart of peninsular India), the area of the Mughals' effective rule was limited to the Indo-Gangetic plain. And even within north India, their sovereignty was always constrained. This, in turn, brings us to a notable feature of India's political history. In striking contrast with Qing China, which extended its sovereign territory from Manchuria to Mongolia, Turkestan, and Tibet to the west, the Mughals, like the Delhi sultans before them, never tried to expand their rule beyond the subcontinent, except for a single, abortive foray into northern Afghanistan. Even within South Asia, Mughal rule was territorially limited. One reason for this was topographical. The Deccan plateau is hemmed in by formidable mountain ranges on its northern and western sides, and punctuated by numerous steep hills. Over the centuries hundreds of hill forts, taking advantage of the region's natural topography, appeared perched atop the region's many scarps. Whether giving refuge to rebels or serving as power bases for local chieftains (*zamindars*), the plateau's numerous fortified centers inhibited the region's conquest by any one state. In north India, by contrast, the wide, flat, and fertile Indo-Gangetic plain—like Egypt's Nile Valley but on a much grander scale—proved relatively easy for cavalry-based armies to control. Yet even in the north, large, centralized states were more often the exception than the rule, suggesting that topography was not the only factor inhibiting the emergence of large, stable empires in the Indian subcontinent.

More fundamentally, and paradoxically, the expansion of states in the Indian subcontinent—whether informed by the Sanskritic or the Persianate model of power and authority—was limited by the very factors that caused them to expand. In the Sanskritic model a righteous king, like a chess player carefully maneuvering his pieces on the board, followed an elaborate geopolitical strategy aimed at creating around his royal court a circle (*mandala*) of subordinate rulers. These might be distant kings, would-be rivals, or even former enemies. As a result, although a king's circle of subordinate rulers might be forged from success in combat, it was maintained by an exchange of honors. The paradox, however, was that in return for gaining public recognition as a supreme overlord, a maharaja had to dispense to his subordinates much of the substance of governance:

administering justice, collecting revenue, raising armies. As a result, the more vassals (dependent states) a king gathered within his realm, thereby expanding his notional sovereign domain, the more effective power he lost. Moreover, because numerous actors were all playing by the same principles on the same geopolitical chessboard, India's political space between roughly the fifth and thirteenth centuries became crowded, with no single power ever able to control anything approaching the greater part of that space.

After the thirteenth century, a similar dynamic limited the territorial reach of Persianate states, including the largest of them all, the Mughals. Notwithstanding that empire's association with images of power and grandness—their very name having entered English as a synonym for a great person or magnate, or indeed anything "big"—the Mughals always interacted with indigenous communities, especially in provinces distant from the imperial center. That, after all, was where imperial officials encountered, and had to engage with, local elites of various sorts: powerful merchants, recalcitrant *zamindars*, petty functionaries, entrenched gentry, village headmen, etc. Recognizing that imperial sovereignty could be established only by sharing its perquisites with a myriad of such local power holders, Mughal officials had constantly to negotiate and compromise with these figures who, for whatever reason, were socially or politically important. This meant, quite simply, that the Mughal state was anything but a Leviathan. Paradoxically, while sharing power with local players served to expand Mughal authority along the periphery of its borders, it was at the expense of further empowering those same players. This had not only diluted central authority but also transformed the character of the empire. In effect, each and every deal made with a local power holder, no matter how petty he might be in the Mughals' vast imperial machine, chipped off a tiny bit of sovereignty from the imperial center.

In a curious way, then, the Persianate model of the Indian sultanate—even in its largest, most majestic, Mughal incarnation—suffered a fate not unlike that of its Sanskrit predecessors. Maharajas of earlier dynastic houses had demonstrated their pretensions to universal dominion by exchanging honors with vassals, which in practice meant authorizing the latter to engage in the substance of governance. In like manner, Mughal officials on the periphery of the realm negotiated with existing power holders in ways that diluted central authority. A notable instance of this is seen in the late seventeenth century when the emperor ʿAlamgir (r. 1658–1707) was campaigning along the Mughals' southern frontiers. Intent upon realizing the old north Indian ambition of conquering the Deccan, the emperor offered inducements to local commanders or chieftains to join the Mughals as imperial *mansabdar*s. But since the principal such inducement was land in north India, much of which had already been assigned to other officers in the form of *jagir*s, the emperor's initiatives effectively disenfranchised older sections of the nobility. Such a policy of "robbing Peter to pay Paul" inevitably created tensions within the imperial service, ultimately contributing to the decay of the empire as a whole.

The same political factors that constrained the territorial expansion of India's largest empire in the early modern era also constrained lesser polities. It would be wrong, however, to view the resulting state of political fragmentation as some sort of failing on the part of Indian states, in contrast to the more consistently centralized empires of their Chinese contemporaries. A decentralized political condition was no more a failing for India then than it was for contemporary European states. Indeed, it is sometimes argued that Europe's smaller, more coherent, and more compact states had a cultural and political dynamism not found in sprawling, top-heavy empires. More states meant more courts, and hence more patronage and opportunities for literati and artists, which raised the overall level of cultural production in both India and Europe. A greater number of royal courts also fostered greater diversity in cultural production, as regional states patronized artistic and literary traditions unique to their regions.

The same principle holds true for technological research and experimentation. During the tumultuous sixteenth century, when gunpowder technology spread throughout India, intense interstate rivalries led to remarkable advances in the making of matchlocks and cannons. The most impressive advances, however, were made not in the sprawling Mughal realm in the north but among the fragmented sultanates of the Deccan plateau. There, continual warfare among antagonistic states led to a sort of arms race. This in turn stimulated extraordinary advances in firearms technology that in some respects were centuries ahead of anything developed in Europe, such as the world's first large cannons mounted atop towering bastions, capable of 360° rotation.

China—Sources of Qing Imperial Ideologies

Both the Mughal and the Qing empires indirectly inherited traditions of universal rulership from Mongol conquerors and rulers of the thirteenth and fourteenth centuries. But universal pretensions in early modern rulership could take a great variety of forms. In Central Asia and across the Iranian plateau, where Turkic-speaking peoples outnumbered the Mongols themselves, the latter were dependent upon and in some sense absorbed into the Turkic mainstream, usually adopting Sunni Islam. Since the Turkic peoples of this region had already been integrated into the Persian literary and ideological world, the Mughals—themselves Persianized Turks—had weak ties with Mongol culture. As a result, even though Babur was distantly descended from Chinggis Khan (r. 1206–27) through his female ancestors, the political traditions that he and his successors brought to India were nested mainly in Persianate court culture and ideology—especially as articulated by Babur's ancestor Timur, as described above. In order to create claims to universal dominion, those traditions tended toward a hybridized, cosmopolitan fusion of their imported ruling practices and local Hindu, and especially Rajput, traditions.

Mongol overlords in China during the Yuan period (1271–1368) continued to use the Mongolian language and religion as their primary tools of government, while the political life of the lineage descended from Chinggis Khan and his grandson Khubilai Khan (r. 1260–94) remained unbroken in parts of Mongolia down to the seventeenth century. After the fall of the Mongols in China and the establishment of the Ming dynasty in 1368, a group of Mongols returned to eastern Mongolia and established the "Northern Yuan" empire. For a century and half the Northern Yuan regime attempted to unite all of Mongolia under its control. Although they failed to do so, they did perpetuate a complex ruling ideology that historians have called "Chinggisid." This ideology included (1) a special role in ceremony and political participation for descendants of Chinggis Khan; (2) the notion of the Mongol supreme ruler, or *khaghan,* as a secular ruler endorsed by Heaven (Tengri), the lineage elites, and the hierarchs of Tibetan Buddhism; and (3) the use of the Tibetan Buddhist Mahākāla cult to transfer the consciousness of Chinggis Khan and other conquerors to the living *khaghan.*

When the Yuan Empire of the Mongols had gained control of Manchuria in the thirteenth century, its rulers appointed traditional local headmen as Yuan officials who were then obliged to render tribute and enforce imperial law. In the centuries after the fall of the Yuan in 1368, Manchuria was divided by regional alliances. They sanctified politically significant occasions by the performance of shamans who could assure the approval of the spirits of mountains, forests, waters, or other natural features. In the seventeenth century, the Qing emperors traced their earliest political ancestor to one of these Yuan-period appointments. In their view, this was one direct source of their ancestral state, which had been organized in the late sixteenth and early seventeenth centuries by Nurgaci (r. 1616–26), who became a leader of a group of native Jurchens (later known as Manchus) in southern Manchuria. Nurgaci's Aisin (or Jin) Khanate, created in 1616, had already absorbed several distinctive bases of authority and legitimacy— namely, the Turkic ideology of the *khan* as a transregional leader and lawgiver, and the Mongol ideology of the *khaghan* as the supreme ruler. He also adapted the northern Asian tradition of the aristocratic estate encompassing people, herds, equipment, and rights, making it the basis of what would later be called the Eight Banners system. In their early forms, the banners were the property of the princes of the ruling council, enrolling families under their authority in military enterprises. By these means the population and the military forces were controlled through one administration, allowing Nurgaci to consolidate his control over the contending villages and federations of the region.

In 1618, just two years after founding the Aisin Khanate, Nurgaci declared war on the Ming Empire. By 1621 he controlled enough of the Ming province of Liaodong to establish a capital in the city of Shenyang (whose name the Manchus translated into Mukden), where he employed Chinese bureaucrats to create a civil infrastructure of his state. These bureaucrats represented Nurgaci as a ruler who revered the traditional Chinese ruling virtues and who could be trusted to govern Liaodong's large population and rich economy. Nurgaci died in 1626 while still pursuing war against the Ming and was succeeded by his son Hong Taiji (r. 1626–43), who initiated a second war against the Chinggisid Khaghanate (a continuation of the Northern Yuan) in eastern Mongolia. In 1634 the war in Mongolia concluded with absorption of the Chinggisid state, its cult objects, its aristocracy, and a good portion of its population. The effect upon the victorious Aisin Khanate was remarkable, as its institutions and nomenclature were changed. The process culminated in the establishment of the Qing Empire in 1636, ruled for the first time by an "emperor" (*huangdi*).

At the moment of its creation, the Qing rulership encompassed the rituals, the rhetoric, and many of the institutions of three systems of rule—the emperors of China, the Great Khans of the Mongols, and the headmen of Manchuria.

The early Qing rulers decided not to have one system of rule supersede another or to blend old and new elements into a hybridized whole. Instead, they increasingly directed their performance of rulership toward different audiences, representing different phases of the Qing conquest. The foundation population, the Jurchens, now known as Manchus, were still governed through the Eight Banners organizations that dated to Nurgaci's earliest days of local rule, before the creation of the Aisin Khanate. The Manchus addressed the Qing rulership in Manchu, while edicts from the emperor came to them in Manchu (or that was the ideal). They mediated their relationships with the emperor and with Heaven through shamanic rituals, and they had a hereditary obligation to remain military slaves of the ruler. For his part, the emperor continued his role as a traditional northeastern khan by practicing Manchu-style shamanism in the imperial compound, by keeping Manchus as his closest bodyguards and retainers, and by personally demonstrating his skills in the traditional military art of horseback archery.

The next ruling personality added to the Qing emperorship was derived from the Mongols and from Mongol systems of rule. These contributions began as early as 1607, when Mongols escaping pressure from the Chinggisid Khaghanate in eastern Mongolia appealed to Nurgaci for support and recognized him by the Mongol title *khaghan*, making him in title the equal of the Chinggisids. Beginning at that time and continuing through the defeat of the Chinggisids in 1634, Mongols of various federations became members of the Aisin aristocracy by marrying into the ruling lineage, and many other Mongols joined the Eight Banners, where special units were eventually created for them. By the time the Qing emperorship emerged in 1636, Hong Taiji ruled the Mongols not only as leader of the Manchus but also as a Mongol ruler in his own right. He inherited the *khaghan* tradition of Chinggis through his mother (a similarity to Babur in some ways) and the distinct role of *cakravartin* (the Buddhist ruler extending enlightenment to all nations, modeled on Emperor Ashoka [r. 268–232 BCE], whose *Edicts* helped spread Buddhism throughout ancient India). Loyal Mongols would thereafter address the Qing rulers in Mongolian, in terms resembling those once used to address the Chinggisid rulers, and accept them as the legitimate heirs to control of Mongolia; those dissenting would discredit the Qing pose as the successors of Chinggis. For their part, the Qing emperors patronized the Tibetan Buddhism that had become the greatest symbol of rule in Mongolia. They also patronized the friendly Mongolian aristocracy and made regular sojourns in Mongolia to hunt with the Mongols and perform their traditional rituals. Mongols outside the Eight Banners were also administered by their own government within the Qing state, the Lifanyuan. As a formal state office the Lifanyuan dated to 1634, though its functions could be traced to the earliest times of Mongol affiliation with the Aisin Khanate.

The last component added to the Qing state and emperorship was the civil government adopted from the Ming and used to administer conquered Chinese-speaking territories. The Chinese political traditions to which Nurgaci appealed after his conquest of Liaodong had been shaped first by the Han Empire in China (206 BCE–220 CE) and taken up in an increasingly conscious way by subsequent empires based there, whether ruled by Chinese, Turks, Tibetans, Kitans, or Jurchens. There was a legal code underlying this model, which in its prescriptions for hierarchy and differentiated punishments based on status probably preserved the basic content of the Han Empire's laws through the centuries. An ideological tradition—by Qing times, based on the Four Books of Confucian scholarship— helped unify imperial officials (see also chapter 5). There was also a ritual structure, bringing together ancient themes of worship of Heaven, Earth, the ancestral spirits, and seasonal changes with specific veneration of Confucius (551–479 BCE). And there was a very strong rhetorical tradition allowing the emperor to express himself as a moral guardian and not as the head of a state based on extraction or coercion. Foremost among the rhetorical themes was that of "benevolent government," according to which the state acted to prevent predation upon the common people by elites, used its powers to protect the people and encourage agriculture, and maintained a harmonious relationship between humanity and Heaven.

Governments fulfilling these ideals were regarded as enjoying the "Mandate of Heaven"—the endorsement of a supreme deity that either sustained the current dynasty or led to its replacement by another. Stability was theoretically achieved not by state coercion but by the recognition of mutual obligations between social classes. This included both the obligation of educated men, empowered either through landowning or through government appointment, to protect the powerless, and the obligation of the powerless to revere the powerful. Over the centuries, realization of these ideals in any particular empire ranged from incidental to negligible, but as an ideology this system was indispensable to Chinese emperorship. Moreover, although the ideology produced strong rulers in relation to the aristocracy or other rival elites, it did not change the dynamics of a tiny state in a huge and complex society. Hence, the ideological appeal to cooperative elites and an acquiescent population were essential to the functioning of China's imperial systems.

There was comparatively little in the way of amalgamation, synthesizing, or fusion among these rulerships before the nineteenth century, in contrast to the Mughal style of rulership, which combined Sanskritic and Persianate traditions into a hybridized whole. This may be because through the reign of the Qianlong emperor (r. 1736–95), the regions conquered by the Qing and contributing the distinctive traditions of legitimacy remained distinct as political districts. Manchuria, China, and Mongolia were all very clearly represented in the legal codes and historical geography of the Qing Empire. In state pronouncements, the emperors generally distinguished clearly among these regions, even if the exact vocabulary varied with time and circumstance. Their distinctness was reinforced by the fact that each region loosely corresponded to a government, or set of departments, within the imperial state. And there was the custom of accommodating the rituals and political practices of both the conquering caste and the majority population (usually Chinese-speaking), dating back to the time of the Northern Wei (386–534) state. Each impersonation was linked to its own places, language, dress, and religious ideas. This pattern was found in other empires based in China, including the Tang (618–906) and Jin (1125–1234). A high priority was placed on keeping these lesser rulerships separately recognizable within the greater rulership, not fragmented or fused together to the point of losing their distinctness, and losing the facility to represent distinct groups who had taken a role in conquest.

One may call this political and ideological tradition "simultaneity," in the sense that the Qing emperor simultaneously addressed each of the empire's three major political communities in its own traditional idiom. This pattern was further elaborated in the eighteenth century, when Tibet was added to the amalgam of political constituencies, albeit with careful excisions. A posture of imperial discipleship to the Tibetan hierarchs, particularly the Dalai Lama, was expressed in imperial language, religion, and architecture. But the people and the territory of Tibet remained a blank in imperial speech and behavior. In the mid-eighteenth century, Qing rulers fashioned another carefully tailored persona for the Xinjiang region. Although it ignored Islam and most of the Xinjiang population, this persona was built on the Uighur language, the history of Turkic-speaking nomads in Xinjiang and western Mongolia, and the genealogies of the very small number of Sufi lineages that had facilitated the Qing conquest of the region.

An outstanding feature of Qing literature and monuments was the parallel placement of multiple languages—usually Manchu, Mongolian, and Chinese, but in the later period also Tibetan and Uighur—carrying more or less the same message, as if the emperor were radiating his meanings to various audiences simultaneously. This style of simultaneous rulership was found in other continental "conquest empires" of Eurasia, perhaps most obviously the Ottoman Empire (1299–1922) and Tsarist Russia (1615–1917). In these instances, two factors seemed to have driven this political and ideological strategy. First, at the initial time of conquest, rulers of the empires had depended upon soldiers and administrators from the newly conquered population. With simultaneously represented rulership, the conquered could see their values of political legitimacy represented alongside those of the conquerors. Second, by representing the political ideologies and cultural values of the separate conquered peoples within their rulership, the Qing, Ottoman, and Russian rulers could influence the identity, beliefs, and practices of their diverse populations. This helped preserve the long-term stability of elites in both empires. Not surprisingly, simultaneous rulership was the mark of an empire of conquest. Once the conquests had ceased and the leadership was consolidated, laws and ceremonies reifying cultural identities became influential in the regulation of status.

How credible did each of the empire's intended audiences find the Qing court's various impersonations? Manchus appear to have taken their relationship to the khan fairly seriously, as it was emblematic of their livelihoods as dependents of the court. Mongol reactions were split between those regarding the Qing emperors as true heirs of Chinggis Khan and those regarding the pose as a tool to undermine Mongol independence. Among Chinese officials and the scholarly class from which they were drawn, there was a general acceptance of the Qing emperors as rulers successfully fulfilling the ideals of benevolent government, specifically by restoring civil order after the failure of the Ming and its successor, the short-lived Shun dynasty (1644). They approved of the fact that the Qing preserved the traditional institutions of annual worship, maintained the examination system, and constantly exhorted the population to honor the traditional hierarchies based on class, generation, and gender. A minority among the Chinese voiced their rejection of the Manchus as barbarian conquerors who, in the mold of the Mongols four hundred years earlier, had come to China only to dominate and exploit. Unlike the Mongols before them, the Qing court sought to discover such acts of treason by conducting home inspections, trials for sedition, and literary inquisitions, and they punished offenders so severely that the opposition remained almost entirely underground.

The Qing Empire in Operation

The Eight Banners had originally administered the entire local population under Nurgaci's control, but as the conquests spread to China the Bannermen became distinct and segregated agents of occupation. They and their families were settled in walled compounds, with their own lands, grazing areas, living quarters, entertainment districts, and graveyards. This created many complications for the imperial state. First, by separating this large portion of the Eight Banners from their traditional livelihoods in the northeast, the court had made all Banner families dependents of the state. Problems in paying their salaries and supplying them with grain became evident almost immediately. At the same time, the state's requirements that Bannermen retain distinct cultural identities did not work. Bannermen were required to live in the garrison compounds, work as soldiers or in military support, speak and write Manchu (or, if they were Mongol, Mongolian) in all official communications, and avoid relations—most specifically marriage—with the locals. Within only a couple of decades of the conquest, the emperors were aware that almost none of these rules was being consistently or universally observed. At the same time, using the Eight Banners as an occupation force severely limited their usefulness in further conquests in Taiwan, Mongolia, Tibet, and Xinjiang, since they were nowhere near the front. New soldiers were constantly recruited from among civilian Chinese, and the state struggled to coordinate its increasingly complex military populations and its campaigns of conquest. In the early eighteenth century a new central coordinating office, the Grand Council, was created, but it could do little to control the cultural identities and outlooks of the Eight Banner soldiers settled in the Chinese provinces.

The Lifanyuan or Frontiers Department—the state office originally created to manage the affairs of Mongols who were not in the Eight Banners—gradually assumed more general duties. It temporarily administered territories that came under direct military control in Xinjiang, and it managed communications between the Qing court and the Dalai Lama, who controlled part of Tibet. Later, the Frontiers Department became the comprehensive instrument for administering the empire's indirect rule over these regions. The department had its own treasury, personnel office, diplomatic reception courts, translation offices, law code, and judicial system. The appointment or confirmation of Mongolian, Turkestani, or Tibetan clerics, tax and tribute collection, and adjudication of disputes were all under its jurisdiction. Perhaps inevitably, the process of conquest and consolidation caused a seepage of its jurisdiction and authority. The Eight Banners supplied most of the officials to the Frontiers Department, whether or not they were appointed to military posts. Military campaigns in western Mongolia and eastern Turkestan required coordination between the Frontiers Department and the policies of the Eight Banners. For a time, parts of the southwestern provinces of Sichuan and Yunnan were administered by the Frontiers Department, owing to the strategic significance of these regions to the Qing position in Tibet. But the imperial policy of assimilating and progressively regularizing the administration of the southwest gradually put these matters under the authority of the civil government.

The civil government, initiated after the capture of the Ming provincial government at Shenyang and later acquired whole with the conquest of Beijing, was largely kept in its Ming form. There were small amendments made to accommodate the emperor's multiple cultural identities, but in general Qing innovations consisted of the introduction of the earlier governments of the Eight Banners and the Lifanyuan. The civil government mainly managed imperial edicts, the criminal courts, census taking, population, and the writing of history. It also administered an examination system, modeled in principle on the traditional examination system by which Chinese officials were made eligible for employment (though there was a translation component for candidates whose official language was Manchu or Mongolian). Officials at the highest level of the Qing bureaucracy, the traditional Hanlin Academy, were expected to read Manchu as well as

Chinese, since both languages were necessary to the business of the imperial court. But at the level of the central offices for history, law, maintenance of public works, and appointments, the bureaucracy of the Qing functioned along the same general lines as had the Ming civil bureaucracy before it. This was true to the point of virtually no increase in the number of county magistrates who had worked under the Ming, despite the fact that the Qing empire grew to be much bigger. The civil bureaucracy used Chinese as its administrative language and addressed the emperor through the same rituals and used the same physical venues in Beijing as had their Ming predecessors. Considerable power devolved to the civilian government during the conquest period. Indeed, by the later seventeenth century, a set of southern provincial regimes had become so independent that the Qing court had to prosecute a civil war to root out secessionist tendencies. Over the course of the eighteenth century, however, the central government reclaimed power through a torrent of literary inquisitions, prosecutions for corruption and factionalism, and a rewriting of seventeenth-century history aimed at discrediting some of the leading bureaucratic lineages of the civil government.

India and China Contrasted: Different Responses to Similar Problems

The Mughals and the Qing were both originally expansive empires of conquest, but their differences are instructive. For their part, the Qing after conquering China conducted repeated wars to conquer all of Mongolia, and they were eventually drawn into Tibet and eastern Turkestan. They also made the first incorporation of Taiwan into an empire based in China, and expended significant resources attempting to expand into Nepal, Burma, and Vietnam. By contrast, the Mughals had far more limited territorial ambitions, restricting their major annexations to the north Indian plain and eastern Afghanistan. It is true that they coveted peninsular India, as had the Delhi sultans before them. Yet the Mughals learned nothing from the Delhi Sultanate's failure to hold Deccani territory that it had conquered in the early fourteenth century. For unlike in north India, peoples south of the Narmada River had never subscribed to the legitimacy of Delhi as India's "natural" capital. Thus, from 1682 to 1707, the emperor ʿAlamgir doggedly and vainly campaigned across the ever-rebellious Deccan plateau, squandering the wealth of an empire that would soon show signs of internal decay.

Both empires also patronized the dominant cultures of their respective subject populations, but in very different ways. In the case of the Qing, the emperor was simultaneously a *khan* to the Bannermen, a *khagan* to the Mongols, and a *huangdi* to the Chinese. Depending on context, he could also be a Mongol hunter, a Daoist priest, a Manchu warrior, a Confucian scholar, or a Buddhist monk. This was a difficult act, to say the least, and not entirely convincing to all subjects all the time, but it appears to have been sufficiently convincing to enough subjects enough of the time, at least before the nineteenth century. After that, the Qing sought to recast themselves as archetypes of a newly recognized "national" culture, but that attempt failed, as did similar attempts in Tsarist Russia and the Ottoman Empire.

In contrast to the Qing practice of fashioning distinct imperial personae, the Mughal emperors worked in a more amalgamizing style, blending the political cultures of their subject populations into a hybridized, composite whole. Thus, aware of the original sources of their legitimacy, they presented themselves as proud heirs to the Central Asian political legacy of Timur ("Tamerlane"). Babur saw himself as institutionalizing in India the very sort of Timurid kingdom that he was unable to establish in his native Central Asia, adopting the same titles by which his ancestor Timur had associated himself with Mongol rule. The Mughals also cultivated a self-image as millennial sovereigns and projected this image onto Timur, whom they called the "Lord of Conjunction." In the seventeenth century emperor Shah Jahan (r. 1627–56), making a clear reference to Timur, grandly referred to himself as the "Second Lord of Conjunction." Reflecting the influence of the Iranian components of their ruling class, Mughal emperors associated their rule with the sun, drawing both on Sufi Illuminationist thought and on ancient Iranian traditions that stressed the primacy of the sun and represented the emperor as embodying emanations of divine light. Accordingly, Akbar replaced the Islamic calendar with the Persian solar calendar, Jahangir (r. 1605–27) commissioned paintings depicting himself enveloped by the sun and the moon, and Shah Jahan was depicted with rays of sunlight striking his halo. From Akbar's time on, Mughal rulers also incorporated a wide spectrum of Rajput political culture, enlisting leading Rajputs into the elite *mansabdari* service corps and Rajput women into the imperial harem. By sitting in small, elevated balconies (*jharokha*) that projected from their palaces where they could be viewed by elites and commoners alike, Akbar and his successors directly participated in a traditional Rajput political ceremony that would have been familiar to all Indians.

With respect to the recruitment of elites and government officials, the Qing and the Mughals faced similar problems but produced differing solutions. In the Qing period, high-ranking officials of the Eight Banners or the Frontiers Department shared a reverence for the emperor that obviated cultural differences, whereas civil officials were largely recruited via China's traditional examination system. Because this system required lifelong immersion in a relatively fixed set of texts, successful candidates shared a public ideological consensus that could transcend private philosophical and cultural differences. The result was a network of local magistrates, working under provincial governors, who could be relied upon to handle local financial and security issues without routine consultation with the capital (though with a rigorous system of reporting local problems). The system therefore served the Qing regime's strategic goals of achieving long-term stability and of reproducing an elite that in theory would be both loyal and competent.

The Mughals, instead of instilling ideological conformity among its ruling elite through something like the Qing's examination system, relied on a highly regulated system of nomination as its primary means of recruiting new talent into the ruling class. High-ranking officers in the *mansabdari* system nominated candidates whose credentials were then examined and vetted by court officials—and in theory by the emperor himself. If approved, these recruits were given appointments, typically in the form of land assignments, or *jagirs*, where they were expected not only to collect revenue but also to recruit, maintain, and lead a specified number of cavalry. Since new recruits to the imperial service were already known to those nominating them and were often related to them by blood, the ruling class gradually took on a distinctly hereditary quality. By the mid-seventeenth century, relatives of powerful nobles entered imperial service not only on the death of their patron-relative but even during his lifetime. In fact, sons of the highest-ranking *mansabdar*s were normally enrolled as *mansabdar*s themselves. Although they could not inherit their fathers' rank or titles and had to begin their careers with a relatively low rank, they were marked for promotion and rapid advancement in the system. India and China thus present a sharp contrast in how they recruited men into their respective ruling classes. Whereas the Mughals were more concerned with reproducing hereditary power and stabilizing a loyal aristocracy, the Qing valued a fluid class of civil officials whose highest priority would always be preservation of the concentrated personal power of the ruler.

In terms of more practical imperial life, Mughal and the Qing rulers were both acutely aware of problems inherent in having a large imperial lineage, especially the problem of succession. But their solutions were different. The very early Qing did not use primogeniture, but followed the old northeast Asian practice whereby a council of princes selected new rulers by merit rather than by birthright. In an attempt to minimize princely rivalry and intrigue, the Kangxi emperor (r. 1661–1722) secretly named a successor among his sons, starting the practice of not revealing the identity of a new emperor until the death of the former one. In other ways—such as establishing imperial court control over the Banners, refusing to invest princes with fiefs, and using a network of spies to keep an eye on aristocrats and high officials—the Qing attempted to prevent the imperial lineage from becoming a political theater. The succession struggles of the late seventeenth century and even the deadly strife between regencies and the imperial lineage in the late nineteenth century show that the emperors were not entirely successful in this; but in comparison to the imperial lineage dramas of the Ottoman and Russian empires, the Qing appear relatively placid.

For specific reasons, however, even the Ottoman and Russian struggles look tame compared to the Mughals, who had more directly inherited Turco-Mongol traditions of imperial succession, according to which a new ruler came to power as a result of violent contests between the sons of a deceased ruler. In order to avoid the destabilizing effects of such struggles, and being well aware of the dangers of Turco-Mongol traditions of allowing princes to govern provinces for long periods of time, the Mughals regularly rotated their princes through provincial appointments. They also required princes to make regular trips to the imperial court to pay paternal homage, in addition to using spies and informants to keep tabs on their political activities. But none of these measures prevented princes from cultivating their own political bases, or violent succession struggles from breaking out after an emperor's death, some becoming fratricidal civil wars. By contrast, neighboring states (i.e., not only the Ottomans but also the Uzbeks and Safavids) avoided such wars either by executing their princes or by confining them in court, thereby depriving them of valuable hands-on experience in governance. Nor did the Mughals adopt primogeniture or any system of succession less traumatic than outright fratricidal struggles. Though sometimes violent, the system did guarantee that new rulers had the benefit of considerable political and military experience before assuming the throne, and that the "best-networked" among competing princes would ultimately reign.

These striking differences in approach to conquest parallel equally striking differences in accommodation of diverse cultural identities within their realms. For example, India and China had very different approaches to the related problem of language and geography. Since Chinese is written in semi-ideographic characters, not phonetically based letters, it was possible from early imperial times for elites of very diverse geographical and dialectal communities to participate—across both space and time—in a common written culture. This continued during the Qing, though the nature of Qing rulership required that in public monuments and various aspects of court administration, Manchu and Mongolian were also prominently used. Particularly in the eighteenth century, the court's determination to keep the Manchu language as the emblem of the conquerors' identity produced the interlocking developments of imperial pressure to standardize the language and to publish dictionaries and primers. This unusual accessibility of written Manchu had an impact at the time and also today, but over time the ability of written Chinese to transcend differences of language and dialect made it the more critical language in most aspects of direct imperial administration, and provided a clear basis for a national language after the Qing demise.

India had nothing like this. While the Mughals endeavored to stamp a sense of imperial uniformity on their realm—and in 1582, Akbar declared Persian the sole language for all levels of the empire's judicial and revenue bureaucracies—their far-flung empire embraced different vernacular language communities. And since all South Asian vernacular languages use phonetic scripts, no one of them could completely suffice for written communication. Persian, though the mother tongue of very few native Indians, became the tool for socioeconomic advancement for upwardly mobile Indians (just as English would do in India under the British Raj). But around the beginning of the second millennium, when India's various vernaculars began to appear in writing and to be used in state bureaucracies, the sovereign territory of states tended to coincide with the distribution of spoken languages. Rulers of the Delhi Sultanate used the transregional Persian language only at the highest level of administration, while conducting their local administration in newly emerging written vernaculars.

Consequently, with that kingdom's decline in the fifteenth century, regional states emerging from its former provinces promoted their respective vernaculars as their official language. The tight relation between language and state is seen in the decline of Persian usage as imperial fortunes themselves began to wane in the eighteenth century, leaving the linguistic foundations of any future state negotiable among the prominent vernaculars. (Linguistic unity and disunity across India and China is discussed further in chapter 4 on language and literature.)

Conclusion

While there are striking differences between the Chinese and Indian early modern states, from attitudes toward territorial expansion, state bureaucracy, and succession to style in governing across vast differences in culture and language, there are ultimately many points on which the Mughal and Qing empires display both structural and familial similarities, largely because the problems they successfully faced were the same. Both regimes were originally outsiders who strongly identified fixed points of historical political centrality and established themselves in cities that had been important capitals since the thirteenth century. For the Qing, Beijing was the political heart of China, largely because it had been from there that Khubilai Khaghan and then the Ming had ruled. In India, from 1206 sovereignty over the Indo-Gangetic plain was closely associated with rule from Delhi. New dynasties aspiring to pan-Indian rule felt compelled to make that city their capital, or at least, in the case of the Mughals, their principal capital.

Both evolved elaborate administrative systems to extract wealth from dense agrarian populations in the form of land taxes, while maintaining powerful, land-based armies combining both traditional and artillery-based elements. Both maintained enduring contact with the peoples of Central and Inner Asia, the great belt of pastoral grasslands stretching from Manchuria to the Caspian Sea. Although the Mughals' connection to the pastoral life (i.e., life where clans followed their herds to seasonal pasture lands) was much stronger than that of the Manchus—who were not nomads but had experience of the political history of the pastoral Mongols—both entered their respective sedentary zones as horse-oriented warrior castes and attempted to retain these identities after assuming rule. But while acting the role of conquerors they also, over time, came to identify in varying degrees with the conquered. They adapted already existing infrastructures for taxation, control of currency, punishment of crime, regulation of internal commerce, and so forth.

Ultimately, the rulerships and the strategies of the Qing and the Mughals were shaped most profoundly by the exigencies of overland conquest. Each remained partly in thrall to a traditional military elite, which not only threatened repeated political fragmentation but also left them unprepared to deal with foreign economic encroachment. Their tiny—with respect to their large populations and complex economies—civil governments never allowed them to generate the revenue that would have permitted modernization. Instead, each regime was financially devastated by cataclysmic civil war. In the case of the Mughals, the exhaustive Deccan campaigns (1682–1707), which the ageing emperor `Alamgir personally directed for twenty-five years against a sea of opponents, devoured imperial resources. In the case of the Qing, the Taiping War (1851–64) claimed between twenty and forty million lives and forced permanent decentralization of its administrative and financial functions.

And finally, in each empire, the penetration of foreign merchant capital further weakened control over domestic affairs. With the conclusion of the Opium War (1839–42), European powers acquired concessions from a weakened Qing court that allowed foreign investments in large-scale projects such as railway construction; by the end of the nineteenth century, the Japanese, Russians, and several Western European powers had all imposed large "spheres of influence" in Qing territory, undermining the court's sovereign authority. In India, investments by Western European trading companies in the seventeenth and eighteenth centuries slowly and quietly integrated coastal economies into economic regimes directed from Amsterdam, Paris, or London. Initially, this went largely unnoticed in the Mughal capital, since Delhi had never conquered much of coastal India in the first place. By the late eighteenth century, however, the penetration of foreign capital in two commercially rich coastal provinces under Mughal rule, Gujarat and Bengal, began having the same corrosive effect on Mughal authority that the penetration of foreign capital would have in nineteenth-century Qing China. By the mid-nineteenth century, both India and China were sufficiently entangled in British imperial trade management that the Europeans could play their weaknesses off against each other. Yet neither empire developed a national style of rulership or a narrative of successful opposition to foreign intrusion that would have made them appear authentic to the subjects they ruled.

For Further Reading

China

Bartlett, Beatrice S. *Monarchs and Ministers: The Grand Council in Mid-Ch'ing China, 1723–1820*. Berkeley: University of California Press, 1992.

Chang, Michael G. *A Court on Horseback: Imperial Touring and the Construction of Qing Rule, 1680–1785*. Cambridge, MA: Harvard University Asia Center, 2007.

Crossley, Pamela Kyle. "The Historical Writing of Qing Imperial Expansion." In *Oxford History of Historical Writing*, Volume 3, 1400–1800, ed. Jose Rabasa, Masayuki Sato, Edoardo Tortarolo, and Daniel Woolf. Oxford: Oxford University Press, March 2012.

———. *A Translucent Mirror: History and Identity in Qing Imperial Ideology*. Berkeley: University of California Press, 1999.

Dai, Yingcong. *The Sichuan Frontier and Tibet: Imperial Strategy in the Early Qing*. Seattle: University of Washington Press, 2009.

Elliott, Mark C. *The Manchu Way: The Eight Banners and Ethnic Identity in Late Imperial China*. Stanford: Stanford University Press, 2001.

Millward, James A. *Beyond the Pass: Economy, Ethnicity, and Empire in Qing Central Asia, 1759–1864*. Stanford: Stanford University Press, 1998.

Perdue, Peter C. *China Marches West: The Qing Conquest of Central Eurasia*. Cambridge: Harvard University (Belknap) Press, 2005.

Rawski, Evelyn S. *The Last Emperors: A Social History of Qing Imperial Institutions*. Berkeley: University of California Press, 2001.

Rowe, William T. *China's Last Empire: The Great Qing*. Cambridge, MA: Harvard University (Belknap) Press, 2009.

Wakeman, Frederic E., Jr. *The Great Enterprise: The Manchu Reconstruction of Imperial Order in Seventeenth-Century China, Volume 2*. Berkeley: University of California Press, 1985.

India

Alam, Muzaffar Alam and Sanjay Subrahmanyam, eds. *The Mughal State, 1526–1750*. New Delhi: Oxford University Press, 1998.

Balabanlilar, Lisa. *Imperial Identity in the Mughal Empire: Memory and Dynastic Politics in Early Modern South and Central Asia*. New York: I. B. Taurus, 2012.

Dale, Stephen F. *The Garden of the Eight Paradises: Babur and the Culture of Empire in Central Asia, Afghanistan and India (1483–1530)*. Leiden: Brill, 2004.

——. *The Muslim Empires of the Ottomans, Safavids, and Mughals*. New York: Cambridge University Press, 2010.

Faruqui, Munis. *Princes of the Mughal Empire, 1504–1719*. Cambridge: Cambridge University Press, 2012.

Habib, Irfan. *The Agrarian System of Mughal India (1556–1707)*. 2nd rev. ed. New Delhi: Oxford University Press, 1999.

Hasan, Farhat. *State and Locality in Mughal India: Power Relations in Western India, c. 1572–1730*. Cambridge: Cambridge University Press, 2004.

Kolff, Dirk H.A. *Naukar, Rajput and Sepoy: The Ethnohistory of the Military Labour Market in Hindustan, 1450–1850*. Cambridge: Cambridge University Press, 1990.

Kulke, Hermann, ed. *The State in India, 1000–1700*. New York: Routledge, 1998.

Moin, Azfar. *The Millennial Sovereign: Sacred Kingship and Sainthood in Islam*. New York: Columbia University Press, 2012.

Phillips, Andrew. "Civilising Missions and the Rise of International Hierarchies in Early Modern Asia." *Millennium: The Journal of International Studies* 42, no. 3 (2014): 697–717.

Talbot, Cynthia. *Precolonial India in Practice: Society, Region, and Identity in Medieval Andhra*. New York: Oxford University Press, 2001.

CHAPTER III

Gender Systems

The Exotic Asian and Other Fallacies

BEVERLY BOSSLER AND RUBY LAL

A juxtaposition of the historical landscapes of early modern India and China (between 1500 and the early nineteenth century) reveals profound differences. China has had a long tradition of political unity and acceptance of an overarching ideology of social and political practice. India is a region with extraordinary ethnic, linguistic, religious, geographical, and political diversity. Political and religious regimes were multiple, and social practice varied with caste, class, region, and religion, rarely conforming to a standard pattern. In comparing China and India, this chapter emphasizes historical trends, events, and individuals that often escape notice. It traces some of the ways gender systems in India and China came to be ascribed, misleadingly and self-servingly, stereotypes associated with "exotic" Asian societies. It brings into view a diverse range of female figures, and the spaces (schools, homes, rooftops) that were the grounds where gender relations were negotiated.

The gender ideologies that shaped India and China seem, on the face of it, notably similar: the seclusion and restriction of women through cruel social and cultural practices such as foot binding in China and *purdah* (seclusion) in India; the sanctioned suicides of young widows in both societies. As you read this chapter, the critical underlying point is to understand the gender systems of China and India as sets of relationships negotiated by human beings rather than static, harsh, and abstract ideologies imposed upon them. Accordingly, this chapter explores some of the ways even the apparently restrictive gender regimes provided emotional rewards and allowed for autonomy of action.

Until recently, the histories of the precolonial Indian and Chinese worlds were written as if the early modern were no more than a preamble to the "modern." This chapter explores more than those terms narrowly concerned with the emergence of a bourgeois, reformist, "modern" China or India. It also explores how notions and norms of gender shape expectations and opportunities for men as well as women. To that end, it presents a more complex picture of gender by insistently documenting "minor" forms of agency where none were thought to have existed and investigating the individual struggles and aspirations that shape all periods of history.

Stereotypes and Western Imperialism

Before examining the historical specificities of gender in early modern China and India, it is essential to point to the history of the emergence of stereotypes and their ongoing legacy. A common moment in the cases of both India and China is when the idea and images of women became inextricably intertwined with Western expansionism. A very specific sense of the exotic and at the same time subdued and dutiful woman was created by an imperialist projection of fantasy and superiority. Again, the time and the landscape of the emergence of actual and imaginary restraints in both societies differ in striking ways.

Eighteenth- and nineteenth-century British colonial writings on India, deemed "histories," constructed a vision of India as a collection of strange, unfathomable societies that had no history. These societies were "idyllic," yet marked by violence, religiosity, indiscipline, divisiveness, laziness, lustfulness, and strangeness—witness the women, *harem*, *zenana*. The Hindi-Urdu word *zenana* (women's quarters among respectable Hindus and Muslims) came to be used interchangeably with the Perso-Arabic word *harem*, which is essentially a descriptive term for the inner, sacred spaces of domestic life in palace societies. Like the zenana, the harem is meant to be the inner domain of women, but the harem could serve as the living space for women across generations and thus was often a larger physical space.

European writings on this luxurious, remote, and inaccessible world became especially pervasive with respect to the imperial societies in India. If the dynasties happen to be Muslim, as was the case of the Mughals, who ruled most of the Indian subcontinent in the sixteenth and seventeenth centuries, then the extravagant and extensive descriptions of royal women and a sexualized harem become the main focus. Harems were depicted as debased polygamous setups where behind secure walls hundreds of veiled women, resting on couches with grapes and wine, black eunuchs in attendance, were waiting for the monarch to appear. Mystery and indulgence encapsulate such histories. In subsequent capital H histories describing the Mughal economy, polity, administration, or empire at large, written by both British and Indian scholars, the experiences and the influence of women were almost entirely wiped out. What could an empire possibly have to do with its women?

Up to the seventeenth century, Europeans rarely advanced general propositions of the "inferiority" of India. At some point in the eighteenth and nineteenth centuries, however, a different kind of statement began to emerge, one that would become part of the standard image of India. This new representation rested upon accounts of specific institutions and practices that were symbolic of the general "barbarity" and "debased" condition of "the East." A new structure of colonial power produced a new structure of knowledge, both explicitly based on a belief in the hierarchy of civilizations. In the pecking order now drawn up, the British (or the British version of Christian civilization) was at the top. Muslims, Hindus, and others ranked far below—with the Muslims sometimes rated better than the Hindus, and the Hindus at times seen as superior to the Muslims. The signs of the inferiority of the latter set were frequently seen in the place assigned to their women. *Purdah*, *sati* (a widow committing suicide after her husband's death), child marriage, and the harem became more or less equivalent symbols of that barbaric "other." Such premises meant a colonial writer would not need to distinguish among these institutions; one "barbaric" practice could stand in for the others.

The equally static image of "premodern" Chinese women and their physical locations and social institutions was likewise shaped by the impressions of European and American traders and missionaries, especially those who began arriving in the eighteenth century. Traders' stories of the mysterious Forbidden City, which was built in the fifteenth century and remains the largest palace complex in the world, included accounts of imperial concubines—women whom the emperor supported and with some of whom he had long-standing romantic and sexual relationships. Earlier stories such as the thirteenth-century *Travels of Marco Polo* had laid the groundwork for a pleasure palace image of concubines who waited on the emperor: "such of them as are of approved beauty, and are good and sound in all respects, are appointed to attend on the Emperor by turns. Thus six of these damsels take their turn for three days and nights, and wait on him when he is in his chamber and when he is in his bed, to serve him in any way, and to be entirely at his orders."

Nineteenth-century writers had somewhat more accurate information, but were no less fascinated by the image of women confined for the emperor's pleasure. Thus the American traveler H. O'Shea observed in 1890,

> Can anything in the jealous and suspicious orient be more religiously secluded than the imperial court of Peking?. . . The "Palace of Earth's Repose" [is] where the empress holds her court and rules over the imperial harem, whose only glimpse of the outside world is what they can see in the imperial flower-garden. . . . In the centre of the garden is an artificial mountain surmounted by a pavilion. . . . From the apex of this hill the unfortunate captives can just catch a glimpse of the roofs of some of the higher buildings outside the Forbidden City. Here the ladies of the court take the only breath of fresh air they can hope for till they reach the allotted age of twenty-five years, when the imperial concubines are free to return to their homes and parents, whom they are never permitted to see during the long years of their gilded slavery. . . . The present young emperor, in addition to his seven lawful concubines, has already no less than one hundred and thirty others in his harem.

These observations echoed long-standing Chinese fantasies of hundreds of beautiful but lonely and neglected palace women, all waiting for the attention of the emperor. Foot binding, arranged marriage, and concubinage attracted a different kind of attention from horrified Christian missionaries. Anxious to convince the populace at home of China's desperate need for "Christian" reforms, they wrote at length of the abuse and misery of Chinese women. Only rarely did missionaries explain the larger ideological system in which the Chinese gender system was embedded—Confucius's "five bonds" of the natural order that outlined the mutual obligations of ruler to ruled, father to son, husband to wife, elder brother to younger brother, and friend to friend. Confucian ideology (like other ideologies throughout the world before the twentieth century) taught that men should have authority over their wives, and ritual propriety dictated that women should obey their fathers, then their husbands, then their sons (in China, this was called the "three followings"). But Confucian emphasis on social harmony and filial piety imposed constraints on men as well as women.

While there were no such clear-cut, time immemorial "three followings" for Indian women, a range of prescriptions abounded. The *Laws of Manu*, composed about 200 to 400, indexes severely restricted property rights for women, the trend of early marriage, preoccupation with chastity, and a growing concern to maintain inheritance in the male line. The eighteenth-century *Guide to the Religious Status and Duties of Women* (*Stridharmapaddhati*), compiled from ancient scripture by the Hindu scholar Tryambakayajvan, emphasized the good wife's utter devotion to her husband: "The good woman regards her husband as a god.... For the husband is god for women; the husband is family; the husband is the goal. There is no goal, no deity but the husband." The duties of the ideal Hindu wife included waking before her husband to prepare breakfast, doing all the housework (even if servants were affordable), and caring for the children. These acts of devotion were believed to contribute to the maintenance of an ordered universe, in the same way that the "three followings" promoted cosmic order and social harmony for the Chinese.

Instead of looking at these practices as historically based and evolving religious traditions—and in India, ones that varied widely by region—they were interpreted by Westerners as signs of inferiority and often used to justify imperialism for the "improvement" of women. Reformers paid little attention, for example, to the matrilineal inheritance that was practiced by by the Nayyars of Kerala and the Bunts and Billava of Karmataka, among others across India, or to evidence of women sacrificing to the gods in ancient India even though later this became associated exclusively with male practice. Similarly, they ignored that foot binding, a favorite Western image of cruelty imposed on Chinese women, had actually originated in the tenth to eleventh centuries as an alluring fashion, and that by the early modern period, it was a sign of social respectability and Chinese identity. Instead, the legacy of exotic debasement oversimplified what were complicated and nonlinear historical developments in gender relations, as will be explored further in this chapter.

Spatial Dimensions of Gender: Harems and Inner Quarters, Walled Gardens and Rooftops

Distinct spaces are central to the making of women and men, and male and female practices, in any society. In China, classical texts from before the first millennium CE advocated a strict separation of family and social life into "inner" (*nei*) and "outer" (*wai*) domains, specifying that women's proper place was inner while men's proper place was in the outer realm. This ideal originated from a basic principle of political economy: if men devoted themselves to plowing the fields while women spun and wove inside the home, the populace would be fed and clothed. But this principle was conjoined with the notion that the family was a microcosm of the universe, which implied that properly ordered relations within the family were critical to the proper functioning of the cosmos. As a result, by no later than the eleventh century the notion that "women are inner, men are outer" was widely understood as a general norm of social organization.

By the early modern period, philosophical principles of gender segregation had long since been incorporated into the architecture of homes and palaces in both China and India. To Western viewers in the nineteenth century and after, these hypervisible Chinese and Indian abodes became signs of constraint and incarceration: the Forbidden City that housed the Chinese court, the sexualized harem, and the inner quarters of the mansions of the elite in both China and India, are some examples. But what did the segregated spaces mean for women and men as the everyday locations of existence? Concepts such as "inner" (private) and "outer" (public) were always relative and fluidly defined. In China and India, proper women would have as little contact as possible with males outside their immediate circle of kin. But among rural families in both societies—who made up the great majority of the population—many tasks typically performed by women (washing clothes; picking tea; raising silkworms) were understood as properly "inner" work, even when those tasks required women to be physically outside. In the Chinese countryside, for example, to be "inner" meant mostly that women generally did not labor in fields growing grain along with men.

In both China and India, male and female domestic spaces were distinctly marked. In Hindu households, physical distance was practiced in relation to older male relatives as well as outsiders. Among the Muslims, physical seclusion was especially observed toward males who were not relatives.

Different male and female spaces—and distinct activities that were tied to being in separate spaces—as well as ritual practices such as covering one's head in various cloth arrangements (throwing a stole casually on, or veiling the head) depending on age, generation, and region were a sign of respect accorded to women. In imperial setups, being veiled, as we'll see, was part of the inaccessibility that marked the status of royal women.

Various spatial terms bring to life the character of the dwellings of the royalty and of the elite. The etymological history of the term *harem*, to take an example from the Mughal palace society that reigned from the mid-sixteenth through the mid-nineteenth centuries, is from the term for the house where the wives and the household live: *haramsara*. The word for the place of sleep—*shabistan*—is used as a synonym for *harem*. Related concepts include: those behind the curtain, not to be seen (*pardeh-giyan*); that which is inside, internal, within, intrinsic (*andarun, andaruni*); and the area around the *Ka`ba* and the garden of the Prophet Muhammad (*Ruzayi Rasul*).

A physically segregated harem came to be institutionalized for the first time in the history of the Mughals under Akbar the Great (r. 1556–1605). Akbar had declared that women of the royal household were to be segregated in a well-ordered, high-walled harem. To ensure their seclusion, he built a large enclosure and gave each woman a separate apartment. According to the first official history of the Mughals, *Akbarnama* (the *History of Akbar*), the chosen historian Abu-l Fazl claimed the harem housed 5,000 women (others have put it at as few as 300). Marital alliances helped him expand his territory and solidify political networks. The seclusion of his harem was part of his presentation of himself as a celestial, almost godly, protector of the people, who assumed the role of infallible spiritual authority. In this way, in the early 1570s, Akbar had begun transforming his imperial image, casting himself as a sacred figure. In the exhaustive *Akbarnama*, Fazl also amplified the emperor's illustrious genealogy. The harem, which Fazl called "the fortunate place of sleep," was further proof of his near-divinity—pure, inviolable, at once glorious and untouchable, as the womenfolk of a godly king should be.

Although the word *zenana* (women's quarters) came to be used interchangeably with *harem*, especially in many nineteenth-century British accounts, it was the inner domain of women, with a more restrictive sense of space and the individuals who inhabit it, and widely used among Muslim and Hindu aristocratic households in northern India. The main entrance to the house was a large gate on the street that opened into a courtyard leading to a front row of rooms—the *mardana* or men's area. Behind the *mardana*, a verandah led to an open courtyard around which the rest of the household quarters would be arranged, perhaps on two floors. The women's sections would most likely have several private rooms on the upper floor and communal rooms, kitchens, and toilet facilities below. Off the courtyard, on the outskirts of the women's area, were storerooms, stables, and servants' quarters, with back doors opening onto the street.

The women's quarters at the Udaipur palace complex of the Mewar Kingdom in western India (who resisted the Mughals for several centuries) maintain an aristocratic flavor not that different from the Mughal women's quarters: it is a multistoried enclosure built around an open courtyard. Likewise, in south India during the Vijayanagara Empire (1336–1646), the ruler Krishnadeva Raya (r. 1509–29) would conduct the public ceremonies of the state from the royal center at the great imperial city of Vijayanagara, but he actually lived in a fortified suburb built supposedly for his favorite queen, Chinnadevi. This practice was different from indigenous Rajput kindoms (e.g., Delhi, Mewar, Kanauj, Ajmer, Bihar, Bengal, Bundelkhand, Malwa, and Chedi) and the subsequent Delhi Sultanate and their Mughal successors. These built walled complexes that held both the court and the domestic areas.

In the mansions of upper-class Chinese families, women likewise resided in the "inner quarters," typically located in the back or on the second story of the house. Their quarters were separate from the main rooms just inside the front gate, where men of the family conducted business or entertained their guests. In a similar fashion, in the elite households of India business matters were carried out in spaces separate from the "inner" domain of women.

Within these nominally restrictive domestic spaces, however, women and men found places for creativity, reflection, and freedom. Among the elite, as among the rest of the populations, creativity and resistance, transgression and adventure continued in "border" spaces—lanes and orchards, forests and riverbanks. Once urban development, market towns, and administrative headquarters became significant, with concentrations of populations of many different classes; rooftops (or, more precisely, the terraces found on the tops of the houses of the well-to-do) took the place of the forest for women of respectable households in much of South Asia, as in the Middle East and North Africa. Rooftops linked neighboring houses, so that women and children could go (unseen) from one to another, sometimes for miles. Apart from allowing for regular passage and communal interaction, such rooftops made it possible for women—and men (especially in male-male attractions)—to access and cultivate, albeit for short whiles, aspects of forbidden life: a glimpse of the loved one, a rendezvous, affectionate embraces that lasted a few minutes, or a lonely communication with the sky.

Thus, rooftops were an extension of the domestic world, in part for reasons of practicality (family members sleeping on the terrace on hot summer nights, women and servants drying clothes, grains, pickles), in part when women chose to make them an extension. They often did, in order to get away from the drudgery of the chores downstairs. At the same time, a woman could get away from domestic chores on the rooftops; she spent time with friends, or just went upstairs—escaping from the mundane—in a mode of introspection, wondering about her life, taking stock of all that was around her. In other words, rooftops provided a different, not-quite-domestic space, under the open sky; looking up at the endless stars and sky might even suggest an erasure of intermediaries between oneself and the infinite, between the devotee and the divine. Painterly traditions from much of India invoke such spaces of freedom and agency, as do any number of fictional accounts, poetry, and architectural spaces.

In China, where the ideal home was built around a courtyard, the courtyard (or in elite homes, walled-off gardens) became a similar site of female sociability and personal independence. Even in modest households, women gathered in the courtyard, which afforded more light than indoors, to spin, sew, and do other chores. The courtyard, though sheltered from outsiders' view, could also provide a covert glimpse of the street, and perhaps of a passing female peddler who could be called in to provide necessities like needles, along with news of the neighborhood. In elite homes, the enclosed garden provided a private space where women and girls of the family—sisters, cousins, and daughters-in-law—could meet and play games, write poetry, and even hold drinking parties, while enjoying the fresh air and open sky.

Domestic Hierarchies, Literacy, and Power

In both China and India, domestic spaces were marked by hierarchies and power relations in which the most extensive authority was vested in the matriarch—the oldest mother, an unmarried aunt, and so on. In neither China nor India did women's position in the "inner" prevent them from controlling household funds: Mughal women had vast landed properties, and commercial and trading interests. In China, the demand for boys and men to concentrate on their studies (in the hope of passing their civil service exam and gaining a job in the powerful and elite Chinese government bureaucracy) meant that management of the household budget was understood as proper women's work. In upper-class families, where a "household" could include several nuclear families as well as many servants, women could end up in charge of considerable sums. In the eighteenth-century novel *The Story of the Stone* (considered one of the great classics of Chinese literature), the senior daughter-in-law, Phoenix, manages household funds, invests in property, and lends out money for profit. The following passage shows the deference paid to the woman who manages the house.

> Prince Chen himself did not feel very well today and was exhausted from the rushing around and night watching of the last few days. He had twinges of pain in his limbs, and limped into the room, supported on a stick, groaning and with difficulty . . . [and] clutching his stick, got down on his knees with difficulty to salute the ladies. . . . But the prince modestly insisted on making his request standing . . . [and] forcing himself to smile . . . asked if Madame Phoenix would be willing to help out by taking over the role of mistress of the house during the weeks of mourning. . . .
>
> Phoenix did not consider the matter for long. She was confident of her ability for the difficult task, and as the princely cousin begged and implored so pathetically, she gave her consent. The prince thanked her with a low bow and straight away gave her full authority in writing. He warmly impressed upon her that she should manage the servants and the palace housekeeping funds quite freely and absolutely at her discretion.

As their financial dealings suggest, even in their harems or inner quarters, women were far from cut off from the outside world. We have numerous examples of senior Mughal women giving advice to kings in matters of governance. In Indian as well as in elite Chinese families, women usually had a group of kinswomen and attendants, maids, and servants with whom to share conversation and other activities. The boundaries of "inner" could encompass visits to the quarters of female friends or relatives, and both Chinese and upper-class Indian women traveled (the latter in extended entourages). Women were central to the arrangements of marriages, which were hardly private affairs: for aristocratic Indian families as for Chinese officials, matrimony brought with it entrenchment of loyalties, which meant political solidarities and support. Marriages, then, like the birth of (male) children, were also political and public affairs.

Although one traditionally minded Chinese patriarch instructed his daughters that each day they should spend time cooking (including making sauces and brewing wine), spinning thread, doing fine embroidery, sewing clothing, and sewing shoes, other moralists advocated for the education of women. In China elite status for men was predicated on the mastery of classical learning, ideally to be deployed in government service. And although the need for women to be literate in the "inner" realm was less obvious, male (and female) scholars throughout history had argued that education of women would help ensure the proper regulation of the family. Thus the revered historian Sima Guang (1019–1086) in his handbook for family life had insisted: "To be a [good] person, everyone must study. How could men and women be different [in this regard]? Accordingly, girls [while still] at home [before marriage] must read the *Classic of Filial Piety*, *The Analects*, the *Classic of Poetry*, and the *Classic of Ritual*, and understand the general meaning."

More practically, in the highly competitive society of early modern China, an elite mother's ability to oversee the early education of her sons had become a tremendous asset. So literacy for women became one element in the elite's ability to reproduce itself. Literacy was sufficiently common among Chinese women of the fifteenth and sixteenth centuries that they comprised an important segment of the bourgeoning markets for novels and other popular literature and poetry. Moralists of this period were more ambivalent about women writing poetry. Although many elite women in early imperial times had become famous poets, by the early modern period some forms of poetry had become associated with courtesans—glamorous and beautiful entertainers who were accomplished in the arts and with whom elite men developed romantic and sexual relationships. Thus writing poetry was deemed inappropriate for gently bred women. That did not stop them, though some made a show of virtuously burning their work. But other women in the late sixteenth century exchanged poems with other women both by letter and in person, and sometimes formed poetry clubs. And although some men complained about the impropriety of women's writings circulating in the outer realm, other men began to collect and publish anthologies of women's poetry. By the late seventeenth century, women as well as men were editing such anthologies.

Indian women's literacy was, in the main, restricted to the private sphere, bound by the distinct rhythms of the men's and women's quarters. It was in the harem or the *haveli* (mansion) that a girl would take her first steps: write the first letter of Persian script, *alif*, literally, commencement. Festivals, ceremonies, and ritual observances would give boys and girls opportunities to interact, directly and indirectly, with the wider community beyond the walls. On these occasions, noble households gave new suits of clothes and sheep or goats to the needy, ensuring that the poorest were able to offer sacrifice and rejoice.

There were no educational requirements or schools for aristocratic Muslim girls or those of other Indian communities. Girls were raised on a rich diet of fascinating moral tales, stressing responsibility and discipline, but suggesting limited possibilities for women. Sometimes fathers (or grandfathers) taught them arithmetic, stories with morals of the heart, and the art of writing. Much of Indian culture was oral. Men of aristocratic households were, of course, taught to read and write, and so were many elite women, but for the latter, the emphasis was on memorizing verses from the Quran. Women would acquire a taste for tales and poetry informally, from listening to stories and poems and memorizing the Quranic verses recited at festivities and gatherings. They were expected to read aloud the elegant, lyrical prose of *Gulistan, The Rose Garden* (1258), by Sadi, the Shakespeare of Persian literature.

Discipline in elite homes often came from dogmatic manuals of instruction that insisted on precise ways of civilized society and practical wisdom. A standard favorite was Nasir al-Din Tusi's *Akhlaq-i Nasiri*, first published in 1235; it was one of the five books that Emperor Akbar had read to him regularly. Among Tusi's prescription for girls:

> In the case of daughters, one must employ . . . whatever is appropriate and fitting to them. They should be brought up to keep close to the house and live in seclusion (*hijab*), cultivating gravity, continence (`*iffat*), modesty and other qualities we have enumerated in the chapter on Wives. They should be prevented from learning to read or write,

but allowed to acquire such accomplishments as are commendable in women.

As to the noble boys, said Tusi, "Let him also from time to time adopt the custom of eating dry bread," Tusi counseled. "Such manners, albeit good in poor men, are even better in rich. . . . He should be accustomed not to drink water while eating and he should on no account be given wine and intoxicating drinks before he reaches early manhood." The boys would be advised not to sleep too much, or during the day, because that produced "deadness of mind" and languor. Walking and movement, riding and exercise were to be "customary pursuits." They were not to boast about wealth or possessions or what they ate or wore, in [an] attempt to be humble and gracious with peers. They would be taught to refrain from arrogance and obstinacy. It was recommended that the tutor who imparted this ethical guidance be intelligent and religious, well-versed in the training of dispositions, "with a reputation for fair speech and gravity, an awe-inspiring manner, manliness and purity; he must also be aware of the characters of kings, the manners involved in associating with them and addressing them." (trans. G. M. Wickens)

The Hindu goddess Saraswati was the patron of learning. Yet women were not to learn the ancient Hindu scriptures (*Vedas*) or study any branch of ancient Hindu law (*Shastras*). No Hindu girls went to the scholars (*pundits*) to study. If any of them did learn Sanskrit, it was within the family, as daughter or sister or, more rarely, wife of a male in a pundit family. If a Hindu girl learned to read and write, this too happened at home, sometimes along with boys but more likely on her own. Learning to sing devotional songs and gaining knowledge of certain scriptures was part of a Hindu girl's education.

In Bengal, Rashundari Devi (c. 1809–1900) wrote her autobiography, which was published in 1868. Obsessed with a desire to read, she stole a page from a book and a sheet of paper from her son and kept them hidden in the kitchen, where she pursued her "education" fervently. She was the first writer—male or female—from Bengal to be published. In *My Life* she would write about the exhaustion of her daily routine and declare, "Women had no freedom. They could not take any decision on their own. Just like any caged bird, women were imprisoned too." Other remarkable women were also able to seize an education. In North India in the late 1840s, teenage

Ashraf-un-nisa went up to the rooftops while everyone was asleep downstairs and taught herself to read and write with twigs and blacking.

> I began to read Urdu fairly well. When I turned to those . . . [lines] that I had earlier copied down without understanding a word. When I read those copies, you cannot imagine my happiness. . . . As I read my own handwriting, I felt more encouraged and . . . told myself, whatever a human being gets, it is on the basis of one's own efforts and desire. . . . Then I turned to those broom twigs and the blacking, regarding them as my teachers, I began to copy from different books. After just a few days of practice, I could write from memory. No one, yet, knew the secret of my writing.

It is a remarkable statement of initiative, independent thinking, and resourcefulness. Far from being criticized, she became a local novelty, writing letters for local women and hearing many stories of their daily lives as a result.

By contrast, boys and men in elite settings were to spend their time in the outer part of their abode. As mentioned, in China, male children from an early age were expected to concentrate on study of the classics and the goal (seldom realized) of obtaining a civil service appointment. Aristocratic Hindu and Muslim boys in India studied classical poetry and heard epic religious accounts, and also engaged in hunting and military training. Strength, dexterity, daring, resolution, and loyalty led to the advancement of noble men. If they were ambitious, being in the Mughal court would be the highest honor. They would then have to be responsible for providing bodies of well-equipped and trained cavalry for campaigns and battles. Being skilled in the martial arts, archery, swordsmanship, riding, and managing elephants and horses, along with the craft of calligraphy and polished discourse, would come in handy. All this alongside memorizing orations, proverbs, poems, anecdotes, dialogues, elegant stories, and witticisms.

Numerous women also had very direct influence on "outer" affairs, at least among the elite. The Mughal Emperor Akbar's mother served as the regent of the empire when he went on a campaign to Kabul. Akbar asked his elderly aunt Gulbadan Begum to write a history of their forefather as a contribution toward the first official history of the Mughal Empire. A generation later, while following in the paths of power laid down by Mughal women, Nur Jahan, the last wife (some argue she was the twentieth) of the fourth Mughal ruler, Jahangir, emerged as the de facto ruler of the empire. She performed both formal and informal rituals of imperial power, although she was not from the Mughal family and had no children with the emperor: indeed, she brought with her a daughter from her first marriage.

Earlier, in the thirteenth century, Queen Rudramadevi, of the Kakatiya dynasty (1163–1323) that unified the Telegana region in south India, took over the reins of the kingdom along with her father. When he died in 1261, Rudrama emerged as a heroic ruler leading her troops against external and internal military challenges. It is suggested that she died in battle in 1289. She is physically represented as a woman in sculpture, but took on male clothing in order to fulfill the warrior role of a male ruler. There are numerous such examples.

In similar fashion, a number of dowager empresses ruled as regents for their imperial sons or nephews in China. The redoubtable Wu Zhao (Wu Zetian, 624–705) of the Tang dynasty (618–907) went so far as to depose her sons one after the other and declare herself "emperor"—for which breach of protocol she was excoriated by later (male) historians. Their biases have made it difficult to assess Wu's effectiveness as a ruler, but scholars today point out that she reigned over an era of peace and prosperity. She also took a number of actions, such as increasing the mourning period for mothers, that enhanced the ritual status of women. In the early modern period, the most famous case of a female regent was the Empress Dowager Cixi (r. 1861–1908), who dominated court politics for much of the later nineteenth century and beyond.

Marriage and Family

In both China and India, gender ideals were significantly influenced by the demands of the patrilineal joint family system. The ideal Chinese family—and in general terms, also many Indian families—was constituted of a senior male and his wife; their adult sons and their wives and children; and the senior male's younger brothers and their wives and children. In the Chinese system, daughters of the household married out, joining their husbands' families; sons ideally stayed with their natal kin for their entire lives, with the eldest (or sometimes the most competent) son taking over as head of the entire group on the patriarch's death. Kinship through males was regarded as far more significant than that through females. The birth of sons, who would perpetuate the father's line for another generation, was highly valued; daughters, who would leave the family when they married, were less so.

The patrilineal joint family was also closely associated with particular types of property rights. By definition, the joint family shared a common budget: all those who worked contributed their earnings to the family head, and in turn all were supported more or less equally. Sons inherited their father's property on an essentially equal basis. Although there is some evidence that in earlier eras daughters in China may have enjoyed some inheritance rights, by the early modern period this was no longer the case. Still, in families of adequate means daughters were expected to be given a dowry sufficient to allow them to make an appropriate marriage. Even after she joined her husband's family, the bride's dowry remained hers (or perhaps her and her husband's) to control; it did not become part of the resources of the larger household. Late imperial writers effusively praised women who, in times of need, offered personal funds from their dowries to their husbands' families. Dowry funds also seem to have served as a kind of insurance for married women if, for some reason, their husbands failed to support them.

When a husband died, his widow had the right to control his property in trust for his children, although she was not usually allowed to sell family land. Prior to the Mongol Yuan dynasty (1260–1368), a childless widow typically returned home, where her parents might arrange another marriage for her. If she chose to stay in her husband's family, she had the right to appoint an heir for him (ideally a kinsman in the appropriate generation of her husband's family). Due to the combined influence of Mongol custom and a resurgent Confucianism, over the course of the thirteenth century the legal rights of widows became increasingly restricted. By the early modern period, the right to choose a new husband for a widow or to appoint an heir for her to raise belonged to the husband's natal kin. This legal decline in widows' rights, however, was frequently ignored in practice; judges recognized that the deceased's kin might not have the best interests of the widow at heart, and so tended to award her the right to choose an heir.

In China, a centralized state with uniform laws upheld this patrilineal model of kinship and gender relations, but regional variations existed. In any number of cases from both India and China, the joint family model was often only a stage in a continuing cycle of family formation and division. In China, most commonly, when the senior male and his wife died (and sometimes even before), his sons divided the household, each taking his share of the property and setting up his own nuclear household with his wife and children. As those children grew into adulthood, the sons would bring in brides and the cycle would be repeated; but it was relatively rare to see extended households headed by brothers. There were also class differences in both societies: many poor families did not have sufficient land or resources to support an extended household, and in such families most sons were forced to strike out on their own, with only the eldest or youngest staying behind to live with the elderly parents. In China, poor families sometimes adopted a "little daughter-in-law": a female infant or young girl who could, on reaching marriageable age, be married to a son in the family without requiring the ruinous expense of a fancy wedding. (And in some regions, this custom became popular even among the better off, for it helped to assure a tractable daughter-in-law.) Moreover, political and financial realities often trumped patrilineal ideology: the popular idea that married women had little to do with their natal families was frequently belied in practice, as wives and mothers deployed their natal kin networks to aid their husbands and sons.

In India, fluidity remained a feature of marital alliances. India's diversity produced flux and adaptation in marriages and social-political relationships at many levels. Kinship practices varied greatly from region to region and across Muslim and Hindu communities, so the patrilineal joint family system was not the only norm. What seems to have been universal was the physical seclusion of women and marriages designed to protect family honor and to maintain caste divisions centered on the chastity of women. *Kanyadan* or the gift of a virgin daughter in marriage, an act through which a man (father) was supposed to gain the highest spiritual merit, became central in the Hindu matrimonial alliances. It is as if marriage became a necessity and women objects to be given. Kanyadan established a unidirectional flow of gifts from the bride's family to the groom's—father to groom— which over time came to acquire a restrictive meaning encompassed in the term "dowry." Recent scholarship has established that the parental gifts must also be considered evidence of the love of parents for their daughters, ensuring their well-being. Others have emphasized that dowry may be related to the inability of women to inherit property and the practice of marrying into a higher caste.

While people's communities were highly localized and men tended to marry women within their communities, this was not always the only marriage norm. When men moved to different regions for trade, for instance, intercaste marriages occurred. There were changes in the community affiliations themselves. When Hindu Rajputs converted to Islam and began to marry Muslims, Hindu and Muslim Rajputs of the same family continued to identify as members of the joint family. The Gonds, a tribal community of central India, alternately fought and married Rajputs to create political alliances—and thus emerged a new identity of Raj Gonds. The Marathas—Hindu clans from the Maharashira state in western India—are a classic example of an agricultural community that moved up from a lower caste status as agricultural workers to an upper one as soldiers and established themselves as rulers in the seventeenth and eighteenth centuries. With all that, of course, marriage patterns shifted even as prescriptions to marry within the tribe persisted.

Consider the Mughal kings. Babur (r. 1526–30), the first Mughal emperor, even in his wanderings over many locations—parts of Central Asia, Afghanistan, and then India—is said to have had no more than ten wives. Humayun (r. 1530–40; 1555–56), the second emperor, probably had five. By the time of Babur's grandson, Akbar the Great (r. 1556–1605), however, new imperial arrangements institutionalized marriage with a prescription to produce children. Beginning with Akbar, the Mughals, who were Muslims, forged marital unions with Hindu Rajputs and other communities. Mughal Emperor Jahangir (r. 1605–27) even had a Tibetan wife. Akbar's chroniclers differ in reporting the number of women (figures range from 300 to 5,000), but they are unanimous in writing about his large harem. Many of Akbar's marriages were conducted with households that had been connected with the Mughals for a long time; others were with the daughters of the Hindu Rajput rulers, several of whom had been defeated by Mughal imperial forces. The genealogical and political concerns at issue in these marriages—exalted lineage, high connections, and reputation—are clearly recorded in the imperial regulations on matrimony. Royal marriage was vital to the strengthening of political partnerships and served as an important mark of the empire's strength and virility, and as a symbol of its regality and new imperial position.

As discussed earlier, Akbar's marriages conspicuously project the process of empire formation. Many are recorded as having taken place in the early part of Akbar's reign, when the need to cement his power was greatest. Even if Akbar's was a self-consciously Muslim polity, seeking legitimacy as a "Muslim" kingdom, the rules that should govern it were not strictly laid down. A great deal of negotiation and readiness to accept newer methods, including in marriages, was therefore necessary. The creation of new traditions is an essential part of history making. Emblematically, Akbar's marriages (and those of his family members) might also be read in another way, as symbolically demonstrating that the world was under the emperor's protection. Those who married him were seen as blessed simply by the fact of such union. As the emperor's favorite historian, Fazl, tells us, imperial marriages were exalted because of the emperor.

Fluidity remained a feature of marital alliances in early modern India. Historical contingency and change produced flux and adaptation in marriages and social-political relationships at many levels of the society. It was only beginning with nineteenth-century census operations that caste identities came to be frozen and a very different question of caste and marriages emerged.

In China, marriages were also a crucial element in the continuity of the patrilineal family. Marriage was understood to be a family affair, and for that reason decisions about an appropriate spouse for a son or daughter were made by the parents, usually with the aid of a matchmaker, either a professional or an acquaintance or friend. Since the alliance was seen as one of families rather than individuals, betrothals were sometimes decided when the future bride and groom were still children, or even still in utero. Patrilineal ideology dictated that marriage with anyone of the same surname was forbidden, but marriage of distaff cousins (a man to his mother's brother's daughter or mother's sister's daughter) was common.

Most Chinese marriages involved the exchange of both dowry (funds and goods brought into the groom's household by the bride) and bride price (funds and goods given to the bride's family by the groom and his family). In upper-class families, a lavish dowry proclaimed the bride's family's social standing and their affection for their daughter. At the lower end of the social scale, dowries diminished and bride price increased, such that marriage came closer to (and was often perceived as) "sale" of the bride to the groom's family.

In the joint family system, marriage usually involved the incorporation of the bride into her new husband's household, rather than the creation of a new household around the couple. In a wealthy or aristocratic household, the new couple might be given a room or small suite of rooms to serve as their private apartments; in a poor farming family, they might have only a separate bed, perhaps shielded by a drape or screen. But in either case, the bride was expected to join the work and routines of her husband's household. Finally, as this scenario implies, the relationship of the married couple to each other was understood to be secondary to their obligations to the family. A woman was expected to defer to and serve her husband, but her diligent service to her parents-in-law was even more important; a man was expected to treat his wife with respect and care, but his obligations to his parents and brothers took precedence over those to his wife. According to this ideology, in an ideal marital relationship the husband and wife would treat each other as "guests"—that is, with politeness and esteem, but without undue familiarity or informality.

This rather austere ideal was of course frequently belied in practice. Many Chinese accounts attest that couples in arranged marriages could and did fall in love, and increasingly from the sixteenth to the eighteenth centuries, Chinese short stories and novels, and gradually more formal writings, touted a romantic ideal of "companionate marriage." A similar trajectory is seen in poetry in India. Even relationships that were less than passionate could be characterized by mutual fondness and appreciation. In commemorative texts, upper-class men often spoke of their wives with deep affection, praising them for service to the family, for clever management of household finances, and for sage advice and encouragement.

As much of the discussion of marriage already suggests, opportunities varied by gender and class in both China and India. The disparities became increasingly extreme in China between the seventeenth and nineteenth centuries, when a combination of female infanticide, the ability of upper-class men to monopolize several women, and social attitudes that frowned on widow remarriage (discussed further later in the chapter) began to have an impact on gender ratios. Although the social expectation had always been that virtually all men and women should marry, opportunities for lower-class men gradually became more limited, while women could increasingly hope to "marry up."

Restrictions that made marriages difficult across class and status, and religion, existed in India, as everywhere else in the world. There were also limitations that prevented marriage across caste. In the eighteenth century, for instance, the *peshwa* (prime minister) in the west Indian state of Maharashtra forbade certain lower classes from implementing a prohibition on widow remarriage in order to undercut possible claims from lower castes for higher caste status.

Inside and Outside Marriage

In the wandering lifestyle of the early Mughals, recognition of the need for marriages, especially the necessity of having children to continue the dynasty, coexisted with the desire and love for male company. The focus was not same-sex relations between people of either sex, but rather practices of affection and attachment that were widely accepted in the society and may have been especially fitting for a peripatetic life and its demands. In the writings of the time, marriages between men and women and homosocial and homoerotic gatherings of both men and women are presented beside each other, with neither being privileged. Babur writes of his longing for a camp boy, Baburi: "Nor power to stay was mine, nor strength to part; I became what you made me, oh thief of my heart." Such verses may represent an idealizing strand in his poetry, but they are also the expression of an almost inaccessible love in a homoerotic literary genre. And we have a striking illustration of his love for his senior wife, Maham Begum, in the memoir of his daughter, Gulbadan.

But imperial needs and prescriptions changed. A few decades later, any such open adventurism, and even the notion of homosexuality, would come to be regarded as transgressive. Babur's grandson, Akbar the Great, severely criticized any display of affection between men. Such imperial practices were likely to have resonance in aristocratic circles, for whom, theoretically, the emperor was the model for conduct. Akbar's response to the affair of `Ali Quli Khan Zaman, an official, with the son of a camel driver suggests that the emperor wanted the wider sexual regime to be like his own. When a report of the liaison was brought to Akbar, he said that a man who was overpowered by lust and passion was disgraceful. He asked `Ali Quli to repent his deeds and make amends by good service and directed him to send the camel driver's son to the court.

Reports from historian Badauni reveal part of this scheme of disciplining deviance: prostitutes were made to live outside the city in a place called Shaitanpura, literally Devilsville! Of course, the emperor maintained several concubines and scores of wives who are unnamed in the imperial records. Akbar's regulations on marriage further bring out his stringent directives. A musician named Gadai had twenty-five children from one wife. According to the *Akbarnama*, he came to the court and petitioned that his wife was sexually abstaining on account of the numerous births (Gadai uses metaphorical allusions and not such transparent words). Fazl says Akbar comforted him by saying that wicked storytellers must have invented what was being said about his wife, and added that if any matrimony produced so many progeny, it was an honor to the parties, not a case for abstention.

In China, if some men and women were able to find love in arranged marriages, there is no doubt that upper-class men enjoyed the greatest freedom to pursue romantic relationships elsewhere. Not only could they take concubines, the flourishing pleasure districts of Chinese cities also provided them with opportunities to pursue romance with women as well as with other men. Courtesans had for centuries been regarded as appropriately elegant romantic partners for elite men. Chinese literature suggests that, in general, courtesan romances were expected to end in a poignant breakup (class barriers made "happily ever after" scenarios unlikely). Still, in the late sixteenth and early seventeenth centuries, several eminent officials enjoyed long-term (and widely celebrated) romances with courtesans, who in some cases became their concubines. The same period also appears to have been a high point of acceptability of male-male romantic relationships. Such relationships had not been unknown in earlier eras, and had never been as stigmatized as they were in the Christian tradition. But after women were barred from the stage in the fourteenth century, male actors who specialized in female roles became increasingly common objects of romance and male desire. Far from requiring equality between partners, and like relationships between men and women, typical male-male romantic relationships in this period were strongly hierarchical: literati patronized poor and socially stigmatized actors, who, like courtesans, had limited power to reject them.

In China, as in India, women of any class who found their marriages emotionally or physically unsatisfying had comparatively few socially acceptable alternatives. For a married woman to have a relationship with a man other than her husband was considered "illicit sex," and potential punishment was severe. Still, legal cases show that fear of punishment did not always outweigh romantic passion, and women's extramarital affairs were a favorite theme of fiction writers. Women's sexual relationships with other women, by contrast, seem not to have been particularly stigmatized.

Although practical considerations of privacy and leisure probably limited such relationships to upper-class women, literary sources show that they were not unheard of in either country.

Quite different from the practice of aristocratic Muslim (and Hindu) men in India, and equally in contrast to common stereotypes of Chinese practice, in late imperial China a man could have only one legal wife at a time (though a man whose wife had died could legally take a second, successor wife). The image of multiple wives in China arises because China also had an elaborate system of concubinage. From the early imperial period, the Chinese state had attempted to regulate household relationships between men and women and drew careful distinctions between wives (who were the legal and ritual partners of their husbands) and concubines (who had lower legal status than wives and indeed were expected to wait upon the legal wife). Concubines, whose main function (at least putatively) was to ensure that the husband's family had plenty of male heirs, were legally to be drawn from the class of "good commoners," and were thus of higher legal status than slave women or entertainers. The law even stipulated that slave women could not become concubines, though an important loophole allowed a man to give a slave her freedom (especially if she had borne a child) and then make her into a concubine. Moreover, all these laws notwithstanding, in practice the status of women in a household depended significantly on the husband's inclinations and behavior. According to law, a concubine could never be elevated to the position of wife, but widowers who treated their concubines as wives were seldom prosecuted. If a husband seriously neglected his wife in favor of a concubine, and the wife had a family that was willing and able to protect her interests, they could take the errant husband to court on her behalf. But if the wife's family was not around and her husband was so infatuated with a concubine that he treated his wife badly, she had little recourse. And even if the wife's parents were around, there was no guarantee the husband would listen to reason: one famous sixteenth-century official recounted how, when he was a small child, his father became enamored of a concubine. Although his mother's relatives took the father to court, the court's only solution was to divide the family. The court gave two thirds of the property to the household composed of the father, his concubine, and the concubine's son, and only the remaining third to the mother, who had to share her household with a married son and daughter-in-law as well as two younger children.

The early Chinese state had envisioned concubines as a perquisite of official status. At the top of the political hierarchy, the Chinese emperor (like his Mughal counterpart) was allowed an almost unlimited number of women, the better to produce heirs to the throne (though, as mentioned, in China even the emperor could have only one legal "wife" [the empress] at a time). Specific regulations varied by period, but in general the highest court officials might legally have as many as nine or ten concubines, and those of lower ranks correspondingly fewer. The lowest ranked officials were allowed only one concubine in addition to one legal wife, and commoners were not legally permitted to have concubines at all. All of this changed in the tenth and early eleventh centuries, however, when the court ceased to regulate concubinage and the institution spread widely in Chinese society. New laws in the early Ming dynasty (1368–1644) stipulated that a commoner male could not take a concubine unless he was over forty years old and sonless, but this law seems to have had virtually no impact on actual practice. From the later imperial period into the early twentieth century, the number of concubines a man could keep depended principally on his ability to support them.

In the Indian subcontinent, given the stratified households with multiple generations, there were differences of status and residential locations between wives and mistresses and slave-servants especially from the late eighteenth and early nineteenth centuries. The wife was always identified with the illustrious lineage, and with the name of the husband; the slave or others such as a concubine would be listed under a generic name. While concubines were present in most palace societies, including that of the Mughals, the annals of Mughal history do not discuss the status of concubines in clear terms—unlike their contemporaries, the Ottomans of Turkey, who had a well-established system of concubinage in place with clear rule and practices of inheritance and succession.

There are plenty of references to the concubines of the Mughals, and to their children. Babur lists his concubines and those of his male relatives. The most striking is the case of the fourth son of the Mughal Emperor Jahangir, named Shahryar, whose mother was a concubine. She remains unnamed in the records, but history shows that the status of Shahryar was the same as that of his brothers. He married the daughter (from a former marriage) of Empress Nur Jahan (his stepmother). The number of marriages that Shahryar's father, Jahangir, had range between eighteen and twenty, depending on the source. At the time of his wedding with Nur Jahan in 1611, Jahangir proclaimed her "the Light of the Palace." In the years that followed, Nur's spectacular ascendancy under the still more exalted title of Nur Jahan, "Light of the World," transformed the character of that marriage itself. Before long, Nur Jahan came to wield supreme power as the acknowledged empress of Mughal India. According to one court historian, Jahangir confessed in a self-mocking mode that he had bestowed the reins of sovereignty on her. Marrying Nur Jahan's daughter would say a lot, even in the absence of clear codes of law, of the place of sons of concubines.

But what was the relationship among and with an aristocrat's several married wives and unmarried retainers? Indeed, what was it like to live in the same domestic complex, neighborhood, or city? By the nineteenth century, a great corpus of writing, especially in Urdu, emerged in which we find details of a landlord's "other interests"—especially his constant visits to the homes of favored courtesans, usually singers and women of great artistic accomplishments. The Urdu novel *Umrao Jaan Ada* (1899) is told as if dictated to the narrator from the memory of a real-life courtesan, Umrao Jaan Ada (though some question her existence), and came to represent a continuation of these earlier practices beyond the Mughal era.

The matter of love deserves a moment's reflection. Expressions of love, friendship, duty—like most other aspects of human life—are conditioned by social environment. People in different times and places often understood (and understand) "love" rather differently from what nineteenth- and twentieth-century romantic novels have made it out to be. In addition, as with marriage, opportunities for love—or shall we say romance?—varied by gender and class, and also over time.

Mira Bai (c. 1498–c. 1547), a Hindu mystic poet of *bhakti* (devotion), exemplifies the many meanings of love. She was married to a local prince and when her husband died, she shocked her family and his by not committing *sati* or going into seclusion. Instead, Mira devoted herself to Krishna as a husband-god (leaving her family and surviving attempts on her life) and is known today for her many songs of mystical devotion:

> For your sake, I gave up all pleasures,
> now why are you making me long for you?
> You create the pang of separation inside the bosom
> so that you can come and quench it?
> O! Lord! Now I will not leave you
> smilingly, call me soon!
> Meera is your servant in birth after birth.

Her self-willed immersion in love of Krishna is seen as her claiming rights and reciprocity, while acknowledging her duties.

Today, in various regions of India, lower-class men and women take recourse to Mira to express and critique their oppression. In the Mewar-Udaipur regions, however, Mira is not publicly worshiped because her name has come to equal promiscuity. Thus Mira is not just a bhakti saint, but a saint who chose to defy social conventions and family prescriptions. She has become an inspiration for freedom to other men and women. Although there is evidence of women in the Islamic mystical Sufi tradition, whether there were any female Sufi mystics in South Asia remains uncertain. However, there were any number of women, including imperial women such as the later Mughal Princess Jahanara (1614–1681), who called for passionate love for God—union with the divine—as the way, beyond the Quran.

The "Woman Question" and Reform

The increasing political power of Europeans over the course of the nineteenth century gave Western critiques of Chinese customs increasing salience in the late nineteenth and early twentieth centuries. Chinese intellectuals, seeking the source of Chinese weakness in the face of Western military power, concluded that the problem lay in the constraining hierarchies of Confucian ideology, and particularly the "oppression" of women as symbolized in cloistering, foot binding, and especially the long-standing practice of female fidelity. Often called in English the "cult of fidelity" or the "cult of chastity," this could take the form of a widow's refusal to remarry, or of "chaste martyrdom," that is, suicide to maintain sexual honor.

Both practices were valorized in very early Chinese texts. As a result of those classical models, throughout the early imperial period a widow's refusal to remarry was considered an honorable course of action. Still, for most of the first millennium, eventual remarriage was accepted for widows of all classes, especially those who were young and childless. Over the course of the twelfth and thirteenth centuries, however, a variety of complicated developments gave greater cultural relevance to the interrelated ideals of chaste martyrdom and widow fidelity. By the thirteenth century fidelity came to be seen as the preeminent female virtue. Monuments to faithful widows and shrines to chaste martyrs dotted the Chinese countryside; local gazetteers devoted whole chapters to commemorating faithful women of the locale; and widow remarriage came to be regarded as a shameful act, to be undertaken by only the most destitute or desperate. In its most extreme manifestations, the cult of fidelity encouraged young girls whose fiancés had died to live out their lives as faithful widows, even though the marriage had never been consummated. And in some regions suicide by young widows became the focus of public spectacles.

Yet whereas twentieth-century discourse in China stressed the ways that the cult of fidelity had restricted women's options and possibilities, sometimes tragically so, recent scholarship has begun to show that the role of the faithful widow also offered women considerable autonomy and opportunities. Among the wealthy, a faithful widow could enjoy economic and personal independence, as well as significant family authority. And at the margins of society, even a poor widow who remained faithful to her husband had earned a measure of social approbation and pride in her own moral integrity. Even suicide, which in the case of women tends to be portrayed as the ultimate expression of hopelessness and self-annihilation, perhaps was understood differently by the women involved. The early Chinese historian Sima Qian had expressed the sentiment "A death can be as light as a feather, or a death can be as weighty as Mount Tai": here suicide is understood as an expression of honor, of self-respect, of agency. In this respect, the suicides of female chaste martyrs were no different from those of male heroes who died for their lords. In other cases, suicide might be understood as an expression of romantic love, as it frequently was in the works of Chinese novelists and playwrights. Finally, we should not discount the possibility that for some women, even those driven to despair by cruel treatment, suicide was an act of agency in being a form of revenge. For in Chinese popular culture, the spirits of those driven to suicide were imbued with supernatural powers, likely to return to haunt their tormenters.

Would-be Chinese "modernizers" called for women to free themselves, to take on new roles in public life, and in the process they depicted "traditional" Chinese women as unrelievedly benighted and downtrodden. Ultimately, this reformist discourse became part of the platform of the Chinese Communist Party, which promised that their policies would "liberate" women as well as men from the evils of the "feudal" Confucian past. Mao himself decried the "feudal-patriarchal system" in his call to arms: "A man in China is usually subjected to the domination of three systems of authority [political authority, family authority, and religious authority]. . . . As for women, in addition to being dominated by these three systems of authority, they are also dominated by the men (the authority of the husband). These four authorities—political, family, religious, and masculine—are the embodiment of the whole feudal-patriarchal ideology and system, and are the four thick ropes binding the Chinese people." The current Chinese government's dedication to portraying itself as the liberator of women has further intensified the image of women in imperial China as helpless and "pathetic."

And now to India. In the 1820s, the debate heated up considerably. Paralleling the Chinese case, by the latter half of the nineteenth century, British colonial rule sought to legitimize conquest and control of territories in India by entrenching it within moral and legal principles based on a hierarchy of civilization, and "improvement" of Indian women came to the fore of discussions. Evangelical missionaries attempted to implant Christian ideals into the Indian family, expressing "concern" about the fate of Indian women. Eventually, many Indian reformers used Western liberal arguments in favor of women's rights. The major objective of the reformers was to promote education of women, promote later marriages, prohibit *sati* and female infanticide, and to some extent, relax *purdah* and restrictions on the mobility of women.

It was in late nineteenth-century India, and in the context of British colonialism, that widow remarriage became an important cause. The "woman question"—with attendant colonial and Hindu reformist agendas—became a symbol of the colonial encounter. Women appeared in these debates only as objects for improvement. The major social tracts and commentaries of the 1860s and after presented a set of rather fixed images of women. Fundamental to these images were clearly defined tracks of respectable domesticity, which were accorded a pivotal position in the animated debate on social reform. Inevitably, therefore, what had to be negotiated was the problem of a "static" woman, confined to the space of the household, duty-bound with familial obligations, even as the drive to make her literate became more and more insistent. In spite of the limitations of the archive, recent scholarship has engaged in an innovative investigation of the debates surrounding the "woman question" as it played out in the nineteenth and early twentieth centuries, producing a powerful assessment of the various sites of reform, as well as the meaning of education. Scholars have begun to challenge the exclusivity of pain, suffering, erasure, and victimization of women in accounts of China's and India's past, and have written instead of playful, creative, sensual, and erotic girls and women.

Conclusion

Different religious beliefs and political configurations meant that the strikingly similar family systems of China and India nonetheless produced very different life experiences for men and women. Ironically, in the twentieth century, when both India and China were marked by efforts to reform (and "modernize") society by reforming women, women became simultaneously symbols of the nation and symbols of society's "backwardness," and gender relations in China and India looked most similar.

In exploring some moments in the gendered history of early modern China and India, we have attempted to provide an alternative view of the domestic spaces, the family, and the diverse range of women figures in these histories. We have addressed explicitly the varying ways that women appear in the archive of historical records and highlighted ways women have attained lives that were different from the prescribed norm. It is largely male authors who underline the models and ethics of life that women must follow. This fact reinforces the point that historically the male has often been claimed as the universal, and everything to do with the female/feminine has been constructed in the terms of that universal. This chapter might be considered a feminist commentary on the workings of the (male) universal: how it produces purported truths about women, what it catalogues, and how and what it erases from the historical records.

For Further Reading

China

Bernhardt, Kathryn. *Women and Property in China.* Stanford: Stanford University Press, 1999.

Bossler, Beverly. *Courtesans, Concubines, and the Cult of Female Fidelity: Gender and Social Change in China, 1000–1400.* Cambridge, MA: Harvard University Asia Center, 2013.

Chang, Kang-i Sun and Haun Saussy, eds. *Women Writers of Traditional China: An Anthology of Poetry and Criticism.* Stanford: Stanford University Press, 1999.

Ebrey, Patricia Buckley. *The Inner Quarters: Marriage and the Lives of Chinese Women in the Sung Period.* Berkeley, Los Angeles, and London: University of California Press, 1993.

Elvin, Mark. "Female Virtue and the State in China." *Past and Present* 104 (August 1984): 111–52.

Fu, Shen. *Six Records of a Floating Life.* Trans. Leonard Pratt et al. London: Penguin, 1983.

Huang, Martin W. *Negotiating Masculinities in Late Imperial China.* Honolulu: University of Hawai'i Press, 2006.

Idema, W. L. and Beata Grant. *The Red Brush: Writing Women of Imperial China.* Cambridge, MA: Harvard University Asia Center, 2004.

Kennedy, Thomas L., ed. *Testimony of a Confucian Woman: The Autobiography of Mrs. Nie Zeng Jifen 1852–1942.* Athens and London: University of Georgia Press, 1993.

Ko, Dorothy. *Teachers of the Inner Chambers: Women and Culture in Seventeenth-Century China.* Stanford: Stanford University Press, 1994.

Mann, Susan. *Precious Records: Women in China's Long Eighteenth Century.* Stanford: Stanford University Press, 1997.

Pruitt, Ida. *A Daughter of Han: The Autobiography of a Chinese Working Woman.* Stanford: Stanford University Press, 1973.

India

Arondekar, Anjali. *For the Record: On Sexuality and the Colonial Archive in India.* Durham and London: Duke University Press, 2009.

Bayly, C. A. *Empire and Information: Intelligence Gathering and Social Communication in India, 1780–1870.* Cambridge: Cambridge University Press, 1996.

Borthwick, Meredith. *The Changing Role of Women in Bengal: 1849–1905.* Princeton, NJ: Princeton University Press, 1984.

Burton, Antoinette. *Dwelling in the Archive: Women Writing House, Home, and History in Late Colonial India.* New York: Oxford University Press, 2003.

Chatterjee, Indrani, ed. *Unfamiliar Relations: Family and History in South Asia.* New Delhi: Permanent Black, 2004.

Devji, Faisal. "Gender and the Politics of Space: The Movement for Women's Reform in Muslim India." *South Asia* 14 (1991): 141–53.

Doniger, Wendy. *The Laws of Manu.* New York: Penguin, 1991.

Fisher, Michael. *The Inordinately Strange Life of Dyce Sombre: Victorian Angol-Indian MP and "Chancery Lunatic."* London: Hurst, 2010.

Forbes, Geraldine. *Women in India*. Cambridge: Cambridge University Press, 1996.
Jamieson, Stephanie. *Sacrificed Wife, Sacrificer's Wife: Women, Ritual and Hospitality in Ancient India*. New York: Oxford University Press, 1996.
Lal, Ruby. *Coming of Age in Nineteenth Century India: The Girl-Child and the Art of Playfulness*. Cambridge and New York: Cambridge University Press, 2013.
———. *Domesticity and Power in the Early Mughal World*. Cambridge and New York: Cambridge University Press, 2005.
Mani, Lata. *Contentious Traditions: The Debate on Sati in Colonial India*. Berkeley: University of California Press, 1998.
Mill, James. *The History of British India*. Vols. I–II. Ed. Horace Hayman Wilson. London, 1858.
Minault, Gail. *Secluded Scholars: Women's Education and Muslim Social Reform in Colonial India*. Delhi: Oxford University Press, 1998.
Mukta, Parita. *Upholding the Common Life: The Community of Mira Bai*. New Delhi: Oxford University Press, 1994.
Rizvi, S.A.A. *Religious and Intellectual History of the Muslims in Akbar's Reign 1556–1605*. New Delhi: Munshiram Manoharlal, 1975.
Sanghari, Kumkum and Sudesh Vaid, eds. *Recasting Women: Essays in Indian Colonial History*. New Brunswick, NJ: Rutgers University Press, 1997.
Sarkar, Tanika. *Hindu Wife, Hindu Nation: Community, Religion, and Cultural Nationalism*. London: Hurst, 2001.
Shulman, David. *Syllables of Sky*. Delhi: Oxford University Press, 1995.
Sinha, Mrinalini. *Specters of Mother India: The Global Restructuring of an Empire*. Durham and London: Duke University Press, 2006.
Spivak, Gayatri Chakravorty. *A Critique of Postcolonial Reason: Toward a History of the Vanishing Present*. Cambridge, MA.: Harvard University Press, 1999.
Teltcher, Kate. *India Inscribed: European and British Writing on India 1600–1800*. Delhi: Oxford University Press, 1997.
Thapar, Romila. *Sakuntala: Texts, Readings, Histories*. London: Anthem Press, 2002.
Vanita, Ruth, and Saleem Kidwai, eds. *Same-Sex Love in India: Readings from Literature and History*. Delhi: Palgrave-Macmillan India, 2000.
Ziegler, Norman P. "Some Notes on Rajput Loyalties During the Mughal Period." In *Kingship and Authority in South Asia*, ed. John F. Richards. Delhi: Oxford University Press, 1998.

PART TWO

CHAPTER IV

Relating the Past

Writing (and Rewriting) History

CYNTHIA BROKAW AND ALLISON BUSCH

In China the study of history has long been celebrated as an essential component of effective governance. History was a "mirror" for the ruler, but also a rich source of models of proper behavior for all: filial sons and daughters, ministers of state, monks, merchants, etc. Imperial governments consistently supported the collection of documents and oversaw the crafting of dynastic histories; at the same time, private scholars might write their own alternative histories as challenges to the state and its historical orthodoxy. In India history was rarely honored as a distinct category of fact-based study or writing, yet Indians did not lack historical imagination. They simply expressed this imagination in different forms and—given the enormous linguistic diversity of the subcontinent—languages. Some rulers of the many separate states of India had their dynastic achievements cut in rock inscriptions. The literati who recorded the past often gave historical events a literary form, weaving together fact and fiction, thereby revealing a conception of history and the writing of history—that is, a historiographical vision—very different from that embraced in either China or the West.

As different as the Indian and Chinese historiographical traditions are, there are nonetheless some points of similarity. Surely there is no merit in the stark contrast drawn by the German philosopher Georg Friedrich Hegel (1770–1831) between the "rational" and "prosaic" Chinese, who, living under the guidance of a strong state, were naturally drawn to historical thinking, and the unruly Hindus, who, given to extreme flights of fancy, supposedly produced no history. Of course the idea that "Hindus have no history" requires serious reevaluation, but it is also a mistake to assume that China's historiographical tradition was any more "rational" than other national/cultural traditions.

Hegel's comment, born of his imperfect knowledge of both India and China and his Eurocentric bias, alerts us, further, to the dangers of judging one culture's historiographical vision by the yardstick of another's view of what history is. Berating Indians for failing to think about history the way the Chinese did adds little to our understanding of the meaning of history in either culture. So too, assuming that history writing in either (or any) culture ought to "measure up" to "modern" standards for the practice of history—the second error that Hegel made—confounds any efforts to comprehend the ways history was used in China and India. Like all cultures, China and India have for centuries been thinking about, using, and reinventing their pasts, but neither has fashioned its histories in conformity to the standards of modern historiography, which were developed in the West in the nineteenth century and now dominate the practice of history throughout the world. This chapter explores how Chinese and Indians "did" history on their own—very different—terms.

Differences: Linguistic, Cultural, and Political

It is perhaps best to start with the factors that created difference.

The first thing to stress about textualizations of India's past is their diversity. The country boasts more than a dozen major languages with historical traditions stretching back centuries and in some cases millennia. Sanskrit was the principal pan-Indic language of letters in the ancient world, and this continued through the end of the first millennium. The later medieval and early modern periods saw the rise of vernacular languages that were more specific to regions (an analogy with Europe would be the shift from Latin to Romance languages). Muslim dynasties with an affinity for Persian culture began to hold sway in north India by the early thirteenth century, bringing further complexities to this linguistic picture. Grappling with Indian history means grappling with multiplicity.

China, in contrast, enjoyed, relatively speaking, a greater degree of linguistic unity and political continuity. Literary or classical Chinese, although it certainly changed significantly over time, served as a written lingua franca from roughly the third century to the early twentieth century; at the very least it enabled widespread textual communication (despite the enormous diversity of spoken languages and dialects) among the educated elite. Most histories were written in this language. And, although China suffered its share of invasions—most notably during the "period of disunion" (third century to late sixth century), when a succession of conquerors took north China; in the thirteenth century, when the Mongols founded the Yuan dynasty; and the seventeenth century, when the Manchus established the Qing—the conquerors adopted many of the political institutions and cultural practices of the Chinese, lending some degree of continuity even to these periods of foreign conquest.

It would be dangerous to exaggerate this linguistic unity and political and cultural continuity. Many fall into the trap, accepting the current nationalistic assertion of the existence of a single, coherent "China" from time immemorial—when in fact sharp regional, economic, linguistic, ethnic, and cultural differences repeatedly threatened the unity of even the most solidly "Chinese" empires. But there is no question that, compared to India, China enjoyed a more unified cultural and political tradition. It also enjoyed—in another sharp contrast with India—a long *written* historical tradition. Writing developed very early in Chinese history. It first appeared on oracle bones in the second millennium BCE; these served both as tools of divination and, once the divination was completed and recorded on the bone, as the archives of the Shang state.

Indian history was less dependent on writing, particularly in the early centuries. The first Indian historians weren't writers at all. Accounts of the civilizational attainments of ancient India often begin with the four Vedas (lit. "knowledge"), a tradition of Sanskrit cosmological and ritual lore though also, arguably, historical lore that, like the Shang oracle bones of China, originated in the second millennium BCE. The Vedas preserve fragmentary genealogies of ancestors and accounts of sacrificial and other activities in the "Land of the Five Rivers" (now the Punjab region of northwestern India). Traces of the past as found in Vedic literature were viewed as an important model for ritual behavior. "Now, Indrota Daivapa Saunaka once performed this sacrifice for Janamejaya Pariksita," runs a typical instance, "and by performing it he extinguished all evildoing" (trans. Julius Eggeling). Later participants in Vedic culture were prompted by such stories—so runs the theory—to engage in the same sacrificial activity, and in so doing they connected to their past. But nobody felt the need to write any of this "history" down. For one thing, writing did not yet exist in India. Most Vedic texts were not committed to writing until the late medieval period; instead, they constituted an oral archive to be transmitted exclusively by Brahmans—traditional India's learned class—through sophisticated recitation practices that continue right down to the present day.

The writing of history was much more prevalent in early Chinese society than it was in India. We can trace its changing technology with some precision. The earliest "histories"—terse chronological accounts of the major events and rituals of the different states of the North China Plain—were probably written by official scribes on bamboo strips, tied together to form a scroll. By the sixth century BCE, silk was also in use, and by the end of the second century CE at the latest, paper had become a popular medium. Writing, as has been noted, is not a prerequisite for historical thinking—oral cultures do have history—but it doubtless provides a handy tool for record keeping and thus the writing of history. Several centuries later, the invention of woodblock printing made the rapid reproduction of texts—and the spread of knowledge and sources for the writing of history—even easier.

But in another way—in its identification with cosmology and ritual—the practice of history in early China was quite similar to that in India. The first Chinese historians were charged with reading the patterns of the heavens through divination and ordering the ruler's sacrifices in harmony with those patterns. The chronologically arranged annals of their observations and activities—in other words, their histories—traced the interrelationship between Heaven and human affairs, particularly as it was mediated through the figure of the king and his ritual performances. Confucius (551–479 BCE) himself was to some extent heir to this tradition, as he hoped to replicate in his day the perfect order of the past, specifically that of the early Zhou dynasty (c. 1045–722 BCE)—the time, in his view, when virtue ruled, every man and woman knew his or her place, and strict observance of ritual created harmony between Heaven and earth.

The Earliest Histories

The Chinese pride themselves on their long historical tradition, pointing—though not entirely accurately—to their "five thousand years of uninterrupted history" and to the role that diviners cum historians played even in

China's first dynasty, the Shang (sixteenth century–c. 1045 BCE). The character that came to mean history (and is part of the modern Chinese term for history) first appeared on Shang oracle bones. Very early China produced several self-conscious records of the past, each suggesting a distinctive understanding of the meaning and uses of history. History in the conventional sense is harder to find in early India; in fact, in contrast to the Chinese, early Indians did not develop a separate category of writing identified as such. The nature of early historical consciousness has to be sought in oral tradition, inscriptions, epics, and other lore, as well as in biographical poetry.

Classical India—Edicts and Epics

While Vedic culture was wholly oral, the advent of writing in India enabled new traditions of rock-cut inscriptions and signs of a recognizably historical impulse, even if nobody cared to coin a name for it. The great emperor Ashoka (r. 268–233 BCE) has often been associated with the first use of writing in India. His early warmongering acts as a king caused immense bloodshed, which he later regretted. In fact, Ashoka's grief over the carnage led him to convert to Buddhism and publicly embrace nonviolence. His famous rock edicts propagated messages both royal and religious throughout the far reaches of the subcontinent. This excerpt from rock edict XIII shows various recognizable historical markers, such as a recording of the emperor's regnal year and a concern to enumerate the dead while at the same time propagating a distinctively Buddhist message of dharma (committing to a morally upright life) and compassion. Note the remorse of the emperor (Priyadarshi is an honorific title that suggests the emperor's magnanimous gaze upon his realm) at the conquering of Kalinga in eastern India:

> The Kalinga country was conquered by King Priyadarshi [Ashoka], Beloved of the Gods, in the eighth year of his reign. One hundred and fifty thousand persons were carried away captive, one hundred thousand were slain, and many times that number died. Immediately after the Kalingas had been conquered, King Priyadarshi became intensely devoted to the study of Dharma, to the love of Dharma, and to the inculcation of Dharma. The Beloved of the Gods, conqueror

of the Kalingas, is moved to remorse now. For he has felt profound sorrow and regret because the conquest of a people previously unconquered involves slaughter, death, and deportation. (trans. Narayanrao Appurao Nikam and Richard McKeon)

Inscriptions would become one of the most powerful vehicles for historical expression in India. And with the new medium of writing came an avalanche of textual expression in the subcontinent. First were the epics.

Much has been made of India's purported lack of history. A lot hinges on terminology and modernist presumptions about the very category. The modern word for history in many Indian languages derives from the Sanskrit word *itihāsa* (*iti ha āsa*, "and so it was"), the genre designator of India's two great epics, the *Mahabharata* and the *Ramayana* (composed roughly between 400 BCE and 200 CE). The *Mahabharata* and *Ramayana* are deeply influential texts that encoded some sense of past-ness for Indians over two millennia. The *Mahabharata* is the great story of the "Bharata" people, from whom Indians considered themselves to have descended after most of human society was wiped out in a cataclysmic war. (A common word for India in modern South Asian languages is "Bharat.") The *Ramayana*, for its part, is the story of the travails of the revered Lord Rama, an exemplary king.

These works of *itihasa* are both more and less than history. Indian epics are encyclopedic and contain many digressions and side notes on a whole range of topics. They are often deeply political texts that grapple incisively with the nature of kingship, the moral order, and the conditions of possibility of civilization itself. Good rule was perceived to be connected to the rectitude of the ruler, and the epics contain long didactic passages on governance and righteousness. As is often the case in this genre, the characters are larger than life. The *Mahabharata* hero Yudhisthira was the son of Dharma or virtue. And the paradigmatic expression for just rule in Classical India was "Rama-rajya," the rule of Rama. India's *itihasa*s also betray more than a whiff of the fantastical and would thus fail many diagnostic tests of today's discipline of history. The *Ramayana* in particular has always been celebrated as India's first work of literature, an early signal that in this thought-world history was deeply inflected by a strong literary impulse. The time frames are also hard to reconcile with historicist frameworks. Although the Classical Indian epics are understood to have taken place in specific *yuga*s or time periods, these were not the same as the ones that humans were currently felt to inhabit. The epic idea of time was cyclical, not linear, since every so often the creator god Brahma awakens from his slumbers to restart cosmic time. In this typical Hindu cosmological imagining, the entire world is destroyed periodically and then created afresh. Everything is recursive. History quite literally repeats itself.

Such conceptualizations of time may be radically different from modern historical perspectives but, like the related genre of the *purana* ("ancient lore"), these powerful stories were for a very long time carriers of the Indian past that were told and retold over many generations. In the *Arthashastra* (c. 100 BCE–100 CE), an authoritative Sanskrit treatise on political life, kings were enjoined to study *itihasa* and *purana*, and later soberminded historians such as Kalhana (twelfth century) established their chronologies starting from the supposed date of the *Mahabharata* war. In India the conjoint term *itihasa-purana* has sometimes been used to designate the earliest layer of history. *Purana*s, like biblical stories, deal with creation, primordial ancestors, royal genealogy, and the exploits of legendary heroes, sages, and kings. They interweave historical material with something closer to what we would call myth (though Indians, tellingly, have no word for the genre and thus for stories that may be paradigmatically but not empirically true), presenting a record of human society that sees itself as deeply connected to spheres of enchantment controlled by divine mandate. (The same is often said of the Homeric worldview of *The Iliad* and *The Odyssey*, the epitome of history-as-literature that created a cultural framework for ancient Greece and is commonly considered the foundation of Western literature.) Often lengthy and prone to digression, the *purana*s recount not only human history but also the narratives of Shiva, Vishnu, and the numerous other deities who populate the Hindu pantheon. Historical records were also likely to be focused on kings.

The early centuries of the Common Era saw a proliferation of inscriptions issued by Indian royal houses. They were primarily used to record donations to communities or temples, but at the same time they were platforms for the proclamations of a king, as with Ashoka, or for articulating the historical shape of a dynasty and even, on occasion, for setting the record straight. The Chalukyas (c. 500–750), one of the most influential Indian dynasties, cultivated an extraordinary historiographical tradition in inscriptional form, often (though not always) in prose. Court historians would recount the great deeds and generosity of ruling kings in the prefaces to stone-carved grants—legal records of official gifts. A typical example from a Chalukyan grant of King Vinayaditya I, precisely dated to the "Scythian Year" 604 (682 CE):

> With cleverness and daring alone he recovered the vast, full royal power that his clan customarily held. He illuminated the quarters of heaven with the variegated, golden white banner of his fame acquired by his defeat of enemy kings who came before him in battle. He took Kanchi (a capital city in South India) directly after defeating the king of the Pallavas, whose conquest had marked the decline of the men of a dynasty spotless as moonbeams. (trans. Sheldon Pollock)

The inscription goes on to compare the Chalukyan king to, among others, Yudhisthira and Bharata of *Mahabharata* fame. Since these proclamations were carved into the very landscape, later court historians would read earlier inscriptions—sometimes traveling to distant temple sites where they were affixed—in order to establish or confirm the historical record. History was, in this sense, a deeply decentralized affair. The contrast with China would be difficult to overstate. Instead of entering the protected halls of a vast state-controlled history office where archives dating back centuries were meticulously kept, an Indian scholar might be expected to roam for miles, combing the hillsides in order to find sporadic references to the dynasties of the past.

Two Models for History in Classical China: The Topical and the Chronicle

A few centuries before India's epic and inscriptional traditions were evolving, Chinese were composing histories—although they too contained elements of the fantastic—much more grounded in the nitty-gritty of human politics and society. Yet they also very much engaged in reflection on the nature of kingship and the relationship between moral order and human society, concerns that preoccupied Indian writers as well. During this period, two very different works of history were produced in China: *Historical Documents* (*Shangshu*) and the *Spring and Autumn Annals* (*Chunqiu*). Each of these books was eventually designated a Classic (*jing*)—that is, they became part of a core group of works interpreted as expressions of the fundamental cosmological, ethical, and political principles of Chinese culture. *Historical Documents,* as its title suggests, is not a chronological history but rather a collection of documents and pronouncements (varying widely in authenticity, though some date to the eleventh century BCE) that set forth the principles of rulership and the moral standards that were to guide political ideology for the next thirty centuries. The foundational concept of the "Mandate of Heaven"—the belief that Heaven grants kingship only to men of proven virtue—is first explained in this work, for example; and its accounts of China's earliest sage-kings and their well-ordered societies, though mythical, provided the models (and the rhetorical flourishes) for later kings and emperors.

The *Spring and Autumn Annals* is a very different sort of history. A chronicle of events in the feudal states of the Central China Plain from the years 722 to 481 BCE, it was written in the compacted, laconic "ritual style" of the earlier annalistic writings—yearly chronicles—that comprised simple notices of battles, royal successions, alliances, and unusual nature phenomena. The work does not appear to offer opportunities for reflection on rulership or ethics. But one tradition of interpretation found hidden meanings: it was argued that Confucius, the work's supposed author, had concealed his judgment of historical events in the terse prose of the *Annals*. Exacting analysis of the text's vocabulary and word order, the titles and proper names employed, and the designation of dates and times, it was believed, would reveal Confucius's "praise and blame" of the feudal rulers—and therefore his vision of correct governance.

The events recorded so sparely in the *Spring and Autumn Annals* were soon fleshed out and elaborated in a companion text, the *Zuo Commentary* (*Zuozhuan*), which, though it probably originated as an independent chronicle, came to be seen as a commentary on the *Annals*. It provides a rich and detailed narrative fully grounded in human action, often interrupted by direct speech. Where the *Spring and Autumn Annals* reports simply, in nine characters, "In summer [721 BCE], in the fifth month, the earl of Zheng overcame Duan in Yan," the *Zuo Commentary* provides a long—541 characters—and exciting story of family hatred and betrayal (Duan was the earl's younger brother and the favorite of their mother, who schemed to ensure that Duan supplanted him as ruler). It can also be considered a work of ethics: a lesson on good rulership (the earl was able to defeat Duan in part because Duan oppressed his people); and an exemplary display of filial piety and familial love (the earl and his mother are reconciled in the end).

Historical Documents and the *Spring and Autumn Annals* (with the *Zuo Commentary*) established two different models—the topical and the chronological—that deeply influenced all later history writing and inspired much debate over the advantages and drawbacks of each form. But the texts share some characteristics that distinguish them clearly from the early histories of India. To be sure, there is the same interest in the principles of good rulership as we find in the *Mahabharata* and the *Ramayana*. But in the Chinese works this interest is grounded in "real"—that is to say, human—time (not the *yugas* or cosmic cycles of the Indian epics) and expressed in quite concrete narratives of "real" rulers. As Confucius is reputed to have said about the *Spring and Autumn Annals*, "I have relied upon actual affairs and added the mind of a true king to them. I think to reveal them in theoretical words is not as profound and clear as in actual affairs" (trans. Stephen W. Durrant).

Biography in Early China and India

This orientation toward actual affairs, coupled with the faith that humans interacted with the cosmos to make history, early ensured that biography, particularly biographies of rulers, officials, and important political figures, became central to the Chinese historiographical tradition. As, over time, the faith in a responsive cosmos faded and human actions came to be seen as the primary drivers of history, biography became the primary vehicle for the expression of historical judgments. Although he did not invent biographical writing, Sima Qian (145–86? BCE) was the first historian to identify "exemplary lives" (*liezhuan*) as a separate genre of historical writing. *Records of the Grand Historian* (*Shiji*), his monumental history of China from the beginnings of time to the late 2nd century BCE, combines a variety of historical genres (annals, chronological tables, genealogies of hereditary houses, topical treatises) with biographies, establishing the form for all later standard histories. But the biographies stand out. Sima Qian often appends his own judgments ("the grand historian comments . . .") at the end, as in the following assessment of Xiang Yu, the aristocratic rebel leader who failed to establish a new dynasty after the fall of the Qin in 207 BCE:

> He boasted and made a show of his own achievements. He was obstinate in his own opinions and did not abide by established

ways. He thought to make himself a dictator, hoping to attack and rule the empire by force. Yet within five years he was dead and his kingdom lost. He met death at Tongcheng, but even at that time he did not wake to or accept responsibility for his errors. "It is Heaven," he declared, "which has destroyed me, and no fault of mine in the use of arms!" Was he not indeed deluded? (trans. Burton Watson)

Sima Qian's evaluations are often much more subtly and artfully rendered. His group biography of assassins, which is analyzed in some detail in chapter 4, conveys a narrative of change—the deterioration of a code of honor in the face of rising *realpolitik*—through the juxtaposition of a series of biographies of increasingly inept assassins. Indeed, Sima Qian often frustrates the reader hoping to find clear-cut "praise and blame" judgments of the sort attributed to Confucius in his compilation of the *Spring and Autumn Annals*. Even today scholars cannot agree on how he evaluates the wealthy men discussed in his "Biographies of Moneymakers": does Sima Qian, a free-market enthusiast, admire these men for their drive and ingenuity in turning profits? Or is he, like a good Confucian, excoriating them for their willingness to do anything—rob graves, trade in dried sheep stomachs, etc.—to make money? This ambiguity troubled later historians; although much admired and much read for his fine prose style, Sima Qian was also much criticized, particularly during the Song (960–1279) and Ming (1368–1644) dynasties, when a heavily Confucianized historiography had become the model, for his failure to embrace the moralizing approach heralded in the *Spring and Autumn Annals*.

Biography plays a central role in Classical Indian historical expression as well, but with one major difference: biography was usually hagiography. Indian biographies, known as *carita*, were not to be written about just anybody: only great men merited them. One was the Buddha. Ashvaghosha's *Buddhacarita* (c. second century CE), among the earliest works of classical Sanskrit literature, tells the story of Prince Siddhartha Gautama (the Buddha), who famously turned away from the world at a young age and adopted an ascetic lifestyle in the search for truth. Written long after the Buddha had died (probably in the fifth century BCE), it contains both lofty praise and moral instruction, celebrating the greatness of a spiritual teacher while simultaneously propounding the tenets of a proselytizing religion. This passage from the scene of the Buddha's birth in the opening canto illustrates the reverential tone:

> He will rescue with the mighty boat of knowledge this stricken world carried away by the current. . . . Upon men in this world who are being scorched by the fire of passion, whose fuel is the objects of the senses, he'll pour relief with the rain of dharma, like a rain cloud pouring down rain, at the end of the summer heat. (trans. Patrick Olivelle)

Kings too were considered worthy of the *carita* genre. Exemplary is Bana's *Harsa-carita* (seventh century), written to honor Harshavardhana (r. 606–647), the ruler of Kanauj in central India. Both the Buddha and Harsha are demonstrably historical figures, which gives these works a different character from much of the *itihasa-purana* enterprise. Bana even tells something of his own story, adding autobiography to the mix. It would be difficult to reconstruct a full account of the reign of Harsha or his times from the *Harsa-carita*, however. Bana was not so much concerned with chronology as with sequencing events—like a writer of fiction would construct a plot—in order to demonstrate how Harsha's own personal charisma had led him to greatness. Kings were idealized figures. They were larger than life, and approaches to their biographies reflect this deeply.

Writing a *carita* on occasion even required some extraordinary fact bending. For instance, when princes violated the rules of primogeniture, where the eldest son is successor to the father, the matter of succession had to be handled with great delicacy, even creativity. This was the case with Harshavardhana, who had usurped the throne of Kanauj from his brother; another celebrated usurper (and fratricide) was famously eulogized by Bilhana in his *Vikramanka-deva-carita* (late eleventh century). Who better than a poet, rather than a fact-mongering historian, to make the case for the new king? Classical Indian poets considered themselves indispensable to rulers because they were responsible for perpetuating the memory of a dynasty in the written record. Poetry, they felt, acted as a mirror in which the fame of a king could be eternally reflected for the generations to come. Court writers were also public relations officers. Just kingship was the ideal, yet most historians were constrained to write from the point of view of the court, no matter how unjust the current king. Their role was not to apportion "praise and blame" in the manner of the ideal Chinese historian, but to shape and disseminate the ideology of the court. Blame, when it was apportioned, was either very subtle or more pointedly directed at previous dynasties. The current king was axiomatically perfect—or such was the logic of the *carita* genre.

But one work from this period does stand out as a work of critical history: Kalhana's *Raja-tarangini* (*River of Kings*, c. 1150), written in Bilhana's homeland of Kashmir during a period of remarkable intellectual ferment. Kalhana was working in a local tradition that superbly combined historiographical inquiry with poetic craftsmanship; again, these were not separate genres (and he clearly labels his historical work a *kavya*, or poem). Still, *River of Kings* stands apart from earlier *carita*s because of Kalhana's approach. He mentions his sources in the opening of the work and pauses to criticize several of his predecessors on both factual and literary grounds. He also records with unprecedented detail and an almost modernist cynicism the fraught political history of Kashmir.

History and the State

It is possible to identify a few striking similarities between the early Indian and Chinese historiographical traditions. Both are grounded at the start in assumptions about the cosmological significance and ritual importance of history. Historical texts transmit notions about the moral responsibilities of rulership that long shaped the rhetoric—if not the actual practice—of governance; interestingly, both traditions shared the notion that history (or in the case of India, literature) served as a mirror to the ruler. Both favored biography as a vehicle of history. And in both traditions, the literary qualities of historical writing were valued: in India literature *was* history, and in China historical works came to have canonical status as treasured classics.

Equally powerful, however, are the differences. In early India, history did not enjoy independent bibliographical status, and the documentary impulse was much weaker than in China. Inscriptions were an important means of recording events, but much of history was truly literature, written as poetry (either epic or *carita*), not prose, as in China. Early Indians did not, as a rule, see records as vital to the workings of the state. Nor did court writers make the claim to be arbiters of political virtue, as Chinese historians did; their role was to glorify the achievements of their royal patrons.

But, although Chinese court historians did not necessarily devote themselves to the production of hagiographical biographies of their rulers, they had other means of promoting the legitimacy of new dynasties and new rulers. From the seventh century on, one of their most important duties was the compilation of a history of the previous dynasty, a "standard" or dynastic history, modeled in form on Sima Qian's *Records of the Grand Historian*, that would explain the failings of the predecessor dynasty and the virtue and wisdom that allowed the current dynastic line to capture the "Mandate of Heaven." In shaping the narrative of dynastic succession, the Chinese imperial governments recognized and exploited the ideological value of history. (They also made it much easier for historians to practice "praise and blame" because, as in India, it was quite safe to "blame" the rulers of previous dynasties for their failings—indeed, that was one of the points of the endeavor.) They were also, of course, providing records of the previous government for current official use, an essential function in a highly bureaucratized state.

For the standard or dynastic histories relied on—and in turn encouraged the maintenance of—a mass of documents and digests compiled by the archivists and historians of the previous dynasty. From 629 on, the recording and collection of documents were the responsibility of officials working in a newly established History Office. This office produced an impressive volume of material: court diaries (chronological accounts of the official business conducted in daily court sessions), records of current government (confidential documents compiled under the supervision of the different ministers), daily calendars (a condensation of court diaries and records of current government), biographical data, and the Veritable Records (annals of the official activities of the previous ruler in a dynasty, compiled from the court diaries, records of current government, and daily calendars kept under his reign). Thus, the compilers of the standard histories had a vast amount of material to work from, and they worked through it with widely varying degrees of dedication and skill. The worst of the standard histories are little more than voluminous cut-and-paste jobs, excerpts from the mass of documents cobbled together by committees of officials. The best are considered among the masterpieces of classical writing. It is unlikely that any but the best were regularly read, although they were kept at court and doubtless used as documentary references.

The documentary-rich foundation of the Chinese imperial state encouraged close imperial oversight—and interference—not so much in the writing of the standard histories (although such interference was certainly not uncommon) as in the record keeping of the current dynasty. To provide just one of many examples: the Yongle emperor (r. 1402–24) of the Ming dynasty, who had usurped the throne from his nephew, saw to it that the Veritable Records of his father, the founder of the dynasty, were rewritten—no fewer than three times—to strengthen his claim to legitimacy; among other falsehoods, he claimed that his mother was the chief consort of the founder. Although the method was different, as during the reign of the Indian monarch Harshavardhana, historians occasionally had to engage in some extraordinary fact bending to please their demanding employers.

Nonetheless, the relationship between the Chinese state and the historian (or record keeper) was one of ambivalence and much potential tension—and in this sense starkly different from that in India during the classical age. Doubtless the concerns of a powerful emperor to assert his legitimacy or burnish his legacy created pressure on the officials in the History Office and other court historians, who may have had little recourse but to "help him shape and disseminate the ideology of the court." Yet at the same time, the historian, the arbiter of "praise and blame" according to the early historiographical tradition, could claim a moral authority and far-ranging judgment that qualified him, like Confucius himself, to evaluate even the mightiest of rulers. History was a "mirror to the ruler"—and the historian held the mirror. Sima Guang (1019–1086), an official (but not an official historian) of the Song dynasty, reminded the ruler of this fact in the very title of his work, *Comprehensive Mirror to Aid in Government* (*Zizhi tongjian*). Throughout the text he drives the message home: all of the almost three hundred chapters end with a series of judgments addressed to the emperor: "Your servant Guang is of the opinion. . . ." Repeatedly he links the moral qualities of the ruler and his officials to the state of the empire, embracing the conventional Confucian faith that good governance depends on the ruler's virtue.

But his narrative is designed to emphasize a practical political message as well: quite simply, the beginning and end dates of the *Comprehensive Mirror* reveal what Sima Guang wants the ruler to see in his "mirror." 403 BCE, when the weak Zhou king ceded power to a regional strongman, marks the beginning of the decline of the great Zhou dynasty; 959 CE marks the eve of the founding of the Song dynasty, the reunification of China under the leadership of a strong ruler, Zhao Kuangyin (r. 960–76). The pointed contrast delivers Sima Guang's message: the emperor was to "mirror" the strong ruler, the founder of his dynasty. Remarkably, for much of the time that Sima Guang was working on his history—with the permission of the emperor—he was also leading the opposition to the reform program endorsed by that same emperor.

Whether functioning as a mirror for the ruler or as a vehicle for political legitimization, history writing in China was seen as the responsibility of the state. The very language of officialdom relied on it: policies were justified by historical precedents and political positions summarized in historical allusions. The determination with which certain rulers pressed their own versions of the past—as well as the quickness of dissenting officials and scholars to turn to historical narratives to express political criticism—reveals the firmness of the belief in the bond between history and political order.

No such bond existed in India. History was irrelevant to the functioning of the state. Rulers—at least until the early modern period—were manifestly uninterested in collecting or preserving large volumes of data. This is a conspicuous difference between the two societies.

Changing Political and Historical Cultures

History writing in India and China in roughly the thirteenth to seventeenth centuries underwent some changes and also followed very different paths. In India, new political developments prompted the spread of different conceptions of history and transformed and strengthened the relationship between historians and the state. In China, however, as official historiography entered a period of decline, there was a proliferation of unofficial histories and an expansion in the understanding of the suitable subjects of history. In both cultures, new dynasties of foreign rulers reshaped the central concerns of historians, both official and private.

Persian Historiography and India's New Political Dispensations

Not long after Kalhana was writing *River of Kings* in the far northwest of the subcontinent, Turkic Muslims established themselves to the south in the Gangetic plain in a political formation that would later come to be known as the Delhi Sultanate (1206–1526). The language of high culture of the new rulers was Persian, which introduced new protocols of courtiers, court poetry, and elite learning as well as sophisticated structures of government administration to the expanding reaches of Islamic society. The Arab conquest of the Persian Empire in 651 had given an impetus to the eastward spread of Islam toward Central and South Asia. A fusion of Arabic, Persian, and Turkic traditions brought additional genres and perspectives to Indian historiography.

The Muslim nobility of India engaged with a variety of texts from the greater Islamic world. Advice literature was especially popular among the courtiers and kings who drew inspiration from Persian culture. These texts often combine historical inquiry with political theory. Advice genres like *akhlaq*, or mirrors for princes—a genre that took the form of annalistic history in China—provide insight into how India's Islamic dynasties responded to cultural, religious, and political difference. Shari'a (Muslim law) was a subject of considerable negotiation in India, where Muslims were never a majority. Persian texts from beyond India, like the thirteenth-century *Nasirian Ethics* of the Azerbaijani author Tusi (who dedicated the book to an Ismaili ruler who also had to confront the problem of religious difference), provided the theoretical foundation for more inclusive policies.

The Perso-Arabic genre most readily equated with the English term "history" is *tarikh* (chronicle). The *tarikh*, like the Indic *carita*, may be associated with a particular ruler. One of the most famous chronicles of the Delhi Sultanate is Zia al-Din Barani's *Tarikh-i firoz shahi* (1357), which concerns the reign of Firoz Shah Tughlak (r. 1351–88). Barani speaks eloquently about the genre of history writing, which he considers the very highest form of learning. This was a view that never would have been defended previously in India, where poetry was preeminent, and to the extent that it served as history was concerned with timeless, paradigmatic truths rather than quotidian facts. One of history's many benefits was its ability to instill good character (for instance in a sultan), a view, we have seen, embraced by Confucian Chinese historians hoping to provide models or "mirrors" of proper governance and ethical conduct to their rulers. For Barani, who also wrote advice literature, history was closely aligned with the principles of Sunni Islam, and ultimately only Muslim historians could be trusted.

The later Mughal period (1526–1857) saw a whole cluster of emperor-specific texts. Two Mughal chronicles, the *Baburnama* (*Account of Babur*) and *Jahangir-nama* (*Account of Jahangir*), were autobiographies, among the very first in the Islamic world. The self-narrative of Babur, the founder of the Mughal dynasty (anomalously written in a dialect of Turkish, his native language, rather than in Persian), tells the story of a prince on the run from Central Asia who finally succeeded in conquering India four years before his death, in 1526. Both Babur's and Jahangir's accounts proceed chronologically and capture a wealth of important diplomatic and military details as well as the more random and incidental moments in daily life, including what often seems like the ingestion of a surprising amount of intoxicants. A fairly typical entry from the diarylike *Jahangir-nama* reads as follows:

> On the eve of Saturday the twenty-first [corresponds to December 3, 1620] the forward camp set out under good auspices in the direction of Agra [a Mughal capital]. Barqandaz Khan was assigned the post of supervisor of the arsenal of the Deccan [southern] army. Shaykh Ishaq was assigned to Kangra [district in the north]. Allahdad Khan Afghan's brothers were released from prison and given an award of a thousand rupees. I sent two white falcons as a gift to [the emperor Jahangir's son] Khurram.
>
> On Thursday the twenty-sixth [December 8] a wine party was held as usual, and the gifts from the ruler of Iran that he had sent with Zaynal Beg were presented for my inspection. I gave Sultan-Husayn of Pakhli an elephant. (trans. Wheeler M. Thackston)

As a rule, Persian chronicles conform more to conventional notions of history than their classical Indic counterparts. Most *tarikh* writers adopt a chronological perspective, even if their unit is the year of the current sultan's reign. Some Persian texts show annalistic features, recording the day-to-day proceedings of the court (*roznama*) in a fashion somewhat reminiscent of the Veritable Records kept at Chinese courts. There are often incidental references to the period's prominent nobility, both Muslim and Hindu, and many take stock of the past from a comprehensive, *longue durée* (long-term) perspective. Dates are given; competing evidence is weighed. Such easily recognizably historiographical concerns and techniques would mean that unlike writings in Sanskrit, the Indo-Persian sources were widely viewed as a legitimate tradition of history writing in the nineteenth century, when modern notions of history began to hold sway.

And yet panegyric (praise) and didacticism (imparting lessons)—often seen as flaws in the more "Hindu" approaches to the past—were demonstrably part of the Persian tradition as well. Like the writers of *carita*s, chroniclers always praised their sultans. Moreover, in Sultanate and Mughal-period India no less than in classical times, the legitimacy of rulers was generally based on perceived divine sanction. In his rock-cut inscriptions, the emperor Ashoka introduced himself as "the beloved of the gods," and in fact most Classical Indian kings considered themselves imbued with a portion of divinity. Abu al-Fazl, author of the *Akbarnama* (*Account of Akbar*), presented his patron as a perfected man connected to the divine presence, aided in part by the norms of a Persian textual culture that was often overlaid with Sufi tropes:

> Heavenly in appearance, he is an earth of stability;
> possessor of universal intelligence, Jalaluddin [glory of the faith].
> Light of the sun of essence and shadow of God, jewel of
> the crown and throne, Akbar Shah.
> Be this ancient world new through him; may his star shed rays of
>   light like the sun. (trans. Wheeler M. Thackston)

Notable here is the idea, shared by the Chinese, that the ruler has in a sense earned divine sanction (or, in the case of Chinese rulers, the Mandate of Heaven) through his moral perfection; he does not enjoy a European-style "divine right" to do as he wishes, but he has the sanction of God because of his special qualities. (The *Akbarnama* is also discussed in chapter 3; Fazl wrote of Akbar's harem as a symbol of near divine status.)

However positive the public perception of the emperor, ruling the vastly diverse territories of India was never easy and insurrection was a common problem for the Mughals, one of the rare Indian dynasties that aimed to bring the whole of the subcontinent under their sway. From the time of Akbar it became a widespread state policy to incorporate highly ranked Hindu vassals into the Mughal bureaucracy, allowing them to remain *raja*s (local kings) in their own dominions. Many of these Rajput chieftains felt understandably conflicted about their loss of political authority under the Mughal dispensation. Some resisted mightily. The sixteenth- and seventeenth-century Persian chronicles often present the enforcing of Mughal authority in didactic terms. Thus, a Hindu raja who rebels against imperial authority and then comes back into the fold is said to have "escaped the cesspool of error" or to have reached "the felicity of his majesty's grace."

For all of the rhetorical flourishes that characterize both Indic and Persian textual culture, the early modern period (largely coextensive with Mughal rule) saw more historiographical accuracy and a much stronger sense of deliberation about the past than ever before. Historical reflection began to accommodate an increased sense of human (as opposed to divine) agency. The standards by which history was to be written also underwent some updating. In the lead-up to his sponsorship of Abu al-Fazl's *Akbarnama*, for instance, Akbar issued an imperial edict exhorting people to share their memories of his father, Humayun, and grandfather, Babur, and the recent political events that had culminated in the successful founding of the Mughal Empire. Emperor Humayun's sister Gulbadan Begum, for instance, wrote the *Humayunnama* (*Account of Humayun*) as a direct result of Akbar's command. The politically astute Akbar, who was acutely aware that he ruled over a diverse population, also became deeply interested in the pre-Muslim Indian past. Not unlike the British colonial rulers who would unseat the Mughals two centuries later, Akbar commissioned translations of a host of Sanskrit texts, notably the *Mahabharata* and *Ramayana*—evidently then seen as histories—into Persian. His court historians presented him as a universal emperor, whose incisive intellect did not allow anything to bypass his critical gaze.

There were naturally tensions between Persian-style historiography and more local visions of the past that had been disseminated through Sanskrit traditions like *itihasa-purana* and the *carita*. Some Mughal-period writers, including Emperor Babur, saw India's Muslim rulers as their only legitimate predecessors, and many Indo-Persian chroniclers rather shortsightedly traced the beginnings of Indian history to the advent of Islam. Others, however, adopted a more wide-ranging perspective, straining to incorporate the events of the *Mahabharata* or the earlier genealogies of Indian kings into their worldview. Occasionally Persian historians, such as Abd al-Qadir Badauni (fl. 1614), appear nonplussed by what they saw as the "preposterous absurdities" of their Hindu sources. Evidently nineteenth-century Europeans were not the only ones to express some degree of exasperation with "Hindu history" or a perceived lack thereof. Badauni was also a severe critic of Akbar. Some of the now much vaunted open-mindedness (in today's India Akbar has become a byword for religious tolerance) of the emperor, including an interest in other religious faiths and his selective adoption of quasi-Hindu practices like vegetarianism and sun worship, could also be perceived as apostasy. Badauni waited until the emperor was dead before he published his history, an indication that dissent would not be tolerated.

More popular, if less verifiable traditions suggest that imperial authority could be questioned, at least in some circles. An entire subgenre of vernacular poetry, for instance, casts Akbar in a less than regal light. Still a favorite in Indian children's bedtime stories is Birbal, considered one of the nine jewels (i.e., luminaries) of Akbar's court. In tale after tale his legendary wit consigns the emperor to the status of an inveterate bumbler.

The early modern state was a paper bureaucracy in ways that were wholly unprecedented for India—but that had been long established in China, as the earlier discussion of court record keeping reveals. In India, inscriptions were common but writing had never fully supplanted orality (witness the transmission of the sacred Vedas). Palm-leaf manuscripts remained for centuries the preferred medium for textual circulation, but paper became more and more dominant as a medium due to Muslim influence (the Muslims had learned paper making from the Chinese in the mid-eighth century). While Indians of all stripes eschewed print (the technology was available to them, but they never chose to adopt it) until the colonizers and missionaries established their presses, literacy was a prized attainment among several social groups: Muslim elites, Brahmans, Jains, and Persianized scribal communities like the Indian Munshis, who helped to keep the Mughal bureaucracy running.

After the sixteenth century there was a huge proliferation of a wide range of documents, and for the first time it is possible to identify a corpus roughly comparable to the sorts of official records kept in China from an early period. This is probably more than an accident of survival, though old documents did not stand a fighting chance in India's tropical climate. The Mughal state does seem to have gathered information on a much larger scale than was the norm in previous times. A whole class of news writers contributed to a burgeoning information economy. Local languages also became more formalized as written traditions, leading to a proliferation of record keeping and new genres of historical writing at India's regional courts.

The Rise of "Unofficial" History in China

From the thirteenth to seventeenth centuries, then, the Indian subcontinent was undergoing political and cultural changes that introduced new approaches to history. Formerly poetry had on occasion been a mirror to the ruler and even a moral guide for governance, but with the exception of inscriptions, Sanskrit textual culture had rarely been a documentary exercise. During the Sultanate and later Mughal periods, as had already taken place much earlier in China, the link between history and the state was reinforced: while the classical *carita* tradition continued in Sanskrit and, eventually, in local Indian languages, new genres of Persian history writing and record keeping were developed to support Muslim rule.

In China at roughly the same time, the practice of history had taken new turns as well, albeit in very different directions and due to very different causes. Official history suffered a decline during this period, in part as a result of the Mongol conquest (to the mid-fourteenth century) and the overzealous efforts of the emperors of the restored Chinese dynasty, the Ming (1368–1644), to limit and control the activities of the History Office and official historians. For most of the dynasty, the histories of the different reigns were not kept, and the standard of history writing was low: the *History of the Yuan Dynasty* (*Yuanshi*), hastily completed within two years of the Ming founding, is considered the worst—or one of the worst—standard histories in terms of both accuracy and style. As one distinguished critic complained, "The national historiography never failed in its task to such an extreme degree as under our dynasty" (trans. On-cho Ng and Q. Edward Wang).

But the poverty of official history seems to have spurred the writing of private or "unofficial" histories (*yeshi*, "histories [written] in the wilderness"). Belying the oft-quoted claim that history in China was "written by officials for officials," literati not employed by the government also contributed significantly to the historical tradition. Although the "unofficial history" genre was certainly not new in the Ming, literati and retired officials of that period produced a striking number, as if to make up for the inadequacies of official history. Tan Qian (1594–1658), author of *Evaluations of the Events of Our Dynasty* (*Guoque*), explicitly stated in his preface that concern about these failures was the motive for his privately compiled annalistic history of the Ming. Criticizing those officials who submitted to the will of the emperor in editing the veritable records, Tan tried to correct the account of the Yongle usurpation by restoring the rightful emperor to the record and praising the actions of officials who had remained loyal to him. But in many ways the flood of unofficial and "miscellaneous histories" written in this period served not just to compensate for the severe limitations of the official record but also to enrich and expand the historical record. Shen Defu's (1578–1642) *Gathered Outside the Wanli Court* (*Wanli yehuo bian*), for example, is a wide-ranging set of observations about politics and life in the capital; and Ye Mengzhu's (1624–c. 1693) *Experiencing the Times* (*Yueshi bian*) records local economic conditions in the Jiangnan area. These works (and many others too numerous to list) reflect a growing interest both in smaller informal, even personal ("I was there") histories covering a short time span, and in historical investigations of topics rarely touched upon in official histories: regional economies, popular customs, material culture, etc.

Local Histories

In this context it is perhaps not surprising that other, more localized forms of history writing began to flourish in China. Gazetteers (*difangzhi*), local surveys of counties, prefectures, and provinces, proliferated in the early modern era, although the genre had originated many centuries before. These were topically organized digests of information—including much historical information—about local geography, administration, educational institutions, ritual and cultural practices, economy, and important figures of local society. Of course these works were political products, in that the court often ordered their compilation (and a presentation of the completed gazetteer to the Imperial Library) as a means of identifying a locality as part of the empire. They also served as valuable sources of local information for magistrates and other officials sent from the center to manage local government. But local scholars and gentry of necessity played leading roles in—and sometimes even initiated—the production of gazetteers, and thus were able to shape the narrative of their native place. In so doing, they had opportunities to provide either alternative interpretations of or important details about local events and conditions not found in central state records. Even official editors might use the gazetteer as a means of indirectly criticizing state policies. Feng Kecan (fl. late seventeenth century), for example, in his gazetteer of Tancheng county, Shandong—where he served as magistrate until cashiered for incompetence—makes clear that the unreasonable fiscal demands of the state doomed his efforts to govern a profoundly impoverished area effectively.

Gazetteers are generally shaped by the concerns of government, both central and local. But other forms of local history—we might even say social history—flourished well outside the purview of the central government. Genealogies (*zongpu, zupu, jiapu*), a genre that originated most likely in the third century CE, began to be produced in significant numbers only in the late Ming and Qing. This was to some extent a response to large-scale social changes: as corporate lineages developed, particularly in south China, genealogies—accounts of a family's history, with lists of its members and ancestral halls and often (highly ritualized) biographies of its most distinguished men and women—became important means of registering lineage members (so as to determine who had access to shared property), defining proper behavior within the lineage, and establishing the standing of the lineage in local society. But these works, whatever their social and economic meanings, were self-consciously identified as histories. Their prefaces routinely introduced the notion that the genealogy form, with its hereditary tables and biographies, derived from Sima Qian's *Records of the Grand Historian*; the latter treated the *guo* or state/empire, the former the *jia* or family—which in Confucian ideology is the prop of the state and the training ground for the ruler.

Localized history also took on special importance in India during the early modern period. Persian remained the imperial language of the Mughals, and Persian historiographical approaches and historical genres governed the writing of history at court. But Persian histories were also written outside the court, and in the regional Indian kingdoms, local histories in various vernaculars proliferated. Examples are legion in Bengali, Telugu, Marathi, and, in the regions closest to Mughal power centers, in various dialects of Hindi.

Many of the Hindi-using literati were Brahman or Jain rather than from scribal castes associated with the imperial bureaucracy, which means they were more likely to be conversant with Sanskrit than Persian. Hindi historians therefore turned to familiar genres like the *carita*, updating the classical past to meet the needs of the Mughal present. Take the *Man-carita* (1595) of Narottam, a biography of Raja Man Singh Kacchwaha, a leading Rajput general under the Mughal emperor Akbar. One impulse behind this text was to construct Man Singh as an ideal Hindu king and Mughal official (the two roles were not incompatible), and Narottam drew on a stock of motifs from the classical *carita* genre. However, the poet-historian was also clearly grappling with an insistent new Mughal political reality that impinged in various ways on his text. Sanskrit poets were on the whole more prone to idealizing, their *carita*s more focused on the timeless than the temporal. Often classical writers were concerned not so much with quotidian details as with establishing something more abstract and generalizable about human potential, presenting an exemplary life story from which future generations stood to learn (and suppressing that which detracted from the mission). The early modern historical writings in Hindi were as a rule more realistic and connected to the here and now. The works were often dated (this was almost never the case in Sanskrit). They were filled with proper names, local family genealogies, and details of specific recent events. Hindi writers also attempted "to shape the narrative of their native place" by including descriptions of their cities and matters of local concern. Still, the authors of vernacular *carita*s did not jettison the literary impulse altogether. The descriptions of their cities read more like poetry than gazetteer, and writers would often showcase a raja's heroic exploits using elaborate poetic techniques. As with Sanskrit, most of the Hindi historical tradition was composed in verse, not prose, so literary demands such as rhyme scheme, alliteration, and genre conventions had a strong claim. Moreover, the western Indian provinces in which many Rajput kingdoms were located boasted a strong bardic tradition; thus, aural-performative flourishes and genealogical concerns—the staple features of bardic tales—also made their way into Hindi historical writing. In performance, bards would have added or subtracted, corroborated or subverted, or in some other manner stamped their own imprint on the narrative.

India's Rajput kings, like their Mughal overlords, also widely turned to more structured record keeping by the seventeenth century. Scribes kept track of more and more facets of society, from marriage and kinship records to daily proceedings at the court. New genres came into being to document events in more matter-of-fact and less poetically embellished ways than had been the norm before. Local courts now routinely had *daftars* (repositories of records) and libraries.

A dramatic example of this new attention to the archive comes from the Jodhpur court of the 1660s. The Jain intellectual Muṃhata Nainsi, a prominent revenue administrator under Maharaja Jaswant Singh (r. 1638–78), began to compile a history of the Rajput polities, including accounts of select Muslim rulers. He naturally had access to the records of his own court but evidently was also able to procure important manuscripts from quite far afield since documentary records were by this period far more readily available. He sifted through this material and evaluated it, compiling the salient details into a comprehensive account of India's major royal houses.

History, Conquest, and Counter-History in the Early Modern Period

As a tradition that ran concurrent with Persian historiography throughout the early modern period, Hindi history writing offered up a combination of perspectives. Some accounts of events were quite congruent with Persian versions that emerged from the Mughal imperial domains. But, at times, a raja who was denounced as a worthless renegade in the imperial paradigms in Hindi became a local hero, celebrated for his bravery and martial ethos. There were thus elements of counterhistory. One writer, Keshavdas (fl. 1600), wrote a narrative poem about the Mughal invasion of his own kingdom (Orchha in central India), telling it from the point of view of a local prince whom he depicted as a martyr. Elsewhere, using the *carita* genre, he recounted elements of recent Mughal history that were connected to political intrigues at his court. In the time-honored tradition of the classical *carita,* the work also served as an opportunity to broadcast the kingly authority of his patron, Bir Singh Deo Bundela (r. 1605–27), who was closely allied to Emperor Jahangir. In a political climate that demanded uncompromising allegiance to the Mughal emperor, regional Hindu rajas and their court writers could still project a sense of sovereignty with a lowercase *s*.

Some Hindi writers also expressed their views of the Mughal Empire. Narottam included a brief biography of Akbar within his *Man-carita*. Clearly he thought highly of the emperor, and his perspective was in this sense quite congruent with imperial records like the Persian *Akbarnama*:

> Akbar is lord of Delhi, praise be unto him.
> He commands respect in the four directions.
> This is Hindu rule, who says it is Turk?
> The kings sing his praises everywhere.
> He (Akbar) always worships Vishnu and bathes in holy Ganges water.
> He doesn't kill living beings. He does not extract rapacious taxes.

Attitudes toward the Mughal authorities varied considerably. Some regional courts chafed against Mughal rule. Bhushan, a Hindi court poet of the Maratha rebel king Shivaji (r. 1674–80), likened serving the empire to chasing a prostitute:

> Working under the Delhi government is like chasing a clever, desirable prostitute.
> She does not stay faithful to one man.
> But Shivaji is under the sway of a woman called "fame."
> The woman who traps everybody else can't touch him.

When vernacular histories served to record dissenting voices, Hindi writers, like their counterparts in China, engaged in praise but also dispensed blame—not, of course, directed at the court that patronized them. In premodern India histories were generally sponsored by courts.

In China, conquest provided a strong impetus for the writing of private histories. These might be acts of dissent or resistance but were just as likely to be serious reflections on the failings of the Chinese state and society. Such was the case after the fall of the Ming dynasty to non-Han conquerors, the Manchus, and the establishment of the Qing dynasty in 1644. The loss of the Mandate of Heaven and its humiliating capture by a "barbarian" people required analysis and explanation: what had gone wrong?

Zhang Dai (1597–1684?) is not the most famous of the historians who struggled with this question, but his example nonetheless nicely demonstrates the almost obsessive interest, as well as the personal passions, it inspired. The pleasure-loving scion of a wealthy and distinguished family of Shaoxing, Zhejiang, in the culturally advanced Jiangnan region, Zhang lived a fairly carefree life until the Manchu invasion. Although impressively well educated, he never succeeded in passing the civil examinations that would have granted him a much coveted official position. In 1628, apparently oblivious to the external threats to Ming rule but keenly aware of the internal weakness of the government of his day, he began writing a history of the Ming from its founding to 1627. This work was interrupted by the conquest, after which Zhang's life changed dramatically: many of his friends lost to military resistance or loyalist suicide, his family's property expropriated, he lived a life of poverty and seclusion in the mountains outside of Shaoxing.

He devoted himself there to the completion of two works that grapple with the Ming fall: *Book in a Stone Casket* (*Shigui cangshu*, 1655) and a sequel (1664), both of which analyze what went wrong in the Ming through biographies of the late Ming emperors. The fate of the dynasty was already set by the time of the greedy and indolent Wanli emperor (r. 1573–1620), who employed eunuchs to "ravish the people of the empire's resources." But only in the reign of the Tianqi emperor (r. 1621–27), Wanli's grandson, did the state of the empire become evidently critical: then, "the illness penetrated into the region of the kidneys: since [the patient] was running out of physical strength, malignant lesions developed in the bones. Shortly, those lesions festered and seeped with pus, and the life was gone." Zhu Yousong, the prince of Fu, who had briefly led resistance to the Manchus as "emperor" of the Ming in 1644 and 1645 (and whom Zhang had briefly followed), was in Zhang's eyes so contemptible that he did not deserve to be included in the legitimate Ming line: "not only stupid but also recklessly promiscuous," he employed evil ministers and doomed any chance of a Ming comeback (trans. Jonathan Spence).

Stone Casket presents a conventional Confucian analysis of the Ming fall as a failure of moral character on the part of the last rulers of the dynasty. Other historians blamed the Ming educated elite for their absorption in airy philosophizing and consequent neglect of good governance. One of the bolder spirits of the day, Wang Fuzhi (1619–1692), who had fought against the Manchus and refused to serve the new dynasty, identified the vicious factionalism of Ming politics as the problem and then went on to baldly deny the sovereignty of the Manchus; citing many historical precedents, he argued that barbarians could never legitimately rule China.

Had Wang Fuzhi's views been widely known in his lifetime (his writings were not published until the nineteenth century), there is no question that he would have suffered at the hands of the Manchu rulers. The state's conviction that control of the historical record was essential to the maintenance of power was nowhere more clearly expressed than in the actions taken in the seventeenth and eighteenth centuries to stamp out any hint of anti-Manchu sentiment in Chinese histories (and eventually to construct a history for the Manchus). When, for example, it came to the attention of the Kangxi emperor (r. 1661–1722) that a Chinese scholar had completed a history of the last years of the Ming dynasty that treated the Southern Ming (established to resist Manchu rule after the Manchus had already conquered China in 1644) as a legitimate government and referred to the Manchu emperors by their personal names (violation of a sacred taboo), he had the text destroyed; its editor's corpse exhumed and burned; the family members of all the scholars who had participated in the work either executed or enslaved; and the printers and purchasers of the work executed, together with any officials who had known of its publication and not reported it to the throne. At total of seventy people were put to death, and many others exiled. It is impossible to find a comparable case in India of such vociferous censorship and retribution. Control over the historical record simply never mattered that much.

The Kangxi, Yongzheng (r. 1723–35), and Qianlong (r. 1736–95) emperors all oversaw campaigns to identify and destroy any historical works (and, indeed, any works at all) that could be construed as anti-Manchu. But, as discussed in chapter 1, the Manchu emperors were also devoted to the construction of a history for the Manchus. Yongzheng and Qianlong took positive steps to manage the historical record by commissioning the compilation of genealogies of the Manchu ruling family and a study of the origins of the Manchu people. The most important of these works, the *Investigation Into Manchu Origins (Manzhou yuanliu kao)*, completed in 1783, provided the Manchus with a written history that confirmed, through scholarly investigation (or so the title claimed), that the Manchus were descendants of the Jurchens, earlier conquerors of north China—and thus had, by virtue of this precedent, a legitimate claim to the governance of China. This argument required the adjustment of some of the Chinese standard histories; the Qianlong emperor saw to it that the histories of the Jin, Liao, and Yuan dynasties were "corrected" to support the conclusions of the *Investigation Into Manchu Origins*.

At the same time that the Qing emperors were insistently shaping both the Chinese and the Manchu historical narrative, scholars outside the court were developing new critical approaches to the study and writing of history. They were by no means the first to think about historical method and source analysis. In the Tang (618–907), Liu Zhiji (661–721), author of the first Chinese work of historiography, *The Study of History (Shitong*, 710), wrote very pointed critiques of Sima Qian's *Records of the Grand Historian* (he found it annoyingly repetitious and wordy) and the work of the Tang History Office, in which he served. Historians adopted a critical attitude toward their sources. Sima Guang and the many editors of his *Comprehensive Mirror for Aid in Governance,* for example, drew on a wide array of sources (over three hundred) and included discussions of disputed points (with textual variants provided) within the *Comprehensive Mirror* (although it is also true that Sima Guang sometimes changed the wording of his primary sources in order to highlight his interpretation of events). And Ming readers were highly critical of the official histories produced at court.

But systematic analysis of errors in the great histories of the past and development of tools for the critical evaluation of sources were phenomena of the high Qing, in particular of the movement of evidential research that called for close philological study of ancient texts, so that their original meanings could be restored. The pioneers in this effort gained practical experience in textual criticism through their work collating texts in the Imperial Printing Office in the mid-eighteenth century; they applied their expertise to the production of several studies of variant readings in the standard histories. By the end of the century, three noted scholars had produced searching philological analyses of inconsistencies in these works; Zhao Yi's (1727–1814) *Notes on the Twenty-Two Histories* (*Nianer shi zhaji*), covering all the standard histories from the Han through the Ming, is the most interesting, as Zhao did not simply point out inconsistencies but also offered more general assessments of each work and, more broadly still, of the nature of historical writing.

The evidential research scholars repudiated the moralizing "praise and blame" historiography promoted by earlier Song and Ming historians; tellingly, they also celebrated Sima Qian for his avoidance of simple moralizing. But the evidential research movement's greatest long-term impact on historical thinking and history writing lay in the methods of critical textual analysis it promoted and the questions it raised about the nature of the Classics. Some of its discoveries called into question long-held assumptions about the sacred nature of these texts; most notable was the conclusive demonstration that the version of *Historical Documents* long believed to be authentic was in fact a forgery of a much later period. By the end of the eighteenth century historian Zhang Xuecheng (1738–1801) had famously declared "the Six Classics are all history."

This view, expressing an eagerness to historicize—and perhaps to desacralize—the Classics, was by no means widely accepted. One of the notable intellectual developments of the nineteenth century was the resurgence of political analysis and policy founded on decoding the *Spring and Autumn Annals*. The sweeping reform program that inspired the famous (and failed) Hundred Days of Reform in 1898 grew out of an esoteric reading of this history Classic, based on the faith that Confucius had hidden his blueprint for political reform in the coded language of the text. The ruler simply had to crack this code, and then he would know how "to overcome the chaos of the age and restore its correctness" by first "governing himself," then "transforming the barbarians" (that is, the Western and Japanese imperialists), and finally uniting all, Chinese and barbarians alike, in a ritual order of "great peace."

Historians of the day, whether skeptically critical of the authenticity of the historiographical tradition or certain that it held the key to China's salvation, were still working very much *within* the tradition and still confident that history—accurately understood—should serve as a guide to present policy. The prominent official Zhang Zhidong (1837–1909), for example, urged careful combing of the dynastic histories for ideas about how to meet contemporary challenges: "Readers of history should focus on exhaustively investigating events and the discussions conducted by the ancients, on searching the causes of rise and decline, the evolution of government, the weight of circumstance, and changes in the mood of the times, in order to benefit the human spirit and intelligence and, when a problem arises, be able to see all possible plans."

The crises of the day could be understood and resolved only by looking into the "mirror" of the past.

Modernity and the Critical Practice of History

Although the specific contexts were very different, the development of "modern" history in both India and China was spurred to some extent by the kind of historical force that so challenged Chinese literati of the late seventeenth century: conquest—or, in the case of China, the threat of conquest. In India, British colonizers initiated the move toward historiographical modernity in the nineteenth century both practically, with the reform of Indian education, and conceptually, since the British presence itself and colonial officers' reconstructions of Indian history spurred Muslims and Hindus alike to reflect upon the putative weakness that had brought them to this impasse of subjection by a foreign power.

The early colonial state drew on many of the resources—record keeping, revenue collection, a Persian-style bureaucracy—that had already been in place since the early days of the Mughal Empire. Like their Mughal predecessors, the British wanted to know their Indian subjects, and turned their attention to history. They combed Persian, Sanskrit, and vernacular texts; they studied inscriptions and mounted archaeological digs; they wrote learned articles in the *Journal of the Royal Asiatic Society*. Doubtless, scholarly values drove some of this spirit of inquiry, but the enterprise as a whole could hardly be called value neutral. One of the more damaging historiographical paradigms of colonial history, consistent with a belief in the "white man's burden" and its so-called civilizing mission, was that a great (if history-averse) Classical Hindu society had been weakened and overrun by rapacious Muslims whose supposed tyranny brought India to its present state of decline. By occupying India the British saw themselves as fostering the country's uplift. This tripartite division of Indian history into Hindu, Muslim, and British periods pitted the two most prominent religious communities against each other. The lead-up to Indian independence was accompanied by massive bloodshed and, eventually, the partition of the country in 1947. Colonial constructions of premodern Indian weakness contributed to a climate where Hindu nationalists felt the need for a militant response to two perceived slights: British occupation and previous centuries of Muslim rule. Here we see some grounds for comparison with China, where a need to understand the Manchu conquest colored Qing-period historiographical inquiry.

Still, there were many different layers to nineteenth-century Indian historiography. Only a few can be signaled here. One towering figure is the Scotsman Colonel James Tod, who served as the British political agent in the Rajput state of Mewar from 1818 to 1822. Tod developed a great affection for Rajput traditions, which culminated in the publication of his influential *Annals and Antiquities of Rajasthan* (1829–32). He is certainly guilty of romanticizing the Rajputs—more than one scholar has suggested that some of his views were conditioned by an appreciation for the historical novels of Sir Walter Scott—but whereas mainstream colonial historiography gave more credence to Muslim historians writing in Persian, Tod was arguably the first to emphasize the importance of the vernacular traditions in Hindi. More problematic, however, was Tod's tendency to present the Mewar Rajputs' oppositional stance against the Mughal Empire in starkly religious terms, as a Hindu dynasty warding off a Muslim threat. This notion of a fundamental Hindu-Muslim enmity between Rajputs and Mughals remains dominant in popular history today.

Another noteworthy historian from the nineteenth century is Shyamaldas, whose *Virvinod* (compiled in the 1870s and 1880s) is an interesting blend of earlier Rajput historiographical thinking with the modern conventions of history writing. Hailing from a family of *caran*s, a caste of traditional bardic professionals, Shyamaldas had been educated in the customary Indian subjects (including *itihasa-purana*) but also became familiar with some of the more modern evidentiary methods of British historiography. Shyamaldas compiled various records and sources, both Indian and British, to compose a new history of the Rajput state of Mewar. He was aware of Tod, his seventeenth-century Jain predecessor Nainsi, British findings, and a plethora of more traditional genres, like the *carita*s. As had become customary in his day, he decried the exaggeration that was held to have distorted much of premodern Indic historiography. This was about as close to Rankean history (the nineteenth-century German intellectual Leopold van Ranke is often considered the founder of modern academic history) as it was possible to come, although the institutional context and conceptualization of the project remained more traditional than the product itself: Shyamaldas was still fully reliant on the patronage of a regional Hindu court, and the title of his book, *Virvinod* ("the joyful exuberances of heroes"), reflects a much earlier textual worldview rather than a self-conscious historian's endeavor.

The academic practice of history—sustained not by courtly patronage but by scholarly institutions—was new to India and a direct product of the colonial education system. History departments began to appear in Indian universities from the 1920s. The Bengali intellectual Jadunath Sarkar (1870–1958) was a pioneering figure in interpreting India's past through the modern techniques of historiography. Sarkar was especially conversant with the Mughal period and produced several influential works that sifted Persian sources but interpreted them in conformance with European methodologies. From then on it would no longer be said of Indians that they do not have "history," at least as the West expected history to be written.

In China, "the move toward historiographical modernity" did not require the reorientation in thinking or the institutional transformation that it did in India, largely because history as conceived and practiced in China more closely resembled the methods of historical study developed in the West. And no outside power had the ability—as the British did in India—to impose a new system of education or disciplinary order on China. To be sure, the Qing government, in its desperate efforts to reform, and later the Republican government, in its push for modernization, were heavily influenced by Western models of education (often filtered through the Japanese experience). But in China history had long been a subject of study, second only to the Classics in importance; it fit very neatly into the curriculum of the modern school system.

But there is no doubt that the dramatic events of the early twentieth century, beginning with the fall of the imperial system in 1911 and the establishment of a republic the following year, encouraged the development of critical historiography. Nationalist students and intellectuals, deeply disturbed by China's weakness, launched a vigorous effort to define a new culture, one strong enough to combat foreign imperialism and grant China a place on the world stage. Most often the leaders of the New Culture Movement argued that the creation of a new culture depended on the repudiation of the old. In historical studies, this trend was expressed as a call to "doubt antiquity" (*yi gu*)—that is, to subject the Chinese histories to rigorous critical investigation, to distinguish myth and propaganda from truth, in order to forge a new, accurate national history.

The "new history" was influenced by trends in Western historiography. Chinese historians who had studied in Germany transmitted the rigorous philological methods of Leopold von Ranke (1795–1886); those who had studied in the United States advocated the principles of the "New American History." Modern archaeological techniques and the comparative method were both Western imports that helped to transform the understanding of early Chinese history and to contextualize it in world history. But there was also another important source for the critical approaches championed by new historians like Gu Jiegang (1893–1980) and Fu Sinian (1896–1950): the Chinese historiographical tradition itself, particularly the work of scholars in the eighteenth-century evidential research movement.

Conclusion

India and China took their own distinctive paths to the past, but they are not as incommensurable as Hegel once proposed. The differences—in language, conception of time, literary form, and the role of the state—are important. Early Indians wrote their histories in rock inscriptions and epic poetry, the Chinese in chronicles and topical histories. The (relatively) unified Chinese state quite early saw the advantages to governing in both the keeping of bureaucratic historical records and controlling the "national" historical narrative. India, without the same degree of centralized governance—or a single common written language—came later to this realization.

Yet the similarities are equally striking. Both cultures believed that written records of past events had cosmological and ritual—and moral—meaning. History also functioned as a "mirror" to the ruler, as it reflected either his glory or his failure to live up to the principles of virtuous governance. Not surprisingly, then, biography was a major historical genre in both cultures. Perhaps because of this shared faith that writing history was a moral endeavor, historians in both cultures, when they disagreed with the governing authority, developed strategies—and, in China, new forms of historical writing—that allowed them to challenge or bypass, with varying degrees of subtlety, efforts at centralized historiographical control.

Well into the twentieth and twenty-first centuries history maintains its status in both China and India as an important—and contested—arena, as both a narrative subject to official oversight and control and a source of resistance and change. The People's Republic of China in its early years closely monitored the writing of history, imposing a Marxist-Leninist framework as rigid—albeit in very different ways—as the dynastic cycle framework of the standard histories. Yet in 1961, the historian Wu Han (1909–1969) famously used the history of the virtuous Ming official Hai Rui (1514–1587) to question Chairman Mao Zedong's policies (although Wu Han suffered the consequences of this challenge with a long prison term that terminated only with his death). The PRC has turned more recently to other ways of shaping history—for example, through the regulation of textbooks and classroom instruction and through the sponsorship of a massive new state-funded "dynastic history" of the Qing. Chinese academic historians routinely produce sophisticated works of "modern" critical history modeled on the evidential research tradition and Western historiography. But the awareness of history as both a mirror for and a political tool of the ruler is still powerful.

History remains too a vital subject in democratic India today, as the country's postcolonial citizens continue to grapple with the complexities of their past. New voices are being heard, as India's feminists, Dalits (formerly known as "untouchables"), and social historians generally bring attention to neglected pasts. Engagement with the past, whatever form it takes, remains vital. The capital of one of Emperor Ashoka's pillars is enshrined on Indian currency notes, a constant reminder to Indians of a revered Buddhist king from the classical period. The state has rarely exerted the same kind of control over the historical record found in modern China, although there have been contestations over what can and cannot be included in history textbooks as well as academic books, particularly on topics to which today's Hindu majority is sensitive. Some politicians have successfully campaigned on a platform of "Rama-rajya," the ideal rule of Rama—not exactly an inclusive platform for a modern pluralistic state, but certainly one that illustrates the ongoing presence of the past in everyday life.

For Further Reading

China

Beasley, W. G. and E. G. Pulleyblank, eds. *Historians of China and Japan*. Oxford: Oxford University Press, 1961.

Durrant, Steven W. *The Cloudy Mirror: Tension and Conflict in the Writings of Sima Qian*. Albany: State University of New York Press, 1995.

Gu Jiegang. *Autobiography of a Chinese Historian: Being the Preface to a Symposium on Ancient Chinese History (Ku Shi Pien)*. Trans. Arthur Hummel. Leiden: E. J. Brill Ltd., 1931.

Legge, James, trans. *The Chinese Classics*. Vol. III: *The Shoo King, or The Book of Historical Documents*. Hong Kong: Hong Kong University Press, 1960.

Li, Wai-yee. *The Readability of the Past in Early Chinese Historiography*. Cambridge, MA: Harvard University Asia Center, 2008.

Ng, On-cho and Q. Edward Wang. *Mirroring the Past: The Writing and Use of History in Imperial China*. Honolulu: University of Hawai'i Press, 2005.

Nivison, David S. *The Life and Thought of Chang Hsüeh-ch'eng*. Stanford: Stanford University Press, 1966.

Schaberg, David. *A Patterned Past: Form and Thought in Early Chinese Historiography*. Cambridge, MA: Harvard University Press, 2001.

Schneider, Laurence. *Ku Chieh-kang and China's New History: Nationalism and the Quest for Alternative Traditions*. Berkeley: University of California Press, 1971.

Sima Qian. *Records of the Grand Historian*. 2 vols. Trans. Burton Watson. New York: Columbia University Press, 1961.

Spence, Jonathan. *Return to Dragon Mountain: Memories of a Late Ming Man*. London: Penguin, 2007.

Twitchett, Denis. *The Writing of Official History Under the T'ang.* Cambridge: Cambridge University Press, 1961.

Wang, Q. Edward. *Inventing China Through History: The May Fourth Approach to Historiography.* Albany: State University of New York Press, 2001.

The Zuo Tradition/Zuozhuan. Trans. Stephen Durrant, Wai-yee Li, and David Schaberg. 2 vols. Seattle: University of Washington Press, 2016.

India

Abu al-Fazl. *The History of Akbar,* Vol 1. Ed. and trans. Wheeler M. Thackston. Cambridge, MA: Harvard University Press, 2015.

Alam, Muzaffar. *The Languages of Political Islam: India 1200–1800.* Chicago: University of Chicago Press, 2004.

Asher, C. and C. Talbot. *India before Europe.* Cambridge: Cambridge University Press, 2006.

Babur. *Bāburnāma.* Trans. Wheeler M. Thackston. New York: The Modern Library, 2002.

Bronner, Y., D. Shulman, and G. Tubb. *Innovations and Turning Points: Toward a History of Kavya Literature.* New Delhi: Oxford University Press, 2014.

Chakrabarti, Dipesh. *The Calling of History: Sir Jadunath Sarkar and His Empire of Truth.* Chicago: University of Chicago Press, 2015.

Deshpande, Prachi. *Creative Pasts: Historical Memory and Identity in Western India, 1700–1960.* New York: Columbia University Press, 2007.

Eaton, Richard Maxwell. *Essays on Islam and Indian History.* New Delhi: Oxford University Press, 2002.

Gulbadan Begum. *Humāyūnnāma.* In *Three Memoirs of Homayun,* ed. Wheeler M. Thackston. Costa Mesa, CA: Mazdas, 2009.

Hardy, Peter. *Historians of Medieval India: Studies in Indo-Muslim Historical Writing.* New Delhi: Munshiram Manoharlal, 1997 [1960].

Jahangir. *Jahāngīrnāma.* Trans. Wheeler M. Thackston. Oxford: Oxford University Press, 1999.

Pathak, Vishwambhar Sharan. *Ancient Historians of India: A Study in Historical Biographies.* New York: Asia Publishing House, 1966.

Pollock, Sheldon. "Pretextures of Time." *History and Theory* 46 (October 2007): 366–83.

Rao, Velcheru Narayana, David Shulman, and Sanjay Subrahmanyam. *Textures of Time: Writing History in South India.* New York: Other Press, 2003.

Talbot, Cynthia. *The Last Hindu Emperor: Prithviraj Chauhan in the Indian Past, 1200–2000.* Cambridge: Cambridge University Press, 2016.

Thapar, Romila. *The Past Before Us: Historical Traditions of Early North India*. Cambridge, MA: Harvard University Press, 2013.

Valmiki. *Ramayana*. 7 vols. Trans. Robert P. Goldman et al. Princeton, NJ: Princeton University Press, 1990–2015.

Vyasa. *The Mahabharata*. Abridged and trans. by John D. Smith. New York: Penguin, 2009.

CHAPTER V

Sorting Out Babel

Literature and Its Changing Languages

STEPHEN OWEN AND SHELDON POLLOCK

"Literary Tradition" in China and India

What makes a literary tradition? Perhaps it is the continuously renewed experience of earlier texts over long spans of time and across large, somehow coherent territory. In the case of China and India, this sort of experience has been in evidence for several thousand years, throughout what have long been the two most populous countries in the world. The poet Yuan Zhen (779–831) celebrated his predecessor Du Fu (712–770) as follows: "When my reading of poetry reached Du Fu, I understood that all things great and small were gathered in it." Yuan Zhen goes on to give an account of the whole poetic tradition, each earlier poet adding something that Du Fu combined into a whole. Grade school students in the People's Republic of China still study texts from 2,500 years ago, including those by Du Fu, if with much vernacular explanation. Similarly, the equally old Indian epics are still very much alive in the subcontinent, though more often in films, comic books, or village pageants than in the Sanskrit of their most ancient versions. A work like the *Mahabharata* seems to have foreseen its own continuous cultural prominence when proclaiming itself a total account of the world: "Whatever is found here may well be found elsewhere; what is not here does not exist."

Given the enormous time and space they have filled, Chinese and Indian literature may appear to be immediately comparable. But that appearance is quickly dispelled when we start to look more closely. Consider just the quotes adduced above. Yuan Zhen implies that fullness is the consequence of a cumulative tradition, whereas the *Mahabharata* seems to assume that it was all there at the beginning. And this first modest contrast is complemented by many others far more consequential. For example, unlike Chinese, there was no single language called "Indian" in which literature was communicated across that time and space, but rather several: Sanskrit, the "perfected" language (from around 1500 BCE until around 1500 CE), along with two languages (or dialects or registers) closely related to it: Prakrit, the "natural" language, and Apabhramsha, the "corrupt," or demotic (both used especially for pastoral themes during the first millennium); and, in the second millennium, Persian, a literary language in India from about the eleventh century onward and the official language of the Mughal Empire (1526–1858). Hindi—called Hindavi, "Indian," by Arabs, Persians, and others, and chosen as the national language in free India in 1950—emerged only around 1500 out of the broad north Indian vernacular and until the modern era did not gain the subcontinentwide presence of Sanskrit or even Persian.

But India's linguistic differences from China are even greater than this. Precisely as occurred in Europe around the same time, a number of languages of smaller spaces came to be used for the production of literature: in the south, Tamil from the early centuries CE, Kannada and Telugu from about the tenth century, Malayalam from the thirteenth; in the north, Bangla, Hindi, Marathi, Oriya, and others from around the fourteenth or fifteenth. This process of differentiation included scripts as well as languages, more than a dozen of them (all derived from a single source, an ancient script called Brahmi, but their relatedness had long since been forgotten), something that again distinguishes India from China but also from Europe, where a single script connected the far-flung areas of "Latin" Christendom. The relationship between linguistic and political differentiation also seems pretty clear. The empirelike states using Sanskrit gave way around the end of the first millennium to regional polities using the vernaculars until the coming of the Mughals, who promoted Persian as the language of learning and culture in the consolidation of their empire in the Indian subcontinent. If these many literatures were not written in a language called "Indian" or in a politically unified region called "India" (a term of non-Indian origin), what in fact makes them "Indian"?

China did have its own, less extreme language diversity tied to linguistic change, but two factors had large consequences: the ideal of a unified state and the writing system of Chinese characters. The unified polity insisted that a number of mutually unintelligible but closely related languages were merely dialects, as early medieval Europe understood the nascent Romance vernaculars as "dialects" of Latin. Chinese characters allowed very different pronunciations across space and time, contributing to the conviction that it was somehow one language. Pronounced in radically different ways in different subregions, the characters contributed to the establishment of Chinese as the most common written language of premodern Korea and Vietnam, and the second written language of premodern Japan. Far more than Sanskrit, written Chinese kept growing and changing; but, until the ideological division between "classical Chinese" and "vernacular Chinese" was institutionalized in the 1920s, linguistic variation in written Chinese was understood by Chinese readers and writers as difference of registers, each proper to a certain kind of writing. Regional variation and linguistic change were manifested primarily though new genres of drama, song, and prose narrative.

Lyric, Like and Unlike

If the time and space across which a literature is produced and continuously reproduced contribute to making a literary tradition, it is thanks to genres that a literature comes to be recognized *as* literature. And if in many respects the genres found in China and India are strikingly incomparable, some, like the short self-contained poem—called "lyric" for ease of reference here, without assuming a category identical across the two traditions—were shared enthusiasms over a very long term. Both traditions show an interest in the emotional force of literature—how emotion is coded in language—and in the closely related phenomenon of implication, how something is conveyed without being said. Both emotion and implication are showcased in the short lyric in China and India; these components do of course exist in the European tradition, but they became a central concern to writers and critics only in more recent times. In addition, literary traditions also require learning, self-reflection, and often theory, and here China and India again show some striking points of convergence.

Let us consider one example each of the sort of lyric poem that these two literary cultures prized, and the kind of learning, on the part of writers and readers, that they both presupposed.

We do not know who wrote this sample Sanskrit poem. It is included in an anthology called the *Amaru-sataka*, or *Hundred Lyrics of Amaru*, but many of the verses in this anthology are elsewhere attributed to other poets—and we have no idea who Amaru was anyway, if he was more than the anthologist and actually a poet to whom some of the poems should be ascribed. We do not know where the *Hundred Lyrics* was written in the vast world that Sanskrit occupied in South Asia (and even Southeast Asia, where the language was also cultivated), since Sanskrit poets typically sought to eliminate any marks of localization. We do not know when it was written. The anthology dates from sometime before the late ninth century, but the sample poem could be from anytime between then and the beginning of the Common Era, when Sanskrit first came to be used for nonscriptural poetry, since marks of temporality were eliminated too. The form of the poem strongly suggests that it is a benediction introducing the collection, but we have no idea what work it may once have introduced. In short, all the tradition has given us is the poem—complete in itself, not a fragment of some larger work—along with a history of interpretations of it. Here is a literal translation:

> The fire of Shiva's arrows, like a husband
> whose betrayal is still fresh, was driven off
> as it tried to clutch their hand, mercilessly struck
> when grasping at their hem, shaken off when stroking
> their hair, spurned spitefully falling at their feet,
> and in the act of embracing rebuffed with force
> by the women of the Triple City, eyes brimming with tears.
> May this fire burn away your sins. (trans. Pollock)

If the who, where, when, and why of the poem is information never preserved, this is not because of the tradition's historical stupidity; detailed data for many other aspects of premodern Indian life are available in other cultural forms, such as inscriptions. The information is missing because none was thought to be necessary for understanding the poem. Sanskrit, considered the language of the gods, was prized precisely because it allowed literature to escape human time and space and live forever. All that was necessary was the learning that the tradition privileged. Part of this learning, the simple part, is the mythological background; the harder part is the aesthetic.

According to legend, the enemies of the gods once built three cities, out of gold, silver, and iron, in heaven, in the sky, and on earth. The great god Shiva destroyed them in an act of violence and heroism—but also compassion, since if Shiva destroyed living beings he did so to save the universe from their wrongdoing. This cosmic act prefigures the possibility for the god's salvation of the individual devotee, however great his own wrongdoing may be. If this little bit of cultural knowledge suffices to make the surface meaning of the poem clear enough, understanding the poem's emotional registers was a challenge no less for traditional readers than for us.

It was entirely within the scope of Sanskrit criticism to ask why God's destructive fire should be compared to a husband, and an unfaithful husband at that, who is seeking forgiveness by ever more desperate actions. This was not, however, a question traditional readers posed. Nor would they have cared to remark on the several ironies here, for example, that the figure of a straying husband is used in connection with the deity who famously elevates asceticism over eroticism, or that one and the same fire should burn away sin destructively in the case of evil and beneficently in the case of a devotee. (See also chapter 3 on fire as a burning away of sin in widow self-immolation.) Most of these questions, along with more general ones about the relationship of lyric poetry to legend or, even more important here, to theology, are of interest typically only to those standing outside the tradition and looking in.

The interest of those inside lay, in part, in the mechanisms of signification, especially literary "implication"—meaning without saying—which was subtly analyzed by Indian thinkers and is beautifully exemplified here: the errant husband is mentioned in the simile but coordinated with the fire only by a series of puns (far more compelling in the original). But what preoccupied them above all was the poem's *rasa* ("taste"), its principal emotional impact: tragic? heroic? erotic? Readers reflected on its rich complexity for centuries. The power of God's cosmic act could be seen as heroic or violent or awe-inspiring, all three emotions being recognized as possible aesthetic tastes, and all were suggested by thinkers from the ninth to the sixteenth centuries. For others it is the tragic that is primary—after all, the wives are tearfully watching as their husbands and children are burned alive. There is further a clear suggestion, conveyed by a simile, of the erotic: the women are repulsing the fire like an unfaithful husband come home to ask forgiveness. How the tragic and the erotic coexist here (since the former presupposes permanent separation, the latter eventual reunion) led to further sophisticated analysis.

What fascinated Indian readers, in short, was not only how a poem makes us feel but also how it *makes feeling* by the processes of verbal representation. For them, the feeling evoked by a poem, far from being a critical fallacy as it was for the American "New Critics," was its very essence, both the horizon of expectation that shaped the creation of literature and the central object of literary criticism. The centuries-long history of reflection on the *rasa*, or emotional impact, of poetry like Amaru's supplies us with another of the diagnostics—besides time and space and genre—of what makes an *Indian* literary culture: a very learned practice, and self-aware tradition, of slow reading.

No Chinese poem is anything like the Amaru poem. While Indian readers of literature were typically uninterested in the specificities of place, time, and historical context—though this typicality can be overstated, given the precise temporal referencing found outside the lyric genre, in for example royal inscriptions (see chapter 5 on inscriptions as historiography)—Chinese readers read a poem in the context of the author, his life, and the larger historical world in which he lived. Du Fu, one of China's greatest poets, documented his life in unprecedented detail. He even added his own notes when he thought that later readers might not know the circumstances behind a poem. For a thousand years every Du Fu poem has been read as part of the "Du Fu story"—a poetic biography set in motion by Du Fu himself. His life was set in a historically tumultuous period of the Tang (618–906, also considered China's golden age of poetry), and that was always the background of his story.

If we cannot date Amaru, much less feel confident that the poem was written by him, there are a remarkable number of Du Fu's more than 1,400 poems that can be dated to the year and season, often to the month and day. A tenuous link may also be found in the interplay between the world on a cosmic scale and the human world close at hand. The "Amaru" poem makes a human situation the simile by which to try to grasp the otherwise inexplicable actions of an omnipotent god. Likewise, in "Staying Over at White Stands Station," Du Fu, on the shore of a vast lake, crosses from *this world* to *that world*, from a journey in the empire, where name and reality are matched, into mythic space through reflection. Du Fu wrote his poem in February 770, the first month of spring and the last year of his life.

Having left his comfortable life in Kuizhou on the Yangzi River, Du Fu went downstream to the great city of Jiangling, hoping to find friends and above all, patrons. Finding his friends but no patrons and in a desperate situation, he took the inexplicable next step—as he often did—setting out southward with his family onto the vastness of Lake Dongting, heading for Changsha in modern Hunan. In this context, passage from *this world* to another world has a particular resonance. The phrase that Du Fu used for this journey onto Lake Dongting, planning to go to the "Southern Deeps," would have evoked for any reader the great parable that opened the ancient philosophical work by Zhuangzi (370–287 BCE) in which the mythic Peng bird, whose wingspan is so large that it covers the sky from horizon to horizon, "plans to go south" to bathe in the "Southern Deeps." In the parable, the "Southern Deeps" represents the sky-pool of heaven, i.e., *that world*. With this parable Zhuangzi, who more often teaches the relativity of perception and value, is satirizing the inability of those who can conceive only of the world close at hand to imagine a universe beyond that.

To return to this world, in late winter of 770, Du Fu found a mooring at White Sands Station in a section of Lake Dongting called Green Grass Lake. These stations were part of the imperial post system, with lodging for travelers on official business. Du Fu had the credentials of a vice-director in the Board of Works, but it was an honorary appointment and evidently not enough to get the old man lodging in the government post station.

STAYING OVER AT WHITE SANDS STATION

I spend night on the water, now still in last sunshine,
the smoke of men's dwellings, and then this pavilion.
Beside the station, sands white as before;
beyond the lake, the grass turns fresh green.
The million images—all springtime's vapor;
on a lone raft, I myself am the wandering star.
Along with the waves, the moonlight boundless,
and on its sparkling I draw near to the Southern Deeps.
   (trans. Owen)

Another old story is also cited by traditional commentators as the source for Du Fu's interesting poetic usage of the "lone raft" and "wandering star":

Zhang Hua (232–300), a court official and poet, tells of a man who every year in mid-autumn saw an empty raft passing down the Yangzi River. One year he boarded the raft and was carried to sea and up around into the Milky Way, the "River of Stars." Following the current, he returned to earth and came to Chengdu in Sichuan, where he consulted a local astronomer, who told him that he had seen a "wandering star" in the heavens earlier. On his "lone raft" at night, amid the shattered reflections of moonlight and starlight, Du Fu sees himself as that "wandering star," ready to launch into Zhang Hua's "River of Stars."

As the poem moves from twilight into darkness, it moves from imperial space to mythic space. At first Du Fu comes over the huge lake, recognizing where to stay by the "smoke of men's dwelling," leading him to the imperial station. Tying his boat up there, he matches the place names with what he sees. White Sands has white sands; and now in early spring Green Grass Lake has newly green grasses. This is imperial space, *down to earth*, where words match experiential perception. We can locate these places on a historical map. But moving into night and reflection in the lake's water, representation links ordinary imperial space to something else. Du Fu's "wandering star" becomes the great Peng, beyond mortal understanding, drawing closer to the "Southern Deeps," where he will bathe in the celestial ocean.

In the classical poetics of the eight-line regulated verse, the fifth and sixth lines are the *turn*. The poem does indeed turn, moving outside the security of imperial space into another dimension. In the second couplet Du Fu matches "image" and "name." In the third couplet all the visible images of the world are "springtime's vapor." For all its simplicity, this is a strange, grand line. The Chinese word Du Fu uses is *qi,* translated here as "vapor," as it often is. For example, steam rising from boiling water is *qi*. But is also a basic term in Chinese cosmology for the cosmic substance that is life energy, which is sometimes coalescing into hard things, sometimes attenuating into invisible gases, and always in flux. The spring scene before him is the momentary shape of spring *qi*—for example, in winter the green grasses that give Green Grass Lake its stable name may not be so green.

Language Dynamics

If the dense learning that marked the two traditions makes them fully comparable with each other, other features set them far apart. The first is the question of social status, which is highly marked in all the Indian literary languages, beginning with Sanskrit. Although all literary languages are, to an appreciable extent, what Henry David Thoreau (in *Walden*) called "father tongues" ("a reserved and select expression . . . which we must be born again in order to speak"), Indian languages are characterized by a range of internal ranking criteria that differentiate them from one another. Sanskrit, for example, could only be acquired in the course of formal education. From the earliest period of its existence it was restricted to use in solemn religious rites—in what is called the Vedic dialect, from the name of the ancient scriptures, Vedas—and was made available for the creation of nonreligious literature perhaps as much as 1,500 years after the composition of the oldest stratum of those scriptures. While restrictions on who could use the perfect language of the gods have been exaggerated in both traditional accounts and modern scholarship, there is no question that those outside the Vedic fold, such as the new religious communities that arose around 500 BCE, in particular the Jains and Buddhists, originally rejected Sanskrit (or were, so to speak, rejected by it), and composed their own religious texts in other languages newly invented for the purpose. But Jains and Buddhists both eventually adopted Sanskrit, whose prestige and universality made it the premier language of literature across South Asia for more than a millennium. This early history is important as well for the example it offers of language restriction and response, a process that would be reenacted time and again in the literary history of India.

In China language was conceived as situated in a hierarchy as a register of social standing, with the range of possible registers restricted by genre. This sounds complicated, but it is instinctive in English: one does not apply for a job in a bank with the English used in rap lyrics. In terms of variation, a dialect is regional, whereas a language is often the claim of a distinct self-governing country. Galician is a Spanish dialect; Portuguese is a language—despite the fact that Galician and Portuguese are far closer than Galician and Spanish. We can map this phenomenon in India, which had many independent regional polities, whereas China, whatever the political situation of the moment, believed in one polity.

One of the most distinctive features of Indian literary history is the interplay between languages that traveled boundlessly—Sanskrit and Persian above all—and those that did not—the dozen or so regional vernaculars with written traditions. This linguistic situation strongly resembles that of Europe, where Latin and the Romance and Germanic vernaculars parallel

Sanskrit and the north Indian vernaculars (Hindi and so on) and south Indian vernaculars (Tamil and so on). This interplay was impossible before such regional languages were constituted as literary languages in the first place, a process inaugurated in southern India in the late centuries of the first millennium (with Tamil as a precocious pioneer) and visible in north India from about the thirteenth century. The constitution of a literary language is not a natural development; it is the result of an act of cultural will, and in India this will was sharpened by two developments, the first and earlier political—the growth of regional polities—and the second and later (and perhaps even a consequence of the first) religious—the emergence of oppositional faith movements that spoke to often very local concerns.

"Vernacularization," as this process is now often termed, was in India initially an elite, courtly affair, as regional political orders sought to replicate the transregional political idioms and practices of Sanskrit. Among the most important of these practices, for its high symbolic value and its practical contribution to moral education, was literature. This cosmopolitan vernacular, as it might be called, of the regional polity gave way in many places to a regional vernacular reaction on the part of religious groups, which sought to displace the courtly with more local—and often militantly anti-Sanskritic—registers.

With few exceptions, the vernacularization of India was essentially complete by the time the Mughal Empire was founded. Although the Mughals originated in Central Asia and were speakers of a Turkic language, they adopted Persian as the language of empire—the language of learning and culture used by much of the courtly culture of the Islamic world after its conquest of Persia. The Mughals thereby changed the fortunes of the language dramatically. In the case of the Lodi dynasty that preceded the Mughals, the semiofficial language was called Hindavi, an early form of today's Hindi. Persian too was in many ways an elite idiom in its Indian embodiment. Despite pervading much of everyday language in north India at the level of vocabulary (by a process still unclear to scholars; the penetration of the bureaucracy has been suggested), its use was essentially literary, as a code of courtiers and religious professionals; Persian was hardly more of an everyday language than Sanskrit. The erosion of Persian beginning in the late eighteenth century, among other factors, led to the creation of a new literary language called Urdu, in which a spoken idiom, largely indistinguishable from Hindi, was refashioned as a literary language embodying Persian genres, tropes, rhetoric, and aesthetic. In all these processes, especially those of from about the sixth to the sixteenth centuries, languages were practically and cognitively instituted as literary by the creation of texts that reflected the values of a dominant earlier literature (Sanskrit or Persian, and much later but in a very similar way, English). In many cases a whole battery of accessories meant to ensure the individuality, unity, and stability of the language developed: dictionaries, grammars, versification manuals, treatises on rhetoric, and individualized scripts.

The Chinese, by contrast, just kept adding new registers. Chan masters from the eighth to tenth centuries were recorded in a new literary (or "antiliterary") register invented to mimic the spoken language. Chan masters for the next millennium tended to echo that vernacular register. Northern plays (*zaju*) of the late thirteenth and fourteenth centuries invented new Chinese characters to represent the sounds of words common in Northern Mandarin. However much Mandarin changed over the next eight centuries, later playwrights of *zaju* never entirely forgot that special language. That vernacular dramatic register of language was quite distinct from the storyteller vernacular register used in fiction, but in many cases both versions of the vernacular register were printed for elite consumers, which led to their durability as the register appropriate to a certain genre.

Although Chinese vernacular registers appeared in roughly the historical period that vernaculars emerged through throughout Eurasia, their emergence cannot be described as a revolution. In China it crept in around the edges of an already heterogeneous literary language, becoming institutionalized as still newer written vernacular registers formed around its edges. Only in the modern period, under the influence of the European model, was the range of written Chinese reconceptualized as a "classical language," *wenyan*, and a "vernacular language," *baihua*. Even when Chinese intellectuals allowed a division in written Chinese, it was into two languages rather than many, and those two languages were seen to have been in a struggle for dominance, with one emerging victorious and the other declared "dead."

The striking contrast with India is that no outside language ever supplanted the use of some version of "Chinese." The Mongols ruled in Chinese, as did the Manchus later, and Manchu was even more the creation of Chinese loanwords than Ottoman Turkish (used in the Ottoman Empire) or Chagatay Turkish (brought by the Mughals from Central Asia), which were both heavily influenced by Persian and Arabic loans. Admittedly, when the Mughals, the Mongols' distant cousins, declared Persian the official language of the empire in the late sixteenth century, it was hardly an outside language that was being introduced, since poets in India had been writing in Persian almost as long as those in Iran proper. But Persian had never been used so assertively as a language of power in India before the Mughals made it so, and for many in Mughal service it was a truly foreign language they had to learn.

What Is "Epic"?

Whereas a number of literary genres beyond the lyric are comparable in the two traditions, some are stunningly different in themselves and in their historical effects. First on this list of differences is the dominant role in India of the epic imagination, one of the key forces that, through circulation of the originals and later vernacular versions, made Indian literature *Indian* in the absence of any single unifying language or script. While the absence of epic in China, like the absence of historiography in India (discussed further in chapter 5), has been a cliché of Orientalism from the time of the German philosopher Georg Frederich Hegel (1770–1831), here is a divergence in genre in the two traditions that markedly contrasts with what unites their lyric poetry.

In India, the two great epic traditions, the *Mahabharata* and the *Ramayana*, have shaped its literature in ways with few parallels in world literature. It is not just that Sanskrit drama, like the Greek, is largely crumbs from the epic table, in that both have plays derived from and heavily influenced by epic tales. Later vernacular literatures also referenced epic themes, as European literature referenced the Bible. Instead, rethinking and rewriting the epics were processes that fundamentally shaped literature—and even founded literary traditions—across Indian time and space.

What is significant about the two great epics from a comparative perspective, accordingly, is not so much their literary characteristics as their literary-historical effects. For the period of its likely origins in the last century or two BCE, the *Ramayana* offers an unprecedented combination of narrative coherence and aesthetic concern over an extended tale of love, loss, and recovery, so much so that the author, Valmiki, was called the *adi-kavi*, or "primal poet," of the Sanskrit tradition. His narrative will be familiar to readers of the romantic epic tradition in the West from the *Odyssey* onward. And to readers of the martial epic tradition in the West from the

Iliad onward the *Mahabharata* will be familiar, both for its style (largely as oral poetry, which makes it older than the *Ramayana* though it is also younger, since it was probably first committed to writing in the early centuries CE) and for its tale of the centrifugal forces of political arrogance and aristocratic pride that ineluctably lead to the chaos of war. The literary-historical consequences of the two works, however, are unfamiliar, if not unique.

Most regional literary traditions in India defined themselves by vernacularizing and localizing one or the other work, their authors often receiving the same sobriquet of "primal poet" in acknowledgment of their inaugurating a new regional tradition of poetry. But the consequences of these epic works were more fundamental than marking the point of vernacular origins. It is no exaggeration to say that the *Ramayana* shaped much of Indian literary history over some two millennia. This holds true for the *Mahabharata* too, though to a lesser degree; dealing as it does with civil war, the most horrific of political failures, it was often viewed as a less normative, even more dangerous text. One exception to this is the *Bhagavad Gita*, an episode in the *Mahabharata* that seeks precisely to invest this failure with positive meaning by offering a new ethics of social action as moral imperative, detached from outcomes. Both epics were held to record actual historical events and exactly as the events occurred, and thereby to make claims to moral significance—for defining dharma, or the right thing to do in one's relations with parents, siblings, spouses, society, polity—of the sort that actuality far more than fictionality carries with it. Akbar the Great, the Mughal emperor of the late sixteenth century, recognized the centrality of both works to the Indian cultural and political order and commissioned their translation into Persian, along with sumptuous illustrations. Their didactic force remains strong up to the present day. The *Ramayana* continues to enjoy a sanctity among many people as a divine text resistant to any modernist historicization, whereas the *Bhagavad Gita* has in some ways become the Bible of India, a status that is no colonial invention but dates from at least the eighth century.

Generation after generation rethought and rewrote the epic narratives in every imaginable genre of written and performative art. These revisions, especially prominent in the case of the *Ramayana*, sought to address what a given era or section of society came to regard as morally problematic. In one reworking offered in a celebrated Sanskrit drama of the early eighth century, the *Uttara-rama-carita* (*Rama's Last Act*) of Bhavabhuti, the heroine,

Sita, herself exiled by her husband, Rama, in the face of rumors about her infidelity during her captivity, is vindicated by the goddess Earth and by the ancient poet himself, who returns to rewrite the end of his story. In some South Indian versions especially of the modern period, the demon king antagonist Ravana, like Milton's Satan, has become far more sympathetic, and even heroic, than the protagonist. In yet other versions, Rama and Sita are represented as brother and sister (the Pali retelling), or Sita as the daughter of Ravana (the Tibetan), or Rama's brother Lakshmana as the wily defeater of Ravana (the oral version of the Dungari Bhils, a community of landless cultivators in northern Gujarat), or Hanuman, the monkey ally of Rama's, as the true hero of the story. Indeed, this last rewrite is found in many Southeast Asian versions, and is faintly visible in the sixteenth-century Chinese novel *Journey to the West* (discussed later in this chapter), a text about Chinese travelers to India that marks the point where our China-India comparison, thanks to the vast dispersion of the *Ramayana*, becomes connection.

China's "lack" of an epic was troubling to earlier scholars, both Chinese and non-Chinese. Hegel assured us that every literature was supposed to have at least one, and the Sanskrit epics were used to confirm the thesis that epic stood at the head of every tradition. Genres are, unfortunately, defined inductively; and characteristics of specific texts have been taken as essential to a genre rather than as interesting possibilities within something more broadly conceived. Epics are supposed to focus on one hero in one great undertaking. In practice, however, the "one hero, one action" definition is contingent on a larger knowledge of surrounding history/myth. We cannot read the *Iliad* without knowing the larger story of the Trojan War. The early epics were taken as not only historically true but also centers of historical knowledge. If, instead, we think of epic as foundational history, then we have grounds for comparison.

Records of the Grand Historian (*Shiji*), written by Sima Qian (145–86? BCE), is not the earliest example of extended historical writing in China, but, like the ancient European and Indian epics, it defined the past and provided material for future iterations of antiquity. It treats China from the mythic past down to Sima Qian's present, the turn of the first century BCE. It is in prose, but prose was already the medium of narrative, and it is beautifully crafted. From the beginning it was a written text, drawing on written sources, many of which we would classify as "prose romance" (where historical material is reconfigured and amplified for the sake of the story)—although to Sima Qian they were "history." Moreover, *Records of the Grand Historian* has an author very much personally engaged in his text, continuing it as a project bequeathed to him by his father and accepting castration (rather than honorable suicide) in order to see the book to completion. Under the circumstances, it is not surprising that he finds echoes of his own case in many of the stories he tells.

In the famous letter explaining why he accepted castration rather than committing suicide, he explains the purpose of the work:

> I have compiled neglected knowledge of former times from all over the world; I have examined these for veracity and have given an account of the principles behind success and defeat, rise and fall. . . . In it I also wanted to fully explore the interaction between Heaven and Man, and to show the continuity of transformations of past and present.

But in the very first of the biographies, which make up more than half the work, he questions the existence of any moral order that would make "the interaction between Heaven and Man" comprehensible.

Perhaps the most striking aspect of the *Records* is that it is not overall linear narrative. It first treats the linear history of the rulers and dynasties, then the histories of the great aristocratic families that ruled the feudal domains. Then there is a dull, but necessary set of tables correlating the histories of the feudal domains, by which a single history became possible. The final and largest section treats "biographies," either in pairs, as did the Greco-Roman essayist Plutarch, or in sets. Ancient China did have prose romances of moderate length treating individuals, but very long poetic or prose narrative is not extant. One earlier, long chronicle history survives, but the commitment to chronicle makes it almost incomprehensible for modern readers because there are many central characters and many continuous "actions," appearing then disappearing, to reappear the following year or years later. The Sanskrit epic, with its very long digressions, still is framed around a single linear narrative.

Ancient China's preference for shorter narratives may have had to do with writing. Writing was slow, reading was slow, and the physical texts—primarily bundles of bamboo slips—were cumbersome. To imagine a text like the *Mahabharata* in China, we would first have to imagine a very large warehouse with a meticulous organization. As elsewhere in the ancient world, memorization was important, but in ancient China it was memorization of shorter texts.

Whatever the reason, ancient China's commitment to shorter narrative led to a different intellectual order. One of the basic forms of narrative is avenging a wrong and setting it right, in which the deferral of action is the space of the narrative. This is the cycle of the Trojan War and of the Sanskrit epics. We can find many parallels in *Records of the Grand Historian*, but it is most explicit in a chapter in the biographies, "The Assassins." In the structure of the chronologically organized short narratives that make up this chapter we see an argument about long duration historical narrative done through short narratives.

The first story is very short, on a general of the domain of Lu in the early seventh century BCE. Cao Mei was known for his physical prowess and was made a general; he repeatedly lost in battle to the neighboring domain of Qi, but the Duke of Lu retained confidence in him. At a treaty ceremony with Duke Huan of Qi, in which Lu was to cede large amounts of its territory to Qi, Cao Mei leaped out of the Lu entourage, took a knife to Duke Huan's throat, and asked him to return the conquered territory to Lu. Duke Huan agreed, and Cao Mei put back his knife and returned to the Lu entourage as if nothing had happened. Duke Huan wanted to go back on his promise, but his advisor Guan Zhong persuaded him that a reputation for honoring his promises was worth more than the territory of Lu he had gained. Duke Huan returned the territory.

If we see no interval between intention and action in the Cao Mei story, in the three stories that follow an increasing deferral of action, accompanied by formalization of a code of honor involving the recognition and trust granted by a superior (hence allowing the assassin to be manipulated by the generosity of a superior). With plotting and the deferral of action, the stories become increasingly complicated.

The last and longest story occurs about four and a half centuries later, when Qin was pressing forward to establish a unified empire. The world of Cao Mei was one of honor and obligation; Qin was a machine of empire. The story of Jing Ke's failed attempt to assassinate the Qin king who would become the First Emperor has been told in movies such as *The Emperor and the Assassin* and *Hero*, but it needs to be understood in its original context.

We have another version of the story in an early prose romance, perhaps not the one Sima Qian was working with, but close. And we can see Sima Qian working with his sources. One of Sima Qian's most telling additions was that as a youth, Jing Ke "loved reading"—the first time that term appears in the tradition. From his knowledge in the story, he seems to have been reading stories of assassin-heroes. Unlike all the previous assassin-heroes, Jing Ke wanted to become a hero like those he had read about. Eventually he met Prince Dan of the domain of Yan, who chose him to assassinate the king of Qin. They discussed the example of Cao Mei, whose story Jing Ke surely knew—without any misgivings that the age of honor was long past. Prince Dan treated Jing Ke royally, and Jing Ke continually deferred taking action until "the time was right." Qin's armies were pressing on Yan, and at last Jing Ke had to go. He concealed his sword in a map as an earlier assassin had concealed his knife in a fish: he was a well-read assassin. He struck, but hesitated, and in the end he died. His last words were that he had failed because he wanted to take the king of Qin hostage and force a promise to turn conquest (and history) back, as Cao Mei had done. This could only have provoked laughter at his naiveté—the king of Qin might make such a promise, but he would never honor it.

We have not one single linear narrative, but five chronologically arranged and historically unrelated stories, echoing one another throughout, with the last story finally coming back to the first. It is a compact way of narrating four and a half centuries of cultural change, in which past narrative itself becomes one agent. This is not extended linear narrative, but a basic way of making significant historical narrative outside of a linear structure, with "one hero, one action."

New Literary Cultures

The early modern period of Chinese and Indian literary history (roughly 1500–1800) introduces as many contrasts between the two traditions as anything in the preceding two millennia.

Printing in China became increasingly common during the Tang dynasty, with large projects beginning in the tenth and eleventh centuries, sponsored by the Buddhist church and the state. China's early modern period should properly be thought of as beginning with the rapid expansion of print culture at the end of the eleventh and through the twelfth century in commercial and private venues. If, for the purposes of comparison, we take 1500 as the date to begin our account, print culture was already fully mature. Manuscripts remained an important venue for circulation (including manuscript copies of printed texts), but printing was ubiquitous. The categories of literary publication covered a wide range of purposes and markets, both domestic and foreign. At one extreme a family might subsidize the printing of the works of a family member, primarily for local prestige and for inclusion of the name among prominent literary figures in local gazetteers. A local official or private scholar could subsidize an imprint for his personal interests—and sometimes make a handsome profit from the enterprise. At another extreme, fiction and other kinds of literature became a commodity that could be sold throughout the empire as well as in Korea, Japan, and Vietnam.

Older plays from the late thirteenth and fourteenth century existed in print, but later aficionados of drama reprinted them as well as more recent plays. The great storytellers' cycles were appearing in printed prose narrative; incidents in those cycles provided plots for drama, much as Indian drama drew on the epics. Later some of those novels spawned fictional spin-offs, followed in the eighteenth century by novels with original plots. Everything from popular songs to joke books to political gossip to travel diaries and manuals for flower cultivation proliferated. Earlier literature was often reprinted, making possible unprecedented access to the literary tradition. Scholars would collect their judgments of earlier and contemporary writing in different genres. Women writers had long been a presence in the tradition, but from the seventeenth century on there began to be circles of women writers. They often circulated their works in manuscript, but increasingly their poetry collections were printed. Numerous anthologies of contemporary and earlier women writers often had prefaces that reflected on traditions of writing by women. If memorization retained primacy of place in India into the nineteenth century, print, supplemented by memorization, dominated China.

Although it is hard to generalize about such textual production on such a scale and in such variety, one consequence bears comparison with India. The distribution system of commercial printing produced a truly national market, which differentiated itself by specialization: it became a culture of aficionados. There were aficionados of particular kinds of writing everywhere: an early seventeenth-century reader might be devoted to travel literature, fourteenth-century plays, and contemporary song lyrics written on the model of song lyrics from five centuries earlier. Certain classical genres were still generally shared by the educated elite. Thus the hypothetical aficionado would have had a basic knowledge of and capacity to compose classical poetry, but might not have been particularly interested in it.

The old classical genres of prose and poetry were often provided with scholarly commentary in print, identifying sources of phrases, explaining allusions, and glossing difficult words. Both the classical and the newer vernacular genres, however, were often also provided with critical commentaries, which became part of the pleasure of reading. Characters were analyzed, structure explained, and parallel passages identified, often with appreciative judgments on the author's skill. A text could be followed by a short essay offering an overall interpretation, and the beginning of a book might contain a section giving a theoretical overview of what to pay attention to in reading, or else a literary historical interpretation.

The issue of rhetorical complexity, which so deeply engaged Indian literary practice and thought, was never a central concern in the Chinese tradition. Classical poetry and the song lyric tradition that matured in the eleventh and twelfth centuries in different ways sought a transparent perfection in writing about experience and emotion. Heavy figuration did exist but was often understood as concealment, adding a degree of intensity by the presumption of that which should not be spoken but had to be.

Such a poetics of transparent authenticity begged for its negation, in irony, parody, and sometimes disillusioned anger. We first see this prominently in the drama and lyrics in the northern vernacular from the end of the thirteenth century. Indeed, the Chinese passion for genuineness in poetry was the shadow of a social world perceived as false and duplicitous, filled with hidden motives and stratagems. Like Elizabethan drama—and indeed, classical Sanskrit—Chinese drama from its inception had its fools (sometimes with a wisdom undercutting the elite characters and sometimes simply foolish) and its more serious characters held up for ridicule.

The *Romance of the Three Kingdoms* is a prose narrative written in a very simple classical style about the struggles for power at the breakup of the Han dynasty (206 BCE–220 CE) around the turn of the third century. This does have its innocent heroes of pure prowess or honor, who often bungle the purposes of the true central figures, the thinkers for whom stratagem and deception are central. *Shuihu zhuan*, variously translated as *Water Margin* or *Men of the Marsh*, concerns righteous bandits of the early twelfth century: these are mostly heroes of prowess, but they too depend on a leader to curb the propensity to chaos they represent.

In our comparative context *Journey to the West*, the sixteenth-century prose narrative of the seventh-century Chinese traveler Xuanzang's journey to India, comes to the fore. The central figure is not the monk Xuanzang himself, but the attendant, Monkey (Sun Wukong, "Monkey Enlightened to Emptiness"), perhaps originally the Indian Hanuman, the monkey hero of the *Ramayana*, but transformed beyond recognition into a figure of endless resourcefulness and willfulness, bound to Xuanzang's service by an iron band around his head that tightens to cause excruciating pain when Xuanzang recites a spell. Monkey and his main counterpart, Pig, (Zhu Bajie), gluttonous, lecherous, and slothful, are obviously Buddhist allegories of the mind and the sensual self, but they are also lively, engaging characters, the necessary servants of Xuanzang, who possesses neither prowess nor resourcefulness, but who does have purpose.

Although these three prose romances all exist in sixteenth-century editions, they have no clear moment of origin. There are earlier versions of episodes in drama and prose, and their transformation continued in later versions—indeed, to the present day. When we come to *Jin Ping Mei*, a spin-off of *Water Margin* that appeared in print in the seventeenth century but clearly circulated in manuscript in the sixteenth century, we can talk about the "novel." Although it is nominally set in the Song dynasty, it represents the domestic and local politics of the nascent bourgeois culture of the Ming. As in many of the short stories circulating in the early seventeenth century, the culture of officialdom is present but no longer central. The male protagonist of *Jin Ping Mei* is a fabulously wealthy pharmacist, while the short stories focus on merchants and vendors, with women as centrally important as the male characters (in striking contrast to the three early prose romances). After *Romance of the Three Kingdoms*, longer fiction was in a version of Mandarin.

Drama circulated primarily within China itself. Classical literature and vernacular fiction circulated throughout East Asia; given the native training in classical Chinese, the classical literature seemed in no way "foreign" in Korea, Japan, and Vietnam. Vernacular fiction, however, required "translation," but its appeal was such that it found translators and adaptors.

Even before China's humiliation in the Opium War (1839–42), the old culture was showing signs of strain from forces both external and internal. Once the treaty ports were established, the cultural encounter with the European powers was under way. The primary cultural mediator, however, came to be Japan, which had a head start in the mass translation of

European texts. After China's humiliating defeat (1894–95), Japan was flooded with Chinese students, who translated Japanese translations of European textual culture and borrowed the Japanese characters for translating European concepts. In contrast to India, where English became a lingua franca, Chinese continued to be the unifying language; but, as had happened long before with the importation of Buddhism, it became a new Chinese with the resources to engage more effectively in its cultural encounter with the West.

In some ways the European periodization of early modernity works no better for India than for China. Changes were under way already in the early second millennium that would mark the later era as very dissimilar to what had gone before. We have seen that the vast vernacularization of the subcontinent began around the start of the second millennium and was everywhere more or less complete by around the sixteenth century. Even in the learned traditions of Sanskrit something new was unmistakably happening. There were the first self-conscious editions of the epics, for example, with a *Mahabharata* prepared in the eleventh century in Kashmir (by a scholar named Devabodha) and the *Ramayana* in thirteenth-century south India (by a scholar named Udali Varadaraja). Then too, the first complete edition of the four Vedas and all their subdivisions came to be produced in a massive work of scholarship in the mid-fourteenth century. A new style of philology, or scholarly reading, came into being as well, signaled by the literary commentary, invented, it seems, in the early years of the millennium.

In dramatic contrast to China—and of course Europe, where the invention would help define the early modern era—printing was of no relevance to India, which remained a manuscript culture, and to some degree an oral culture, well into the colonial era (the bardic tradition of western India was vibrant as late as the eighteenth century; see chapter 5). This manuscript culture, especially during the Mughal period, was hugely successful in achieving both astonishing accuracy and widespread dissemination of texts. While admittedly works could be expanded, interpolated, and otherwise changed from the original, practices were in place designed to ensure almost absolute accuracy in handwritten reproduction. Thus the many hundreds of copies of the great Bengali poetic biography of the mystic Caitanya (1486–1534), the *Caitanya-carit-amrta* (*Nectar of the Life of Caitanya*, by Krishnadasa Kaviraj, last quarter of the sixteenth century), were produced with complete uniformity. Equally remarkable, the most important

Hindi work, *Ram-carit-manas* (*The Sacred Lake of Rama's Deeds*, by Tulsidas, c. 1575), was disseminated largely through oral performance across north India, yet the manuscripts of the work show remarkably little variation. Dissemination likewise astonishes with its breadth and relative speed. A celebrated poem like the *Gita-govinda* (*Song of Govinda*) of Jayadeva, for example, which was produced in Bengal in Eastern India in the twelfth century, could be found in Rajasthan, more than a thousand miles to the west, within a century.

Printing was irrelevant to this world not because it was unknown but because it was deemed unnecessary. North Indians were made aware of block printing by the Tibetans, who learned it from China as early as the ninth century. Pandits from the holy city of Varanasi who visited the Fifth Dalai Lama's court (in 1642 and later) helped to correct texts published in Lhasa, so we can be sure some were familiar with printing. Books were produced by moveable-type printing in Goa in the 1550s by the Portuguese (who were present on India's west coast from the end of the fifteenth century), but significantly, the experiment was short-lived and did not spread. If the Mughals did not know about printing firsthand, they were certainly exposed to printed books brought by European travelers, yet they had no interest in making their own. Perhaps the Mughals' indifference was related to their calligraphic tradition, which was unsuited to mechanical reproduction, but this would not explain the indifference of Hindus or Jains, for whom calligraphy was never a central cultural value.

Of a piece with this indifference to print is the relative unimportance of paper. Although introduced into the Indian subcontinent from Western Asia sometime in the thirteenth century (earlier introductions from Tibet never caught on), paper took centuries to make an impact, unlike its history in the European and Islamic world, where, by providing a cheap alternative to parchment, paper dramatically opened up communication practices. The state the Mughals ruled from the late sixteenth century on came to be called a *kagaj-raj*, or paper empire, and Islamic-style culture in India naturally conformed to the book practices of the Persian and Arab world. With many new textual collectivities entering Indian literary history in the early modern period—a good example are the Sikhs, a monotheistic religious community that originated in India in the late fifteenth century—the sheer amount of paper manuscript material did increase. But this happened very gradually and unevenly across the subcontinent, and whether it was a direct consequence of the availability of paper is open to debate. In fact, long after the introduction of paper and well into the modern era scribes in many parts of India continued to prefer older writing materials, especially palmyra leaf in the south (which actually seems to have seen an increase of use during this period) and birch bark in the north, in just the same way as writing itself continued to be supplemented by oral reproduction, which literacy typically undermined in other world regions.

The early modern epoch shows a remarkable efflorescence of several new literary cultures, among them Persian. As noted earlier, poets in India had been writing in the language almost as long as poets in Iran itself—though of course India and Iran were far less sharply bounded than they have become in the modern era—and major figures mark those early centuries, including perhaps the greatest, Amir Khusrau (1253–1325). But the language of power in those early centuries of the Delhi Sultanate (c. 1192–1526) and regional Islamic polities were the vernaculars, which had only recently emerged as literary codes. The Mughals, however, actively fashioned Persian into the language of the state and court culture, though poets and singers who used Sanskrit and Hindi were equally welcome and often crowned with distinguished titles, and the sultanate attracted men of learning from across India and even from Iran as poets left the Iranian Safavid state, whether for political or religious reasons remains unclear.

With the rise of Indian Persian poetry, the question raised earlier—what makes Indian literature Indian, if anything other than the fact of being produced in India—is posed once again. The concept of *sabk-i hindi*, or the "Indian style," which has often been used to characterize this literature, is now understood to be a category of nineteenth-century nationalist Iranian vintage, according to which real Persian literature could only be composed by Persians in Persia, not one developed by the early modern writers or readers themselves. (To some extent, in fact, the "Indian" style can be found among Safavid poets in Iran.) Yet there is something about Indo-Persian poetry that sets it off from the classical works of the poets and literary men of classical Persian, Saadi (c. 1200–1292?), for example, or Hafez (1315–1390), and draws it closer to the formal concerns of a broader Indic tradition. Syntactical innovations such as extended nominal compounding are the formal hallmark of Sanskrit court literature in particular; the studied use of *iham*, or double entendre, is very similar to *shlesha*, or the simultaneous "embrace" of two meanings; *kaifiyat* (the term itself is an invention of eighteenth-century Urdu writers) is something close to the Sanskrit notion of *rasa*, the emotional impact of a literary work; dense metaphoricity is of the kind theorized in Sanskrit rhetoric and largely unfamiliar from the Iranian style. Consider the complexity of the image Bedil Dehlavi (1642–1720) uses in this poem:

> What was it
> that plucked at the strings of your heart
> that you came here
> to divert yourself among such as me, and us?
> You are the springtime
> of another world. How is it
> that you're here, in *this* garden? (trans. Shamsur Rahman Faruqi)

This is unlike almost anything in Persian found outside of India. A similar kind of distinctive and innovative style marks Indo-Persian prose, best exemplified in the work of the greatest intellectual at Akbar's court, the historian Abu'l-Fazl (1551–1602). The following is the opening of his *History of Akbar* (*Akbarnama*) (see also chapters 3 and 5), where he recounts receiving the commission to compose the work:

> Day after day this determination took shape, and the threads of success were coming together until, from the court of all excellence, an order was given for the patronage of this favored one, Abu'l-Fazl, son of Mubarak, who had placed the cap of utter devotion on the head of his heart and shaken the eighteen thousand worlds from the sleeve of loyalty. (trans. Wheeler M. Thackston)

If the consolidation of Persian as a dominant language of literature in India in the early modern era was a consequence of its consecration by the Mughals as a dominant language of power, its life was tied inextricably to that power and would end with it. This did not occur with finality until after the full dissolution of the Mughal Empire with the Indian Rebellion of 1857, but signs of Persian's loss of cultural energy were visible earlier. As a consequence of this loss a widespread north Indian vernacular, eventually named Urdu, was gradually upgraded to a literary language through incorporation of major elements of Persian literary culture, including vocabulary, rhetoric, motifs, and of course script. Urdu was used to produce a literature of astonishing subtlety and sophistication—and self-revelation, as in the poetry of Mohammad Taqi "Mir" (1725–1810):

> There was a time when Mir—before tyranny killed him—was young.
> His style of poetry aroused tumult and lamentation.
> The page on which his poetry was inscribed was a packet of magic.
> He recited his *ghazal* and people raptly gazed at his face. A strange and wondrous sight it was.
> In Delhi, on whichever street he would wander, with afflicted heart,
> there walked with him a noise and turmoil like Doomsday.
>
> He wasn't ever downcast, like dust sodden with water:
> he was a storm, a terrible wonderful thing; a clamor that shook the whole world.
> . . .
> Was anyone in the world, Mir, ignorant of you?
> And yet when you ceased to be, no name or trace of you was to be found. (trans. Faruqi)

Another register of this same North Indian vernacular would appropriate the vocabulary, rhetoric, motifs, and what had emerged as the dominant script of Sanskrit literary culture. This language would come to be called Hindi, and while literary experiments in Hindi can be found as early as the late fourteenth century (not by Hindus, however, but by Sufis), beginning in the late sixteenth century poets began to produce a literary corpus of such depth that the language would eventually replace Sanskrit as the principal courtly and religious idiom across the north. Key figures of the early history of Hindi include the court poet Keshavdas (1555–1617), and two authors of devotional literature, Surdas (1483?–1573?), poet of lyrics in praise of the god Krishna, and Tulsidas (1532–1623), author of a *Ramayana* epic. The dividing line between the courtly and the devotional cannot always be clearly drawn. Situated right on this line is the following poem by Surdas, which develops a motif of the legend of god come to earth as the cowherd Krishna (also called Mohan, Shyam), who has departed for the city of Mathura, leaving the young women of Braj, his village, brokenhearted. One of the women speaks here, with a conceit that testifies less to the fervor of the devotee than to the sophistication of the imagist:

> Mathura's wells must be clogged with my letters.
> Mohan, for his part, sends not a one,
>   and mine are never returned.
> Messengers traveling there from Braj
>   seem to forget to search him out,
> Or maybe Shyam silences them with some palaver,
>   or maybe they perish halfway there.
> Maybe a cloudburst has soaked all the paper,
>   or all the ink has dried, or a forest fire
>   has burned all the shoots that make all the quills,
> Or the scribes, says Sur, have gone blind
>   from all their writing: cataract-doors
>   have closed and blocked their eyes. (trans. John Stratton Hawley)

The differentiation of Urdu and Hindi was a slow process and, in the early modern era, never clearly enunciated. There is much evidence that the two literary cultures were broadly overlapping: Hindi poets could make use of Persian-Urdu vocabulary and sometimes script, and Persian and Urdu poets would adopt motifs and narratives from the Hindi tradition. It was mainly in the twentieth century, perhaps only in mid-century, with the importation of a nationalism that required single peoples with single languages and scripts, that the process was complete, with Hindi becoming the national language of India and Urdu that of Pakistan.

Poetry would continue to dominate the literary cultures of the region. To be sure, prose genres are available, from the massive Persian histories of the Mughals to the mid-sixteenth-century Telugu romances, such as the *Kalapurnodayamu* (*The Sound of the Kiss*) of Pingali Suranna (identified by its recent translators as "in a certain sense, the first Indian novel," though in fact it is in mixed prose and verse, and many of the elements of the tale are very old). But storytelling was typically oral. Not until the beginning of the nineteenth century and at the behest of British scholars at Fort William College in Calcutta were the vast Urdu linked story collections known as *dastan* committed to writing, the most celebrated being Khalil Ali Khan

Ashk's *Dastan-e Amir Hamza*, starring the paternal uncle of the Prophet (1801). Other older genres either disappeared or ceased to be produced. Especially curious is the fate of Sanskrit drama. The high tradition of theater marked by the works of Kalidasa (fourth–fifth century) declined over the following millennium, so that by the end of the precolonial era (c. 1800) it was only the one-act monologue (*bhana*) that was still being composed. Very few vernacular dramatic traditions are known, one being the *kuravanci*, a dance-drama genre involving lovelorn ladies and bird-catcher fortune-tellers, cultivated in Tanjore (from where the story that was to become the basis for Mozart's most famous opera, *The Magic Flute*, was exported in the mid-eighteenth century). But something must have lived on, though the genealogy has never been fully traced; larger-scale Sanskrit dramas from the courts of seventeenth-century Rajasthan and Tamil Nadu—perhaps the tip of an iceberg—remain largely unstudied or often unpublished. The spectacular, and spectacularly successful, play by Agha Hasan Amanat, *Court of Indra* (*Indersabha*, 1853), the first Urdu drama, did not come out of nowhere; and it was to go somewhere indeed, influencing the Parsi theater of Bombay and thereby the future Bollywood film industry.

The kinds of literary processes we have sketched in north India were replicated, to be sure with all the variations produced by particular histories and regional genius, across India during the early modern period. Devotional poetry of great intensity was promoted in temple and village side by side with the courtly productions much sought after for edification, adornment, and pleasure by small kingdoms, whether in Bengal or Maharashtra, Andhra Pradesh or Nepal. While works in Sanskrit and Persian continued to be written, they now were complemented, if not overshadowed by vernacular literary composition. The unimpeded reproduction of long-standing convention in idiom, theme, and genre may suggest stasis to those outside the literary cultures, as it did to the British colonialists, who labeled "decadent" anything incompatible with their own Victorian Protestant values. But to those within, such reproduction often conceals the dynamism of small refinements that the "intelligence of tradition" such as the Indian elevates as the hallmark of literary mastery.

Visitors from the West had been coming to India for millennia—Persians, Greeks, Romans . . . Danish, Dutch, English, French—and often left their mark on literary culture; the similarities between Sanskrit and Greek drama, for example, have long intrigued scholars. But the consolidation of British rule after 1800 and absorption of India into the British Empire after 1857 enabled European language and literary practice to completely transform the Indian literary landscape. For one thing, the deepest structures of literary feeling began to mutate. Realism, historicism, Romantic authenticity, social improvement—all these largely new values came with colonial modernity. For another, the languages of literature themselves were to modernize—those that could not would be pronounced decadent or dead—so much so that, in a way strikingly different from what happened in China, readers without special training would increasingly be cut off from the works of their literary past. Traditions cultivated with such loving care by Indian poets and critics for a thousand years or more would simply be swept away, and left in their wake was an ever-thickening cloud of obliviousness of what had come before, and an ever more anxious uncertainty about the open road ahead.

Conclusion

Direct comparison of non-Western literary traditions must address both a general and a particular challenge. The former lies in the fact that literary traditions are evolving rather than stable systems, which accordingly cannot be captured, without serious distortion, in the sort of freeze-frame narrative required of the comparative method, with its fixed objects. The particular challenge of comparing outside the West means acknowledging that its categories and norms are actually just historical particulars rather than timeless universals, and that accordingly, other categories and norms are to be expected, and difference is not to be regarded as deficiency.

It is a truism that identity is constructed by comparison; through comparison, diverse communities find some sort of unity. Comparison with India and China was one means, among others of course, by which the fractious polities of the western end of Eurasia became "Europe" and "the West" to begin with. The essentialized commonality given India by Europe and the work of Indian intellectuals themselves created the cultural construct that made a modern "Indian" identity possible. That same process gave China what it had always wanted, an imagined unified "Chinese" identity. To throw "China and India" as a comparison set into the familiar clichés complicates things. India and Europe share the epic in the conventional sense; China and Europe share early modern print culture; China and India share a fascination with mood and feeling. The stability of binary comparison disintegrates.

The literary cultures of China and India do share a range of phenomena that is broad and deep. The commonalities of their larger environment are indeed striking. Both China and India possessed learned traditions of great historical depth and continuity, which were tasked with similar responsibilities of editing, preserving, commenting on, and critiquing literary works. In both, common social functions—the praise of princes and patrons, for example—worked themselves out in different ways. We find comparable dynamics of literary gatherings and literary societies, richly documented in different places at different times. We find comparable town and village performance traditions, again each working with its own resources. Many genres are familiar to both cultures: for example, what we have discussed under the heading of "lyric" or "drama," without being too troubled by the use of Western categories.

Other genres confront us with precisely the threat of European conceptual domination that we have to navigate with care. If we follow Hegel on what constitutes an "epic," for example, there is no epic in China; if we ask instead what kind of historical, imaginative, and political work certain texts perform, then a Chinese epic emerges as readily as an Indian one.

At the same time, the contrasts between these two cultures are undeniable and consequential. They can be found everywhere, from the most material level of literary culture to the most abstract. A salient example of the former is provided by the role of paper and printing. In China, these produced a transformation that many scholars have seen as the start of modernity. In India, printing was known but rejected, and paper continued to be supplemented by—and in many areas ignored in favor of—traditional materials, palm leaf and birch bark. By contrast, new forms of literary practice, including vernacular language use and the growth of commentaries for new reading publics, combined to produce something of an early modernity around the same time.

In China, a single language, or script language, was used for literary culture for more than two millennia, though vernacular registers developed in different locales and venues. In India, after some 1,500 years of Sanskrit's dominance, new regional languages burst into prominence and were cultivated for literary purposes, as were later new transregional languages, Persian and Hindi. In China, the unity of the language produced an imagined unified literary culture, divided by special interests in different forms.

In India, that unity, to the degree it existed, emerged out of a shared concern with a pool of narratives, motifs, allusions, and expressive techniques. In China, the same script was read everywhere the literary culture extended, but everywhere the language was spoken differently. In India, Sanskrit was spoken everywhere more or less similarly, with wide mutual intelligibility, but it was read everywhere in different scripts. In China, poetry could not be understood without a detailed historical apparatus, identifying the poet and when and where he wrote. In India, poetry could not be understood with a historical apparatus; it was meant precisely to express what was beyond time and place.

Literature is a form of life, and Chinese and Indian literary traditions have long embodied larger trends in Chinese and Indian life. These show commonalities but also profound differences, with regard to the importance and nature of historical imagination, for example; the relationship between culture and state; and the very nature of language itself. Many of these trends continue; indeed, no better exemplar exists for understanding what the past of China and India means to their present than their deep historical literary cultures.

For Further Reading

China

Denecke, Wiebke, Wai-yee Li, and Xiaofei Tian. *The Oxford Handbook of Classical Chinese Literature*. Oxford: Oxford University Press, 2017.

Durrant, Stephen. *The Cloudy Mirror: Tension and Conflict in the Writings of Sima Qian*. Albany: State University of New York Press, 1995.

Hanan, Patrick. *The Chinese Vernacular Story*. Cambridge, MA: Harvard University Press, 1981.

Li, Wai-yee. *The Readability of the Past in Early Chinese Historiography*. Cambridge, MA: Harvard Asia Center, 2008.

Lu, Tina. "The Literary Culture of the Late Ming." In *Cambridge History of Chinese Literature*, vol. 2, ed. Kang-I Sun Chang. Cambridge: Cambridge University Press, 2010.

Owen, Stephen. *Readings in Chinese Literary Thought*. Cambridge, MA: Harvard University Press, 1992.

———. *Traditional Chinese Poetry and Poetics: An Omen of the World*. Madison: University of Wisconsin Press, 1985.

Tian, Xiaofei. *Tao Yuanming and Manuscript Culture: The Record of a Dusty Table*. Seattle: University of Washington Press, 2013.

West, Stephen H. "Literature from the Late Jin to the Early Ming: Ca. 1230–1275." In *Cambridge History of Chinese Literature*, vol. 1, ed. Stephen Owen, 619–648. Cambridge: Cambridge University Press, 2010.

West, Stephen H. and Wilt L. Idema. *Monks, Bandits, Lovers, and Immortals: Eleven Early Chinese Plays*. Indianapolis: Hackett, 2010.

India

Bronner, Yigal, et al. *Innovations and Turning Points: Toward a History of Kavya Literature*. New York: Oxford University Press, 2014.

Busch, Allison. *Poetry of Kings: The Classical Hindi Literature of Mughal India*. New York: Oxford University Press, 2011.

Ingalls, Daniel H. H. *Sanskrit Poetry from Vidyakara's Treasury*. Cambridge, MA: Harvard University Press, 2000.

Orsini, Francesca, ed. *Before the Divide: Hindi and Urdu Literary Culture*. New Delhi: Orient Blackswan, 2010.

Pollock, Sheldon. *The Language of the Gods in the World of Men: Sanskrit, Culture, and Power in Premodern India*. Berkeley: University of California Press, 2006.

——. *Reader on Rasa: A Historical Sourcebook of Classical Indian Aesthetics*. New York: Columbia University Press, 2015.

——, ed. *Literary Cultures in History: Reconstructions from South Asia*. Berkeley: University of California Press, 2003.

Pritchett, Francis. *Nets of Awareness: Urdu Poetry and Its Critics*. Berkeley: University of California Press, 1994.

Ramanujan, A. K. "Three Hundred Rāmāyaṇas: Five Examples and Three Thoughts on Translation." In *The Collected Essays of A. K. Ramanujan*, 131–60. Delhi: Oxford University Press, 2004.

Russell, Ralph and Khurshidul Islam. *Three Mughal Poets: Mir, Sauda, Mir Hasan*. Cambridge, MA: Harvard University Press, 1968.

Sharma, Sunil. *Mughal Arcadia: Persian Literature in an Indian Court*. Cambridge, MA: Harvard University Press, 2017.

Shulman, David. *Tamil: A Biography*. Cambridge, MA: Harvard University Press, 2016.

PART THREE

CHAPTER VI

Big Science

Classicism and Conquest

BENJAMIN ELMAN AND CHRISTOPHER MINKOWSKI

"Science" is an especially loaded term in English, freighted with triumphant meanings connected to the rise of a new form of knowledge in Europe in the early modern period and associated with institutions that promoted a rapidly moving forefront of discovery and communication. Too often, the history of science is told as a story about getting there first: who first had the stirrup; who first understood the mobile nature of the planets; who borrowed, or stole, iron metallurgy from whom; and so on. Triumphant intellectual and technical achievements secure a nation's standing on the scientific league table. They have become a currency of national prestige and honor in our global present. This is not a bad thing: it enables scientists to win state support for projects that may require many years of their lives and yield no guaranteed result. But in this invidious climate, where modern nations have become the unit of analysis for the history of science, cognitive fantasies are rife on all sides, and historical understanding the loser.

Like their counterparts elsewhere, some Indian Brahmans and Chinese scholars have claimed, both in the past and in the present, that all things new and good have come from their own lands. Gunpowder, the compass, paper, silk, cotton textiles, zero and Arabic numerals, decimals, and sugar are usually reeled off as examples and attributed to Asian precociousness. The proud parents are right, up to a point. Viewed in another way, such claims are "not even wrong," to borrow the phrase of the Nobel Laureate in physics Wolfgang Pauli. From the perspective of an interconnected, continentwide history of the flow of sciences across space and time, such claims answer a question that is only of parochial interest. They drive the conversation toward comparing the sciences of India and China with those of modern Europe, not with each other. India and China made substantial and enduring contributions to the sciences, both worldwide and at home. This chapter will explore the setting in which they did so, and how much of their work was shared.

The Sciences and Their Basis in India and China

In this chapter we use a definition of "science" that is intentionally broad. It takes in all the disciplines of systematized rational inquiry in the Indian and Chinese cultural spheres, ranging from philology to jurisprudence to astronomy and astrology—the astral sciences being particularly important. Accordingly, a variety of terms drawn from the language of our own day are used to designate these subjects, such as "disciplines," "knowledge systems," "sciences," "arts," "learned traditions," and their variants. Terms such as "discipline" do double service, furthermore, in referring not just to intellectual content but also to contexts—the institutional, social, and even professional dimensions. These were not the terms known to the scientists of India and China themselves, of course, who used such Sanskrit designations as *shastra* (authoritative body of knowledge), *vidya* (lore), and *vijnana* (experiential understanding), and Chinese designations for knowledge frameworks such as *gezhi* (investigating and extending knowledge), *bowuxue* (broad knowledge of things), and *shiwuxue* (studies of contemporary affairs).

In antiquity, both Indian and Chinese scholars recognized this broader scope of what constituted rational, disciplinary knowledge. In Brahmanical India, conservative opinion about education had by the sixth century converged on an ideal curriculum of fourteen sciences (*vidya*): the four Vedas (the sacred texts of the Brahmans) and their six limbs (*anga*)—language analysis (*vyakarana*), etymology (*nirukta*), phonetics (*shiksha*), ritual (*kalpa*), metrics (*chandas*), and astronomy (*jyotisha*)—along with their four subordinate limbs, (*upanga*) law and moral philosophy (*dharma*), discourse analysis and scriptural hermeneutics (*mimamsa*), logic and epistemology (*nyaya*), and mythology (*purana*).

The Chinese terms *gezhi* and *bowu* set the framework for Sinitic knowledge. They could at times have a generic sense and at others could refer to types of content. "Affairs" represented the concretization of the objects of knowledge, just as things were of the world. For example, the scholar Zhu Xi (1130–1200), the dominant voice of the late imperial classical consensus, proposed a uniform methodology to accumulate knowledge and wisdom in both the cultural/moral and natural/political realms: "The essence of Confucian teaching is to put the investigation of principles first, because each individual thing maintains its own coherence (*li*). This must be first understood, and then the phenomena of the mind will be seen to have in each case a standard by which their character may be estimated."

He did not delineate a precise classificatory system within which "investigating things" (*gewu*) represented a particular kind of knowledge, i.e, calendrical or mathematical, social or political, cultural or religious. For Zhu Xi, *gezhi* (extending knowledge) and *bowu* (broad knowledge of things) were opposed to each other, because the former was guided by moral purpose while the latter was just aimless erudition. Thus the classification of the sciences in China emphasized the method of studying them and their moral value.

Classification in India, on the other hand, emphasized and enumerated the differences in content. The *Lalitavistara*, the *Long Story of the Playful Deeds (of the Buddha)*, for example, provides early testimony to this abundance of skills and lores. The text, an account of the life of the Buddha that circulated in Asia in all the classical languages of Buddhism in the first millennium, tells how the young Buddha to be, even before he attended school, demonstrated his knowledge of sixty-four different writing systems and of a hundred arts and sciences (*vidya*), both worldly and sacred, many of which do not appear in the short list of Indian sciences mentioned above. His mastery, developed in his previous lives, ranged from archery and swimming to aromatics and music to comedy and politics to leisure and the physiognomy of elephants.

As the description of the Buddha's education in the *Lalitavistara* suggests, in both India and China the sciences abounded, and the profusion in forms of knowledge was put into some order by arranging them into enumerated groups. A few such groups include the Six Arts of the Chinese scholars (rites, music, archery, charioteering, calligraphy, and mathematics) and the Fourteen Sciences of the Indian pundits.

When the Buddhist monk Xuanzang (602–664), visited India in the early seventh century, he noticed among the Buddhists five sciences (*vidya*), general studies that educated a scholar and prepared him for further learning. These were the sciences of words; of arts, mechanics, and the calendar; of health; of the theory of proof; and of the inner man. The Brahmans, meanwhile, he said, had four of their own disciplines connected with the Vedas (*Veda-shastra*): medicine, ritual, public decorum and military arts, and science and incantations. On Brahmanical knowledge, Xuanzang did not do very well, describing only what he managed to understand of four subordinate Vedic practices. But he did correctly notice a crucial fact about the Brahmanical world of learning: that the Brahmans conceived of their disciplines as springing from the Vedas and as both supported by the Vedas in their authority and supporting the Vedas in turn.

Xuanzang's description of separate Brahmanical sciences captured another important fact: that there was something like a distinction between sacred and secular sciences. The Brahmans called some disciplines worldly ones (*laukika*), such as poetry and aesthetics. These were made by mere humans and subject to error. To these subjects and to others such as metrics, lexicography, grammar, and the theory of proof, Indian scholars of many backgrounds, not just Brahmanical ones, made contributions that all accepted.

In China too, during the Tang (618–907) and Song (960–1280) revivals, a profound conservatism reigned in classical knowledge. The community of the learned, the literati, cultivated the study of political statecraft in secular disciplines whose four major fields were the classics (such as *Poetry, Change, Documents, Annals,* and *Rituals*), histories, literature, and the "masters" (such as the astronomers, mathematicians, agriculturalists, and physicians). Medicine and mathematics had their own classics. The sacred sciences, such as astrology and numerology, also flourished. These were frequently but not exclusively associated with medicine and alchemy, the preserve of the Buddhists and the Daoists (see the next chapter on religions of China and India). Both secular and sacred disciplines prospered: the secular as shared and open discourses, the sacred as rhetorically closed ones. Scholars and monks were more often inclusive than exclusive in their pursuit of followers. Xenophobia of the Christianized European variety, although not unknown in imperial China, was unusual.

For long periods in both India and China, scientific thought was primarily textual thought. An Indian thinker in any discipline normally communicated his ideas, however original, by commenting on a preexisting "root" text, a classic work that everyone knew. Others would react by commenting on his work in turn, or by composing an alternative commentary on the root text. The most fundamental sciences, therefore, were those that enabled and regulated this mode of thought. A triad of sciences were considered essential to the study of all others, the sciences of word, sentence, and proof (*pada, vakya, pramana*), that is, of language analysis (*vyakarana*), scriptural hermeneutics (*mimamsa*), and epistemology (*nyaya*). These three disciplines produced the most extensive and continuous literatures. All three reached a summit of esteem in the early modern period, when they were treated as the queens of the sciences.

Classical learning based on the Confucian Classics flourished among elites in Song China, as did Veda-based learning among the literate castes in medieval India. Here too, engagement with the classics was the primary mode of systematic thought. The classic-centered view of things in both India and China reflected conservatism about knowledge. It did not rule out innovation, but it did modulate and regulate the forms that innovation could take.

A typical Chinese official living in the latter days of the Song period could remark that no learning was to be preferred to the "Learning of the Way" (*daoxue*) that Zhu Xi and his followers had propagated as the vision of the highest good—an investigation of the principal elements of human nature as the foundation for a moral universe within which humans were the prime beneficiaries: "Human nature is the all-comprehensive substance of the supreme ultimate, and in its essence is indefinable; but within it are innumerable coherences (*li*). To these, then, the names love, righteousness, reverence, and wisdom are given."

This was the general attitude, but not all valued classical study. Under the Mongol regime (1280–1368) the literati turned to a new manner of learning. Textuality became the clearest marker dividing elites and the lower classes. Literati increasingly compiled texts by excerpting antiquarian writings in new compendia to exhibit their erudition and encyclopedic knowledge.

In China an "empire of words on paper" spread via the wide use of woodblock printing. Printing increased the velocity of both secular and sacred domains of knowledge. The growth of the influence of printing in China did not find a counterpart in India, where hand-copying texts remained the principal engine of publication and circulation down to the colonial period. Scribes sustained a brisk, continentwide circulation of scientific literature, though this network could break down at times of political upheaval. Block printing of texts, learned from the Chinese, was not taken up in any extensive way except as adapted to the manufacture of textiles.

Institutions

As other chapters in this volume show, institutions in both India and China—the state, the family, the monastery, and the religious movement—supported and shaped the sciences. There was an ongoing difference between the two lands in the extent of the state's involvement, as discussed more thoroughly in chapter 1. In general, Chinese political order was more centralized; the government intervened more directly to regulate the activities of the literate classes and to keep them uniform across the imperial region. Already in the ancient period the state and its scholars gave classical Chinese this durability by endowing it with a uniform writing system that made a special register of the Chinese language independent of local pronunciation or written variation. Through sustained philological refinement, generations of scholars made classical Chinese accessible to mastery by educated readers and writers working in different regions and in different eras. Classical Chinese became the preferred elite language for discussions of law, statecraft, sciences, and medicine, though in China's borderlands, Mongols, Khitan, Jurchen, Tibetans, and Manchus developed their own scripts for writing their spoken languages, which they used in lieu of Chinese writing for their sciences, administration, literature, and religious purposes. But classical Chinese was the one route to the civil examinations, the allegedly meritocratic gateway to the civil service, which remained primarily the domain of aristocrats because of their dominance in written learning. The state reinforced its social prerogatives by scheduling periodic examinations in the Tang capital and only accepted candidates via recommendation. During the Song and, later, the Ming (1368–1644) eras, such examinations were for the first time held in the 17–18 provinces, 140 prefectures, and 1,350 counties, thereby opening them up to local elites, not just capital and courtly elites, though not yet to artisans, peasants, monks, or women.

The effect of this opening was decisive. Europeans first marveled at the educational achievements of the Chinese in the sixteenth century when

Catholic missionaries, especially Jesuits, wrote approvingly of the civil examinations then regularly held under the auspices of the Ming government. In the absence of alternative careers of comparable social status and political prestige, the goal of becoming an official took priority. The civil service recruitment system achieved for education in imperial China a degree of standardization and local importance unparalleled in the early modern world. But this classical ethos carried over into the domains of medicine, law, literature, fiscal policy, and military affairs. Imperial rulers and Chinese elites believed that ancient wisdom, properly inculcated, tempered men as leaders and prepared them for wielding political power.

The power of classical learning and statecraft to motivate millions of Chinese to become public officials serving far from home and family is only one part of the story, however. Only 5 percent of the candidates would see their hopes realized. A more important part of the story is what became of the 95 percent who would not. The authority of the classical language empowered the civil examinations to serve as a sociocultural gyroscope that oriented the minds of those who failed. More than just the thousands of classical literate officials, the examination system produced millions of literate students who, after repeated failures, became doctors, Buddhist or Daoist priests, pettifoggers long distrusted by the state, teachers, notaries, merchants, and lineage managers of large kinship groups (see further below), not to mention astronomers, mathematicians, printers, and publishers.

The Chinese civil service examination system had far-reaching effects on modes of writing, thinking, and textual production as well. Chinese scholars created, published, and studied reference encyclopedias (*leishu*) and daily-use compendia (*riyong leishu*), which they found to be invaluable in preparing for the civil examinations or for collecting the source materials needed to carry out their administrative activities. During the Song dynasty, these traditional collections transmitted a specific epistemological approach for investigating things, events, and phenomena. The textual approach to natural studies and practical knowledge culminated in the creation of encyclopedias and collectanea (*congshu*, lit., "a library of books") that served as knowledge repositories simulating "textual museums." Rather than microcosms of nature, as in early modern European museums, the late Ming encyclopedias simulated a textual museum of marvels.

The tendency of modern historians to concentrate on individuals in the development of classical learning has hidden the place that family and lineage occupied in late imperial China. Although the civil service examinations made upward mobility possible, Chinese lineages and clans invested "cultural capital" in ensuring that their children dominated the next generation of professional scholars. The male children of literati monopolized the imperial civil examinations. Chinese schools that prepared students for the examinations were in fact private and depended upon great lineages of literati for their maintenance. Classical scholars, as individuals, did not construct a vision of their political culture out of nothing.

Their mentalities were embedded in a larger social structure whose premise was the centrality of kinship ties. In day-to-day affairs, the local social elites were defined mainly by their kinship relations and by the cultural resources that formed and maintained lineages. Keeping sciences such as medicine, astronomy, and mathematics within the family line, and thus within the lineage, was a frequent strategy to continue the success of a descent group in the civil service examinations. But compared with the role family lineages played in the education of scholars and scientists in India, the Chinese literati appear to have been formed in more open educational structures.

Indian states devolved power to local and regional administrations and were more intentionally pluralist and less interventionist than the Chinese. This was reflected in a greater plurality and decentralization of traditions, in which striking uniformities of discourse and method were nevertheless maintained in other ways. Given the multitiered and delegatory structure of the political order, there was nothing like the centralized and standardized examination system of Song China. In place of such structures, India relied on the relatively steady state of family prestige and status. Those who became learned pundits were eligible to do so by virtue of being born into a scholarly caste and family. Indian states, both large and small, left much of the regulation of the knowledge order to the literate classes, which maintained lineages of learning through family and caste structures, as well as through monastic organizations and religious movements.

In India, most of the learned were Brahmans. But there were also non-Brahmans in significant numbers: leaders of religious movements; monks, both Buddhist and Jain; and members of a scribal caste, the Kayasthas, who in later centuries specialized in Persian literacy. Rulers provided roles for the learned as adornments to their courts. They honored the pundits who had the best reputation as scholars, offering titles and emoluments. They also staged events at which celebrated figures would perform, reciting poetry (usually poetry that reflected well on the ruler) or engaging in philosophical and theological debates. Royal or courtly patronage often drove fashions in subjects and in literary styles. Some kingdoms attempted a more systematic and widespread patronage of Brahmanical learning. Following earlier examples, the Mughal rulers (1526–1857) dispersed wealth to the pundits in Banaras, channeling it through large monthly stipends given to the most prominent Brahmans in the city, such as Kavindracharya Sarasvati, a monk celebrated in contemporary documents for his generosity to the city's learned specialists.

Gifts honoring scholarly or artistic brilliance could be made hereditary through granting the land revenue from an agricultural village to a family, thereby ensuring leisure from work for generations of lucky scholars. Some Brahmans supported themselves through other kinds of literate labor, private priestly jobs or teaching, or administrative service to a ruler.

By comparison to China, this approach allowed for a more self-regulated and plural intellectual world. At the same time, the literature produced by Sanskritic scientists is remarkable for the almost total regularity of its grammatical usage and the continuity of its disciplinary methods, employed everywhere in the cosmopolitan sphere, across many centuries. So uniform are the orientation and method of Sanskrit scientific texts that one cannot usually identify the period or location of an author unless he happens to mention it.

Sanskrit as the perfected instrument of scholarly discourse did not happen naturally or inevitably. It was brought about by the efforts of learned custodians who developed a battery of linguistic sciences and scholastic arts: grammar, phonetics, phonology, etymology, hermeneutics, lexicography, prosody, rhetoric, and so on. Sanskrit's dominance as the language of the sciences and learning sustained it for a thousand years, until Persian came to rival it in the court of the Delhi sultans and the Mughals. Later, in the British imperial period, English displaced both in institutional primacy.

The Vedas were hereditary—a Brahman learned the same Vedic text as his father—but other sciences were not. Learning often passed through families, while outside of families there were small schools in temples, monasteries, and sometimes state buildings. But scholarly acumen was not hereditary, and many famous scholars were the first in their family to take up a discipline. Most scholars in most periods mastered more than one.

Disciplines of knowledge were regulated by the participants, who, as in China, belonged to lineages. Direct study with a guru, a master of the discipline, was the prerequisite for entry into the community of scholarship. The guru had himself been a pupil of an earlier master, and he taught others, one's "guru brothers." Families played an equally important role. Extended Brahman families worked together to cultivate a collective reputation as reliable and learned authorities. In the Mughal period especially, learned families could become transregional corporate concerns, operating like the trading families of the mercantile castes (*banya*). One branch of a Brahman family would maintain a foothold back in the Deccan, on the old land grant, while the most talented would go up to Banaras, the international center, there to rely on the cousins already based in the city. Other cousins might try their luck in regional kingdoms on the rise, for example Tanjore in the south of India.

The Yuan/Sultanate Transition

This picture of how the sciences were maintained in India and China was shattered in both lands at about the same time, with the establishment of imperial conquest dynasties in Delhi and in Beijing in the twelfth and thirteenth centuries. The conquerors were in both cases descendants of Turkic warriors from the Eurasian steppes. Both new dynasties displaced the old intellectual and administrative elite and introduced new forms of knowledge, communicated in new languages. The old knowledge elites of India and China responded in different ways to their displacement. In both cases they returned to something like their old prominence but never regained it entirely.

For the Han Chinese literati, the new developments accompanied the beginning of the Yuan period (1280–1368). When the Mongols took power, the literati who had dominated the institutions of learning under the previous Song state could no longer look forward to official appointments. In the face of the Mongol monopoly of political power via appointments of outsiders such as Muslims, Persians, and other Central Asians, the cultured Chinese elites sought in classical learning an alternate form of legitimacy for their social status. As mentioned earlier, new types of classical encyclopedias developed. Owing to the steady expansion of printing and literacy, and to the corresponding proliferation of a bookish print culture, some of the new encyclopedias reached a broader readership than ever before. Using the encyclopedic form, compilers increasingly applied the ideals of "investigating things and extending knowledge" (*gewu zhizhi*) beyond the classical corpus to medicine and mathematics.

The establishment of the Delhi Sultanate in 1206 marked the transition in India from the Sanskritic model of political authority to the Persianate one (described above in chapter 1). Initially the rulers disrupted, and even physically destroyed, old institutions of Sanskritic learning, turning the courtly experts, Brahmans, out of their places. The sultans introduced a competing knowledge order, communicated in Arabic and Persian, which was connected to a different and expansive Islamic community of learning whose center was farther west, not in India.

This period of Brahmanical dislocation coincided with a new turn among the pundits to devotional religious movements based around temples, or to movements of yogis or tantriks, in which powerful god-men and deities took on the role of the now missing king figure of the Brahmanical political ideal. Regional courts beyond the reach of Delhi, the southern Vijayanagara kingdom for example, represented themselves as bulwarks of Vedic and Brahmanical education and scholarship. With the blending of Persianate and Sanskritic models of political authority in later centuries, Brahmans and Brahmanical learning were reintroduced into the courts of most kingdoms, including the imperial ones. The Mughals actively sought to include the pundits in their courtly activities, but there the Brahmans represented only one alternative among several.

In most of the Sanskrit scientific literature of this period, there is complete silence about the competing knowledge disciplines in Arabic and Persian. Such silence amounted to a willful ignoring of the competitors, a strategy of not recognizing their authority. The literature of *jyotisha*, the science of the celestial luminaries, provides one notable exception. There the contributions of the *yavana*s, Persian-Arabic astronomers, were taken up for consideration and adaptation. That brings us to the central topic of our study.

The Transformation of Calendrical Knowledge

Similar forms of knowledge have arisen independently in different places in the world. Some, such as the textual practices that confront texts at close range, seem to emerge spontaneously in literate societies that prize and preserve their classics. On the other hand, some forms of systematic empirical knowledge, such as astronomical knowledge, can move from country to country through the protective membranes of cultural difference. A telling example of portable knowledge is encapsulated in the story of the state calendars of India and China.

From around 1250 to 1750, both India and China received an infusion of mathematical expertise and experts who worked in the idiom of the Arabic and Persian astral sciences. The creation of this new Eurasian zone of contact resulted from the expansion of the domain of the Mongols, the descendants of Chinggis Khan. The later part of the story of transmission is complicated by an additional flow of knowledge, between Europe and Asia. The vector for the introduction of European knowledge into China, and to some extent into India, was the Jesuit order.

Our focus here is on how the classical scholars—the Chinese literati, the Islamic scholars, and the Indian pundits—reacted to the availability of new science. We will draw attention to the interaction between the state and the literati, pundits, Jesuits, and others, in the creation of technical knowledge.

Why should rulers care about the calendar? What does it mean for a calendar to be accurate? The modern reader should not forget how relatively recently the world began to reckon time by a globally uniform standard, or how political that change was. Even today, not everyone follows the common calendar, not exclusively. Why is the Greenwich observatory the point through which we think zero degrees of earthly longitude passes? Why is the time we use expressed as "mean time"? When does a day begin? When does the year begin, and how long does it last? When does a month begin and end?

The answers to all of these questions depend on a web of social agreements. Someone has had to decide the answers and persuade others to adopt them. Being reliable always helps in persuasion, but how does one judge who is reliable? The international scientific community took a long time to agree to the contemporary system. There was no universal agreement before that, but a consensus emerged in Asia around 1250. It fell to rulers to establish the standards within their kingdom, just as the national observatories in each country do today. All standards have been imperfect and subject to correction. In the old days, the imperfections were greater.

Technical knowledge of the heavens mattered for both Chinese empires and Indian kingdoms. Since antiquity, the Chinese Mandate of Heaven had measured a dynasty's worth. It was the emperor's ritual responsibility to establish an accurate calendar based on a system of computational astronomy. The state calendar specified economic, social, political, and religious rituals. Its accuracy demonstrated the ruler's authority over the agrarian cycle, affirmed the cosmic order, and normalized relations with other rulers. Like Rome's Julian calendar, the symbolic power of the calendar to order daily life via time keeping affirmed the effectiveness of the dynasty in power, especially a Chinese dynasty founded by those considered foreigners, such as the Yuan under the Mongols and later the Qing (1644–1912) under the Manchus. The calendar was recorded and organized in light of the emperor's reign. His legitimacy was narrated using historical events associated with a specific year of his era. In India, systems for maintaining calendars were less centralized, being spread among the learned community. But the ritual importance was equally great, as the eleventh-century Arab astronomer Al-Biruni remarked in his *Kitab al-Hind*, a study of India's sciences. Rulers kept *jyotisha* pundits at court to determine the calendar for state ritual functions, and the calendars set by the court astronomers carried weight in the kingdom.

Most Indian and Chinese calendars, past and present, have made use of a lunar-solar year, that is, a year that coordinates the lunar months (from full moon to full moon or new moon to new moon) with the passage of the annual solar cycle through the equinoxes and solstices. By comparison, the Western, now global, calendar is a strictly solar one. Its months have nothing to do with the position of the moon. The Muslim Hijra calendar, on the other hand, is purely lunar. The date of its new year has nothing to do with the seasons. The most common Indian calendars celebrate the start of the year with a new moon (or full moon) that falls close to the spring equinox. The Chinese calendar celebrates the start of the new year on the second new moon after the winter solstice. Every year, the New Year celebration according to the Indian or Chinese calendar falls on a different day according to the Western calendar.

Keeping a lunar-solar calendar accurate, that is, in conformity with what people can see for themselves of the passage of the seasons, eclipses, and the cycle of the moon, is difficult. The solstices and equinoxes have to fall on the same day of the calendar, or nearly, while the twelve lunar months should fall in the same season that they do every year, and coincide with the full moons that people can see. For that one needs very accurate values for the length of the year and of the month, and a system of intercalating lunar and solar cycles. That is where the astronomical sciences come in.

The Astral Sciences in India and China

Both India and China had long-standing astronomical traditions. The differences between them follow the more general pattern: in China the state controlled the practice of astronomy centrally; in India there were several traditions spread around the subcontinent, in conversation with one another, following the same general model of science.

In India, *jyotisha* had, in its traditional enumeration, three subdivisions: positional astronomy, astrology, and divination. Mathematics came under astronomy and developed primarily to serve it, as is evident from the strength of its geometric, trigonometric, and algorithmic components. These sciences were used primarily for two purposes: calendar keeping, that is, determining the timing of seasons, the dates of festivals, and so on, and astrology and divination.

For much of its history, the practitioner of *jyotisha* had a lower status among scientific occupations. Nevertheless, *jyotisha* pundits were an indispensable presence at court. In the countryside, there was a calculator in almost every village, for the lunar day of the Indian calendar was determined by the moment of sunrise and was therefore variable by longitude and latitude. In the premodern era, one needed an expert on the spot. Astrologers in small towns and villages could also support themselves by private consultations and by performing ritual pacifications of a client's angry planets. For this reason, an unusually large number of texts for end users survive for this science: tables, almanacs, and other ready-calculation works that enable a local astronomer to calculate the position of the planets for a local position without having to start from scratch.

The plurality of Indian intellectual activity in general is reflected in the multiplicity of Indian astronomical systems (*paksha*). Varahamihira, the eminent Indian astronomer and astrologer of the sixth century, knew of five schools of thought that preceded him. Later there were five other ones, all with a pan-regional reach, each prominent in a different area. The main three that survived into the early modern era were connected with the creator god, Brahma; with the sun god, Surya; and with the brilliant south Indian astronomer of the fifth century, Aryabhata. These systems use different parameters and algorithms and posit different geometric models, different values for the sine, and so on. The outcome of all this variety was that there were always different dating systems available, different epoch dates, and rival predictions of the moment of eclipses, of the correct date for religious festivals, and so on. As a result, across the continent even today, there are different traditional calendars current, and calendar makers working in different traditions can decide that a major festival like Diwali (the festival of lights that takes place on a new moon in mid-autumn) should be celebrated on different days, or even in different months.

In China, astronomy and the calendar system had been a major feature of political statecraft since the ancient Zhou dynasty (1145–221 BCE). The state declared a monopoly on the subjects. Classical scholars living during the Han dynasties (206 BCE–220 CE), who drew on the canonical Five Classics associated with Confucius (551–479 BCE), upheld this proprietary attitude. The exact sciences were thereby closely linked to the classical texts known as the "Canon of Mathematics," which closely imitated the "Medical Classics" as a state product and as the ruler's prerogative. The classics in mathematics comprised problem-solving techniques based on arithmetic, geometry, algebra, trigonometry, and measurement principles. During the Tang and Song, mathematics was included in the civil examinations.

In the era of the Song and later of the Yuan dynasties, astronomy and the accuracy of the Chinese calendar were brought to an unprecedented level through mathematics. To the long-standing "Ten Mathematical Classics" combining arithmetic, geometry, and algebra (compiled in the seventh century) were added the new, seminal works of Qin Jiushao (1202–1261) on polynomial algebra and other topics, as well as Li Ye's (1192–1279) solving of polynomial equations of one variable in his *Sea Mirror of Circle Measurements* (*Ceyuan haijing*). They heralded a new direction for solving differential equations to several unknowns and to several powers.

Although many of these seminal Chinese works were wrongly presumed lost by the middle of the Ming dynasty, Qin's and Li's likely reliance on the introduction of Islamic algebra in China in the thirteenth century, as in contemporary Europe, had apparently made possible a Song–Yuan breakthrough in the calendrical computation deployed circa 1280 under the Mongols.

Observatories

The story of knowledge transfer to be told here is about a style of science developed by an Arab astronomer in the employ of the pagan Mongol Hulagu Khan (1218–1265, r. 1256–65), ruler of the Ilkhanate kingdom

(1256–1335), which stretched from Syria to present-day western Pakistan. Hulagu, the grandson of Chinggis Khan, is best known for the conquest, at the head of a huge Mongol army, of Baghdad and of Syria. It is said that Hulagu relied on astrologers in his military planning. Most notable among them was the celebrated Arab polymath Nasir ud Din al-Tusi (1201–1274). Al-Tusi ingratiated himself sufficiently with Hulagu to persuade him that he needed improved planetary tables, that is, tables showing the position of each planet at set intervals of time, together with values for the planet's daily speed.

Tables were the means by which al-Tusi predicted the positions of the planets relative to the fixed stars, on the basis of which he could cast horoscopes. Faulty predictions, he claimed, were due to faulty knowledge of planetary positions. Faulty knowledge of planetary positions was due in turn to relying on the inherited astronomical literature. Improvement required building an observatory and assembling a team of specialists to work at it. So began what would become a model for state-supported "big science" for kingdoms in central, western, and southern Asia for some time to come—a large, team-driven, long-term astronomy project.

Put in charge, al-Tusi brought together a team of specialists at Maragha, in western Azerbaijan, today in Iran. The specialists were mostly experts in Arabic and Persian sciences and drawn from different regions of the Arab world. But there were other scientific traditions and regions represented, among them China's. Al-Tusi assembled a library of scientific works drawn from different traditions, including the Greek and Indian works already known to Arab scientists. He promoted translations of texts from other traditions into Arabic and Persian, fostered the synthesis of scientific ideas, created innovations in geometric representations and in other mathematical techniques, and most important, oversaw the construction of the Maragha observatory in 1259 CE. This included handheld observational devices as well as large masonry instruments.

The advantages of a masonry observatory, in theory, lie in two things: first, its fixity allows for the accumulation of observations made in the same spot with the same instrument. A long-term science project depends on just such data. The one in Maragha lasted for nearly sixty years, continuing after al-Tusi and Hulagu were both gone. Second, there was thought to be an advantage in largeness, in that one could make finer calibrations on the larger measurement field and read off the position of a shadow or sighting that much more precisely.

The Hulagu–Tusi model for a big scientific project—an observatory, an international team of experts, a motivation to revise existing parameters and algorithms—represented the culmination of several developments in Islamic science. The most significant was the very idea of a unified approach, in which observations and theory creation were integrated into an ongoing program. The earlier astronomical science of the Greeks and Indians did use observational evidence, but more as a form of verification. This coordinated approach to science was emulated by subsequent rulers in Inner Asia and spilled out into other regions. Al-Tusi also pioneered a new mathematics of planetary theory that supplanted Ptolemy's. His new mathematics and the principles behind it reached Copernicus and informed his development of a heliocentric (sun-centered) planetary theory.

All of this astronomical activity culminated in the creation of an astronomical treatise named after Hulagu, the *Zij Il-Khani*, or the "astronomical handbook of the subordinate Khan" (i.e., the Viceroy, a title of Hulagu). The *zij* was the primary form of authoritative astronomical publication in the Persian-Arabic scientific world, and had been so even before Hulagu and al-Tusi. The *zij* contained everything an astronomer or astrologer needed to determine the position of the stars, sun, moon, and planets at any moment, including the time of their appearances or disappearances and of their conjunctions or eclipses, without the need for observing the heavens.

The *Zij Il-Khani* included instructions for converting dates between six different eras and calendars: the Muslim Hijra (purely lunar), the Persian Yazdigird (purely solar), the Seleucid (Hellenistic), the Jewish (lunar-solar), the Maliki (purely solar), and the Chinese Uighur calendars. The *Zij Il-Khani* made some use of the tables of earlier *zij*s, but incorporated the Maragha observations, most obviously in its table of 60 stars and table of 245 geographic locations.

The big science model of Hulagu's observatory had different destinies in India and China. Khubilai Khan (r. 1260–94), Hulagu's brother, expanded the Yuan dynasty to south China in 1271, becoming emperor of all of China in 1280 from his capital in Beijing. There Khubilai picked Hulagu's model up immediately; it formed part of the same dynastic vision of the role of the state. He reconfigured the Chinese Astronomy Bureau, which had been part of the bureaucracy of the Chinese emperors since the Han period a thousand years earlier, and commissioned the construction of an observatory at Beijing. The Mongol Bureau had four departments: astrological interpretations, timekeeping, Islamic methods, and mathematical astronomy. The personnel of the Islamic department were segregated from the literati astronomers. The Islamic department, the innovation of Khubilai, reckoned time and calculated planetary positions using the Persian-Arabic scientific system. This became the preferred system during the Yuan era in China and into the Ming period as well.

The astronomers in Beijing were in close contact with their counterparts in Maragha. The Chinese dynastic histories record the appearance in 1267 in Khubilai's court of a visitor whom they refer to as Zha-ma-lu-ding. This was the Persian astronomer Jamal ud-Din (fl. thirteenth century). He had come from Maragha, bringing a number of instruments, most of which had parallels in the handheld instruments that were in use at the observatory there. The astronomical instruments that Jamal al-Din described at the Yuan capital were the most advanced of their time. There were state-of-the-art versions of an armillary sphere, of a parallactic ruler, of sundials for equal hours and unequal hours, of a terrestrial globe offering a map of the known world, of a celestial sphere that constituted a star chart, and of an astrolabe. The arrival of these instruments influenced the design of Guo Shoujing's (1231–1316) "simplified instrument" (*jianyi*) (a cross between an armillary sphere and an astrolabe) and of his large masonry gnomon towers, built at the bureau in Beijing.

The chief outcome of Khubilai's new, internationalized astronomy department was the creation and promulgation of a new calendar in 1280, the Yuan dynasty's Season-Granting Calendar (*Shoushou li*). The new calendar followed soon after the *Zij Il-Khani* and is structurally parallel to it. It represented a Chinese-Indian-Islamic synthesis under the greater Pax Mongolica. The Mongols were still not Muslim at this point, so it was a matter not of importing "their own" science into China but of creating an amalgam of the sciences that they had encountered in the expansion of their realm.

Meanwhile, Ulugh Beg (r. 1411–49), a grandson of Timur, played a pivotal role in the transmission to India of Il Khanid theory and practice. Ulugh Beg was a governor of the Timurid Empire (1370–1507) in its old capital, Samarkand (in modern-day Uzbekistan). He founded a college there and followed the model of Hulagu in mounting a big astronomy project, again in hopes of producing better astronomical tables. He assembled an international team of experts and accumulated a library, which included copies of many of al-Tusi's works, among them the *Zij Il Khani*.

He fostered translations and constructed a large masonry observatory in 1420. The result in 1441 was the "New Zij of the Sultan," the *Zij Jadid Sultani*, which included a famously good table of 994 star positions.

The *Zij* survives in many copies, in Turkish, Arabic, and Persian, and may have been the most widely used of all *zijs*. Among the celebrated Arabic astronomers who worked on it for Ulugh Beg were Ali Qushji (1403–1474), the natural scientist, and Jamshid Ghiyas ud Din al-Kashi (1380–1429), the astronomer and polymath. Al-Kashi was the principal medium of intellectual connection with the Maragha observatory. Before Ulugh Beg's team completed the *Zij Jadid Sultani*, he produced his own work, the *Khaqani Zij*, which was based on but aimed to correct problems in al-Tusi's *Zij Il Khani*.

Debate Over the Late Ming Calendar

Reforms associated with the Yuan calendar introduced many innovations. For instance, the Season-Granting astronomy system applied new computational techniques of a trigonometric nature to convert the equatorial coordinates observed on the celestial sphere into numerical equations solvable by artisans deploying counting rods (*chousuan*). The compilers of the new calendar also recognized the computational differences in the procedures for positioning lunar and solar movements. This led to a gradual understanding of the conditions in which eclipses took place. The success of the new Season-Granting calendar in predicting celestial events eventually led to complacency in the Astronomy Bureau, however. The civil service examinations were cut back; literati lineages were sidelined and went into other professions; and the Mongol rulers brought in outsiders to serve as their middle-level bureaucrats.

When the Ming dynasty came to power in 1368, they carried on the Yuan dynasty's Season Granting astronomical system, updating it and renaming it the Grand Concordance Calendar (*Datong li*) in 1371 in order to make it their own. But civil servants with Confucian classical learning were now rare in the highest levels of government. Initially the Ming maintained the organization of the Astronomy Bureau that the Yuan had instituted, but the Islamic office was eliminated in 1398, though Muslim personnel were absorbed into the overall bureau to provide an Islamic calendar for the millions of Muslims in China, many of whom had served the Yuan dynasty.

As early as 1465, Ming officials recognized that their calendar was falling behind and that the work coming out of the Astronomy Bureau was prone to unacceptable errors. Inertia prevailed until the late Ming, however, because the Yuan–Ming calendar had achieved unprecedented success. Nevertheless, the 1280 calendar's parameters had small discrepancies, which accumulated over a long period. Its value for the mean duration of a lunar month, for example, was 29.53086 days. The modern value is 29.53059. This difference, albeit tiny, would after 310 years add up to an error of a full day. Discussions ensued. Some called for new personnel and better management of the bureau's offices, but not for reform of the calendrical system, which was considered unnecessary. The scientists in this period appear to have lost track of the idea of the coordinated and ongoing program of theory and practice instituted at Maragha.

In 1478, the Astronomy Bureau staff acknowledged in a memorial that its observational instruments were out of date. Minor errors in computation were explained away because the bureau's predictions were still sufficiently accurate. A series of inaccurate predictions in 1517–18, however, exposed the bureau to criticism for underpredicting solar eclipses, an ominous sign for the dynasty. The winter alignment of the five visible planets that was observable in 1524, while an auspicious event, further raised concern about the accuracy of the bureau's predictions. The straw that broke the camel's back came in 1592 when the Ministry of Rites charged that the Astronomy Bureau had erred by a full day when predicting a lunar eclipse, which meant that the Relief Ceremony congratulating the emperor for his cosmic virtue had to be rescheduled. An error of a full day also affected ceremonies tied to the first day of the month, season, and the New Year.

In 1596, Wang Honghui (1542–1601?), a scholar-official at the Ministry of Rites, broached to a Jesuit missionary based in the southern capital of Nanjing, Matteo Ricci (1552–1610), the possibility that he might contribute to calendar reform discussions. Several of the Jesuits who arrived in China in the 1580s had studied in Rome when major calendrical problems bedeviled the Church in Europe, especially the controversy over the calculation of the date for Easter. Pope Gregory XIII (1502–1585) appointed the German Jesuit Christoph Clavius (1538–1612), a leading mathematician and churchman, to the Gregorian reform commission. With the promulgation of the Gregorian calendar in 1582, the Church achieved a reliable method for determining the proper date for Easter. Astronomers such as Clavius were already aware of Copernicus's (1473–1543) sun-centered (heliocentric) challenge to the earth-centered (geocentric) model of the solar system but were wary of using it. The papal furor over Galileo in 1616 would directly affect the Jesuits' role as transmitters of European astronomy to Ming and Qing China.

Jesuits such as Clavius were insiders in the Gregorian reforms, whereas Jesuit missionaries were always outsiders in Ming China, opposed by native Chinese in the Ming bureaucracy and by the Muslim staff in the Astronomy Bureau. Clavius's followers and, later, the students of Tycho Brahe (1546–1601) and Johannes Kepler (1571–1630) could understand why an accurate and up-to-date calendar mattered to the Ming and Qing state. More importantly, Ricci, Adam Schall (1591–1666), and Ferdinand Verbiest (1623–1688) understood the important role the new Christian calendar played in unifying the faith in early modern Europe.

In the 1630s, the government's willingness to recruit new talent for the bureau opened the door for the Ming and Qing dynasties to accept Jesuits as calendrical experts, just as earlier rulers had accepted Indians, Persians, and Muslim specialists. To gain support for the missionary enterprise, the later Jesuits followed Ricci's lead and presented themselves as specialists in mathematical astronomy. At first, Jesuit astronomy represented the last stage of the Ptolemaic system. It was replaced in the 1630s by the earth- and sun-centered (geoheliocentric) system devised by Tycho Brahe at the end of the sixteenth century in which the planets revolved around the sun, while the sun revolved around the earth. In the face of the Copernican challenge, this development represented a compromise position beyond Ptolemy's increasingly discredited geocentrism, but one not yet acknowledging Copernican heliocentrism.

The Tychonic age in the Astronomy Bureau meant that Chinese specialists by the 1630s had available to them a rich new toolkit of computational techniques, more accurate observations, a new view of the cosmos, and the latest precision instruments that went beyond those available to the Gregorian reformers in Europe a generation earlier. In addition, the Jesuits introduced trigonometric tables and translated the Englishman Henry Briggs's (1556–1630) *Arithmetica Logarithmica*, which was published in Chinese in 1624. Nikolaus Smogulecki (1611–1656) and his collaborator Xue Fengzuo (1600–1680) introduced trigonometric logarithms in the early Qing. In an astronomical work, circa 1656, which pioneered spherical trigonometry and logarithms in China, Smogolenski introduced the latest European method for calculating eclipses. The use of both arithmetical and

Figure 6.1 Ferdinand Verbiest's 1699 Silver Armillary Sphere in the Jesuits' Beijing Observatory. Woodblock print

trigonometric logarithms enhanced the ease of astronomical calculations. Acceptance of a portion of European *scientia* was possible in Ming and Qing China because Chinese literati themselves had long-standing and commensurable interests in natural phenomena, which had undergone a significant revival in the sixteenth century.

The Mughals and the Calendar

Many things changed in India with the advent of the Mughal dynasty, which had extended its sway over most of the subcontinent by the beginning of the seventeenth century. Descendants of Timur and Chinggis Khan, the early emperors (Babur, Humayun, and Akbar) all consulted astrologers and made use of *zij* science to maintain their calendars. Akbar had the *Zij Jadid Sultani,* compiled in 1441 under Ulugh Beg, recast so that its epoch date coincided with his ascension to the throne. Persian-Arabic astronomy was the official system for creating calendars in the court throughout the Mughal period, but the emperors began to involve the *jyotisha* pundits as well. Outside the court, the rest of society continued to use the variety of traditional Indian calendric methods.

The first of the four Great Mughal emperors, Akbar (1542–1605), is best remembered for his cultural politics of "soft power." Akbar's strategy was to Indianize the dynasty by fostering a courtly atmosphere of cultural blending. The emperor and other high nobles of the court intermarried with Hindu princely families and fostered in their courts and salons blended forms of art, architecture, music, poetry, and science. There were Hindu and Jain Indian artists, scholars, and scientists at court, as guests or as retainers. Akbar took advice from astronomer-astrologers, both specialists in Arabic-Persian astral sciences and specialists in Sanskritic astral sciences. They were consulted especially for the casting of birth horoscopes and for recommendations of moments that would be propitious for undertakings.

The Jesuits were invited to Akbar's court, but not to discuss astronomy. Akbar wished to include them in a religious dialogue that he promoted at his court among representatives of the various religions of India. The idea of using astronomy as an entrée to the court was either not contemplated by the Jesuits, or if tried, was unsuccessful. The Jesuit reliance on astronomy for proselytization was unique to China.

Shah Jahan (1592–1666), Akbar's grandson, continued the cultural policy of engagement with Indian arts and learning, and during his reign a number of the dialogues set in motion by Akbar reached their culmination. The city of Hindu pilgrimage, Banaras, returned to its dominant status as the seat of Brahmanical learning for most of the subcontinent, after periods during which its main temples had been demolished and its learned community scattered. With the revival of Banaras as the preeminent site of learning, the traffic of specialists between the city and Delhi resumed, through which many pundits become regulars at the Mughal court. Like Akbar before him, Shah Jahan gave titles and honors to leading pundits of the city, calling them "chief pundit" or "preceptor of the world," and so on.

An example of this special engagement can be found in the creation of Shah Jahan's *zij*, the *Zij Shah Jahan*. In 1629, one of Shah Jahan's relatives and courtiers commissioned a pundit, Nityananda, to translate the *Zij Shah Jahan* into Sanskrit, in the hope of promulgating it among the Sanskritic scientists. Nityananda produced the *Siddhanta-sindhu*, the "ocean (*sindhu*) of astronomical treatises (*siddhanta*)," in the 1630s. In 1639 Nityānanda completed another Sanskritic treatise, the *Siddhanta-sarva-raja*, the "emperor among treatises." This later work offered an argument for the appropriation of the astronomy of the Persian-Arabic astronomers, the *yavana*s, and freely incorporated elements of their astronomical system.

Nityananda's work was part of a more general tendency among *jyotisha* experts of the period, expressed in impulses toward revision, restoration, and, in some places, rethinking the foundations of the science. The presence of the *yavana* sciences, though not necessarily their specific content, drove this tendency to a considerable extent. Not every pundit was interested in the Islamic alternative, but many were aware of it, and more than a few authors discussed its challenge explicitly. Both newness of thinking and the resistance to it were expressions of the energies awakened in early modern India.

In the astral sciences, some pundits like Nityananda explicitly described and discussed features of the *yavanas*' astronomy and astrology. Other *jyotisha*s adapted the *yavanas*' science less noisily. Kamalakara, a *jyotisha* pundit in Benares in the seventeenth century, made use of Ulugh Beg's geographical coordinates for a number of cities, including Kabul and Samarkand, when compiling a list of longitudes and latitudes. He also mentioned Ulugh Beg's values for the table of sines. Among the writings of the astronomers in the Kerala school, beginning with Parameshwara in the late fourteenth century, the most far-reaching reflection on Brahmanical astronomy appears. The *jyotisha*s in the Kerala school are also famous for proposing a radical rethinking of planetary theory, particularly stressing the coordination of theory and practice.

Not until the opening decades of the eighteenth century did an Indian ruler undertake a state astronomical project in the spirit of, and on the scale of, the projects at Maragha and at Samarkand. It required an exceptional ruler to do so. Jaisingh II (r. 1699–1743), the Hindu Maharaja of Amber, had as a boy received the sobriquet *sawai* from the Mughal emperor, Aurangzeb. Aurangzeb gave him this byname, which means "one and a quarter," on the spur of the moment, finding the young Jaisingh that much more clever than anyone else.

The Mughal rulers who succeeded Aurangzeb did not wield the same power from the center that the Great Mughals had. Although there was still a Mughal ruler on the throne—Muhammad Shah, the great-grandson of Aurangzeb—by the 1720s, Jaisingh had emerged as one of the dominant figures in the empire. Thus when Jaisingh undertook to create the *zij* for the Mughal emperor, the *Zij Muhammad Shahi*, he was making a political statement, as had his Mongol and Manchu contemporaries in China.

Jaisingh had a lifelong passion for astronomy, both Brahmanical and Islamicate. When he set about creating a new *zij* in the early 1720s, therefore, he wanted to make a thorough job of it, and to base it on observed planetary positions. For this purpose he brought together a team of experts in the different versions of astronomy, just as Hulagu and Ulugh Beg had done. He assembled a library of scientific books and manuscripts, most of which remain in the palace of the planned city that he built, which was called Jaipur after him. Jaisingh commissioned translations into Sanskrit of al-Tusi's versions of Greek mathematical and astronomical works: Ptolemy's *Almagest*, Euclid's *Elements*, and Theodosius's *Spherics*. He had copies of the *zij* works that had been produced in Maragha, Samarkand, and Delhi. While the development of his knowledge base went on, Jaisingh commissioned the construction of masonry observatories in five cities, among them Jaipur, his own capital, and Delhi, the capital of the Mughal ruler. The observatory in Jaipur was the largest, and the one that Jaisingh used to best effect. It was made up of sixteen different masonry instruments, the largest standing nearly twenty-three yards high.

Jaisingh brought in European astronomy and mathematics through the involvement of the Jesuits, some 150 years after their successes in Beijing. Portuguese Jesuits from Agra who visited Jaisingh in 1727 were guided by

Figure 6.2 Masonry observatory built by Sawai Jaisingh II in Delhi in the early eighteenth century.
Photograph by Lala Deen Dayal, 1880

his obvious interests and informed him about progress in European astronomy and mathematics. Soon after, Jaisingh sent an expedition to Portugal, led by the Jesuit Manuel Figuereido, with instructions to bring back European astronomical instruments and books, together with some astronomers. The expedition returned in 1730 with books, especially the *Astronomical Tables* (*Tabulae Astronomicae*) of the French scientist Phillippe de la Hire. They also brought a non-Jesuit astronomer called Pedro da Silva. Jaisingh ordered a Sanskrit translation of the *Tables*.

The resultant translation in versified Sanskrit was a botched job, unfortunately but not surprisingly, since Indian astronomers at that time did not use logarithms, upon which de la Hire's tables were based. Logarithms were barely a hundred years old in Europe, though already influential in Ming China because of the presence of Jesuits with mathematical talents there. Da Silva did not understand them either, apparently, for he appears to have been unable to give the pundit translator, Kevalarama, any help with them.

Accordingly Jaisingh wrote to the Jesuits on the other side of the country, in the French outpost of Chandranagar in Bengal, asking them questions about de la Hire's *Tables*. The communication with the Chandranagar Jesuits seems to have improved the understanding of de la Hire at the Jaipur institute. A fresh, more accurate prose translation of the *Tables* into Sanskrit was generated. This gave better results. The tables for the sun, moon, and planets that were published in the *Zij Muhammad Shahi* in the later 1730s were influenced by de la Hire's tables, as these were adapted and verified at the observatory.

Although de la Hire does not say so in his text, his diagrams make clear that he based his calculations on the heliocentric model of the universe popularized by Galileo, and this was understood by the pundits in Jaisingh's court. Thus European science made its entrance via the Jesuits only at this late date. But the science that emerged at Jaipur was distinctive for its integrated and blended form. Jaisingh aimed at a single science, produced from a fresh observational program and the accumulated knowledge of three distinct traditions. Throughout his project Jaisingh worked primarily in the idiom of Sanskrit. In this way, he brought the *jyotisha* experts into the mainstream of thought in his institute, while radically revising their thinking. The interesting possibility of scientific creativity through blending that arose in Jaisingh's institute was not continued on the same scale or with the same success afterward, probably because of political upheavals in Jaisingh's kingdom after his death and in India more generally.

Denouement: The English and Science in India

Later the tables turned, when the educational policy of the British made European science standard in the school curriculum. British science, as made available in public lectures in Calcutta by Newtonians such as James Dinwiddie, attracted greater interest in India than it did in China, at least until the 1840s.

In 1793 Britain sent its first diplomatic mission to China, turning its attention eastward after the loss of its American colonies. The much ballyhooed Macartney Mission was led by George Macartney (1737–1806), who famously touted Britain's colonial power by saying that the British Empire was one on which "the sun never sets." When the mission ended in 1794, the ship's Scottish mechanic and astronomer, James Dinwiddie (1746–1815), was sent to the hub of British power and trade in India, Calcutta, with samples of tea and other Chinese plants. Dinwiddie also took some of his technical "toys" along to Calcutta, where he taught for over a decade at Fort William College, the British East India Company's academy.

In Calcutta, Dinwiddie achieved a lucrative career as a mathematics teacher and astronomy lecturer. He returned to England in 1806 after having made a good living teaching "public science" to British traders, British East India Company officials, artists, women, and contemporary Indian elites by presenting the essentials for a unified understanding of Newtonian mechanics. This turn toward British engineering and careers in experimentation and manufactures represented a movement away from traditional artisanship in India.

In this the destinies of India and China began to follow different trajectories. Mughal India increasingly became an English satellite and the economic foundation for the British Empire. China under the Manchus, however, maintained an orbit beyond the control of London until the Opium War (1839–42) resulted in the establishment of treaty ports that overwhelmed China's international trading network.

Comparative Points

What comparisons can we draw from our discussion of astronomy and the calendar in early modern China vis-à-vis India? The centralized bureaucratic control of the calendar-making system in imperial China led to different results compared with the dispersed arrangements in India. A clear and unified calendrical system served to legitimate the Chinese goal to unify the realm with the cosmos, a goal the decentralized northern and southern India polities did not share. The Mughals certainly had a state calendar, their *zij* calendar, but it included sections on how to convert to other calendars in the realm. The Chinese simply allowed for separate calendar offices in their main bureau.

Over time both sides tended to deal with the content of their astronomical sciences differently, dividing up or unifying knowledge according to their social, political, economic, and religious idiosyncrasies. Such forms of segregation among the strands of science, or their amalgamation, tell us the extent to which developments out in the countryside were following—or not—what was happening at the center. China and India reveal both tendencies at work, but the dynamics at play in each operated differently according to the dictates of time and space, and according to political locations in the center or at the periphery of the space-time continuum.

There were differences between East and South Asia in their moments of relative "openness" versus "closed-mindedness" toward the outside. Long before the Pax Mongolica, India had been a part of the shared story of the sciences in Asia, while China was more involved mainly during the Mongol era, when the Indian *jyotisha* pundits were only sporadically involved. In the era of European expansion and the coming of the Jesuits, moreover, the Chinese were relatively more open to the Jesuit outsiders in their midst, while the Indians under the Mughals were less interested in, perhaps even uninformed about, the new knowledge systems associated with early modern Europe.

A final question arises from this comparative history, about the selective nature of connectedness. Why was astronomical and calendric science so amenable to transfer? Though obviously foreign and understood as such, it was nevertheless introduced into the scientific establishment of both imperial capitals at Delhi and Beijing, while other sciences were not. The philology of canonical texts, for example, the technical art of verifying the authenticity and accuracy of classic works, was a discipline that evolved in both literate cultures. Philology came to have enormous political significance in securing royal claims to authority, but it did not travel between India and China, neither directly nor through intermediaries in some larger network. Is there something about astronomy and the exact sciences, wherever practiced, that is special, perhaps in being detachable from its context in a way that other sciences are not, or in being reality convergent, while other sciences, like textual criticism, can only be internally coherent?

Or could it have had to do with earlier connections? Indian *jyotisha* had a shared pedigree with astral sciences in western Asia and the Mediterranean, participating in the adaptation and re-exportation of Babylonian and Greco-Babylonian science. Features of Indian astronomy and mathematics had been taken up and spread into the Islamic world from the middle of the first millennium. Thus the Islamic science that came into India in the period of the Delhi Sultanate was a familiar form, a visiting wealthy cousin, with an entrée at court that the *jyotisha* science had lost. China, meanwhile, had developed more independently up to the moment of the Yuan. Yet that explanation would seem to run counter to the history. One might have expected the Indians, confronted with an entirely recognizable rival, to have seized on Islamic science wholesale, carefully evaluating it for any apparent improvements. This happened only much later. The initial reaction was more inactive, a frosty silence. Perhaps the novelty fascinated the Chinese more. Already in the eleventh century the Arab astronomer Al-Biruni had castigated the Indian astronomers for their complacency.

Yet these explanations overlook the political arrangements that seem to be involved in the different treatments of different sciences. Subjects that interested the state, fed into its model of state authority, and were promoted by competitor states elsewhere did well at moving; others that weren't did not. In any case, a successful transfer requires preexisting common ground. The new transplant requires some basis in which it can take root, some past scientific activity that makes the new arrival at least partly comprehensible, and some political support that drives an interest in finding better answers to questions that were already being asked. And the global visibility of celestial events, such as solar eclipses, made it impossible for the Chinese or Indian empires to falsify and thereby finesse their knowledge of the heavens from day into night, or vice versa.

Conclusion

Although this chapter includes familiar terminology, it does not suppose that the Indian and Chinese disciplines map neatly onto their European equivalents, or onto each other. Nor have we spoken here of all the arts, sciences, skills, and techniques that were cultivated and used in India and China. We have not been able to do justice even to the disciplines of the elites, much less to other systems of knowledge, of which there were many. Yet the scientific disciplines of India and China, and the social settings that supported them, can be usefully compared in many ways. After all, their history is not entirely separate. There were episodes when India and China were in scientific contact, and episodes when they participated in a much larger zone of exchange.

As early as the seventh century, Chinese monks made their way to India in the hope of finding records of more of the Buddha's teachings. They took back with them other, non-Buddhist forms of knowledge as well. Indians learned from their neighbors to the west, the *yavana*s, a term that at different times has referred to Scythians, Persians, Hellenes, and Afghans. In turn, the two countries exported knowledge, to Japan and Korea in the east and to Inner Asia, Iran, and Mesopotamia. That is only the local story. Systems of knowledge, and the technical languages in which to communicate them, have flowed across Eurasia since at least the days of the Achaemenid Empire (550–330 BCE). Sciences traveled in the aftermath of conquests by horsemen from the Inner Asian steppes, who were led by such warlords as Chinggis Khan and Timur. There were flows in the early modern world of trade that linked Europe with Asia by both sea and land, when Jesuits first arrived in the East circa 1550. This trading world gave way by 1800 to new European empires in Asia and culminated with the establishment of English-medium education in India, Burma, Ceylon, and Hong Kong.

While India and China had many comparable developments in their sciences, their political institutions and social organizations supported the sciences in different ways. This had a telling effect on their respective destinies. For the calendrical sciences, for example, political plurality in India fostered scientific variety, which presented rival states with competing cosmologies and an array of different calendars. In contrast, China's singular state monopoly of the imperial calendar ensured radical uniformity—in both accuracy and error. Over the centuries, the responses of experts in these two scientific cultures to the influx of new knowledge varied, both in their preferences—what sort of knowledge interested them—and in their timing—at what moments they were more open to knowledge from outside.

In each society, furthermore, there were different reactions: some scholars complacently ignored the new European knowledge while others eagerly adopted it. Some, deeply suspicious, actively rejected the outsider's science, while others judiciously, and sometimes undetectably, absorbed it. In the early modern period (roughly 1350 to 1750), the introduction of outside sciences reached new heights in both China and India, and long-distance contact troubled local waters. There were too many expectations of the European embassies in Asia for them to bear the weighty political responsibilities assigned to them. Astronomical tricks and tokens of mechanical exchange, accompanied by technicians to set up and maintain the science displays, proved to hardly overawe the Manchu court, for example, due to the incommensurability of the meaning of the gift exchanges for the two sides. But the seventeenth and eighteenth centuries have been considered not just as a late imperial prelude to the end of traditional China and India but also as a harbinger of things to come.

Earlier scholars have been so determined to explain why modern science, technology, and medicine arrived late in China and India that until recently the "Needham Question"—Why did a divided Europe, and not imperial China or Mughal India, develop modern science first?—dominated thinking on the subject. This overly determined "failure question" has been paralleled by scholarly efforts in other fields to explain why neither India nor China developed capitalism, modern industry, or democracy before Europe did. We are now entering a new era that explores early modern science in East Asia and South Asia in more active rather than simply receptive terms. By problematizing the narrative of the "rise of the West" circa 1500–1800, we can begin to see things in Asia regionally, as they developed from the inside.

China and India's role in the early modern world's globalism has been forgotten, replaced with an illusory, self-justifying hindsight. Such hindsight has frayed recently. It no longer has much traction, if for no other reason than that the vast majority of engineers and scientists trained in the twenty-first century, whether at home or abroad, are Chinese and Indians.

For Further Reading

China

Elman, Benjamin. *A Cultural History of Modern Science in China*. Cambridge, MA: Harvard University Press, 2006.

Frumer, Yulia. *Making Time: Astronomical Time Measurement in Tokugawa Japan*. Chicago: University of Chicago Press, 2018.

Hart, Roger. *Imagined Civilizations: China, the West, and Their First Encounter*. Baltimore, MD: Johns Hopkins University Press, 2013.

Hashimoto, Keizō. *Hsü Kuang-ch'i and Astronomical Reform*. Osaka: Kansai University Press, 1988.

Jenko, Leigh. *Changing Referents: Learning Across Space and Time in China and the West*. Oxford: Oxford University Press, 2015.

Needham, Joseph, et al. *Science and Civilization in China*. Cambridge: Cambridge University Press, 1957.

Peterson, Willard. "Western Natural Philosophy Published in Late Ming China." *Proceedings of the American Philosophical Society* 117, no. 4 (August 1973): 295–322.

Pomeranz, Kenneth. *The Great Divergence: China, Europe, and the Making of the Modern World Economy*. Princeton, NJ: Princeton University Press, 2000.

India

Hartner, Willy. "The Astronomical Instruments of Cha-ma-lu-ting, Their Identification, and Their Relations to the Instruments of the Observatory of Maragha." *Isis* 41, no. 2 (1950): 184–94.

Lightman, Bernard, et al., eds. *The Circulation of Knowledge Between Britain, India, and China: The Early-Modern World to the Twentieth Century*. Leiden; Boston: E. J. Brill, 2013.

Minkowski, Christopher. "Learned Brahmins and the Mughal Court: The Jyotiṣas." In *Religious Interactions in Mughal India*, ed. Vasudha Dalmia and Munis Faruqui, 102–34. New Delhi: Oxford University Press, 2014.

O'Hanlon, Rosalind. "Contested Conjunctures: Brahman Communities and 'Early Modernity' in India." *The American Historical Review* 118, no. 3 (2013): 765–87.

Pankeneir, David. "Planetary Portent of 1524 in China and Europe." *Journal of World History* 20, no. 3 (September 2009): 339–75.

Pingree, David. "An Astronomer's Progress." *Proceedings of the American Philosophical Society* 143, no. 1 (1999): 73–85.

Plofker, Kim. *Mathematics in India*. Princeton, NJ; Oxford: Princeton University Press, 2009.

Pollock, Sheldon. *The Language of the Gods in the World of Men: Sanskrit, Culture, and Power in Premodern India*. Berkeley; London: University of California Press, 2006.

Schaffer, Simon. "The Asiatic Enlightenment of British Astronomy." In *The Brokered World: Go-Betweens and Global Intelligence*, ed. Simon Schaffer et al., 49–104. Sagamore Beach, MA: Science History Publications, 2009.

Sharma, Virendra Nath. *Sawai Jai Singh and His Astronomy.* Delhi: Motilal Banarsidass, 1995.

Other

Daston, Lorraine, and Glenn Most. "History of Science and History of Philologies." *Isis* 106, no. 2 (2015): 378–390.

CHAPTER VII

Pilgrims in Search of Religion

ZVI BEN-DOR BENITE AND RICHARD H. DAVIS

In 629 CE the young Chinese Buddhist pilgrim Xuanzang set out from the Tang capital city of Chang'an (modern Xi'an), traveling westward in hopes of reaching India, the ancient birthplace of his faith. He hoped to recover a superior form of Buddhism in its place of origin, to help reform the Buddhism of China. After following the Silk Road, he headed south through the Hindu Kush Mountains and into India. Along the Ganges River plains he was able to see for himself the great sites of the Buddha's life and lore, like Sarnath, Bodh Gaya, Rajagriha, and Kushinagara. He visited and studied at the greatest centers of Buddhist learning, and he stayed for several years at the university-like Nalanda monastery, said to be home to ten thousand monks. Later he went south as well, through the Deccan as far as Kanchipuram in Tamilnad. Throughout his travels the monk was an acute observer of geography, social mores, and especially religious traditions and institutions, both Buddhist and otherwise. After sixteen years he returned to China in 645, laden with Buddhist manuscripts and relics, and received a hero's welcome in Chang'an. The Tang emperor persuaded Xuanzang to record his observations in a detailed travelogue, the *Da Tang xiyuji* (*Record of Western Realms*) (646), which continues to serve as a significant primary source for the history of early South Asia. The "pilgrimage to India" became a potent motif in the Chinese imagination. The geographical barriers between China and India were a major hindrance limiting commercial and political relations between the two. Therefore, to a greater extent religion, broadly defined, is the main characteristic of the exchanges between China and India before the mid-nineteenth century.

In the early seventeenth century, another peripatetic observer explored the diversity of South Asian religions and completed his account, the *Dabestan-e Madaheb* (*School of Religious Doctrines*), in 1655. The writer, whom historians now identify tentatively as Maubad Zulfiqar Ardastani, presented himself simply as a Persian, from modern-day Iran, and he was probably a follower of the Iranian prophet Zoroaster (fl. fifth century BCE). He traveled from Kashmir in the north to the Coromandel coast of the south, from Gujarat on the west coast to Orissa on the east, over a period of many years, in an attempt to examine and record the religious beliefs of South Asians in his time. In the *Dabestan* he claims to set them forth "without omission and diminution, without hatred, envy, or scorn, and without taking a part for the one, or against the other side of the question." His fair-minded account reflects the abundant variety of religious doctrines to be found in India in the mid-seventeenth century.

Another traveler in early modern Asia, the Jesuit missionary Matteo Ricci (1552–1610), set out from Italy in 1578 to spread the Christian religion in the East. His first stop was Portuguese Goa and the southwest coast of India, where he completed his education and received his ordination. In 1582 he moved on to Macao to begin his preparatory study of Chinese language and culture. Once in China, Ricci first adopted the shaven head and garb of a Buddhist monk and later changed to the robes of a Confucian scholar in his efforts to present his message in an appearance familiar to the Chinese of his time. One could say that he was steeped in what he thought was Chinese religion from the very first moment and was certainly preoccupied with religious issues. Throughout his thirty years in China, Ricci paid close attention to the religious life he was able to observe there. He recorded his observations in his journals, published in Europe shortly after his death. Much of his interest in Chinese religion, of course, was instrumental. What could be of value to his aim of transplanting Catholicism to China? But in the effort, he also studied China and its society.

These three pilgrims traveling in India and China, each with their own agendas, explored the myriad religious institutions, beliefs, practices, and texts to be found in these complex civilizations. Imagine traveling in India and China in the early modern period. In contrast to the real, proselytizing Matteo Ricci, imagine yourself as a more neutral observer of Asian religions and ask more general questions about the religious phenomena. Who regulates religious life, and how do the political powers of the time relate to religious institutions? What forms of divinity are recognized, and how do humans establish relations with them? What are the cosmological visions within which religions operate? Who are the religious specialists who devote their lives to sacred matters? What scriptures are honored, and how are they transmitted? And first, what are the main religions of India and China?

In Search of World Religions in Early Modern Asia

Nowadays it has become conventional to designate several distinct major "world religions." The recent *Norton Anthology of World Religions* (2014), for instance, recognizes six: Buddhism, Christianity, Hinduism, Islam, Judaism, and Taoism. This classification suggests that these religions are stable entities over time, with worldwide and historical significance. They are said to have canons of venerable scriptures and boundaries of doctrine that distinguish them from one another and from other lesser religions. Moreover, they are portrayed as organized worldwide communities to which persons belong as members, and these memberships can be given demographic quantification. So a recent Pew Research Center survey of the "Global Religious Landscape" (2012) found Christianity to be the largest world religion, with 2.2 billion adherents, Islam second with 1.6 billion, then Hinduism and Buddhism. The Sikh religion, seldom granted "world religion" status, came in fifth, ahead of both Judaism and Taoism in pure numbers.

In early modern India, our European pilgrim would have readily found examples of these major religions. But he or she would also have observed that the reality was more complex and fluid than a modern notion of unitary religions would suggest. A European traveler would have found small numbers of people adhering to religions familiar to him. These were communities who had originally migrated from the Middle East to Asia centuries before and maintained their faiths in new regions. Enclaves of Jewish trading groups were established along the Indian coasts. In southern India, the first Portuguese explorers and traders in the late fifteenth century found venerable communities of Christians. But these were strange Christians who conducted services in the Syriac language, not Latin, and brought their bishops from Mesopotamia, not Rome. Were they even Christians? Inquiries and even inquisitions were instigated to turn these unfamiliar Christians into more recognizable ones. Many Syriac Christians, however, determinedly kept to their own version of the faith. The moderate growth of Christianity in India would only come later, through the initiative of European missionaries like Matteo Ricci and the many who followed in his wake.

Like India, early modern China had its Jewish community. Persian and perhaps Yemeni Jewish merchants had come centuries earlier and maintained themselves through trade. So too, there were Christians in China even before the arrival of the European monks who traveled to the Mongol Empire and to China during the thirteenth century. These were Nestorian Christians, who had fled eastward from the Near East when they were persecuted by the Byzantines, who subscribed to a different kind of Christianity. Matteo Ricci was curious about the Nestorians and even tried to meet with some, but he stands out among his colleagues. In early modern times, both India and China proved resistant to the large-scale conversions that European missionaries—Jesuits, Franciscans, and Dominicans—hoped to accomplish.

Much more important for the religious history of Asia were two other proselytizing world religions that made significant historical impacts in both India and China, namely Buddhism and Islam.

First established in northern India several centuries before the Common Era, Buddhism expanded throughout the Indian subcontinent. In India it often became the dominant religious orientation among ruling elites and wealthy merchant classes. From India it spread outward, across the Himalayas. Itinerant Buddhist monks brought it north to China in the early centuries of the Common Era, where it took firm root and sometimes enjoyed state patronage. But by early modern times, Buddhism had largely disappeared from the Indian religious landscape. The great congregations of Buddhist monks and nuns that Xuanzang had met in the seventh century were no more. Many of the monumental Buddhist structures, the towering stupas (dome-shaped Buddhist shrines) that Xuanzang had recorded, had fallen into ruin or been taken over for other uses. At Bodh Gaya, the great 160-foot Buddhist temple that marked the site of the Buddha's enlightenment was now occupied by a Hindu order of ascetics and their followers. Only in a few outlying regions of South Asia—notably the southern island of Sri Lanka and the Himalayan plateaus of Tibet to the north—was

Buddhism still a major part of the religious landscape. The reasons for the decline of Buddhism in India are not certain, though the emergence of new forms of Hinduism and the arrival of warrior groups from the Middle East affiliated with Islam both contributed to its decline.

In China, by contrast, Buddhism persisted in early modern times as a significant religious force, so much so that Matteo Ricci dressed himself as a Buddhist monk in order to present himself to the Chinese in the guise of a religious teacher. Established Buddhism had reached the peak of its strength and influence in China during Tang times, several centuries after its arrival. Around the ninth century it was delivered a major blow by the state when Chinese rulers embraced Daoism and began to persecute Buddhists. This diminished the material and political power of Buddhism in China, but it remained quite strong and omnipresent in early modern times. Buddhist temples and shrines stood everywhere. Buddhist monks roamed the land or lived in large monasteries, treating the people's spiritual and medical needs.

In earlier centuries many Chinese Buddhists had made pilgrimages to India's Buddhist homeland. They brought back with them immense numbers of Buddhist scriptures, as well as Indian works in many fields of knowledge. As a result, during the first millennium, there had been strong cultural ties between India and China. The great Chinese novel *Journey to the West* (*Xiyuji*), published shortly before Ricci's arrival in the seventeenth century, celebrated this era of vigorous exchange (in which Xuanzang's *Da Tang xiyuji*, discussed earlier in this chapter, was an emblematic example of a much larger phenomena). *Journey to the West* mixed elements from Chinese folk religion and lore, mythology, Daoism, and Buddhism while telling the tale of Xuanzang's expedition to India a millennium before. The novel is above all a testimony to the place that India, China's West, occupied in the Chinese religious imagination. By early modern times, however, direct ties had disappeared. Over the centuries, China had become the new emanating center of Buddhism, which spread from there into Japan, Korea, and Vietnam.

Islam was another matter. Rising in Arabia in the early seventh century, roughly contemporary with Xuanzang's travels, Islam became the most dynamic religious force throughout much of the world in medieval times, from 700 to 1700. Some have called this the "Islamic millennium." Spreading east from its original home, Islam established a significant presence in both India and China. This dynamic, world-spanning religious orientation had profound effects on the religious landscape. But there were also important differences in the nature of its presence in the two areas.

In India many of the most powerful polities from the thirteenth century through early modern times adopted Islam. In the seventeenth century the dominant power of northern India was the Mughal Empire (1526–1857), and their Muslim mosques and tombs dominated the landscape. This imperial support of Islam also provided the basis for extensive religious, literary, and intellectual interactions between India and the Middle East. Instead of Buddhist monks crossing the Himalayas between China and India, Muslim religious specialists now circulated across the vast Islamic world from northern Africa to India.

The dominance of Muslim polities in much of India did not always lead to widespread conversions. In fact, ruling powers like the Mughals generally took little direct interest in proselytizing. Only in a few peripheral areas of South Asia did Islam become a majority faith: in the Sindh, Kashmir, and parts of Bengal. But this was most often the fruit of locally based efforts, often by the mystically oriented Sufis. As a result, Islam took on a remarkable diversity of local and regional forms in early modern India. Only much later, beginning in the nineteenth century, would there be widespread efforts to create a more unified, "purified" Islamic community in India.

This was less the case in China, though there too dynasties linked to Islam enjoyed periods of state power. The Tang (618–907) and Song (960–1279) dynasties maintained very good relations with the rising Islamic world to the west. Merchants were tolerated and allowed to settle in major cities, buy land for religious purposes, and practice freely. Since interaction with the local population was rather limited, Islam did not spread into the Chinese hinterland. Only during the Mongol conquests of China was there a massive influx of Muslims into many areas. Indeed, at this time mostly mercenaries, merchants, and migrants moved to China in large numbers. Toward the end of Mongol rule, roughly during the fourteenth century, the localized form of Islam, Chinese Islam, began to emerge. As in India, the mystical Sufis—first in the form of Sufi thought and later in the form of Sufi orders—played a crucial role in the emergence of localized Islam in China through interactions with local practices and religions.

Despite the presence of these expansive cosmopolitan religions, the most common religious orientations in both India and China of the early modern period were homegrown. We call the most prevalent form of homegrown religion in India Hinduism. But it is important to keep in mind that this is a modern designation, and the suggestion that it represents a unitary organized religious formation throughout history is highly misleading. The seventeenth-century author of the *Dabestan*, for one, observes that "there are many systems of religion, and innumerable creeds and ceremonies" among those he classifies as Hindu. The term "Hindu" has a complicated history, but it did not come into broad general usage in South Asia as a sign of religious identity prior to the census-taking activities of the colonial British in the nineteenth century. The beliefs and practices that have come to be included under that capacious religious category are too diverse to allow any single definition, although scholars and modern-day Hindus continue to try. In the seventeenth century, likewise, our pilgrim in search of religion would have been able to find some unifying aspects, as well as bewildering variety, among the diverse beliefs and practices of those whom, following modern usage, we will call Hindus.

The most evident feature of religion in early modern South Asia was the coexistence of Hinduism and Islam. In demographic terms, South Asia had a majority Hindu population, but most Hindus found themselves under political rule associated with Islam. Each had its own sacred canon of texts, its religious specialists, its characteristic patterns of worship, and its forms of religious architecture. There is no doubt that these two religious formations differed greatly in historical background and orientation. An outside observer would have quickly recognized the contrasts.

The juxtaposition of Hinduism and Islam within South Asian religious history has led many to overstate the conflict between them. Colonial-period British historians, Hindu nationalists in India, and American political scientists have all sought to pose Hinduism and Islam as antithetical civilizational opponents, locked in perpetual conflict. Any observer in late eighteenth- to early nineteenth-century India, however, would have readily seen that these lines were not so clearly drawn and the rumors of everlasting conflict were greatly exaggerated. Both religions were internally diverse, ranging from the rigorously orthodox to the highly eclectic or syncretic. If they maintained clear centers of orthodoxy, they also became fuzzy and indistinct away from those centers. Moreover, there was a great deal of mutual observation, borrowing, and adaptation across religious lines. In some cases, such as that of Sikhism, the process of interaction and critique led eventually to the formation of entirely new religious communities. The concern with singular religious identities is a modern preoccupation. Most religious practitioners in early modern South Asia lived in the fuzzy regions.

Like India, China would have appeared as a huge repository of many world religions. Buddhism was only the first of many. In addition to the communities of Jews and Christians, many other religious orientations persisted. Manichaeism, once a globally very popular dualistic religion concerned with the forces of good and evil, had entered China several centuries after Buddhism, mostly after a number of Central Asian peoples adopted it. Zoroastrianism also came from the west, via the Silk Road, and took hold in certain areas in China in the sixth century. Other religions came in the form of small or large migrations. Some were simply present in China for a while and disappeared. Manichaeism, for instance, thrived in certain areas for several centuries but was eventually banned during the early part of the Ming dynasty (1368–1644) and disappeared. Many others took root and stirred the religious scene in China in different ways—becoming localized, interacting with other religions, and developing new ones.

In China, religious categories like "Daoism" and "Confucianism" largely represent the efforts of European observers to identify religious formations with clear doctrines, founding texts, and ecclesiastical institutions, parallel to those they believed to exist in the West. Daoism is a complex religion concerned with immortality, longevity, and alchemical and meditative techniques designed to escape or transcend this-worldly body, time, and space. It became established in China about two thousand years ago, but its roots are much older. Many Daoist rituals and gods can be traced back to very early times, thousands of years before its appearance as a religion. As an escapist movement seeking to get away from this world, Daoism first appeared in the sixth century BCE, a time of constant war and incessant strife. This is also when the enigmatic text that gave this religion its name, the *Daodejing,* or the *Classic of the Way and Virtue,* was composed. The *Daodejing* is the basis for what is known as Daoist "philosophy," a scholarly tradition centered on commentary and exegesis of Daoist texts, but it is also the central sacred text of the Daoist religion. Its putative author, the "Old Master" Laozi (fl. sixth century BCE), is a god in the Daoist religion.

Confucianism is in many ways much harder to classify as a religion. On the one hand, it appeared to Jesuit observers like Ricci as a philosophical and political system designed to maintain proper social order. On the other, it involved a great number of rituals that were in effect religious practices.

Europeans spent a long time debating the nature of Confucianism during the so-called Chinese Rites Controversy. In the end, Ricci could not tell if the Confucian literati were religious or not. And for a long time no one in Europe could really tell what was the nature of the religious scene in China.

In essence, Confucianism is several things at once. First, it is a seemingly well-bounded keyword that is a scholarly construct, much like "Hinduism" in India. Second, it is an ethical system based on the canonical writings of Confucius (551–479 BCE) and some of his disciples. But it is also an elaborate system of rituals and religious practices bringing together common worshipers and elites into the same temple. To be sure, Confucius himself did not intend to create a new religion. But his teachings and his own image became attached to specific religious practices in China.

But the diversity of actual religious beliefs and practices and the willingness of Chinese people to adopt various useful rites without concern for religious boundaries rendered these classifications superfluous. More commonly historians of religion now employ the plural and the simple geographic designation "religions of China" to avoid undue reification. Indeed, as the real Matteo Ricci noted, it is not always certain just what is and is not "religious" in China. He had a hard time classifying China's religions and understanding them in relation to one another. In many cases, he refers to what he sees in China in the sixteenth century as the "corrupted" forms of an original "ur-religion" of China that existed thousands of years before.

Religion at the Centers of Power

In premodern states around the world, religion commonly played a major role within the political sphere. (The division between the "private" and "public" spheres and the notion that religion belongs only in the former is a modern idea that emerged and took hold mostly in Europe.) That role, however, could take many differing forms. Ruling elites might consult with religious specialists in setting policy. Those with religious training might serve in key advisory capacities at court. Priests might perform public rites to confer religious authority on rulers. Sovereigns might patronize religious institutions or utilize the resources of the state to construct grandiose religious structures, out of personal piety or a desire to gain favor. In some cases, rulers might claim a divine mandate, or even divine status, on their own behalf. In early modern India and China, a European observer would have seen several contrasting relationships between religion and the state, much as one would have seen in early modern Europe.

The seventh-century Chinese Buddhist pilgrim Xuanzang was invited to meet Harshavardhana, the most powerful ruler of northern India at the time, and together they participated in a lavish Buddhist festival. For a seventeenth-century visitor, the dominant power on the Indian subcontinent was the Mughal Empire, centered in the northern cities of Agra, Lahore, and the new Shahjahanabad (Delhi). While the Mughal state was not as centralized as its Chinese neighbor at the time, it ruled over a large portion of southern Asia. Through its effective system of taxation, the Mughals were able to accrue tremendous resources, and they used them to construct opulent new urban landscapes, including religious buildings, that astonished all visitors. To build a mosque is a great act of piety for Muslims, assuring the patron of a place in paradise, and members of the Mughal court sponsored myriad mosques in the large urban centers of northern India.

The Mughal rulers were Islamic in their affiliation, yet they ruled over a population that remained predominantly non-Muslim. Thus, their ruling policies toward other religious communities had broad repercussions throughout north Indian society.

Historians sometimes distinguish two contrasting orientations among Islamic rulers in South Asia: "India-centered" (inclusive, mystical) and "Mecca-centered" (exclusive, prophetic). Among Mughal rulers, Akbar (r. 1556–1605) best exemplifies the India-centric style. He is remembered for broad policies of tolerance toward other religious groups and for a compelling curiosity about his Hindu subjects. Under Akbar's rule Hindu elites were incorporated into the Mughal administration, and Akbar supervised the translation and illustration of classic Hindu works from Sanskrit into Persian. Himself a spiritual seeker, he initiated a series of religious discussions in his court. Initially the participants were Muslim theologians of the various branches of Islam, but Akbar later expanded the colloquium to include Brahmins, Zoroastrians, Jains, Sikhs, and Portuguese Catholic missionaries. This was one of the first "parliaments of world religions" in world history.

This inclusive policy was controversial, however, and orthodox Muslim critics chastised the Mughal court for failing to adhere more strictly to

Islamic principles. In the mid-seventeenth century, Akbar's grandson Shah Jahan (r. 1628–56) adopted a more Mecca-centric style. His rule emphasized lavish patronage of Muslim institutions and festivals and discouraged demonstrations of Hindu religiosity in the public sphere. Between Shah Jahan's sons Dara Shikoh and Aurangzeb, who were contending for power in the 1650s, the contrast in orientation was dramatic. The eldest son, Dara Shikoh, was deeply involved in the study of Hindu and Sufi ideas, and sought a "confluence of the two oceans" of Islam and Hinduism. To this end he translated the Upanishads, the philosophical portion of the Vedas, into Persian and postulated that these were the "hidden books" referred to in the Quran. But the victor in the succession battle, Aurangzeb, adopted a much more exclusive approach. As a devout Sunni Muslim, he promoted a more austere style, without his father's love of opulence, and he discouraged any new Hindu constructions. Aurangzeb is often portrayed as a zealous Muslim iconoclast for his destruction of Hindu temples in Mathura and Benares. This legacy of Mughal temple spoliation has figured heavily in modern Hindu nationalist mobilizations. However, for the most part, any acts of temple desecration by Mughal rulers were more political than religious in their motivation.

Beyond the reaches of Mughal power, particularly in southern India, Hindu kings ruled smaller polities. They followed an older style of Indic sovereignty. These regional rulers would direct state resources not to mosques or tombs but to the construction and expansion of Hindu temples. In the seventeenth century Hindu temple construction was at a peak in the south. Often this took the form of adding on to existing temple centers, expanding them into temple complexes with new shrines, towers, halls, and walls. In old Kanchipuram, where Xuanzang had seen ten thousand Buddhist monks and numerous Buddhist stupas in the seventh century, a seventeenth-century pilgrim would have been astonished by the massive temple complexes devoted to the Hindu gods Shiva and Vishnu.

Like the Mughal emperors, Hindu regional kings in early modern India presided over mixed-faith populations. In southern India, communities of Muslims, Christians, and Jews lived next door to Hindus. Hindu kings adopted tolerant practices, seeking to incorporate the varied social and religious groups within an ordered, hierarchical kingdom. But along with tolerance came a policy of ranking. Kings or other officials might participate in the festivals or patronize the religious projects of minority faith communities but would reserve their most lavish support for the Hindu god or goddess they particularly favored. To a visitor from early modern Europe, where devastating religious wars were fresh in memory, the Muslim and Hindu polities of South Asia would have appeared remarkably relaxed about matters of faith.

In China, the relationships between religion(s) and the state were equally complicated. To make things simple, as we must, we probably better use the terms "orthodoxy" and "heterodoxy" to characterize the most basic way the state and religion interacted in China. The state had the power to declare certain religions or religious orders heterodox and then ban them, and it did so many times during China's long history. (In fact, almost every religion in China was declared heterodox at some point by someone.) What was orthodox is a complicated question in itself, since no one religion was designated as such. With few exceptions, China's rulers did not have a clearly defined religious identity (Muslim or Hindu) as in India. But they played a central role in the rather elusively defined religion of the Chinese state. Since the earliest days of the empire, the emperor of China was considered Son of Heaven (*Tianzi*) and holder of the Mandate of Heaven, whose main function was to maintain the cosmic balance between Heaven and earth (discussed further under "Cosmology" in this chapter). The emperor was in a certain respect the "high priest" of the state religion and had to perform specific rituals in dedicated temples. This did not mean that he could not be also a devout Buddhist (as many were), or a follower of Daoist practices (as some were), or both. In fact, emperors and the state tended to interfere heavily in almost every other religious practice and order in China. The campaign against Buddhism during the Tang and the ban on Manichaeism during the early Ming are just two examples of many state-sponsored campaigns against religion in general or specific religions or cults in China from ancient times to today.

But more than they liked to ban religions and campaign against them, Chinese rulers loved to patronize religions. Like in India, this tendency was in part a policy dictated by China's massive religious diversity. From ancient times, Chinese courts entertained members or representatives of various religions and ethnic groups and engaged them through ritual and direct communication to varying degrees. Ming rulers, for instance, were cognizant of Islam's status and power in Asian—during the rise of the Timurids, the Mughals, and other post-Mongol empires—and patronized it to a certain extent. The Ming founder, Taizu (r. 1368–98), a Buddhist monk at some point of his early life, banned Manichaeism but tolerated

Islam and even married a Muslim woman. His son, the Ming Yongle emperor (r. 1402–24), sponsored the renovation of many mosques in China. This way, he was also able to dictate their architectural transformation—from Middle Eastern style to Chinese. The Qing-Manchu rulers, who were "foreigners" and not Han Chinese, heavily patronized Tibetan Buddhism and presented themselves as central figures in almost every other religion they encountered. The Qianlong emperor of Qing (r. 1736–96), for instance, claimed to be "all things to all his many peoples." He could appear as a Manchu warrior, Buddhist deity, Daoist monk, Confucian writer, father, son, ascetic recluse, hunter, banquet host, beardless youth, and future ancestor. This partly instrumental attitude toward religion was the main reason Qing emperors allowed Jesuit fathers and European men who followed Ricci to China to stay at court and even do some proselytization in China.

Of course, this is an ideal image of state-religion relations. Emperors did not hesitate to attack practitioners of religions they patronized when they needed to. Moreover, members of certain religious groups responded in different ways to state patronage. The Yongzheng emperor (r. 1722–35), whose father befriended the Jesuits in the court, tried to ban Christianity at some point, declaring it heterodoxy. The Qianlong emperor once built a mosque in Beijing, but since it was facing the throne (northward) and not Mecca, no Muslim ever attended it for prayer. During the nineteenth century, the most devastating rebellions against the state were religiously inspired. The political savvy that eighteenth-century Manchu emperors exhibited when it came to religion did not really help or work in later times.

Divinity

When we think of "gods" in the early modern Indian and Chinese context, we must remember that they do not resemble the divine as we know it in most Western traditions. It is perhaps easier to explain the essential difference through the Chinese case. Chinese gods did not necessarily create the world or teach humans law. They are not necessarily in charge of specific human functions or natural phenomena, as is the Greek pantheon. So it should also be clear that the word "god" itself is not always accurate. In addition to *Tian*, "Heaven," whose special nature and status will be discussed below, one crucial word that is important to know in this context is "*di*," which implies sovereignty, kingship, or lordship of the highest nature. Of much less importance is the term *xian*, usually referring to immortals. But the most common Chinese word that is also translated as "god" is *shen*, a word that in different contexts has a wide spectrum of meanings such as "deity," "mysterious," "soul," "spirit," "unspecified divine essence," "spiritual being," "spirit," "mind," and "consciousness." The Chinese have more than one god; indeed, there is a whole pantheon in China. These "shens" could be local or national deities; deified clan progenitors or ancestors, or just nature gods.

In India, Hindus likewise recognized a plethora of gods. Some were of only local importance, while others claimed a pan-Indian following. Minor godlings or local goddesses often presided over matters close to the everyday lives and welfare of their votaries: health and sickness, fields and livestock, and other matters of physical well-being. Pan-Indian gods, such as Vishnu, Shiva, and the goddess Devi, took on more complex identities and roles among their followers. Around each of them grew an enormous corpus of religious literature, relating narratives of godly exploits, guides for proper ritual procedures, and theological accounts of the world. Many Hindus considered one or another of these pan-Indian deities to be universal and supreme over all others.

This highest deity was considered both transcendent and physically manifest. For those who believed Vishnu to be supreme, theologians would insist that Vishnu was an autonomous and ultimate agent of the entire cosmos. Yet in contrast to the God of the Abrahamic religions, Vishnu simultaneously made himself present in the world in countless possible physical forms. His followers stressed Vishnu's accessible personhood. He could incarnate himself in godly human beings like Rama and Krishna, whose full and eventful lives on earth were told and retold among believers. He could likewise make himself palpably present in the sculpted icons of shrines and temples, available to be seen and honored by devotees. And he might also appear, in more subtle form, within the innermost hearts of the faithful. In this way Vishnu became easily accessible to human followers, all the while retaining his ultimate supremacy.

The largest and most evident Hindu institutions in the larger towns and royal centers were devoted to these principal pan-Indian gods. They were depicted as the ruling sovereigns in an immense divine court, surrounded by their attending deities and other sacred beings of all sorts. In the theology of divine instantiation, the ruling god at the center of the temple was also made incarnate, through ritual means, to receive the offerings of his or her human devotees.

With such a diversity of divine possibilities, worshipers could make tactical religious decisions. One god might offer agricultural abundance while a goddess was especially adept at preventing smallpox. A fierce goddess might patrol the village borders. Still another deity might provide the best route toward final salvation. To meet this-worldly vicissitudes and otherworldly aims as well, Hindus in early modern India had many options. This tactical religiosity included local Sufi establishments as well as Hindu shrines, for when it came to spiritual power no group had a monopoly and religious boundaries were unimportant. For most, there was no need for an exclusive commitment to any one divine figure or institution.

An early modern observer from Christian Europe would have found this religious orientation alien and troubling. The abundance of several high gods, multiple manifestations, and attending troupes of lesser deities could appear overwhelmingly complicated to outside observers. European travelers of the seventeenth century, such as Sir Thomas Herbert, regularly observed that the Hindus must be worshiping the devil in their prayers directed toward misshapen and horrible idols. Catholic missionaries like Matteo Ricci roundly condemned the idolatry of the Indians. So too, orthodox South Asian Muslims might regard the multiplicity of images and representations of gods among their Hindu neighbors as a violation of the fundamental Islamic principle of *tawhid* (that there is no God but the one true God). The concept expresses the exclusive divinity of Allah, or what we call "monotheism" in its Islamic understanding.

For their part, orthodox Indian Muslims were firm: there was one god for them, called Allah. All other claimants to divinity were considered to be false gods. This supreme deity was unequivocally the transcendent, all-powerful creator of the universe, its sustainer, and the one who would render final judgment on all creatures. In contrast to the Hindu deities, so promiscuous and visible in their manifestations, Allah was not to be represented in any material image. In orthodox circles, making an image was considered an unwarranted infringement on Allah's exclusive creative prerogative.

For Muslims, one of Allah's interventions in the world was especially important. In the years 609 to 632, Allah revealed to his final and greatest prophet, Muhammad, a series of messages. Muhammad faithfully recorded these revelations, and they came to be codified and transmitted as the

Quran, the central religious scripture for all Muslims. The most prized human interactions with the divine, accordingly, did not involve visual or material exchanges as among the Hindus, but rather verbal prayer. This central religious action could be performed either individually or in large congregations of the faithful, in mosques. In essence, Muslim prayer was a direct and personal act.

Any traveler in seventeenth-century South Asia would have readily observed the striking differences between multiple Hindu gods in their iconographic efflorescence and the austere Allah, singular and unrepresentable. An older colonial-era historiography divided Indian history into Hindu and Muslim periods, as if these represented wholly distinct civilizations. The seventeenth century, in this view, was part of the Muslim period, soon to be supplanted by the British period. But the religious story of early modern South Asia lies just as much in the great internal diversity of these two major religious formations, and in the sharing, interaction, and mutual adaptations, as in the contrasts between them. Our pilgrim would undoubtedly have noticed many examples of this complex religious interaction, especially as he journeyed away from the Mughal political centers like Delhi and Agra.

In the Bengali region, for example, the cult of Satya Pir celebrated a legendary Sufi holy man, a wandering mendicant dressed in rags. This irascible figure deployed his spiritual power on behalf of anyone who offered the proper tokens of respect to his aniconic form—whether the worshiper was Muslim or Hindu, male or female, upper or lower class. Satya Pir, it was believed, could restore one's wealth or health, and Bengalis of all types worshiped him simply because to do so was effective. Further, the worship of Satya Pir did not in any way interfere with devotion to Allah, Vishnu, Shiva, or any other divine figure. He simply provided one more ready-to-hand religious option. The cult of Satya Pir, with his ecumenical following, dates back at least to the sixteenth century. But in the seventeenth century, Bengali Hindus began to assert that this Muslim holy man was also an incarnation of the god Vishnu, known as Satya Narayanan.

One would have encountered similar syncretic cults and practices throughout South Asia in the early modern period. Religious boundaries were not firmly fixed, just as the identity of the Sufi saint could merge with the Hindu god. It was only later, in the nineteenth century, that Bengali Muslims began to withdraw their patronage of Satya Pir as out of keeping with a more exclusive definition of Islam.

Turning our attention back to China, the most important feature of the divine pantheon there is its bureaucratized nature. If the gods in a Hindu temple mirrored an Indian royal court, Chinese divinities reflected the dominant bureaucratic empire prevalent through most of the country's history. If earthly power was bureaucratic, then it made sense to think of divine power in similar terms. Just as the government appointed local officials, it used to appoint city gods, in charge of protecting the city and judging its dead just as the city magistrates would judge its living. The inhabitants of that city would perform specific rituals for the god who would function as its heavenly official. This was a measure intended not only to regulate religious life in China but also to enhance the power of the government. The emperor had the authority to appoint both earthly and heavenly officials. Since Chinese officials mostly attained their positions through learning and success in examinations, the Chinese pantheon included a special god—Wenchangdi, a name that implies cultural prosperity—in charge of the examinations. Students and scholars used to worship this god intensely in temples and at home. Dutiful Wenchangdi, for his part, liked to appear in students' dreams just before they took important examinations. After such appearances they usually passed with flying colors.

Another, more ubiquitous, important symbol of the bureaucratic nature of the Chinese pantheon was the common practice of the ritual burning of "paper money" (paper printed to look like and represent money) and other written documents. The priest who performed the burning, in this instance, became a bureaucrat of sorts in the heavenly world. Just as written documents—petitions, for example—were used to communicate with earthly officials, so too were they used with the heavenly officials. In addition to or instead of prayer, the petitioner wrote a document that was transmitted to the divine world, where it functioned like an earthly petition, through burning.

A story about Prince Li Shimin, the future second emperor of the Tang dynasty (Emperor Taizong, r. 626–49), relates how he once fell into the netherworld. There is a Chinese hell, and even though it is mostly Buddhist, it is massively bureaucratized. The prince was able to redeem his life by borrowing some money from the huge account of paper money that two particularly devout poor peasants held there. When he returned to the world of the living, the prince paid the debt by paying the couple real money. They became immensely rich.

Interestingly enough, the Chinese bureaucratized pantheon was not the home of divine mandarins. Contrary to the real Chinese traditional bureaucratic world, whose heroes were officials and scholars, the divine realm was populated with gods of another nature. One of those to whom scholars and students also turned for help was Guandi, the god of war. But the quintessential expression of the difference between the earthly and heavenly realms in this regard was the role of females and women in the latter. In addition to the aforementioned Guanyin, who began as a male god in India and transformed into a female god in China, there were several other powerful female gods such as the deity known as Mazu, "Queen Mother of the West," who had a paradise of her own and can make people immortal. Furthermore, it is easy to see why the goddesses in charge of fertility were female, but Mazu, the god of the sailors, was also female. Nuwa, an archer, the ancient god who created humanity, was also female. Remarkably, both Mazu and Guanyin were women who preferred not to fulfill their duty in the traditional Chinese society. The former chose to die just before her wedding, and the latter was executed by her father after she refused his order to get married. Another crucial difference from the earthly bureaucratic world was the presence of warriors like the gods Qiye and Baye (Lords Seven and Eight), best friends who were military generals. Finally, there was the Monkey God Sunwukong, a monkey known for his mischief in Heaven and even for his attempts to steal the throne from the ruler of Heaven, the Jade Emperor.

What are the Chinese gods? The simple answer is that most of the Chinese gods are people. They are most often depicted as people, as opposed to unusual creators or amorphous beings (although there are some of those entities as well in China). These deities are either real people who lived in the past and became gods at some point after their death, or figures from Chinese mythologies or even novels that were deified at some point after their appearance in Chinese culture. The class of "smaller" local earth gods (*Tudigong*) is a great example. Unlike many of the gods above who are "universal" in their reach, the local earth god is lowly and modest, its duty is to protect the people in a specific locale—a city, a village, even a neighborhood—from evil demons and hungry ghosts. In many cases well-known Chinese personalities are "appointed" after their death to serve as local earth gods. The god of the city of Hangzhou, for instance, is Zhou Xin, a strict but honest and decent judge from the Ming dynasty. Zhou was particularly effective in fighting corrupt officials and defending the people. When he was murdered, as sometimes was the fate of upright Chinese bureaucrats, the emperor dreamed that Zhou Xin became the god of the city of Hangzhou, whose inhabitants promptly erected a temple for him. Han Yu (768–824), a famous Tang period poet and thinker, is the main local god of the city of Chongqing, presiding over a hierarchy of dozens of neighborhood gods. However, the locals are usually more interested in the protection city gods have to offer than in their specific biographies.

There are other types of gods who were people. We have seen the examples of the two generals and the female gods Mazu and Guanyin. Mazu, known to have a "real" name and real "biography," is supposed to have been a woman who lived during the Song dynasty. So real is Mazu that she became famous most recently when two 6-foot statues of her were flown from China to Malaysia sitting in the business class section of the plane. The airline even issued a boarding pass for each statue. A god known as Star Lord of Prosperity, who is in charge of success, particularly of officials in the bureaucracy, is identified as a man who lived in ancient times. Similarly, Immortal Woman He, the only female god in a Daoist group known as the Eight Immortals, each of whom possesses a certain supernatural power, was born at some point during the Tang dynasty and ascended to Heaven on a specific day. Conversely, as already mentioned above, the Monkey God Sunwukong began his career as a figure in the classical epic novel *Journey to the West* (sixteenth century). To this list we must add the gods that came to China from elsewhere. First and foremost is Buddha Amitabha (the main celestial buddha, in Chinese, *A-mi-tuo-fu*). Buddha was not alone. Other, lesser-known, Indian-born gods made their way to China and became part of its pantheon. The child god Nezha, for instance, is the Chinese version of the Indian child god Nalak-bara. Also present, albeit to a much lesser degree, are Allah, who came with the Muslims who emigrated to China, and Jesus and his holy father (and mother). But in China the famous Western divinity is not necessarily the same "person." Chinese Muslim thinkers attempted, beginning in the early eighteenth century, to establish some mystical relationship between Allah and some Chinese cosmic powers (such as the yin and yang), but they never claimed that he was equal to or the same as any other Chinese god, including Heaven. The Jesuits from Ricci's order, on the other hand, were famous for their attempt to establish some form of similarity between the Chinese deity and the

Western god. We have no evidence that any Chinese Jew ever bothered with this issue.

Perhaps the strongest sign of the connection between divinities and bureaucracy in China is the literary genre centered on the adventures and lives of gods that emerged in popular literature during the early modern period, a time of rising literacy. Among the "gods and demons fiction" (*shenmo xiaoshou*), one can count novels such as *The Investiture of the Gods* (*Fengshen Yanyi*), a late sixteenth-century creation about mostly Daoist gods. But the most famous is *Journey to the West*, discussed earlier in this chapter—the fictionalized account of the aforementioned pilgrim Xuanzang's trip to India. During the Qing and modern periods, this literature developed into another genre of satires and comedies that served more than anything else as a form of social commentary. This literary genre centered on gods tells us something about the rather "instrumental" approach to divinities in China: many of them simply exist in order to serve humans rather than to be served or worshiped.

Cosmologies

In order to complete the divine picture in China we must bring in the basic cosmology—as opposed to just Chinese mythology—within which the heavenly and earthly realms and everything in between them operate. Chinese cosmology, the theory about the ways the universe works, probably had been evolving for millennia before it was fully articulated during the Han dynasty. The timing is not incidental. The Han period was the first time in Chinese history that an imperial power was strong enough and lived long enough to articulate a theory that incorporated Chinese mythology, religious practices, and ideas about theology, ethics, and politics into a package that reflected and suited the interests of the political structure embodied in the empire. This cosmology, which we cannot present here in full detail, became in turn the basis for the religion of the state. From early on the Chinese have identified two major corresponding and complementary powers operating in the universe: the yin and the yang. The yang force, understood to be "male," is famously associated with heaven/the sky, light, the sun, day, summer, the father, dryness, and the south. The yin force, understood to be "female," is associated with the earth, darkness, the moon, night, winter, the mother, wetness, and the north. The universe exists only as result of the mutual and complementary relationship between these two forces. Chinese mythology tells us that the god Pangu, a hairy giant with horns, created the heavens and the earth, indeed, the universe, by separating the yin and the yang with one swing of his giant axe.

Far more important than Pangu are Heaven and Earth, whose relationship, like the yin and yang, is also mutual and complementary. Of the two, Heaven receives much more attention as a deity even though "Earth" (*di*) is also a divinity and was worshiped as such before the twentieth century. The Chinese emperor performed specific rituals in two temples—one dedicated to Heaven and the other to Earth—that are located in the capital Beijing and can be visited today. Heaven, or *Tian*, is a mysterious divine entity that is not entirely Chinese and has some Inner Asian origins as well. It was introduced during the Zhou dynasty, which began on the outskirts of the ancient Chinese world. It is often synonymous with the god Shangdi (Lord on High), the "supreme god" during the times before the Zhou dynasty, which was merged with Heaven after the rise of the Zhou. But Heaven is not just a "Lord on High." It is not a usual god with a persona of its own who stands outside the universe, creates worlds, gives laws, or sends prophets and messengers to humankind. Rather, Heaven is part of the universe and as a key element in a relationship between earthly politics and ethics, and divine providence. Through its specific position within this relationship, Heaven shapes life on earth and gives it meaning. Perhaps the most famous expression of this principle is the term "Mandate of Heaven," mentioned earlier in this chapter, which implies that Heaven confers its mandate to govern and rule all that is under Heaven (*Tianxia*)—or at least China—upon an upright and moral man and oversees his conduct as ruler. Heaven does not speak to humans but has ways to signal its pleasure or displeasure. Unusual celestial phenomena or sightings of mythological animals such as the yellow dragon, the phoenix, or the unicorn were interpreted as signals that Heaven was pleased with the conduct of the emperor. Different imperial courts throughout Chinese history tried their best to report as many sightings of good omens as they could. Conversely, signs of heavenly discontent were often beyond their control. Natural and social disasters such as floods, earthquakes, droughts, famines, and wars were often interpreted as signs that Heaven was displeased with the ruler and that his position on the throne was in danger. "Heaven cracks, earth shakes," ran the slogan. Such beliefs were prevalent not only in premodern or imperial times. When a massive earthquake devastated the city of Tangshan in July 1976, killing hundreds of thousands of people, it was widely believed to be a sign of extreme heavenly discontent with the political goings-on in China at the time.

Chinese cosmology is therefore a closed system in which the relationships among the various elements are mutual, complementary, and interdependent. This explains why the aforementioned trio of politics, ethics, and divine providence is so crucial. All of this places a great deal of responsibility on the ruler of China, who is viewed as the crucial link between Heaven and Earth and whose conduct maintains the delicate cosmic balance. The other side of the equation is clear: imperial misconduct disrupts the balance and leads to chaos. In other words, the responsibility on the emperor's shoulders and the meaning of his rulership is not only political but also religious: the emperor is not only the ruler of China but also the Son of Heaven. We can now also understand why the emperor worshiped in two temples dedicated to Heaven and Earth, and how the upright judge Zhou Xin became a city god through the direct intervention of the emperor. Popular religion required a god to protect the city; imperial values and powers determined its identity.

Hindu cosmological visions were articulated in the Puranas (ancient texts compiled in written form between the third and tenth centuries), though as in China they were the result of a long gestation. Also as in China, Hindu cosmology located the state within an expansive setting, and so provided an implicit religious theory of rule.

Puranic cosmologies in India aver that the entire cosmos emanates from a single being, identified as the supreme overlord. That overlord might be Vishnu, Shiva, or some other deity, depending on one's orientation. Thus, the cosmic order is grounded in that figure. But emanation is not a once-and-for-all creation. Rather, Hindus envision emanation to be a recurrent phenomenon, occurring in succession with dissolutions. The cosmos expands and contracts, comes into phenomenal being and then dissolves and reenters the supreme overlord. We live in just one of these "emanational periods." The complementary forces of emanation and dissolution are not the same as yin and yang, but like that Chinese pair they create the cosmic dynamism in our world.

A Hindu worshiper of Vishnu understands the world to be a realization of the divine order grounded in the being of that god. And just as Vishnu acts as the supreme lord of the entire cosmos, other beings may exercise lordship over other, subordinate portions of that cosmos. One god might rule the underworld, others protect the directions, and still others exercise dominion over other parts of the known world. Not just gods, but also humans may rule. Here is where cosmological vision and royal politics connect. The king, as ruler over his (or rarely, queen over her) domain, acts as a subordinate lord on a part of earth within Vishnu's overarching cosmos. Kingship is imagined as an exercise of lordship modeled on that of Vishnu at the highest level. The ruler should emulate Vishnu in his virtuous act of bringing order to the world. For that reason, kings might claim to have a portion of Vishnu, or to be an emanation of Vishnu or even an incarnation of one of Vishnu's incarnations, as a way of proclaiming their own semidivine status.

In Hindu Puranic cosmology, the various domains of the world are imagined as linked, continuous, and hierarchical. Lesser domains are included within Vishnu's overarching cosmic domain. And at the other end, the earthly ruler could imagine himself as lord within whose domain were smaller encompassed lords and lordships. The cosmological theory of lordship also provides a way of understanding the more fragmentary polities of medieval and early modern India, as compared to the relatively stable state in China. Just as the cosmic order as a whole submits to the recurring processes of emanation and dissolution, so too royal domains rise and fall according to cyclical logic. This is not to say that kings did not seek to create stable structures in their kingdoms, of course, but there was a recognition of the ever-looming threat of destruction.

Religious Specialists

A pilgrim in search of religion in early modern Asia would naturally have sought out the religious specialists who devoted themselves fully to spiritual practices and the maintenance of religious institutions.

A seventeenth-century traveler would not have seen the large congregations of Buddhist monks and nuns in India that Xuanzang had encountered a millennium earlier, but he certainly would have been able to find a great variety of other dedicated religious specialists. By long-standing Indic tradition, one class dominated among the orthodox Hindus: the Brahman class. According to ancient texts, still regularly cited, Brahmans were born from the mouth of the primordial being at the time of creation, while other social classes originated from other portions of this great being. Their birth as Brahmans, it was believed, gave them special competence for religious practices like the transmission and recitation of sacred scriptures and the performance of sacrificial rituals. In ancient times the Brahmans had organized themselves as an intellectual and priestly elite, especially concerned with continuing the ancient traditions of the Vedic scriptures and the Sanskrit language. From this had grown the many disciplines of knowledge in classical India, and Brahmans had maintained a proprietary interest in these intellectual fields over many centuries. In early modern India members of the Brahman class operated schools for the transmission of religious and intellectual texts, acted as priests in Hindu temples, and served as ministers and advisers at royal courts.

The hegemony of the Brahman class within the religious sphere, however, had never been complete. In ancient times religious leaders like the Buddha Shakyamuni and Mahavira (founder of the Jain religious tradition), both members of the warrior class, had specifically questioned brahmanic claims to religious preeminence. Membership in the Buddhist and Jain monastic orders had been deliberately open to all strata of society. So too in early modern India, the traveler would have encountered numerous spiritual communities whose founders and leaders were not of the Brahman class and who vigorously criticized any brahmanic claims to superiority.

Among Hindus, many of the most dynamic religious communities revolved around *bhakti* poet-saints. *Bhakti* is usually translated as "devotion," but its semantic range also stresses the idea of "participation" with the divine. In many regions of the subcontinent, medieval poet-saints sang of a more direct, emotional, and unmediated human relationship with God, quite different from the priest-led ritual programs of the Brahmans. In contrast to the restrictive brahmanic codes of purity, this participation was specifically inclusive. The *bhakti* poet-saints came from all classes and genders. Among the best known north Indian poets were a low-class weaver (Kabir), a leather worker (Ravidas), and a female princess (Mirabai). And they sang not in the learned language of Sanskrit, but in the more accessible vernacular languages of their regions.

Of all poet-saints of India, the one who exercised the greatest long-term influence was Nanak (1469–1538), a singer of God without form, who came to be the founder of a major world religion, Sikhism. A member of a Hindu merchant class, Nanak lived in the Punjab region northwest of Delhi. Later biographies narrate a major revelation that came to Nanak at age thirty. One day he entered a river to perform ablutions and did not emerge. For three days Nanak disappeared. His family and villagers searched but could find no body. Finally, Nanak reappeared from the river and declared to the astonished observers, "There is no Hindu. There is no Muslim." With this his religious ministry began. Nanak traveled around the Punjab region accompanied by a Muslim musician and gradually composed a large body of contemplative songs outlining the theological system that would become fundamental for the Sikh religion. He gathered followers, and just before death he appointed a successor, a second Guru to the growing community of "Sikhs" or students.

By the mid-seventeenth century, the Sikhs were a powerful religious and political force in the region. The community had attracted a large following especially among the local Jat agricultural class of northern India. To help consolidate the community, the leaders had constructed a central shrine in Amritsar, later rebuilt as the Golden Temple. The fifth Guru had assembled the hymns of Guru Nanak and other early Gurus, as well as those of other north Indian poet-saints compatible with basic Sikh principles, and canonized the collection as Sikh scripture. As an expanding regional power, the Sikhs had come into periodic conflict with the Mughals, and the Sikh Gurus of the seventeenth century increasingly adopted a more courtly and militant style. By this time the Sikhs had started to identify themselves as members of a distinct religious community, separate from both Hinduism and Islam.

The devotional poems of Nanak and Kabir are equally dismissive of the Hindu brahmanic establishment and of the Muslim *ulama*, the most prominent religious specialists within orthodox Muslim circles. These scholars of Islam were the experts on matters of faith and religious law. As with the Brahmans, the primary claim to religious authority of the *ulama* rested on their learning and training in a traditional curriculum. And also like the Brahmans, the *ulama* enjoyed a high social status within the Muslim community, though they did not have a myth of divine origin to buttress it. To maintain their standing, members of *ulama* families tended to marry within their clan. Muslim religious scholars could occupy a variety of ritual, educational, and ministerial positions: as preachers and prayer leaders in mosques, as instructors in Islamic schools, and as advisers at court.

A seventeenth-century traveler in South Asia would have encountered other Muslim religious specialists as well. Islam in India took on diverse local forms. Especially outside the urban centers associated with Mughal authority, one would more likely have observed Sufi shrines and religious centers. Among Sufi groups, the *shaykh* or *pir* served as the spiritual center, parallel to the Hindu devotional poet-saints. Sufis organized themselves into fraternities headed by *shaykh*s, who would be responsible for leading the group and guiding disciples. In South Asia, the most vigorous Sufi network was the Chishti order, introduced into India by Moinuddin Chisthi (1141–1236), who traveled from Afghanistan to India in the late twelfth century and established his center at Ajmer in Rajasthan. *Shaykhs* like Moinuddin Chisthi were viewed as particularly charismatic figures whose spiritual authority rested on direct intuitive experience of the divine. This experience conferred on them a special power or *barrakat*, which could continue even after death. This is why the tombs of the most esteemed Sufi saints in India, like Moinuddin Chisthi in Ajmer and Nizam al-Din Awliya in Delhi, remained vigorous and dynamic centers of Sufi devotional practice well into the seventeenth century and up to today.

Among both the Hindu and Muslim religions in South Asia there were also seekers who had renounced social life in order to pursue religious quests. India had always accommodated wandering holy men, mendicants, and ascetics. In the fifth century BCE, the Buddha Shakyamuni had followed a life of social renunciation, homelessness, ascetic practices, and apprenticeship with other seekers before founding his own community of monastic renouncers. In the seventeenth century CE, homeless mendicants still wandered the roads of South Asia. A traveler would encounter Muslim fakirs and Hindu yogis and sadhus, all operating largely outside everyday society in their quest for transformative religious insight or experience. Among these wandering seekers, religious identity—Hindu or Muslim—was not especially important. A fakir could just as easily be a sadhu. More important were the signs of ascetic dedication in pursuit of a higher spiritual purpose. Here and there one of these mendicants might—like the Buddha long ago or Satya Pir more recently—gain a special reputation for insight or spiritual power and become the center of a new group of followers or disciples.

Curiously, one of the noticeable motifs in Chinese portraiture is the image of the foreign ascetic—a man clearly identified as foreign by a large nose and plenty of body hair. There were ascetics and mendicants in China, but asceticism was never so prevalent as in India. The emphasis on commitment to society and values such as filial piety kept people within their communities and families particularly during the Late Imperial period. The state certainly preferred to see its Buddhists and Daoists placed permanently in recognized, and officially patronized, temples or monasteries, living within communities of monks. Nevertheless, traveling ascetics and mendicants did play a role in Chinese social and religious life. Buddhist and Daoist monks traveled the land and offered spiritual and sometimes medical support to commoners in return for food and temporary shelter. For the most part, such people were tolerated and respected by the local population and officials. But there were episodes in Chinese history when traveling mendicants were persecuted. In one famous case during the eighteenth century, traveling Buddhist monks were the subject of strange allegations and persecution—people thought they were stealing their souls by clipping their pigtails.

In early modern China, one encountered Chinese religious clergy or functionaries (monks, priests, shamans, etc.) who seemed familiar. Matteo Ricci knew similar aspects of religious life in Europe. But the Jesuit Ricci also had to contend with a less familiar type of specialist, those associated with Confucianism. The great sage Confucius, who lived in the sixth century BCE, formed the basis of an ethical tradition that emphasized the learning of written texts and order in society. This tradition became in turn the foundation of the Chinese political-bureaucratic system in imperial and particularly late imperial times. Ricci was fascinated with the Chinese officials, the mandarins, and the literati elite of China. He concluded that they did not really have a religion. They seemed to be interested in ethics and in learning and governing. He noticed that they treated the religions of the people with disdain and often called them "superstitions" (*mixin*). Ricci learned quickly that the mandarins expressed hostility toward Buddhists and the Daoists, and he removed his orange cloth at some point. But he also noticed the deep impact Confucian tradition had on Chinese religions. Many religious practices tended to "behave" like, or even imitate, the bureaucracy.

Ricci also noticed that while the mandarins insisted on the this-worldly aspects of their tradition, they actually shared a great deal with the commoners. They encouraged the cult of Confucius as a holy man, or even as a god, and built temples for him that they shared with the commoners. Yet the literati prayed, like the simplest superstitious commoner, to special gods so they could succeed in their examinations and careers. They also worshiped their deceased ancestors like anyone else in China. Ricci also noticed that officials were, like the emperor himself at the top, committed to performing a large number of religious ceremonies. These rites were part of their duties as state officials and were regulated by a special ministry—the Ministry of Rites—located in the central government. In the end, Ricci could not tell if the Confucian literati were religious or not. And for a long time no one in Europe could really tell what was the nature of the religious scene in China.

Religious Scriptures

In the seventh century Xuanzang believed that the religious tradition of Buddhism was embodied and transmitted not just by religious specialists but also in the form of fundamental texts, verbal works that set out the basic premises, beliefs, and aims of the tradition. Many of these texts were said to be the direct words of the Buddha Shakyamuni himself, remembered and transmitted by his closest disciples. For this reason, Xuanzang spent much of his time in India studying and laboriously copying numerous Buddhist works. When he returned to China he brought with him some six hundred Sanskrit works and spent much of the remainder of his life translating them into Chinese.

In the seventeenth century, the major religious communities of India also cherished certain scriptures above all others. Many of these scriptures were ancient. For Muslims, the Quran contained the revelations that the Prophet Muhammad received from Allah, through the Arabic-speaking intermediary angel Gabriel, in and around Mecca from the year 609 until 632, when Muhammad died. For orthodox Hindus, the four Vedas were the paradigmatic sacred scriptures. The term *veda* denotes knowledge, and these ancient knowledge texts had been compiled in South Asia from roughly 1500 to 300 BCE, in an early form of the Sanskrit language. These fundamental scriptures had their own claims to special authority, their own human guardians, their own distinctive modes of transmission and promulgation, and their own ever-growing bodies of learned commentary and ancillary expansions. Like many fundamental religious works, however, the Quran and the Vedas allowed for multiple paths of interpretation, so their interpretive practices often led in quite different directions.

But in India new scriptures kept appearing. Among worshipers of the gods Shiva and Vishnu, for example, bodies of texts claimed to record the direct teachings of these preeminent deities. Among the various regional devotional groups, the compendia of vernacular-language hymns of the poet-saints, supplemented by hagiographical narratives of their god-centered lives, received the highest esteem. Among them, the most notable was the new scripture of the Sikhs. In the early seventeenth century, the fifth Sikh Guru, Arjan Das, assembled the large collection of hymns composed by Nanak and the other early Sikh Gurus into a compilation called the *Guru Granth Sahib* (*Revered Book of the Teachers*). Arjan had his chief scribe write it all down to preserve it intact. Though it was made up of oral song compositions, the *Guru Granth Sahib* was from this point on a written scripture, in contrast to the oral Vedas. Yet it was also meant to be sung. Almost every hymn within the collection was set to a particular musical form for proper performance. Sikhs viewed this recitative practice as a way to maintain the presence of the founding gurus, and later, in the eighteenth century, the *Guru Granth Sahib* took the place of any living guru as the highest religious authority. In Sikh temples, called Gurdwaras (or "doors to the Guru"), the printed *Guru Granth Sahib* is enshrined on an altar and honored with much the same liturgical attention that Hindus might devote to images of their deities.

In the Chinese case scripture plays a much less defined role in religious life. The Confucian Classics are central in the life of the intellectual elites as objects of study, but certainly not as sacred scripture. Confucius, on the other hand, is a god of sorts among commoners, far more important in this respect than the texts associated with him. We have seen how the historical tale of the monk Xuanzang turned into a novel a millennium later and how the novel produced a god—the monkey god. We have seen also many gods that were once real people and therefore no part of any recognized or well-defined scriptural tradition.

In the Daoist case, the *Daodejing* is important. But one would hardly say that the text itself is a central scripture. The fact that Laozi, as a deity of sorts, plays a major role in Daoist rituals further shows that scripture matters less. In Chinese Buddhism things are very different. While commoners simply worshiped, monks and priests treated the Buddhist sutras as sacred texts and as scripture. In some cases, sutras such the famous Lotus Sutra (the *Saddharma Pundarika Sutra* or the *Fahuajing*) were used as the basis for significant political activity. Truly standing out is the Quran, which for many, but not all, Chinese Muslims is a sacred scripture. Islam in China is exceptional in being a religion centered almost exclusively on a sacred text.

Conclusion

In the early modern period China and India were no longer in close cultural contact with each other as they had been in earlier times through the efforts of Indian and Chinese Buddhists, and a great deal within the religious realm separates the two and does not allow for an easy or smooth integration and comparison. But a global perspective brings to the fore several shared issues. These must be understood in general regional terms covering territory much larger than China and India alone—South East Asia, the Eastern Indian Ocean, Japan and Korea, and in recent decades the world itself.

China and India were religious powerhouses with regard to East Asia and Southeast Asia. Of course, both countries also absorbed a great deal from their immediate and distant environment. But thanks to their enormity and power, religious ideas, traditions, movements, and institutions that were formed in India and China shaped the religious history of the entire region. In the major case of Buddhism, the two had constituted a religious regional "power couple"—Buddhism was first formed in India but gained tremendous momentum in China, where it flourished and thrived. Without China's political and cultural dominance Buddhism would have had a very different history in Asia. The territory once known as Indo-China—now comprising several modern states—got this name in large part because of the religious impact both China and India had on it over the years.

Diversity is another important shared feature, and it powerfully characterizes religion in both countries, particularly from a global perspective. Not only are there many religions in China and India, there are also numerous gods and different types of supernatural beings. This diverse divine scene corresponds to numerous religious institutions, traditions, forms of practice, and practitioners. This does not mean that there were no specifically dominant religions in China and India. Different states and regimes in both countries certainly tried to identify some religions and practices as more dominant and therefore more favorable than others. But religious diversity in both countries was so strong that most governments found it necessary to be more all-encompassing and inclusive. This was the case, we can say with some reservation, even when the ruling elites were clearly identified by a specific religion—the Mughals in India are the quintessential example. Diversity also played a key role in "breeding" new religions and new forms of religious practice. Sikhism in India and Zen

Buddhism in China are but two very clear examples of religions produced by religious encounters. Religious diversity also meant a great degree of mobility of divinities, practices, and practitioners and worshipers. Although most religions had clearly defined elite institutions and traditions, boundaries between them were for the most part quite porous, and commoners crossed with great creativity and agility. This does not mean that the state in both countries refrained from interfering and regulating religion. Governments in China and India were heavily involved in religious life on almost all levels. Rulers assumed religious titles, and rulership itself had religious properties attached to it. Rulers and officials also worshiped in state-sponsored places and patronized religious institutions from the imperial level down to the lowest levels of society.

A third, crucial aspect that both countries seem to have shared is the lack of a clear concept for religion. This is evident from the diversity in vocabulary—there are numerous words that function as "religion" in different contexts, and not one can be said to clearly define religion in the European-Christian sense of the word. This diversity in vocabulary and the diffuseness that characterizes words related to religions reflect the condition of religious diversity. At the same time, they also contribute to it. This also is probably why religions in these countries resisted classification for many centuries and even now. Herein perhaps lies the most decisive change in the history of religion and religious in both countries in recent times—the introduction of Western ideas about "religion" in the wake of the encounter between China and India and the early modern and modern West. One cannot appreciate the history of religions in China and India from the early modern period on without understanding the impact of the two countries' encounter with European culture and later, with European domination.

Perhaps more important than simply "making Christians," Western influence on both China and India came with the introduction of the category "religion" itself as it emerged in Europe during the early modern and modern period. In both countries the introduction of the term was accompanied by an effort to classify belief systems, institutions, and ideas as *religions*—Hinduism, Buddhism, Daoism, Jainism, etc. This process also meant separating religions from one another and classifying others as philosophies—Confucianism is probably the best example. The fact that the process of recognizing religions in China and India rested on European experience and thought often leaves us confused when we think about religions in these countries, and many of them often seem to change their guise between philosophy and religion.

Finally, the process of recognizing and classifying religions in China and India had a tremendous impact of the political history of these countries. In China, modern governments—both Nationalist and Communist—initiated several major campaigns against religion and religious activity. These peaked during the Cultural Revolution of 1966–1976. In India, the process of recognizing and separating religions opened major rifts between Hindus and Muslims, resulting in the brutal break of the subcontinent into "Islamic" and "Hindu" states.

For Further Reading

India and China

Keown, Damien. *Buddhism: A Very Short Introduction*. Oxford: Oxford University Press, 2013.

Kieschnick, John and Meir Shahar. *India in the Chinese Imagination: Myth, Religion, and Thought*. Philadelphia: University of Pennsylvania Press, 2014.

China

Gardner, Daniel K. *Confucianism: A Very Short Introduction*. Oxford: Oxford University Press, 2014.

Lagerwey, Pierre Marsone. *Modern Chinese Religion II: 1850–2015*. Leiden: Brill, 2016.

Maspero, Henri and Frank A. Kierman. *Taoism and Chinese Religion*. Melbourne: Quirin Press, 2014.

Miller, James. *Daoism: A Short Introduction*. Oxford: Oneworld, 2005.

Shahar, Meir and Robert P. Weller. *Unruly Gods: Divinity and Society in China*. Honolulu: University of Hawai'i Press, 1996.

Thompson, Laurence G. *Chinese Religion: An Introduction*. Belmont: Wadsworth, 1999.

Yao, Xinzhong and Yanxia Zhao. *Chinese Religion: A Contextual Approach*. London: Continuum, 2010.

India

Asher, Catherine B. and Cynthia Talbot. *India Before Europe*. Cambridge: Cambridge University Press, 2006.

Davis, Richard H. *The Bhagavad Gita: A Biography*. Princeton, NJ: Princeton University Press, 2015.

Jaffrelot, Christophe. *Religion, Caste, and Politics in India*. New York: Columbia University Press, 2011.

Knott, Kim. *Hinduism: A Very Short Introduction*. Oxford: Oxford University Press, 2016.

Laine, James W. *Meta-Religion: Religion and Power in World History*. Berkeley: University of California Press, 2014.

Madan, Triloki N. *Religion in India*. Delhi: Oxford University Press, 2012.

CHAPTER VIII

Art and Vision

Varieties of World Making

MOLLY AITKEN AND EUGENE WANG

"Asia is One" famously began the Japanese scholar Okakura Kakuzo's *Ideals of the East*. Written in English in 1904, the book added Kakuzo's voice to a heated international conversation that was then crystallizing stereotypes about Eastern cultures to produce a compelling idea of Asia. This idea was formulated as a powerful rejoinder to the experience of Western political, economic, and technological dominance. It defined Asia and the West through decisive oppositions: Asia was to be viewed as spiritual, peaceful, idealistic, and traditional, opposed to a materialistic, aggressive, empirical, modern West. Numerous Westerners colluded in this idea because it conveyed a hope that Asia might save humanity's soul.

"Asia knows nothing of the fierce joys of a time-devouring locomotion," wrote Kakuzo, "but she has still the far deeper travel-culture of the pilgrimage and the wandering monk." Here was the promotion of Asian spirituality that still resonates across the globe today. Kakuzo understood the ideals of the East to be rooted in its religiosity, but he was principally interested in the visual arts and was Japan's most active and vocal advocate of a worldwide movement to return to premodern aesthetic values. This chapter explores Chinese and Indian art with a Japanese scholar, because, whereas Buddhism had disseminated the arts of India into China and Japan in the first millennium, Japan led the movement, called Nihonga, to create a pan-Asian, neotraditional art in the early twentieth century, partly under Kakuzo's impetus. The quintessential pictorial values of this movement were wash and haze.

Haze: A Flashpoint

Nihonga's starting point was the rejection of oil paint, the medium of European academic naturalism, in favor of watercolor, which had traditionally been composed of vegetable and mineral pigments mixed with a water-soluble binder. While watercolor was a minor art in Europe, it had been the medium of high art in China, Japan, and India. Watercolor washes, which were created by thinning pigment with water, could suggest light effects and evoke physical and emotional depths (fig. 8.1). In Nihonga painting, washes were typically hazy, a quality that Nihonga teachers conveyed to their Chinese and Indian students, making haze, for a brief time, the most evident visual manifestation of "Asia as One." Many of its early twentieth-century proponents treated haze as the expression of both a disembodied spirituality, the essence of Asia's heritage, and the ideal qualities of an Asian modernity-in-the-making, thus enabling the perfect marriage of past and present.

The pictorial quality of haze is a flashpoint for a comparison of Chinese and Indian art because it enabled the first significant cultural rendezvous for China and India, by way of Japan, since the Buddhist exchanges of many centuries before. Although haze briefly became a moving expression of transnational Asian unity, from a twenty-first-century perspective, it mediates a very different history of local particularity and incommensurability. In retrospect, haze did not signify identically in early 1900s India and China, and, because it was tied to a rhetoric of cultural authenticity, it offers a precise foil against which to explore the distinct premodern arts of China and India that national artists and critics sought to bring back to the present. Japan's Nihonga painters conceived of haze as a rejection of Chinese line, but China had been experimenting with haze for centuries. Meanwhile, India's premodern painters had traditionally been committed to pictorial clarity. Haze materializes for us what the ideas of the past and present meant in different parts of Asia at the moment, around 1900, when an international idea of Asia was coming most forcefully into being.

To define their hazy-style paintings as the embodiment of Japanese modernity, the Japanese Nihonga artists resorted to a convenient reductionism.

Figure 8.1 Yokoyama Taikan (1868–1958). *Moonlight in the Woods.* 1904–1905. Unmounted; ink and light color on silk, 75.8 x 51.2 cm.
Museum of Fine Arts, Boston. Accession number 27.806

Chinese painting came down to the core value of lines. Traditional Japanese painting, exemplified by the Kano school and seen as an offshoot of the Chinese tradition, was characterized likewise. Nihonga painters preferred washes over lines. The opposition of formal qualities thus became contentious. Wash (modernity) was pitched against lines (tradition). The nebulous wash makes it possible to create a hazy effect, thereby highlighting the light-and-shadow interplay. Traditional Chinese and Japanese painting was seen as lacking in this quality, a staple feature in Western painting. Wash-derived haze, therefore, was the Nihonga artists' link to the modern West and their means of forging national identity. They could thus assume their modern stance by aligning with the Western spirit; meanwhile, they could stake out an Eastern home turf by continuing the time-honored traditional brush-and-ink medium distinct from Western oil painting.

How Chinese Art Discovered Haze

To be sure, the Japanese *morotai* artists (*morotai*—"hazy style"—was originally a term used derisively by critics) projected a skewed view of traditional Chinese painting. However, this view serves as a viable prism to frame the complex tradition of Chinese art. The reduction of Chinese painting to lines is a convenient half-truth. The line-versus-wash opposition, staged by the Nihonga artists around the turn of the twentieth century as a central divide between tradition and modernity, is, in fact, a recurrent leitmotif in the long tradition of Chinese art. More specifically, the line-versus-ink problem makes an easy story of the formation of the very medium of Chinese brush-and-ink painting.

Chinese art discovered haze three times—respectively in the fifth, twelfth, and twentieth centuries—for different reasons. Each time it was a revolution and marked a departure from the entrenched practice, thereby blazing new paths in Chinese art. The first instance was inspired, in part, by a proverbial shadow image. Accounts of a proverbial Shadow Cave in the region of Nagarahāra (west of the present-day Jalalabad, Afghanistan) reached China around 400 CE. The cave lore has it that Shakyamuni Buddha, having subjugated a poisonous dragon, leaped into the grotto wall where he stayed as a shadow image, visible only from a distance. The Shadow Cave fired Chinese imagination, attracting a succession of Chinese monk-pilgrims from the fifth to the seventh centuries. An eminent monk named Huiyuan (334–416) even built a replica cave on Mount Lu with its own shadow image—a painted icon—inside. The painting is no longer extant. Its properties can be inferred from eulogies to this "Shadow Image" composed by Huiyuan and his community. It exhibits notable formal qualities such as chiaroscuro. Much was invested in indistinct optical and atmospheric qualities such as "darkness," "dimness," "obscurity," and "void" to offset the luminous forms of "manifestations." These formal qualities were thoroughly alien and refreshing to Chinese pictorial sensibility, long accustomed to drawn contours. Now hazy treatment began to soften those hardened contours. The newfound interest was a marked departure from traditional Chinese surface-oriented curvilinear painting. Cave paintings in Dunhuang of the fifth through seventh centuries, precisely the time frame when the Chinese interest in Shadow Cave was at its height, corroborate this new visual interest in haze registered in the writings by Huiyuan and his circles.

The second surge of interest in haze was around the eleventh and twelfth centuries. In contrast to the first wave that swept through cave shrines, this time the revolution occurred in a different medium, i.e., the surface of scrolls. While the history of Chinese art can be traced back millennia, the medium of brush-and-ink painting mounted on paper or silk scrolls, fans, or album leaves holds the pride of place. It is now often readily recognized as the distinct epitome of "Chinese art." Its long history notwithstanding, not till the period spanning roughly the tenth through fourteenth centuries did the scroll format bearing brush-and-ink painting come to fruition as a full-fledged medium. Nearly all potential formal properties were explored and grounds covered in this period. Artists of subsequent periods essentially worked within the parameters already defined.

Several factors contributed to the formation of the medium. The emergence of landscape in the tenth and eleventh centuries as a self-sufficient genre was a decisive turning point. The art of painting, long regarded as the domain of artisanal practice, changed complexion when literary elites co-opted the medium as an expressive means of cultural pursuit of self-cultivation or a material token that facilitated in-group communication and exchanges. Paper as an increasingly favored medium for painting made it possible for the brush-wielding painters to fully explore its solvent properties to accommodate "ink plays" and other visual effects.

The line-and-wash, or more precisely, brush-and-ink dynamics became an issue in the Northern Song (960–1127). Landscape theorists of the time spoke of the "brush" and "ink" as distinct categories of formal qualities. Here "brush" (*bi*) means linear tracings of the ink-loaded and wrist-controlled brush tip whose movement articulates contours of depicted images; it also encompasses the texturing strokes (*cun*) applied in areas circumscribed by brushed contour lines to spell out complexions, volume, and substance. "Ink" (*mo*), by contrast, refers to expansive, amorphous, and contourless water-diluted washes used to lend tonalities and resonance to the painting. It is typically used to depict moods and shades of mists, clouds, and the haze of dawn and dusk.

Three regional traditions dominated eleventh-century landscape painting: the northwest tradition best represented by Fan Kuan (fl. 990–1020); the east coast tradition following the style of Li Cheng (919–967); and the southeast (lower Yangtze River valley) tradition exemplified by Dong Yuan and Juran (tenth century). Of the three, the latter two displayed distinct interest in hazy effects. While no single extant work can be securely attributed to Li Cheng, Dong Yuan, and Juran, eleventh-century written accounts testify to this pictorial impulse. By the second half of the eleventh century, this interest had grown considerably. To Guo Xi (c. 1020–c. 1090), a painter from the central plain who served as the artist-in-residence under Emperor Shenzong (r. 1068–1085), there was practically no such thing as a fixed landscape out there except its variable aspects contingent upon particular moments in seasons, moments of the day, and weather conditions: "Mists and haze [on mountains] in a real landscape differ through the seasons." Landscapists were advised to observe changing aspects of nature and capture the perceptual effects accordingly.

The growing interest in the hazy effect in the eleventh century hastened the trend toward monochrome-ink landscape. This trend ought to be seen against the backdrop of the rise of landscape, first intimated in the eighth century. The dominant mode then was the colorist blue-and-green or gold-and-green landscape (fig. 8.2). The operative colors are mostly mineral and vegetable pigments: azurite blue, malachite green, umber, and so forth. The "golden" effect is created through the use of vegetable color of rattan yellow. The colorist effect of the eighth-century landscape registers a cultural preoccupation with the heightened experience of transcendent existence. The aspiration for the imaginary land of the immortals in Tang (618–907) times did not amount to rejection of earthly life. Rather, it was a sublimated reflection of an aristocratic taste for material opulence in times of prosperity. The blue-and-green landscape born of this cultural milieu

Figure 8.2 Anon. *Emperor Minghuang's Journey to Shu*. Song copy of eighth-century work. Ink and colors on silk, 55.9 × 81 cm.
National Palace Museum, Taipei

bears the imprint of the pursuit of sensorial stimuli, an interest epitomized by refinement of minerals for life-prolonging elixirs. The transcendent landscape was thus conceived as a fantastic and otherworldly realm: continuous lines with the effect of hard-etched tracings define strange shapes of rockeries. Azurite blue and malachite green cover the linear-circumscribed surfaces. Clouds integral to this transcendent landscape are not the nebulous affairs we see in later artworks. Instead, they are hard-edged curvilinear patterns.

The Song landscape took on a radically different complexion. Broader access to upward social mobility through imperial recruitment examinations had done much to level the ground for aspiring degree candidates from all walks of life, including those with humble origins. The new elite class abhorred the jaded aristocratic taste of the previous ages. Outgrowing the uniform blue-and-green landscapes of opulence, they preferred a landscape of personal visions and subjective moods (fig. 8.3). It is no surprise that painters of the second half of the eleventh century compared landscape moods to human physiognomy, feelings, and states of minds. As

Figure 8.3 Guo Xi (ca. 1020–ca. 1090). *Early Spring.* 1072. Hanging scroll, ink and light color on silk, 158.3 x 108.1 cm.
National Palace Museum, Taipei

the eleventh-century landscape painter Guo Xi put it: "A mountain has water as blood, foliage as hair, haze and clouds as its spirit and character."

Paradoxically, a confluence of seemingly conflicting trends and impulses spurred the growing pictorial interest in haze. On the one hand, the increasing empirical-mindedness fostered observational interest and naturalist sensibility. On the other hand, the introspective literary culture shaped a more subjective and interiorized mode of viewing the world and artistic means of registering that subjectivity. An instruction given by a seasoned painter to a student regarding ways of picturing landscapes epitomizes the eleventh-century interest in the empirical art of observation. As Shen Gua (1031–1095) notes:

> You should first look for a damaged wall, and then stretch plain silk against it. Gaze at it day and night. When you have looked for a sufficient length of time, you will see through the silk the high and low parts, or curves and angles, on the surface of the wall, which will take on the appearance of landscape. As you hold this in your mind and your eyes consider it, the high parts will become mountains and the low parts, water; crevices will become valleys and cracks, torrents; the prominent parts will seem to be the foreground and the obscure, the distance. As your spirit leads and your imagination constructs, you will see *indistinctly* the images of human beings, birds, grasses, and trees, flying or moving about. Once they are complete in your eyes, then follow your imagination to command your brush.

The tenor of the instruction is both highly observation-derived empiricism and imaginative subjective construction.

The artistic investment in haze also reflects the deepening of literary culture in the eleventh century. The area south of the Yangtze River, the land of the Southern Tang that the Song (960–1269) conquered, had been a wellspring of sophisticated literary refinement for some time. The cultural reorientation under the Northern Song in the form of downplaying military or martial swagger in favor of civility led to a "southern turn." The reputation of tenth-century painters such as Dong Yuan (934–962) and Juran (fl. tenth century), whose names had remained relatively obscure in the first half of the eleventh century, soared in the second half. The hazy landscapes growing out of the humid and mellow southern environs became a viable model for emulation by painters beyond the south-of-Yangtze region. As noted by the learned statesman, poet, and cosmologist Shen Gua (1031–1095), Dong's landscapes were too cursory for close viewing; their forms emerge only if seen from afar. They typically feature "distant views with autumnal mists," or evening scenes with villages "half-obscured in the deep distance."

The increased interest in haze led to the currency of the misty and dreamy Xiao-and-Xiang river scenes in the Song. Inspired by the lore of Qu Yuan (343–278 BCE) and the ancient southern rhapsodic tradition, the imaginary topography evokes the landscape of the humid south, suffused with sorrowful emotive tonality and shades of subjective moods. This accounts for the gloom of the Xiao-Xiang landscape. Most of the eight set scenes are rain-drenched, overcast, or dim dusk views. Hazy landscapes by Song Di (c. 1015–c.1080), the leading practitioner of the landscape mode, are said to display "a touch of somber, atmospheric, dismal and pale complexion." The popularity of this misty landscape was such that painters vied with one another to make the hazy scenes even hazier. The same critic who appreciated the poetic overtones of the Xiao-Xiang landscape complained: "[These evening scenes] are hard to figure out. It is impossible to paint the bell sound, to begin with. And to show the Xiao-Xiang [riverscape] at night! And then to add rain on top of that! What can one see?" While no firmly datable eleventh-century Xiao-Xiang landscape paintings are extant, surviving twelfth-century works testify to the trend. Brushed lines still articulate landscape forms and figures. However, massive spreads of ink washes in various shades and tonalities pervade the composition to the extent that they threaten to overwhelm and obscure all those brush-articulated forms.

Mi Versus Ni

The much-touted Mi-style landscape epitomizes this larger trend. Traditional art historical accounts commonly lionize and credit Mi Fu (1051–1107) and Mi Youren (1074–1151), father and son, as innovative trailblazers who inaugurated the "ink play" tradition of rendering hazy cloudy-mountain landscapes. No credible painting by Mi Fu has survived. Extant paintings by Mi Youren present cloudy landscapes almost devoid of any brushed contour lines (fig. 8.4). Shades of ink, highlighted by dots, spell vague forms of gentle cone-shaped hills eroded by unpainted blank passages

Figure 8.4 Mi Youren (1074–1151). *Cloudy Mountains.* 12th century. Handscroll; ink on paper, 27.6 × 57 cm.
Metropolitan Museum of Art, New York

that suggest clouds, mist, and vapors. Mi Youren calls these instances of "ink play." The edginess of the Mi cloudy landscape was self-conscious mutiny against the well-wrought professionalism and artisanal practice of painting that had prevailed up to the eleventh century. Modeling of correct forms, careful handling of details, fixation on verisimilitude, and so on were seen as signs of excess of craftsmanship that stifled individual creativity. In fact, many eleventh-century literary elites had voiced discontent with what they saw as the mindless professional craftsmanship that had impoverished the art of painting. Mi style's freakishness epitomized this growing literary-elitist discontent. Renouncing technical requirements of traditional painting practice, Mi Fu used "twists of paper, sugarcane husks, and lotus pods" for his inky effect. While he is credited with this idiosyncratic practice, it signals a larger trend sketched above. The cloudy landscapes Mi Fu executed through unconventional means had synergy with the aforementioned practice based on observing the protrusions and crevices of plain silk over a damaged wall, the currency of picturing the gloomy Xiao-and-Xiang river-scenes, and so forth.

The Mi-style cloudy landscape has ever since been a landmark in the history of Chinese painting. Seventeenth-century theorists touted the two Mis as major instigators of the literati painting tradition premised on literary elitist self-cultivation and deliberate amateurism; it thrived on deskilling and renouncing professional fastidiousness and artisanal polish. This familiar account obscures the fact that the cloudy landscape was in fact part of a large trend in the twelfth century. Professional painters also participated, and its revival in the thirteenth and fourteenth centuries was largely due to the innovation of an influential Mongol elitist patron named Gao Kegong (1248–1310) who both practiced and modified this subgenre. Moreover, the literati theory does not quite explain a curious contradiction. The cloudy landscape ink play reached its most freakish excess in the second half of the thirteenth century. The Xiao-Xiang landscapes painted by Muqi Fachang (1210?–1269?) and Yujian Rofen (late thirteenth c.) fully live up to the literary sense of "ink play." They are dramatically abbreviated ink passages vaguely suggesting landscape forms. The bravura of willfully splashed and flung ink caused the fourteenth-century literati's ire. As the fourteenth-century critic Tang Hou notes: "The recent painter Muqi, the monk Fachang, made ink plays (which are) coarse and ugly, and without ancient method."

The pendulum of taste swung in the Yuan dynasty (1271–1368). Chinese literary elites became introspective and reflective about the morals of dynastic fall. They abhorred the cavalier flung-ink excess and frivolity of the "recent" (*jinshi*) style of previous generations and pursued an alternative aesthetic standard in the name of "ancient flavor." While the "antiquity" they aspired toward in theory might have stretched all the way back to pre-Tang and Tang times, in real practice, Northern Song precedents were the available models they could access. Even when it came to that legacy, the Yuan literati's aesthetic preference was selective. They singled out the primacy of brush line that dominated Northern Song painting, as opposed to the prevalence of washes that ran out of hand in the Southern Song (1127–1279)—the ink play "Recentism" which they despised. Works by Zhao Mengfu (1254–1322), Huang Gongwang (1269–1354), and Ni Zan (1301–1374) best exemplify the Yuan landscape aesthetics (fig. 8.5). Using dry and center-brushed strokes, the Yuan literati perfected the brush-centric mode of painting. Ink washes were sparingly used, if at all, except by Wu Zhen (1280–1354) and Fang Congyi (1302–1393). Thus for subsequent centuries, critics speak of Song-and-Yuan opposition in selective and grossly overgeneralized terms. The wash-centric Song—to be more precise, Southern Song—is pitched against the brush-centric Yuan; the freewheeling insouciance of the "Song" (i.e., Southern Song) is opposed to the austerity and reticence of the Yuan.

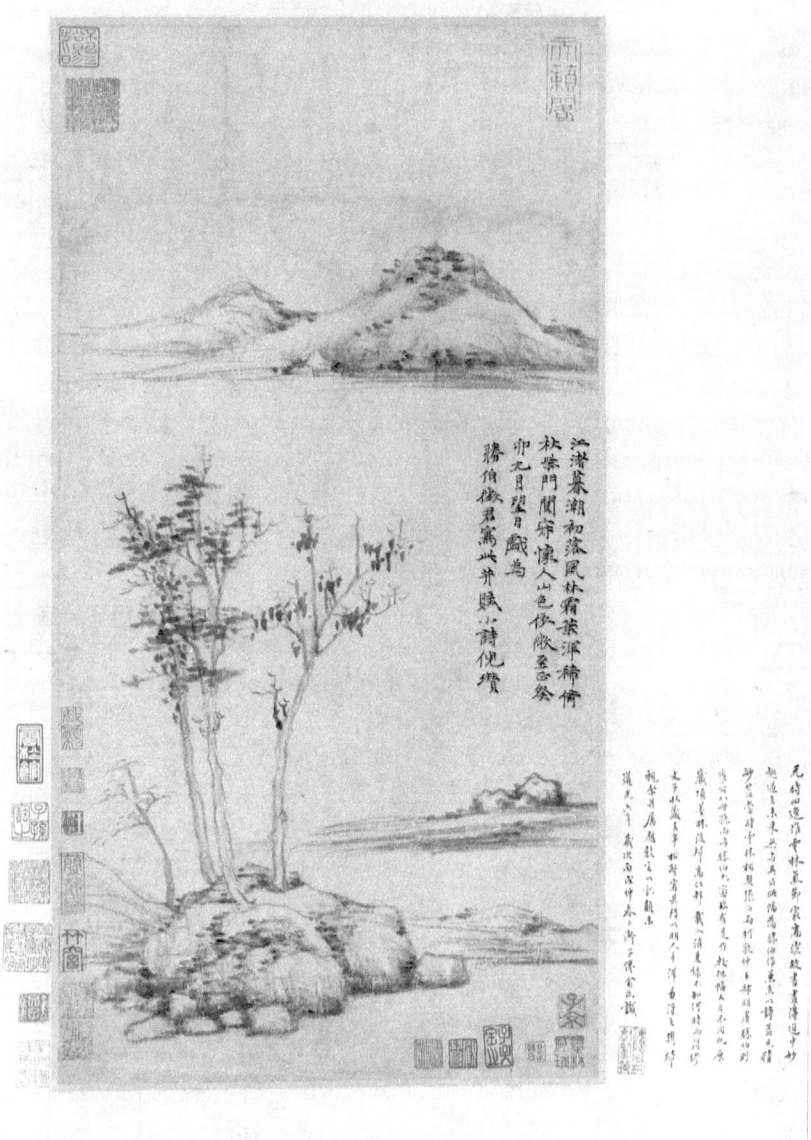

Figure 8.5 Ni Zan (1306–1374). *Wind among the Trees on the Riverbank.* 1363. Hanging scroll; ink on paper, 59.1 x 31.1 cm.
Metropolitan Museum of Art, New York

This opposition cuts too many corners in view of historical reality. But the uncluttered paradigm formulated as such is a convenient framework for subsequent ages. A neat opposition, Mi versus Ni, could thus be posited as two distinct exemplary stylistic models. The Mi mode (Song) is a handy shorthand reference to the wash-centric method; the Ni (Yuan) mode epitomizes the dry brush-centric mode.

The choice of Mi or Ni became a matter of contention for late Ming theorists and artists, whose master narrative of Chinese art is still with us. It is pointless to recapitulate the deeply flawed and often misleading art-historical storyline constructed by Dong Qichang (1555–1636) and his south-of-Yangtze circle. Suffice it to say that in Dong's scheme that pitches literati against professionals over centuries, the foremost great masters populating the lineage of literati tradition include both Mi and Ni. Dong's own painting practice also shows his alignment with both landscape models. However, Dong discriminated between the two modes. His embrace of the Ni model was total and wholehearted. While theoretically touting the Mi model, he was ambivalent about it. If not handled well, he warned, its debonair tendency might run out of hand.

Yet the wash-centric Mi style spoke to the rampant late Ming "intuitive individualism." The libertine attitude, the cultivation of individual freedom, the hedonistic insouciance of the time found the liberal washes a fitting expression. The Mi-style wash-centric mode had its revival, especially with cavalier literati like Li Liufang (1575–1629). Meanwhile, the elitist valorization of Yuan painting reached its apex, making the dry-brushed Ni model the unrivaled aesthetic standard and staple of good taste. The two models—the wash-centric Mi and the dry-brushed Ni—coexisted without posing too much of a problem of choices for the Ming. They spoke to different needs. It was only in the early Qing that allegiance to either mode took on more suggestive stances and overtones.

For many early Qing artists in the wake of the traumatic dynastic change, finding a fitting style for picturing state of mind and moods was a challenge and problem. Ni and Mi were two viable formal models. The late Ming valorization of Ni-style landscape as the ultimate in good taste ensured its continued prevalence in the early Qing. In the hands of painters such as the monk Hongren (1610–1664), the sparse compositions created through the taut formal economy of dry-brushed linear brevity convey a deep sense of austerity and reticence. To be sure, its stoicism amounts to a fitting portrayal of the mood of the time. Some, however, found this dry-brush minimalism wanting. The drastic dynastic change created the urgency for expressive venting. The time-honored conceit of poetry as "voiced picture" and painting as "muted poetry" took on renewed energy, except that painting now aspired toward the condition of poetic voice. To Yun Shouping (1633–1690), for instance, the art of painting was about capturing "the howling amid old trees against a bleak sky." It was not uncommon for a painter to derive his composition from a song.

This explains some early Qing complaints about the Ni-style landscape model and its seventeenth-century derivatives. It was seen as too muted, lacking in the expressive voice effect that early Qing artists desired. Backlash against the Ni model gathered momentum. Wang Duo (1592–1652) categorically dismissed it: "Though with pale flavor, the likes of Ni Yunlin suffer from dryness and drabness, much like a frail sick man about to breathe his last. It is said to possess some lithe ease and [adorable] fragility. This is just too much."

For some early Qing painters, therefore, the problem with the Ni landscape model was its "deadening stillness." The sparse landscape delineated by abbreviated dry-brushed contours may have mirrored the loyalists' eremitic impulse in the face of the bleak and depressing early Qing political landscape. Its downside is just as apparent. It did not lend itself as a cathartic channel for venting pent-up frustration. In short, it did not have a voice. Early Qing artists needed a more forthcoming and expressive visual idiom.

This is where the Mi-style wash-centrism appeared to fit the bill. Its fluid ink washes are melodious and heavier in tonal effects. However, much as it was consistently exalted, the Mi-style model was fraught with problems for seventeenth-century painters. The hallmarks of the cloudscape are easily recognizable: contourless forms, liberal ink washes, and so on. They were also easily imitable: the casual, quick, and effusive application of ink washes instantly create a Mi, or quasi-Mi, cloudscape effect. Much as Dong Qichang, the late-Ming arbiter of taste, exalted the Mi model and practiced the Mi style, he was wary of its potential travesty for fear of "lapsing into casual frivolity."

The polarizing political climate of the Ming-Qing transition made individual subscription to a particular stylistic model a contentious issue. Stylistic choices in the late Ming carried no grave consequences. Personal temperament predisposed one to identify with a certain received model, either Ni or Mi. However, much was at stake with such choices in the early Qing.

According to the historian Frederic Wakeman, two character types became distinct in the early Qing: the "Romantics" and "Stoics." The "Romantics" were by temperament "generous, bold, and expressive." Exemplary "Romantics," such as Qian Qianyi (1582–1664) and Wu Weiye (1609–1671), were among the most celebrated poets of the time. Both served the Southern Ming regime and went on to become "twice-serving" officials in the Qing government, even though they felt deeply conflicted. By contrast, "Stoics" possessed "intransigent integrity." They were inclined toward controlling and regulating excessive emotions. With strong conviction in rational order and responsibility, they were committed to public duties. Exemplary "Stoics," such as Chen Zilong (1608–1647), Gu Yanwu (1613–1682), and Wan Shouqi (1603–1652), all turned out to be uncompromising Ming loyalists. To a large extent, the "Romantics" had a spiritual affinity with the wash-centricism of the Mi model, and the "Stoics" were aligned with the sparse and dry Ni model.

The Romantics faced a dilemma. Those who had succumbed to the lure of the romantic abandon of the Mi model in the late Ming abruptly recanted their former ways after the dynastic change. The morning-after sobering up led to a critical rejection of this stylistic flamboyance, unfitting for a graver time. The Stoics had their problem as well. The "deadening stillness" of the dry-brushed sparse Ni model failed to speak to the urgent expressive need of "the howling amid old trees against a bleak sky." So neither the Mi nor Ni model quite fit the early Qing. The Ni model was too muted; the Mi model was too insouciant. The challenge for artists of the time was therefore: How to have both stoic gravitas and expressive forthrightness? How to both sulk and sing?

Gong Xian (1618–1689) provided a solution by having it both ways (fig. 8.6). He compensated for the Ni-style sparseness with the Mi-style heaviness. Conversely, he treated the Mi tonality in the manner of the Ni dryness. His "wash" has no use for the moisture expected of ink washes. Instead it is a palimpsest of layers of dry-brushed dark tones. The formal device thus provides a perfect solution to the dilemma outlined above: namely, to find a way to both sulk and sing. The posturing and semblance of wash carries the force of release, flow, and resonance, thereby feeding the impression of singing qualities. However, as soon as the wash posturing signals melodies, the singing impulse is kept in check. Drying up the wash forestalls the overflow, levity, and profligacy and adds gravitas to the

Figure 8.6 Gong Xian (1619–1689). *Lone Tree in a Mountainous Lake*. 1671. Album leaf, ink and watercolor on paper; silk mount, 24.45 x 45.09 cm.
The Nelson-Atkins Museum of Art, Kansas [Object number 60-36/10]

picture. So the total effect is one of release and check, singing and its suppression.

In broad historical perspective, Gong's heavily inked landscape points to the roads not taken. It suggests, first of all, affinity with chiaroscuro. European prints brought by Jesuits commanded attention in seventeenth-century China. Whether Gong borrowed a page from the European playbook or not, he did not acknowledge it, as he was primarily interested in fashioning a distinct visual language that spoke to the cultural dynamics of his time. The Mi cloudscape was his professed source of inspiration, but he actually turned the model on its head. Instead of haze and mist, Gong's palimpsest of ink layers showcases illuminated spots of pristine white, accented by the surrounding black mass. The effect, as Gong states, is that of moonlit luminance, the trailing sounds of bells and chimes from distant Buddhist monasteries, the hard-earned lull after stormy spells. Neither European influence nor the Mi-style tradition fully explains Gong's landscape style, though they may have informed it. Gong's language of ink grew out of the early Qing turmoil. The chastening black-and-white contrast evokes the precious stillness in the imaginary soundscape. It is a formal stance that transcends its circumstances and time. Gong was so ahead of his time that his contemporaries hardly understood him; not until the late nineteenth and early twentieth century was he rediscovered. His visual idiom was embraced by twentieth-century Chinese painters, foremost among them Huang Binhong (1865–1955).

Haze and Modernity

The medium of Chinese painting became an increasingly contentious issue in the twentieth century. For millennia, its practitioners and viewers had never felt compelled to consider its distinct set of material and formal properties in a self-enclosed cultural context. The question of what constituted *Chinese* art had never been an issue. Encounters with art forms of other cultures in the previous centuries had never quite shaken the Chinese self-confidence in their own art. The Western powers' intrusion in China in the early decades of the century, however, made the reckoning inevitable. The increased foreign presence and the opening of the coastal treaty port cities heightened the awareness of Western art forms. Moreover, larger cross-cultural comparative perspectives, strongly affected by social Darwinism, framed the Chinese reckoning with the respective merits of the Eastern and Western art traditions. Humiliation following repeated military defeats by the Western powers prompted a deep soul-searching among Chinese intellectuals. This colored their perception of art traditions. Radical political reformers such as Kang Youwei (1858–1927) and Chen Duxiu (1879–1942) made art a contentious political-cultural issue. They lambasted traditional Chinese painting, as exemplified by the landscape paintings of the exalted Four Wangs of early Qing, i.e., Wang Shimin (1592–1680), Wang Jian (1598–1677), Wang Hui (1632–1717), and Wang Yuanqi (1642–1715). The critics correlated art traditions with cultural strengths and weaknesses. They considered Western art more compelling because it was perceived as the embodiment of advanced science and technology. In contrast, they deplored traditional Chinese art for its effete and anemic tenor symptomatic of the spiritual malaise that had long plagued China. Its indifference to effects of verisimilitude was seen as evidence of its deficiency in scientific rigor and technological prowess.

The self-strengthening push motivated many Chinese students to seek education abroad. In the 1900s, Japan was the closest outlet for modern

Western knowledge. The first group of Chinese seeking art training in Japan came mostly from southeast China. Most notable among them were Gao Jianfu (1879–1951), his younger brother Gao Qifeng (1889–1933), and Chen Shuren (1884–1948), all from Guangdong. The three were to be the backbone of the Lingnan School, the first vanguard group in twentieth-century China to reform art. Their sojourn in Japan shaped their artistic vision and had a lasting impact on their careers in China.

 The Gao brothers in Japan found it easy to warm up to the liberal use of wash and technical treatment of light and shadows. However, they refused to renounce brush lines as a key property of ink painting. Even though they were based in Tokyo, they did not fully embrace the Japanese premise of the hazy-style aesthetics. Kyoto, not the more fashionable Tokyo, resonated with the Cantonese students. The Kyoto-based Shijō School founded by Maruyama Ōkyo (1733–1795) and Matsumura Goshun (1752–1811) had more to offer. Ōkyo and his followers had, a century or so earlier, practiced a syncretism by drawing on diverse resources. Constrained by the Tokugawa shogunate's (1600–1868) exclusion policy that denied them direct access to European art, they relied on what came through Nagasaki, the only open port. Illustrated books containing Dutch copperplate engravings with camera obscura effects and Chinese Suzhou prints with stereoscopic qualities derived from European *vues d'optique* gave them hints about how to produce paintings with verisimilitude effects. If Ōkyo provided the model of illusionism, Goshun supplied lyricism. The Japanese Nanga School style, descendant of Yuan-Ming Chinese literati painting, was Goshun's source of inspiration for his brand of pictorial style, suffused with poetic sensitivity and emotional resonance. Takeuchi Seihō (1864–1942) updated the Ōkyo School legacy for the Chinese. His exposure to European art during his tour of Europe in 1900 allowed him to renew and reenergize the Shijō School tradition with techniques of the European landscape painters J.M.W. Turner and Camille Corot.

 The Shijō School tradition, with its balance between technical mastery of close empirical observation of the physical world and emotionally resonant wash-derived lyricism, decidedly recalls the Song tradition. This resonance was not lost on the Cantonese painters. They thus advocated for a return to that tradition—a radical revisionist view at the time. Literati arbiters of taste from the fourteenth to seventeenth centuries had perpetuated the story of the Yuan literati triumph over the Song professionals. Sparse and austere Yuan brush-centrism trumped the effusive wash-centrism of the Southern Song over the centuries. Although the Southern Song wash-centrism had been largely sidelined in the canon of Chinese art, it survived in the wash-centric aesthetics that held on in Japan all the way to modern times. The Meiji (1868–1912) appropriation of European watercolors further reinforced it. These resources informed the hazy style in the 1900s, inspiration for the young Cantonese artists. To some extent, modern Japanese art reacquainted the students with Southern Song wash-centrism. The history of Chinese art thus completed a curious circle, with a loop in Japan.

Haze, however, both linked the Chinese and Japanese artists and set them apart. While haze spelled cultural identity for the Japanese *morotai* practitioners seeking to distance themselves from both Sino-Japanese tradition and modern Western power, for the southern Chinese artists—all zealous political activists around 1911—it was a visual trope to gauge the Chinese political climate. A rousing line from the *Classic of Poetry*—one of the five Confucian Classics—provided the cue: "Wind and rain create a somber haze; the rooster never lets up crowing." The trope dominated the southern revolutionary periodicals in the 1900s. The supplement of a southern daily paper was pointedly titled *Record of Crowing Against Haze*. The inaugural issue of another southern newspaper, titled *Southern Wind*, features a rooster atop a rock, crowing and hailing the rising sun. The caption described the political climate in China at the time, trapped in a "pitch-black chamber." The lamentation—when would "this long night ever see light again?"—turns to the joy of hearing the rooster's crow, signaling the dawn. The Guangdong intellectual Liu Shifu (1884–1915), an ardent anarchist who had organized the China Assassination Group in 1910, founded the Crowing-Against-Haze Society in 1913 and published a journal, *Record of Crowing Against Haze*. The trope was a rallying call for the southern assassination groups aiming at bringing down first Qing officials and subsequently reactionary government officials and warlords who betrayed revolutionary ideals.

Paintings by the Gao brothers, while resonant with this trope, explore the haze for complex effects. For one thing, haze fit rhetorically into the fashioning of the progressive artists' self-image. They saw themselves as avant-garde harbingers of enlightenment, charged with the mission to shine piercing light on the hazy gloom, to expose the hidden reality, to illuminate for the public, and to awaken the masses from collective slumber in the "pitch-dark chamber." The artists' self-regard as Promethean figures bringing light to the dark world harmonized with the Chinese reformers' turn-of-the-century quest for modern technology. Photography and other optical devices were thus part of the modernizing technological apparatus that the Cantonese artists keenly embraced. Gao Jianfu studied entomology in Japan and was fascinated with microscopic lenses. Gao Qifeng (1889–1933) and other Cantonese vanguard artists were avid photographers. One of Gao Qifeng's paintings presents a photographer aiming his camera at hazy gloom in dark woods as if it were a penetrating searchlight. The camera lens reinforced the Cantonese artists' keen interest in capturing the acuity of observational techniques.

The Cantonese artists also created psychologically charged hazy paintings. Their compositions typically feature a low-hanging moon—a device derived from Shibata Zeshin (1807–1891)—except that the moon is veiled in haze. The hazy background offset an oversized insect, e.g., a grasshopper, in the foreground, as epitomized by Gao Jianfu's *Autumn Melodies* (1914) (fig. 8.7). The distinctness of the foregrounded grasshopper is thus pitched against the haziness of the background moon, resulting in a photographic effect, a technologically mediated vision processed through a camera lens. The visual drama thus stems from the low-hanging moon serving as a backlighting source, illuminating and exposing the foregrounded grasshopper, a vulnerable subject put on the spot. The exposure and the grasshopper's precarious perch on the grass stem hint at some recent or imminent violent act—patches of red color smeared over the surface ominously suggest blood stains. It is not clear what kind of killing is involved. Given the Gao brothers' predilection for painting ominous owls in hazy moonlit nights, we know that someone is in for a killing. The painting is fraught with ominous foreboding. In view of the long Chinese tradition of enjoying the Mid-Autumn Festival of drinking in moonlight, we have come a long way. With the moonlit night now unsettled by a nervous apprehension, it is no surprise that a few years later, one of the best-known fictive characters of twentieth-century China went mad. The neurotic first-person narrator of Lu Xun's *Madman's Diary* (1918) sees murderous intent in the glistening of his neighbor's eyes in the moonlight. To him, anything can happen now. That is maddening. Thus began the new page of modern Chinese history—all with the haze in the moonlit night.

Figure 8.7 Gao Jianfu (1879–1951). *Autumn Melodies.* 1914. Hanging scroll; ink and color on paper, 132.5 x 63 cm.
Li Xiongcai Collection, Guangdong, China

Bengal School Haze

Nostalgia for the past bound India's nationalist painters to Japan's. A decade after Japan's Nihonga return to tradition, their movement was paralleled in India when, in 1896, the English art historian E. B. Havell (1861–1934) enlisted the support of the Indian artist Abanindranath Tagore (1871–1951) to develop a new style of traditionalist painting for India. Tagore, already an artist, would become an art historian and administrator committed to art education policy. In 1901, Tagore met the Nihonga leader Kakuzo in Calcutta and opened a dialogue between Japanese and Indian artists and intellectuals that would be sustained over decades.

Kakuzo, Tagore, and their circles sought to redress sweeping changes in art patronage and aesthetic values. The British Raj had introduced to India art schools and a culture of salons and art criticism, which institutionalized European techniques and styles and supplanted traditional patronage structures. Photography and lithography had accelerated the spread of realism in the subcontinent's visual arts, radically revising, if not upending earlier courtly idioms. Meanwhile, Japan's Meiji government had been Westernizing the country with systematic rigor that had made it possible to dismantle and rebuild the country's cultural and political institutions in a little over two decades. In the process, European academic oil painting had all but replaced Japan's native painting lineages. By the 1880s, a tragic sense of cultural loss, inflamed by nationalist rhetoric, was virtually necessitating a backlash against the perceived cultural hegemony of the West in both Japan and India. Kakuzo, Tagore, and their circles made watercolor painting central to this backlash. In close conversation with Nihonga painters, Tagore founded what would be called the Bengal School of painting to resurrect India's premodern aesthetic and cultural values for its present.

Soon after his meeting with Tagore, Kakuzo sent the Nihonga painters Yokoyama Taikan and Hishida Shunso to India to study subcontinental art. They stayed at the Tagore household, where Tagore was astonished to see their techniques: "It was when I saw [Taikan] doing his work that the idea of wash-painting struck me, because I used to find Taikan moistening his piece of paper several times in water. I dipped not only my paper but also the painting in water, took it out and found that it had a very good effect. From that time the wash-painting took on."

Taikan and Shunso would later move away from extreme blurriness, and Nihonga painters would generally prefer a more sedate haziness, but Tagore assumed the technique was an authentic, venerably Japanese tradition, and embraced it as essential to his vision of Asian art (fig. 8.8).

Haze enabled a complex rhetoric in Indian art. In contrast to the illusionism of academic painting, which Asian nationalists had identified as a symptom of Western materialism, haze suggested the spiritual transcendence of the material world taught by Eastern sages. In contrast to the clear, rational, industrial present, for Indian intellectuals, haze suggested the depths of a lost, emotional, intuitive past. The translucent hazes of early Bengal School painting either let white paper glow through or comprised luminous washes scumbled over layers of shadow. Their seemingly spiritual brilliance dissolved forms rather than defining them. Radiant expanses of haze were seen to express artistic genius, which Tagore felt traditional court art had suppressed, and they seemed moody, a quality Tagore prized and that made them capable of reinvigorating ancient imagery with modern psychological depth. The figures of Bengal School painting often peer into hazes that express their inner thoughts and feelings, recapitulating the artist's ruminative mood and inviting viewers to enter the reverie. Haze could be deemed simultaneously Chinese, Japanese, and Indian, modern and ancient, brilliant and obscure, optimistic and melancholy because it was the formal expression of indefinability. Its indefiniteness and its capacity to suggest spatial and psychological infinitude married perfectly with large ideas and aspirations.

Tagore was hailed as a "bridge to the past," but haze was not a traditional Indian technique. While suggesting the incompleteness of memory and the vagueness of imagery eroded by time, haze was also for India a modern editorial process that abstracted Bengal School painting from two fundamental values of its premodern models: clarity and physical embodiment. In the Indian context, these values were rooted in premodern religious and ideological certainties that were politically impossible in the early 1900s, and an eroticism that the embarrassed, still Victorian sentiments of the day could not rehabilitate to national or Asian advantage. Tagore was probably aware that the qualities of clarity and embodiment would complicate the material/spiritual dichotomy that charged East/West rhetoric and still infuses our stereotypes. Clarity and embodiment were hardly materialist qualities in the capitalist sense, but they were emphatically material.

In India, haze solved a semantic problem that the debt to traditional arts had raised, namely how to suggest immaterial qualities when the traditional

Figure 8.8 Abanindranath Tagore, Bharat Mata, 1905, watercolor on paper Rabindra Bharati Society

emphasis on line and two-dimensionality tended to emphasize the planarity of the pictorial surface—literally superficiality. The logic of this planarity had been forgotten: Mughal and Rajput court painting was poorly understood in early twentieth-century India because it had lost patronage, its practitioners had severely dwindled, and Mughal India had no tradition of writing about art that could have carried its intellectual underpinnings into the present.

To the extent that haze was a strategy for creating literal, semantic, and psychological depths in Bengal School painting, it replaced a range of premodern means for achieving similar ends. A history of India's premodern painting can thus be written in response to what modern haze obscured.

Emotions in Painting at Ajanta

Much of India's residential architecture was built of impermanent materials, and, unlike the Chinese, Indians did not bury their dead in tombs before the Islamic period, so very little painting exists from the first millennium. What has survived, however, is extraordinary. The circa fifth-century Buddhist caves at Ajanta in Maharashtra boast India's best preserved early murals. These enlivened monastic residences and spaces for worship with tales from the Buddha's final and previous lives and with the celestial beings who celebrated his teachings.

Buddhism teaches that the material world is illusory and that enlightenment lies in realizing nonduality, a no-thingness that Buddhists describe as *sunyata* or emptiness. Notwithstanding their beliefs, the Buddhists embraced a basic aesthetic attitude, shared by other religions and the elite, that physical beauty was an attribute of virtue and was powerfully auspicious. Although for Buddhists beauty was a delusion that could arouse false attachment, it was also a sign of goodness and powerfully effective within the illusory world of those who had not yet reached buddhahood. The Buddha was said to be a beautiful man, and Buddhist monasteries strove to be beautiful places with sweet-scented flowering gardens. Sensuous, fecund, youthful ideals peopled early Ajanta's murals, along with the auspicious forms of fat-bellied dwarves, curling vines, pots full of flowers, and cornucopias spilling gems. These tend to come as a surprise to modern students of Buddhism.

Ajanta's painted figures were conceived in close relationship with three-dimensional sculpture. Shading, virtuosic foreshortening, and curving lines that thickened and thinned as they wrapped around forms to emphasize their corporeality made India's early painted bodies seem as volumetric as its sculptures. Studying the Ajanta murals was a rite of passage for Bengal School artists, who made it fundamental to their neotraditional art, but the browns, grays, ochers, and dusky greens they adopted from the murals were the tints of age; the murals would once have shone with worldly color. Even today, they still palpably breathe and sway. Bodies undulate with life and eyes dart in multiple directions to fill the spaces between figures with longing, teasing, anger, and wonder.

These paintings depended on the magic of clear, tangibly fleshy, animated bodies to effect blessings. Indeed, the circa sixth- to seventh-century art treatise, the *Citra-sutra*, tells us that a well-wrought figure could "assure prosperity to the creative craftsman as well as the ruler of the realm." However, it was equally the embodiment of intangibilities such as emotion that made Ajanta's paintings aesthetically powerful. Rendering emotions was a principal aim of the painter's art. Painting treatises followed the model of poetry in instructing painters to create emotions in and through bodies. In poetry, and to the extent possible in painting, physical gestures and reactions, like wide eyes, hair standing on end, and flesh that expanded and contracted with the state of the heart worked with settings and times of the day and year to externalize feelings as nine universal aesthetic moods.

Therefore, emotions ran high in Ajanta's murals. One painter depicted a young queen looking seductively into the eyes of her saintly husband, hoping to seduce him away from his desire for renunciation. Another rendered a maidservant sneaking a sideways glance at a conversation she perhaps shouldn't hear but wants to (fig. 8.9). Pressured to become a monk, the Buddha's young half-brother Nanda was shown with his head askew, supported in the palm of his hand, his eyes flat with the disappointment of his future. His wife, insensate on learning he has become a monk, was painted falling into a friend's arms. Painters at the time were advised not to picture sad or violent scenes in a domestic setting, because they would bring bad luck, but the Ajanta painters did not hesitate to convey the enticements and the pain of the illusory world of attachment in the context of monastic caves.

In contrast to these emotionally unsettling scenes, an image of the Buddha occupied the heart of many caves (fig. 8.10). He was depicted without adornment, eyes calm or lowered, body perfectly symmetrical around an

Figure 8.9 Detail of the maidservants' faces in the *Mahajanaka Jataka*, Ajanta caves, Cave I, Main Hall, circa fifth century CE, mural
Photo: © Asian Art Archives, University of Michigan

axis against which the cave's myriad other images turned and twisted. He embodied a peace, offered in his teachings, that transcended the moods wrought by worldly attachments. Thus, Ajanta's paintings and sculptures gorgeously rendered a dichotomy between bodily passion and bodily transcendence through renunciation. This dichotomy would remain—in myriad forms—a prevalent theme of India's visual arts until the colonial period, when it foundered in encounters with Christian attitudes to the body.

However materially and emotionally present Ajanta's world seems, it was not intended to replicate mundane realities. The art of painting had developed a host of strategies to picture an ideal world. One was the visual

Figure 8.10 Buddha, Ajanta Caves, Cave 4, circa fifth century CE
Photo: © Asian Art Archives, University of Michigan

approximation of metaphors. Painting treatises urged painters to draw a beautiful woman's eye like a lotus and a woman's waist like a narrow-waisted drum. Anger should look with a round conch-shell eye, and an elite man's arm should resemble the branches of the banyan tree. Thus painting operated in a poetic register, leading viewers beyond what they could see to trains of association that deepened and charged its imagery. Volumetric form created the illusion of material depth, but scenes were emotionally and poetically suggestive and ultimately committed to a metaphysics of form as delusion. No haze in these murals, but depths indeed.

Mughal and Rajput Painting

A radically different mode of painting emerged in the fifteenth century with the arrival in India of paintings on paper from the Persian-speaking world. Although the well-known Islamic injunction against figuration was consistently obeyed in religious contexts such as mosques and Qurans, figurative painting was a cherished pleasure among the Central and Western Asian Muslim elite. This pleasure was brought to India for the entertainment of Muslims who had begun to command sizeable kingdoms in India from the twelfth century onward. Painting became an especially important and exquisitely refined art under the Mughals (1556–1858), who ruled most of the subcontinent until the early eighteenth century and whose intellectual and aesthetic culture dominated north India until the mid-nineteenth century. During this period Hindu kings, known as Rajputs, also fostered painting workshops, out of which stylistically distinctive regional traditions evolved that were in conversation with Mughal painting but also sustained Indian aesthetic values developed during the centuries before Mughal rule. The artists of the Bengal School looked as much to these Mughal and Rajput paintings as to the Ajanta murals for their traditional "Indian" style.

At the heart of Mughal and Rajput paintings were the miniature surface patterns, precise lines, and colorful planes of the Persian tradition. Persian paintings were made to be held in the hand, and they celebrate the tangible flatness of the paper between the viewer's fingers. They are vehemently two-dimensional, so backgrounds tip up, leaving objects and people to float, while angles, when they refer to spatial depth, tend confoundingly to terminate in counterangles or in horizontals, which adhere flatly to the page. Volumes are only hinted at, and objects have little or no shadow. Colors are confectionary. One inspiration was the highly esteemed art of ornamenting texts, which art historians call book illumination. Persian and Mughal painters were often trained in the illuminator's minute geometries, arabesques, and flora and fauna, and used their ornamental schema in figurative scenes as well as around texts. Another inspiration for Persian pictorial conventions may have been the Islamic injunction against figuration. In its unrealities, the painted world did not claim to rival God but rather to celebrate his creations. Thus, poets praised Persian painters for seeing beyond the material world to express hidden meanings and higher truths.

With their emphasis on planarity, Mughal and Rajput paintings do not seem obviously in dialogue with temple sculpture of their era, except insofar as they adapted iconic temple figurations to the painted page. In the sixteenth century, temple sculpture still looked round and fleshy, though it had become increasingly stylized since the days of Ajanta. Painting and sculpture had diverged, but the capacity of sculpture to embody divinity in India continued to have a significant effect on the two-dimensional arts, which would widely be accepted as a vehicle for divine presence. Many of India's sectarian communities shared a vision of the divine as ultimately formless, but also understood the divine to enter physically into the world through manifold, more or less physically defined forms. For example, Shiva's most powerful incarnation was the almost aniconic *lingam*, but he could also be worshiped as a princely hero or a fierce, unkempt, yet still achingly beautiful ascetic. The rise of intense personal modes of religious devotion in India encouraged representations of the divine in highly adorable or seductive forms. Devotional poetry sometimes treated gods as lovers, so that renunciation of the world frequently became an erotically charged experience. By the time painting on paper was emerging as a significant art in India, the erotic mood was dominating religious and courtly arts. Instead of the sculptural, swaying bodies of the Ajanta tradition, however, other forms for embodying moods were developing that were better suited to the Persianate planar page.

Mughal and Rajput paintings, like Persian paintings, were meant to be experienced as materially opulent objects. Pigments were finely ground from mineral and vegetable ingredients such as mercury, arsenic, lapis lazuli, malachite, dyed lac from the lac insect, chalk, and the famous *gaogoli*, reputedly made from distilled cow urine. Colors were laid down in even planes to fill each area of a composition, like enamel in cloisonée. Depending on the workshop, a painting would then be more or less burnished from the back to smooth each plane of color. Colors responded variously to this process: mercury red shone like glass, chalk became marmoreal, and lapis lazuli glittered with tiny facets. Over this subtle geography of surfaces, the artist drew his lines, touched in details, applied raised dots of white for pearls, and painted areas of pure twenty-four-karat gold into jewelry, clothing, haloes, and sunsets. The gold was itself burnished to a high shine and sometimes pricked or scored for texture. In addition, a few regional traditions embedded tiny gems or bits of iridescent green beetle wing in the surfaces of paintings. These surfaces come to life in the hand when they are turned at changing angles to the light. Thus the enticements of the painting as a material object are a starting point for Mughal and Rajput traditions: strategies for evoking physical, semantic, or emotional depth necessarily take into account the depthlessness of these paintings' planarity and the tactile qualities of their adorned surfaces.

Adornment was intrinsic to Indian beauty: the painted page was akin to the human body in that neither could bring good to the world if it was plain. The illuminated passages of pattern in Mughal paintings were believed to originate with Ali, the Prophet's son-in-law, and beautiful craft in the Hindu tradition was a tribute to Vishvakarma, the divine builder and craftsman, as well as to painting's ideal and often divine heroes and heroines. A few regional styles cultivated looser lines, and imperial painters did not hesitate to picture the grim realities of battle, but Mughal and Rajput painting worked with a basic expectation that painting should be adorned and should adorn, and its painters were therefore (when properly rewarded) precise in their craft.

Although a few Chinese motifs entered into Mughal painting through Persia, haze would have been anathema to these opulent traditions. Precise, slender lines demarcated each painted form from the next to achieve maximum legibility. Shading was less prominent than at Ajanta, but even there it had never swallowed the definiteness of line. Indian painters had always sought clarity. True, Mughal painters took atmospheric perspective from European art and harnessed fading and bluing to diminution in order to create distance, but their object was to open up sometimes impossibly deep tracks of mostly defined hills, valleys, towns and riverscapes. The bird's-eye views of Mughal paintings let you see more into the horizon than is physically possible. Nor can one speak of the expressive skies in Rajput painting as hazy. Artists washed wet streaks of red into swathes of wet white, blue, and black to create swirling, moody skies, but these were not hazy. They too glistened with their burnished textures, obviously puddled into one another at the surface of the page.

Outline was a function of clarity in these traditions. Even when they were copying European prints, Mughal artists lightened shadows and reinforced outlines to ensure that each form was defined as distinct from the next. The Mughals did not care to envelop figures in atmosphere. Color-coordinated palettes sometimes created a poetic flavor of dawn, dusk, or midnight but rarely subsumed line. Indeed, even in nighttime scenes, figures typically glowed with their own light, as if under the noon sun.

This desire for clarity in painting did not signal materialism in the modern sense, or a lack of the semantic and emotional depth that the nationalists would later open up with haze. Mughal and Rajput paintings played against their gorgeous surfaces with depths achieved through other means. From the Persian tradition came the idea that gifted painters expressed otherwise hidden truths. A famous Indian court poet praised one painting master as he who could lift "the veil from the face of the beautiful," meaning the sacred. Mystical forms of Islam dominated courtly life, and painters drew extensively on poetic conventions to suggest underlying meanings. Images of wine drinking and gardens, for example, could hint at devotional intoxication and the gardens of paradise. Likewise, paintings of beautiful women could be read as triggers for a love that would ultimately transcend its mortal object to reach toward god, or as models for the unchecked passion of the mystic seeker after the divine. Imperial portraiture was rife with allusions to the emperor's status as a saint and as the "shadow of God on earth," starting with his halo but including a panoply of imperial symbols like the chenar tree and the purple iris. Painters were responsible for picturing the dreams god had sent their emperor, which meant revealing sacred imagery normally hidden to everyone else.

Mughal painting embodied the world far more tangibly than did Persian painting. Imperial masters studied European imagery and adapted many of its techniques to their own needs. Shading, intuitive perspective, extensive study of nature, and individuation made for a naturalism that diverged from the Persian tradition and from earlier Indic idealism, though Mughal painters adapted this naturalism to Persianate surfaces and consistently eschewed full-blown chiaroscuro and the spatial illusionism of European one-point perspective. Since the early twentieth century, this naturalism has earned Mughal artists a reputation for being materialists, but it makes no cultural sense to read their imagery as locked to a love of the mundane. Take the example of an early seventeenth-century party scene, which at first glance portrays individuals engaged in sensual pleasures and friendship (fig. 8.11). There is a love of material beauty here: one can almost smell the flowers and feel the cool spray of the fountain. However,

Figure 8.11 A Garden Gathering with Two Princes and a Sleeping Cat, ascribed to Govardhan, Mughal, c. 1630–40
From The Minto Album, Chester Beatty Library, CBL In 07A.8

highly allusive poetic imagery suggests concealed meanings. Two cypress trees, which typically signified the beloved in Persian poetry, and a brightly flowering bush frame a middle-aged man in the garb of a mystic seeker, drawing our attention to his intense gaze on the young man before him. The young man holds a stem of narcissus, a symbol of the beloved's eyes. In the Persian tradition, ideal love was between an older and a younger man, and the presence at the party of men in religious garb further suggests the yearning here is the mystic's for the divine beloved—indeed, young men were invited to gatherings to inspire spiritual intensity. Another young man looks out at us, pointing to a book, urging us to look for deeper meaning. While such images of beauty and pleasure tempted viewers with hedonistic attachment to sensual delights, they, like Mughal poetry, offered countless paths to the informed to see beyond their material seductions to the immateriality of Islamic divinity. This kind of aesthetic mysticism was typical of a premodern world in which spiritual and secular were not distinct categories of being but were experienced as a range of possibilities and moods.

If iconography was a primary cue to the semantic depth of Persian and Mughal painting, Rajput painters carried forward several poetic ideals that informed the Ajanta murals, striving more to intensify mood than to symbolize. While no absolute distinction separates Mughal from Rajput painting (the two were deeply intertwined), Rajput patrons, who also valued pre-Mughal aesthetic conventions, were open to extremes of stylization and abstraction that imperial Mughal painters avoided, and they relished paintings of poetic ideals that had no truck with daily life. Because the most stylized of these paintings are not naturalistic, they were once labeled more "spiritual" than Mughal painting, yet they are, in their way, every bit as materially embodied; spiritual and material were not contradictory in their world. A superb example of this eye-opening end of the pictorial spectrum from a far northern court in the foothills of the Himalayas (fig. 8.12) depicts the Hindu god Krishna returning to his beloved Radha, freshly picked lotus in hand. He is framed in a field of burning yellow, the color of sun poured as elixir, while she awaits, tense and erect, within a chamber of forest greens, evening indigo, and subdued red; silver, gold, and white pavilions cluster above her like towers within battlements. She has read the signs: he had been to their trysting place and she was not there. She has missed this opportunity for love. A black pillar marks the divide between them, between heat and cool, male and female, free and enclosed; it is the space of longing. With its expressively divided halves, the composition is

Figure 8.12 Krishna and Radha as the *anusayana nayika* who is anxious that her lover has met another at their trysting place, page from an illustrated *Rasa-manjari*, circa 1660–70, Basohli, Rajput, opaque watercolor on paper
Victoria and Albert Museum, London

simplicity itself. The trees and flowers are patterned, the figures abstracted to planes of color within robust curves, and the eyes impossibly large to resemble lotus petals, drawing on the metaphoric imagery that dated back to before Ajanta.

As at Ajanta, emotion is exteriorized in Rajput paintings. Vines hugging trees, pairs of birds, peacocks crying in the rain, thunderstorms electric with gold lightning, palettes that render mood in color harmonies and contrasts, compositions that abstract the tense divisions between lovers into divided frames: these are among the many strategies to awaken the mood of the work of art in the body of the responsive connoisseur. Mood was called *rasa* ("taste" or "juice"), and the word for the connoisseur was *rasika*, meaning the taster. (See also the discussion of *rasa* in Indian literature, chapter 4.) To taste the work of art was often to taste the sensuous perfections of divine beauty. The god Krishna, especially in north India, was viewed as aesthetic mood embodied. For many of his devotees during these centuries, Krishna was potentially taste-able, touchable, olfactory, and audible. Thus the twelfth-century poet Jayadeva wrote of the "moonlight gleaming on [Krishna's] teeth" to dispel the darkness, and of how his "moon face" lured the "nightbird eyes" of his mortal beloved Radha to "taste nectar from [his] quivering lips" (*Gita-govinda*, Part 10, Song 19).

Even without reference to religion, Indian painting acted in a world in which memories, fantasies, and desires were perceived to have lives of their own that could be as effective, overwhelming, and true in their way as flesh and blood matter. According to prominent Indic schools of thought, cosmic mind came before matter, and matter was never matter-of-fact. Thus, classical Indian literature was full of portraits that tenuously, if at all resembled their subjects, but functioned as if they were resemblances through the vividness of the imagined visions they called into play. Not surprisingly, mirrors were a favorite theme, but instead of opposing the true to the false, they served to highlight the instability of all imagery, even that contoured by our own skin.

Ideal, imagined, and transcendent realms could be signaled through abstraction and stylization, as in figure 8.12, but they did not need to be. Artists in the Pahari hills, whose forefathers painted like this artist, awoke dreamy perfections and the same spectrum of emotional intensity using Mughal-inspired techniques for rendering comparatively naturalistic effects, like those exemplified in figure 8.11. The spectrum in Mughal and Rajput painting between naturalism and stylized abstraction is striking and was certainly conscious and meaningful. In these traditions of volume and surface, there is a decided straddling of real appearances and unearthly ideals. Nevertheless, these polarities may be overplayed in the scholarship and are still poorly understood.

It does not work to simplify the Mughal as a Muslim and the Rajput as a Hindu tradition. Muslims and Hindus held different beliefs, but in India, many celebrated one another's holidays, and they dipped deeply into one another's cultural rituals and forms. Islamic mysticism in India probed Hindu love stories, the relationship of the god Krishna and his beloved Radha, and the yogic practices of Hindu and Jain renunciants to augment their spiritual quests. Meanwhile, as Hindu and Muslim courtly elite became connoisseurs of one another's artistic traditions, their artists became expert in both Persianate and Indic iconographic and aesthetic repertoires, and their artworks were enjoyed at parties where Muslims and Hindus socialized together. The more scholarship wades into these relationships, the more difficult it becomes to summarize what Mughal versus Rajput was without erring toward a simplistic story of Muslim/Hindu difference or syncretism—in other words, without sacrificing critical nuance. Even now, these are touchy matters for many.

Taking a broad view, however, one sees a preoccupation in Mughal and Rajput painting alike with the nature of material attachment and desire. What did it mean to render the things of this world for aesthetic appreciation? What was beauty? Two of painting's dominant themes were love and renunciation. Open a Mughal album of paintings and calligraphy and you will find pictures of beautiful men, women, and lovers interspersed with representations of Muslim and Hindu holy men, mystical Persian love poetry, and passages from the Quran. Open a Rajput series of illustrations representing musical modes, a highly popular genre, and you will find a similar preponderance of ideal men, women, and lovers with saints. In the backgrounds of many Rajput love scenes, tiny ascetics gather in their ashrams. Love and renunciation were visually counterpoised: lovers were young, smooth skinned, thin waisted, and swaying hipped, decked in jewelry and bedazzling in silks; saints were naked, skinny, tangle haired and ashen. The dusty saints of Rajput painting could be beautiful in their renunciant garb and were often adorned by reverential artists with gems they would never actually have worn. At other times, however, they were more like Mughal representations of saints, with protruding ribs and cheekbones, looking like death in their gauntness. In either case, renunciation of the flesh and its attachments was precisely and vividly known through clear, palpably embodied imagery. Renunciation was pictured as a vividly physical experience.

For the Islamic mystic, passionate love for another might start the spiritual quest and offer a taste of the divine, but union with god was ultimately achieved in death. Erotic union in Hindu mysticism was a means to dissolve the self in the divine, and death was not a common theme. However, both conceptions offered paths that decidedly merged mental and emotional with physical experiences. Here was the transformative threshold of painting: the power to move viewers by making as if present what could not be materially grasped. It was up to viewers to pass through the sensual thresholds of paintings to achieve the transcendent experiences the works alluded to beyond their materiality. Thus the fundamental polarity in Mughal and Rajput painting was between what was visible and felt in the hand and what lay beyond physical grasp for the imagination to apprehend. In the early twentieth century, haze was folding into the painted surface some of this beyondness that Mughal and Rajput painters had alluded to in other ways.

Mughal and Rajput portraiture comprehended the mundane, ideal, imagined, and sacred as constitutive of one another. Portraits documented contemporary faces, events, and places, but as ideals. Emperors and kings were haloed and cast as exemplary heroes and lovers. Hindu kings were often conflated with the god Krishna. Meanwhile, royalty was shown to preside over courts that enacted assemblies, hunts, festivals, and processions in perfect concord. Nothing was ugly in this world; nothing went wrong. The tangible and intangible were interleaved formally as well as iconographically in these paintings. The halo in portraiture glittered in the viewer's world as literal rather than represented wealth and concretized the very real presence of the divine, as it radiated from kings and emperors, but viewers understood the halo was not visible in its represented or in their real world; they expected a painting to depict different kinds of reality simultaneously. So too, the lotus eye that flattered kings in seventeeth- and eighteenth-century Rajput painting was obviously a physical impossibility, but it denoted real perfection while alluding to a poetic convention existing outside the painting in the informed viewer's mind. Meanwhile, portraits could convey something of the presence of those they portrayed to the extent that, in exceptional circumstances, they were even worshiped. As a result, even pictures that purported on first glance to portray real people and places were ingeniously sprung with multiple, ontologically distinct states of being. Understanding this helps one make sense of how Mughal and Rajput masters could bring seemingly contradictory formal conventions like planar patterns, poetic motifs, deep landscapes, realistic faces, and glittering gold, into meaningful coherence.

Unlike the Bengal School's ruminative moods that invited viewers into psychological reverie, premodern artists did not strive for psychologically expressive styles to invest their works with eccentricity or to allude to their own states of mind. Court artists were connoisseurs who used the medium of painting to address men and women schooled in a shared repertoire of knowledge, ideas, and tastes. No cultural distinction existed between art and craft, and Indian painters were ambiguously artisans and poets. Many early Mughal masters who served in the imperial workshops also socialized as courtiers with the elite and sometimes held high-level bureaucratic positions. They were charged with devising ways to illustrate subjects that had never been illustrated before, and they often deployed elite iconography in newly playful ways, particularly in the form of courtly panegyric. Late sixteenth- and early seventeenth-century artists like Basawan, Miskin, Govardhan, Bichitr, and Payag became legendary.

Mughal artists painted in dialogue with one another and with the masterpieces of the past, but the trajectory of this dialogue foundered in the later seventeenth century. The emperor Aurangzeb (r. 1658–1707) seems to have dispersed many of his artists, ostensibly for religious reasons, though he continued to patronize portraiture, and painting thrived among the nobility. In any case, the succession war following Aurangzeb's death indisputably sent Mughal authority into sharp decline, resulting in a substantial decentralization of culture. In the ensuing century, artists working for a wide array of local rulers developed additional, marvelously idiosyncratic stylizations in pursuit of ever more effective ways to express abstract ideals and to intensify emotional states. Instances of wateriness and brushiness can be found among these myriad experiments, but clarity remained a dominant value. Artists like Nihal Chand, Nainsukh, and Chokha were exceedingly innovative and achieved a considerable measure of local fame. At the same time, the ability to imitate the work of earlier masters seems to have become an admired skill in its own right, and at Muslim courts, especially at Lucknow, there was a palpable nostalgia (which several successful painters commercialized) for a golden period of painting that had been lost with imperial authority.

A Return to the Past

All of this mastery notwithstanding, the continued absence of oeuvres dedicated to distinctive artistic personalities encouraged early twentieth-century scholars to look back and perceive an ethos of anonymity in India's pre- and early modern arts. They exalted the nameless Indian master who had been content to make art for god and king without reference to himself. In this way, India's nationalist art historians, foremost among them Ananda Coomaraswamy (1877–1957), critiqued the Western romance of the individual genius at the same time that the haze of Bengal School artists implicitly celebrated it.

The artist Abdul Rahman Chughtai (1897–1975) once pictured a Chinese man in traditional dress staring over the ocean at a hazy moonlit night (fig. 8.13). It seems as if the Chinese man sees as Chughtai himself sees,

Figure 8.13 Chinese Man in Moonlight, Abdur Rahman Chughtai (1899–1975), date unknown, watercolor
Private collection. Image courtesy of Oliver Forge and Brendan Lynch Ltd.

with nostalgia for the past and hope for the future, with the psychological sensitivity of the modern genius and the melancholy of Asian loss. Such images helped export the idea of Asia to the West, but it was a hazy idea: Asia as mystery, sentiment, spirit over matter, the place of dreams. So far as we know, Chughtai was unaware that his Chinese counterparts were longing for revolution to illuminate the "somber haze" of their "long night." Chughtai had other dreams. He did not, in fact, see with Chinese eyes.

Over time, many in India would reject Bengal School haze as effeminate and sentimental. Line would be preferred to haze, with Amrita Sher Gil (1913–1941) returning to Rajput line, Jamini Roy (1887–1972) finding backbone and strength in the lines of India's folk art, and Nandalal Bose (1882–1966)—bringing us full circle—celebrating Chinese line with the conviction that "Line is the soul of Eastern painting." Planarity and fields of color would also come back into style, and haze would become a passing phase with little enduring effect on the subcontinent's art. And yet, however hazy, histories of Chinese and Indian painting owed much to this late nineteenth to early twentieth century moment when painting became a matter of political consequence for international dialogue.

Conclusion

While the stories of Chinese and Indian art can hardly be tersely encapsulated without risking gross essentialism or ahistorical reductionism, some distinct problems emerge out of the comparison of the two traditions. There is first of all the striking difference in generic interests. Following a long tradition of figural painting, landscape came to dominate pictorial interest in the second millennium in China. By contrast, figural painting remained the primary preoccupation of the Indian tradition throughout. This may be accounted for by different cultural permutations. The growing interest in eremitism as a rhetorical stance and the use of landscape to represent emotional states are among the forces that sustain the Chinese preoccupation with landscape. Although eremitism is a powerful ideal in India too, the emphasis is on the bodily rigors of asceticism and the embodied passions of the mystical seeker rather than on landscapes of seclusion.

Both Chinese and Indian art are heavily allusive with regard to earlier models, but in different ways. In China, especially in the second millennium, painters see themselves as perpetrators of ancient precedents even if such models are often imagined or reconstructed. Indian literature follows the Chinese model fairly closely, with later authors writing in response to earlier legendary ones, but painters take a different path, typically recapitulating models that are rich with semantic and emotional associations but only sometimes linked to remembered individuals. Muslim and Hindu painters work side by side in Mughal-period workshops, and they are not guided by a single authoritative mythology about their art. Like Chinese painters, they have knowledge and respect for earlier masters and work with a strong sense of tradition, but they do not paint in concert with a discourse on painting.

The distinct treatments of line and wash (haze) in China and India did not develop programmatically, and they become historicized at different times and for different reasons. In retrospect, the early twentieth-century Japanese identification of line as the quintessential quality of Chinese pictorial art has a point, albeit a caricatured one. Line is a formal mainstay in Chinese painting. That line—as opposed to the indistinct wash—is the mainstay of Chinese art may have to do with a long-standing perceptual habit trained on brush-produced writing, i.e., calligraphic practice. By way of empathy, the linear modulation evokes psychological interiority and emotional states. Over time, wash is added to lend more nuance to the shades of inner states.

Line is also reliably present in Indian painting. However, Indian painting embraces an aesthetic that prefers to universalize rather than individualize emotion. For the most part, line delineates forms rather than revealing through its thickness, thinness, and density the pressures and movements of an individual hand. Line does not memorialize the painter's emotional experience. Thus while attention to internal experiences is commonly understood as a salient quality of Asian art, it is apparent that Chinese and Indian art conceived of emotion in aesthetic domains differently and accomplished emotional effects through different formal means.

That haze became the main storyline in this chapter is due to a reconstruction of different stages of history in China and India. In China, that reconstruction started in seventeenth-century art historical reflection. In India, art historical reconstruction began only in the colonial period, and haze was the first formal device to be developed as an art historically self-conscious step from the past toward the future. Therefore, as we look back from the twentieth century on to those painting histories that Chinese and Indian intellectuals sought to reclaim as their national heritages, we are juxtaposing two very different kinds of analysis.

Haze flourished in the early twentieth century as the pictorial condition for concord in Asia. Japanese haze had been predicated on European watercolor techniques; China and Japan had long, rich premodern histories of hazy effects; and haziness also demonstrated the potential expressiveness of modern art. However much haze sums up a substantial part of Chinese art, highlighting a key and constant dynamic that runs throughout the history of Chinese painting, the mimetic impulse strong in Western art was never much of a real concern. That accounts for what makes Chinese art so distinct. The implication that haze was Indian, however, reveals an overwhelming dissimilarity between Chinese and Indian premodern traditions, despite their multiple points of contiguity. For India, revision of its cultural traditions was needed to bring it into conversation with the rest of the world. But because haze was familiar to all parties in the early 1900s, it made a pictorial conversation possible across oceans, mountains, and political borders. The promise of a shared vision, however, turned out to be a hazy dream.

For Further Reading

China

Cahill, James. *The Compelling Image: Nature and Style in Seventeenth-Century Chinese Painting.* Cambridge, MA: Harvard University Press, 1982.

Chou, Ju Hsi and Anita Chung. *Silent Poetry: Chinese Paintings from the Collection of the Cleveland Museum of Art.* New Haven and London: Yale University Press, 2015.

Clunas, Craig. *Pictures and Visuality in Early Modern China.* Princeton, NJ: Princeton University Press, 1997.

Wang, Eugene. "'The Disarrayed Hills Conceal an Old Monastery': Poetry/Painting Dynamics in Northern Song." In *The Rhetoric of Hiddenness in Traditional Chinese Culture*, ed. Paula M Varsano, 279–302. Albany: State University of New York Press, 2016.

———. "The Elegiac Cicada: Problems of Historical Interpretation of Yuan Painting." *Ars Orientalis* 37 (2009): 176–94.

———. "'Picture Idea' and Its Cultural Dynamics in Northern Song China." *The Art Bulletin* LXXXIX, no. 3 (2007): 463–81.

———. "Sketch Conceptualism as Modernist Contingency." In *Chinese Art: Modern Expressions*, ed. Maxwell Hearn and Judith Smith, 102–61. New York: The Metropolitan Museum of Art, 2001.

Wu, Hung. *The Double Screen: Medium and Representation in Chinese Painting.* Chicago: University of Chicago Press, 1996.

———. *A Story of Ruins: Presence and Absence in Chinese Art and Visual Culture.* Princeton, NJ: Princeton University Press, 2012.

India

Aitken, Molly. *The Intelligence of Tradition in Rajput Court Painting.* New Haven: Yale University Press, 2010.

Cummings, Joan. *Indian Painting from Cave Temples to the Colonial Period.* Boston: Museum of Fine Arts, 2006.

Goswamy, B. N. *Essence of Indian Art.* San Francisco: Asian Art Museum of San Francisco, 1986.

Miller, Barbara Stoler, ed. and trans. *Love Song of the Dark Lord: Jayadeva's Gitagovinda.* New York: Columbia University Press, 1977.

Mitter, Partha. *Art and Nationalism in Colonial India, 1850–1922: Occidental Orientations.* Cambridge: Cambridge University Press, 1994.

Pollock, Sheldon. *A Rasa Reader: Classical Indian Aesthetics.* New York: Columbia University Press, 2016.

Singh, Kavita. *Real Birds in Imagined Gardens: Mughal Painting Between Persia and Europe.* Los Angeles: J. Paul Getty Trust, 2017.

Sivaramamurti, C. *Chitrasutra of the Vishnudharmottara.* New Delhi: Kanak, 1978.

Afterword

The Act of Comparing (Both Sides, Now)

DIPESH CHAKRABARTY AND HAUN SAUSSY

Haun Saussy

> We are the first generation to see the clouds from both sides. . . . This is bound to change something, somewhere.
> —SAUL BELLOW, *HENDERSON THE RAIN KING*

This book is a new take on an old problem.

Whether in humanities, history, or the sciences, *the history of the problem* is always worth looking into: how is it that something becomes a fixed reference point of argument? And what, for the sake of advancing understanding, might we change in the terms of the question? Although no one will ever solve the riddle of Homer's identity, for example, or puzzle out what came before the Big Bang, we can learn a lot from the way the questions have been posed.

The leading question of this book—what do the histories of India and China have to say about each other?—has perplexed Europeans since as far back as the Enlightenment and regularly stirred people in Asia to reflection. On the Western side, it was Hegel who molded India-and-China into a unit of thought, not content to let them sit side by side empirically. Together they form "the Oriental World." As Hegel tells the story in his *Philosophy of History*, these two ancient civilizations "lie, as it were, still outside the World's History, as the mere presupposition of elements whose combination must be waited for to constitute their vital progress." "Combination," however, must be preceded by a characterization of the separate elements.

The "character of the Chinese people," in Hegel's view, is such "that everything which belongs to Spirit—unconstrained morality, in practice and theory, Heart, inward Religion, Science and Art properly so-called—is alien to it." And so "the *Spirit* of the [Chinese] constitution . . . has always remained . . . the immediate unity of the substantial Spirit and the Individual; but this is equivalent to the Spirit of the Family, which is here extended over the most populous of countries. . . . In China the Universal Will immediately commands what the Individual is to do, and the latter complies and obeys with proportionate renunciation of reflection and personal independence." The only individual possessing free will in China is the emperor, the patriarch.

The pivot comes in the next chapter: "In contrast with the Chinese State, which presents only the most prosaic Understanding, India is the region of phantasy and sensibility." To the Chinese patriarchy—the empire reduced to an extension of its emperor—corresponds a symmetrical personification of India. And what a personification!

> There is a beauty of a peculiar kind in women, in which their countenance presents a transparency of skin, a light and lovely roseate hue, which is unlike the complexion of mere health and vital vigor—a more refined bloom, breathed, as it were, by the soul within—and in which the features, the light of the eye, the position of the mouth, appear soft, yielding, and relaxed. This almost unearthly beauty is perceived in women in those days which immediately succeed childbirth; when freedom from the burden of pregnancy and the pains of travail is added to the joy of soul that welcomes the gift of a beloved infant. . . . Such a beauty we find also in its loveliest form in the Indian World; a beauty of enervation in which all that is rough, rigid, and contradictory is dissolved, and we have only the soul in a state of emotion—a soul, however, in which the death of free self-reliant Spirit is perceptible. For should we approach the charm of this Flower-life—a charm rich in imagination and genius—in which its whole environment and all its relations are permeated by the rose-breath of the Soul, and the World is transformed into a Garden of Love—should we look at it more closely, and examine it in the light of Human Dignity and Freedom—the more attractive the first sight

of it had been, so much the more unworthy shall we ultimately find it in every respect.

Where China is stubbornly earthbound and literal, India, for Hegel, is an opium dream. On crossing the Himalaya the philosophical tourist might at first revel in the free play of fantasy and the theological imagination of the Indians, but Hegel insists that

> the Divine is thereby made bizarre, confused, and ridiculous. These dreams are not mere fables—a play of the imagination, in which the soul only revelled in fantastic gambols: it is lost in them; hurried to and fro by these reveries, as by something that exists really and seriously for it. It is delivered over to these limited objects as to its Lords and Gods. Everything, therefore—Sun, Moon, Stars, the Ganges, the Indus, Beasts, Flowers—everything is a God to it. And while, in this deification, the finite loses its consistency and substantiality, intelligent conception of it is impossible.

The political form of this unconstrained imagination is a proliferation of divisions that makes a proper State, as Hegel conceives of one, impossible, and leaves India an assortment of disunited castes that falls to the first determined invader. If China is monolithic,

> among the Hindus, on the contrary—instead of this Unity—Diversity is the fundamental characteristic. Religion, War, Handicraft, Trade, yes, even the most trivial occupations are parceled out with rigid separation—constituting as they do the import of the one will which they involve, and whose various requirements they exhaust. With this is bound up a monstrous, irrational imagination, which attaches the moral value and character of men to an infinity of outward actions as empty in point of intellect as of feeling; sets aside all respect for the welfare of man, and even makes a duty of the cruelest and severest contravention of it. Those distinctions being rigidly maintained, nothing remains for the one universal will of the State but pure caprice.

"If China may be regarded as nothing else but a State, Hindu political existence presents us with a people, but *no State*." "This makes [Indians] incapable of writing History. All that happens is dissipated in their minds into confused dreams."

I have presented these excerpts at some length in order to alert the reader to the persistence of these commonplaces in present-day discussion. As several contributors to this volume observe, much of what Hegel said about India or China was off the mark. Indeed, betting against Hegel is usually a safe policy. But it's not enough to say that he was wrong: on something as vast and momentous as the China-India comparison, he could only be vastly and momentously wrong. And durably so.

Hegel is not entirely to blame for the India-and-China topos. He merely gave it a vivid, condensed, and widely circulated form, focused by the pairing of the two places. Herder's somewhat earlier account of world history, *Outlines of a Philosophy of the History of Man*, which draws from Montesquieu's climate theory of government and overlays it with a typology of races and a chronicle of invasions, ranks the Indians among the most "well-formed people" of the world but bemoans the barbaric treatment they have undergone at the hands of the Mughals, the English, and their own priestly castes:

> The Hindus are the gentlest race of mankind. They intentionally injure nothing that breathes; they respect everything that has life; and support themselves by the most innocent food, milk, rice, and the nutritious plants and fruits that their country affords. . . . Temperance and quiet, gentle feelings and peaceful meditation, are conspicuous in their labors and enjoyments, their morals and mythology, their arts, and even their patience under the severest tyranny. Happy lambs! why could not Nature feed you careless and undisturbed on your native plains?

The abundance of the country is to blame for the frequent invasions that India has experienced, and the latest, that of Europeans, is for Herder an offense against cosmic justice that will eventually be reversed.

> From remote times the trade to the East Indies was a very lucrative branch of commerce: the industrious, contented peoples gave of their treasures by sea and land to other nations an abundance of precious articles; and, in consequence of their remote situation, remained in tolerable peace and tranquility; till at length Europeans, from whom nothing is remote, came, and established empires of their own among

them. All the information, and all the merchandise, that they have brought us thence by no means compensate the evil they have done to a nation by whom they were never offended. Yet in this the hand of Fate prevails.

In any case, Herder sees European political dominance as affecting only superficially the customs of the Hindus, customs that will endure, Herder believes, "as long as a Hindu shall exist." In general, it is Herder's message that "the culture [*Kultur*] of a people [or race: *Volk*] is the flower of its existence [*Dasein*]; its display is pleasing indeed, but transitory."

No such indulgence is shown the Chinese. In them is recognizable "the form of the Kalmyks and Mughals," peoples of the Asian steppes about whom Herder has nothing good to say. "Climate has merely reduced the broad face, little black eyes, stump nose, and thin beard, to a softer, rounder form; and the taste of the Chinese seems to be as much a consequence of ill-constructed organs, as despotism is of their form of government, and barbarism of their philosophy." It is a case of arrested development. If Herder is committed to a theory of culture flowering atop racial distinctions, the Chinese serve that theory insofar as they are not considered to have freed themselves, through cultural development, from their physical givens. Based on "false, enfeebling customs," "the mode of education pursued by the Chinese has conspired with their national character to render them just what they are, and nothing more." In China "music and astronomy, poetry and tactics, painting and architecture, are as they were centuries ago, the children of its eternal laws, and unalterably childish institutions. The empire is an embalmed mummy, wrapped in silk, and painted with hieroglyphics: its internal circulation is that of a dormouse in its winter sleep." Unlike the Hindus, the Chinese can expect no delayed recompense from fate.

The elements are sensibly the same as in Hegel's account of the respective parts of the "Oriental World." But Hegel adds to Herder's stock of information the conceit of China and India being two symmetrical, opposite, inseparable parts of the same immaturity of the human race, two fragments calling out to each other but incapable of achieving the synthesis that in Hegel's world history can only be attained by (of course) Greece. Herder's essentialism—his attribution to races or nations permanent characters that historical events only manifest, but do not change—is augmented in Hegel by a *folie à deux* dynamic: whatever characteristics signal China, their opposites will signal India, and vice versa. The "Oriental World" is a hall of mirrors, but its observer—Hegel the narrator—stands apart from its axis of symmetrical reflection, occupying a third dimension known as Spirit. The denizens of India and China cannot possibly raise themselves to that dimension.

Since Edward Said's 1978 book, *Orientalism*, it has become customary to tag such views of the countries and cultures outside Europe as instances of a locally specific variant of the European superiority complex. Nothing is more discredited today than "orientalism"; no one wants to be denounced as "orientalizing" or as "self-orientalizing." But the present use of the word as a term of abuse occludes its history. "Orientalism" is a back-formation from the term "orientalist." As a Slavist is a person who studies the language, culture, and history of the Slavs, and a Persianist someone who studies those of the Persians, one may deduce that an Orientalist is (or was, pre-1978) a person who studies the languages, cultures, and histories of the Orient. In this understanding, "Orientalism" is whatever Orientalists do; it is their specialist knowledge. But "-ism" has another, more treacherous connotation. By a sort of pun, Said asserted that the study of the East by non-Easterners is an "-ism" in the other sense: a fixed set of doctrines comparable to communism or exclusionism, and so not a way of knowing at all. This assertion has been accepted in the English-speaking world to such a degree that many journals and academic departments have changed their names to avoid the suggestion of being complicit with the racism, colonialism, exploitation, and other crimes of the Eastward-venturing West.

The contributors to this book long ago recognized the need to reject "Orientalism" in Said's sense and have often contributed to dislodging the ethnocentric views that go by that name. ("Colonialism is evil" is the part of Said's argument that everyone accepts; "Western scholarship on the East is always implicitly allied with colonialism" is the controversial part.) But it is not by rejecting *unfavorable* views of the East that they accomplish the rebuttal of Hegel and other exponents of the "Oriental World" built on the polarity India-and-China. Uniformly reverential views of India or China are little better than dismissive ones. The problem is how the topic of cultural and historical discussion is to be shaped. Fifteen years before Said's book, the Egyptian political scientist Anouar Abdel-Malek had already diagnosed the trick of considering the "East" under essentializing descriptions as "an object . . . passive, non-participating . . . non-active, non-autonomous, non-sovereign with regard to itself." But Abdel-Malek's use of the term "orientalism" itself was neutral; he called for changes in the discipline, not for making it a new term of opprobrium.

Essentialism, one of the most persistent infections of historiography, requires a persistent treatment. A doubled, symmetrical, self-replicating essentialism is all the more dangerous. The authors of this book have identified essentializing as the danger and devised various strategies for blocking it.

Admittedly, China and India are different, and the features that distinguish them do tend to fall into certain thematic patterns, occasionally inventoried in the chapters of this book for the sake of drawing parallels and distinctions: unity versus plurality, history versus epic, politics versus the divine. But the parallels must be seen as belonging to the observers and to the act of comparison rather than to the objects themselves. "Comparison with India and China was one means, among others of course, by which the fractious polities of the western end of Eurasia became 'Europe' and 'the West' to begin with," as Owen and Pollock observe in chapter 5. Turning India and China into stable protagonists of a story running over millennia was necessary to create a parallel narrative about "the West," magically endowed with similar stability and narrative centrality. To describe the maneuver is almost to undo it.

In another strategy, the discovery of diversity within "India" and "China" helps to turn the previous monoliths into composites having many working parts: thus Crossley and Eaton find in chapter 2 that Indian history contains the contrary pulls of Sanskrit and Persian models of empire, and in Chinese history templates for imperial governance strongly differentiate the Song, say, from the Qing. This internal diversity permits internal hybridity as well, as when the Persian vertical kingship adopts the marriage strategies of Rajput alliance-based kingship.

In chapter 1, Guha and Pomeranz defy an interpretation of history based on culture or ideology from the start, by showing how economy, culture, and politics develop from interactions with the environment. Affordances of water, soil, seasons, cultivated plants, draft animals, and the like set limits to the explanatory power of culture, or as Hegel would call it, Spirit.

Thus—and in many other ways throughout this book—comparison detaches the parts from supposed cultural wholes and shows how they operate differently under differing conditions. In virtually every chapter, the China/India symmetry integral to the "Oriental World" is relegated to the background and the autonomy of the parts reaffirmed. Indian history and Chinese history, or the histories of any subparts of either realm, are adequate to making sense on their own; they are not fragmentary Sphinxes awaiting an answer that can only come from outside. Comparison between them thus serves not to reinforce the traditional list of opposites but to suggest endemic causal mechanisms, alternative scenarios, and path dependencies that can explain the similarities between Indian and Chinese histories, point to their differences, and define the common factors' sphere of validity. The logic of essential national personalities is most effectively undercut by retracing, as several chapters in this book do, those seemingly permanent characteristics to a set of distal events: if X had not happened (and it was not inevitable that it happen), the outcome Y would have been different (and it could have been different).

Such reconstructions and discriminations show us how to think about our thinking about India and China—a different activity from showing us how to think about India and China, which was Herder's and Hegel's aim.

The Europeans of the nascent colonial age were not the only ones to think about the East or to take it as a cultural unit. Their contemporaries among Chinese intellectuals also thought about the conditions of their own state formation through thinking about India, just as Indian intellectuals discovered their culture through observing its differences with China and Japan. According to a recent study by Liu Xi, Liang Qichao, a young firebrand of the 1898 imperial reform movement, wrote in 1896 that "India, the nation with the world's most ancient history, suffered the fate of becoming a British colony due to its stubbornness in sticking to traditions and refusing to reform." (A word to the wise.) Liang's mentor, the statesman Kang Youwei, exiled after the repression of the 1898 reforms, visited India in 1901–1903 and 1909. While there he corresponded with Liang on the future reorganization of China, envisioned by some as a democracy, by others as a federation of states or an empire under a constitutional monarch. Liang held "that China was too large in size and suggested that the 18 provinces of China be given autonomy and made into 18 states. Kang was shocked to hear this and succeeded," during one exchange in September 1900, "in convincing Liang that his suggestion would bring about the fall of China." In 1902, writing to Liang from Darjeeling, Kang put the same argument somewhat differently. This time, as described by Liu Xi,

> Kang provided a review of modern Indian history, noting the collapse of the Mughal Empire, beginning with the British conquest of Bengal in the 1750s and 1760s and extending until the conquest of Punjab and the final annexation of Awadh in the 1840s and 1850s.

Through recounting this history, he elaborated his argument that India's suffering as a colonized country was due to the separation and disunity among the "provinces." . . . He referred to the struggles in China to warn that similar misfortunes to those of India could befall China. . . .

[Kang] suggested that India was superior to China with regard to size, population, scientific knowledge, religion and philosophy, agriculture, foreign trade on both land and sea routes, literature, arts and architecture and the physical strength of the people. The two states, he considered, were on the same level of competitiveness in terms of rule of law, culture and social rites. . . . In sum, he concluded that even though India may be superior in terms of its civilizational development, size and population, it still became a colonized nation, chiefly because of the autonomy of its "provinces."

Kang's version of India, like Liang's, was a "virtual history" constructed out of a sense of China's existential peril. Another virtual history, this one written by Liang Qichao in the early years of the Chinese Republic, reaches back fifteen hundred years to the apex of Indian-Chinese cultural interaction as a model for the cosmopolitanism Liang desired to see modern China adopt in its dealings with the rest of the world:

As for a warm reception given to foreign cultures, an open-minded receptivity toward them, and the sense that translating was an honorable endeavor—all that came only with the introduction of Buddhism. . . . The stronger the receptivity of a nation's culture, the greater its power of growth: this is a constant principle. Our nation's receptivity to cultures outside it was exhibited principally in the epoch of the introduction of Buddhist teachings. . . . We are today in a second age of translation, and those who are engaged in that work should aspire to look to the ancients without shame!

The China-India pairing served various ends in the thinking of Chinese writers. In every case it reflects an image of China back to itself—sometimes an ideal, sometimes a warning. Even Hu Shi's violent rejection of everything Indian-derived in Chinese culture was, like the other virtual histories mentioned here, an attempt to find "indigenous or alternative modernities" (to quote Kamal Sheel) in answer to imported modernity.

Constructions of India are a powerful means of thinking through possible Chinas, and the same must be true of Indian constructions of China. So the constellation of "China-and-India" is not limited to Western discourse. But the Chinese and Indian attempts to think through that constellation are also responses to the Western phantasm of an "Oriental world," which we are still in some necessity of refuting. As the "Oriental world" recedes, different meanings will emerge from the discursive pairing of China and India, that much is sure.

We see that India-and-China was constructed for the particular psycho-geographic needs of a history designed to be at once Eurocentric and a "world history." But does the term "construction" magically dispel the construct? Hardly; once it is in the air, we may ask if it is still in fact meaningful to say that someone was wrong about China or India, or to attempt to bring forth a real China or India that would batter down the sand castle versions. Such hopes are probably misplaced. Authenticity has a political attraction and sometimes a cultural one. I read recently of a Finnish nationalist party that calls itself, simply, "The True Finns." But it is best to recognize that as interpreters of the past, we do not have a choice between a real Finland, China, or India and a "constructed" one; the best we can do is construct ours more wisely, more precisely, with greater respect for the friability of facts and the limits of our own understanding. Is there a China or India to be known apart from acts of construction pertaining to them? As Chinese or Indians, we may indeed feel that there is; as economists, as historians, as readers of literary texts we may be persuaded of the identity and continuity of those large containers of events: China in the year 764 does have a causal connection to China in the year 1764, though no one would simply pronounce them identical. Let us consider the interests in play. A personal identity for human beings in the modern period usually involves a state, and states have tirelessly claimed the prestige that derives from population, military might, natural resources, and economic development, as well as from culture and history (laying claim to the longest history, the most famous writers, the biggest epics, the most memorable lyrics, the most recognizable paintings, the most sublime landscapes—whatever, in the current parlance, rates as "iconic"). Such investment in collective identities is not usually compatible with much complexity or internal diversity. Cultural essentialism in politics appears as ethnic or religious nationalism. Fascist movements have long been aware that people will take great risks and revise their moral calculus for the rewards, not always tangible, of membership in a "great race" (not to say a master race). Critics, historians, and philologists have the unwelcome task of cutting these pretensions down to size, wounding national and individual narcissism.

There is something defensive about the essentialist style of thinking about history and nation, giving them fixed identities and interests. The literary scholar Erich Auerbach noticed a curious relationship between the subtlety of twentieth-century fiction and the crudity of twentieth-century political falsehoods. Could it be that a novel like *Ulysses*, which Erich Aueurbach claims (in his *Mimesis*) "makes severe demands on the reader's patience and learning by its dizzying whirl of motifs, wealth of words and concepts, perpetual playing upon their countless associations, and the ever re-aroused but never satisfied doubt as to what order is ultimately hidden behind so much apparent arbitrariness," is a secret sharer with "the temptation to entrust oneself to a sect which solved all problems with a single formula, whose power of suggestion imposed solidarity, and which ostracized everything which would not fit in and submit?" The same dynamic can be seen in the history of the West's attempts to understand its neighbors. The depth of recorded history and the mass of untranslated documents from China and India that impinged on the consciousness of Europeans in the two centuries before 1800 certainly had the dimensions to precipitate a defensive reaction in the form of the "single formula" that solved all the problems of Chinese chronology, Hindu theology, Buddhist logic, and the like. Great complexity begets the desire for great simplicity—at least in the minds of those who can sense the complexity but are not equal to the task of grasping it. If we take Hegel's utterances as reflecting a hermeneutics of cognitive limitation—as expressing their own conditions of possibility—then what he has to say about these two major world civilizations accurately depicts the processing power of a relatively well-informed nineteenth-century European confronted with more information than he or his contemporaries could handle. "The East knew and to the present day knows only that *One* is free": the single word that will name and transfix China and India is "Despotism." But is it not the attraction of a concept like "despotism" to be despotic in nature, imposing its uniformity on unruly empirical data?

One of the more useful things that we can do today is to identify the gestures of Hegelian history and be vigilant to resist them, one by one. The narcissistic defense is needed only if foreignness is felt as a threat. Hegel would not have exiled the Indians and Chinese into the primitive past if he had not needed to deny that they were engaged, alongside him and perhaps with no less vivid perception, in the sum of actions that make up a world. About that Kang Youwei, Liang Qichao, Hu Shih, and the many other historians, thinkers, and writers who have reflected on India-and-China in the Chinese language had no need to be deceived.

Dipesh Chakrabarty

Haun Saussy is right to say that this book is a "new take on an old problem." Comparing China and India unfavorably with regard to the West—as he shows—has long been a part of the process through which a "modern" West has constructed its own identity. It has also shown up, as Saussy suggests, certain failures of the cognitive frameworks through which European intellectuals of the nineteenth century—especially those committed to grasping the world through a unitary framework—to deal with major cultural and historical differences without consigning them to some inferior status in history. The editors of this book agree with him, and the essays collected here all address this problem in one way or another. Comparison with India and China produced what Owen and Pollock describe as "the long history of mistaken normativity," as "most comparison of large-scale cultural (or social or political) phenomena has usually privileged the West as the comparative partner, with the rest represented as deviation." The theme is announced right at the beginning in the introduction to this book, where Elman and Pollock ascribe this "self-justifying hindsight" squarely to Europe's imperial hubris:

> A crucial aspect of the colonial sort of comparativism is the defining status given to the European "standard" (the *secundum comparatum*, to use the technical term of Western rhetoric, to which *biaozhun* in Chinese and *upamana* in Indic correspond), and the assertion that everything compared with it (the *primum comparandum*, Chinese *mofang*, "model to be emulated," Indic *upameya*, "thing-to-be-compared") was not just different but deviant and even deficient. Western–non-Western comparison, from Hegel until very recently, would typically and without hesitation—and usually without self-awareness—incorporate this constitutive aspect of inequality.

The aspiration to critique the West for its historiographical blind spots is, of course, not unique to this book. A long line of scholars—from Donald Lach to Martin Bernal and for that matter Benjamin Elman himself—have for decades now sought to remind us of what European intellectual and scientific traditions owe to non-European ideas and institutions. In their introduction, Elman and Pollock go on to articulate a more ambitious aspiration—to introduce a "certain distance from the paradigmatic nature of the comparatum (for example, the Homeric epic, which for Hegel was the standard of comparison for all epics everywhere), unsettling its self-evident nature, so that it becomes just one case among other possibilities, and hence 'estranged'." While this book shares with other works descriptive and analytical tactics common to the strategy of comparison, it highlights the importance of the estranging—defamiliarizing—function of comparison. The "dominant concern, whether implicitly or explicitly [of the book]," Elman and Pollock say, "has been with estrangement." But of "a special kind." For, "not only does cosmopolitan comparison require that we actively try to bracket the Western objects—paintings, poems, power formations, whatever—that have functioned as the standards, in order to gain as undistorted a view as possible of the non-Western objects of comparison. But it also leaves us with objects that wind up estranging—sometimes profoundly estranging—each other."

Not every essay in this book pursues this ambition self-consciously. But there are some comparative strategies common to them all: they put similar sets of questions, for example, to Indian and Chinese histories for the "early modern" period and then juxtapose the information gleaned to highlight some particular contrasts. Some of the contrasts are not surprising and constitute the core of academic folklores about the two regions. In chapter 4, Brokaw and Busch's observation that "there is no question that, compared to India, China enjoyed a more unified cultural and political tradition [and that it] . . . also enjoyed—in another sharp contrast with India—a long *written* historical tradition"; or the contrast put forward by Crossley and Eaton in chapter 2 between India's fragment polity and the Chinese tendency toward centralization will not, as such, take readers by surprise. At the same time, some large similarities also will not surprise readers, and the editors themselves have acknowledged and highlighted some of them—for instance, in the introduction: "The prominence and consequences of patrilocal residence (women always moved to the home of their husband's family); the correlation between status and control (the higher the status of women, the more stringent their confinement in China, the stricter the ban on widow remarriage in India); the control of women's bodies (foot binding in China, widow burning in India); ingrained popular conceptions of the place of women in society; and, not least, the difficulty of using sources predominantly produced by men to grasp the real issues of concern to women—all these phenomena seem to be constant across the two regions, and to be largely unaffected by cultural particularity."

The more intriguing issue is what direct comparison between India and China for the early modern period—and undertaken without any reference to Western categories—yields. Of course, there were many instances of direct commerce in goods and (religious) ideas—Buddhism, for instance—between China and India, long before any Europeans turned up in either country with business propositions. But as Tansen Sen's recent study of episodes such as the Tang court's "second embassy to Kanauj [January–February 644 CE]" or "the emergence of Mount Wutai as the present dwelling of Manjusri" shows, the ensuing processes of literal and cultural translation were neither disinterested nor guarantees against any "manipulation" of texts. Elman and Pollock are, of course, aware that their argument for "direct" comparison comes after global institutions have undergone a deep process of Europeanization that followed from the historical process of expansion of Europe. They make the arresting point that the outcome of an exercise of direct comparison today is "less straightforward to characterize in terms of knowledge." They write: "The category of estrangement made possible by non-Western comparison . . . will be of greater interest to the general reader than how comparison has caused us to rethink received categories like 'religion' or to discover stable patterns of structural constraint." What emerges from such "mutual illumination of objects of analysis" are objects, institutions, and practices "that can now be seen to be equally different: neither deficient nor deviant in the light of some standard regarded as perfect, often radically different from one another." Juxtaposition that is not burdened by any "misapprehensions about the essential nature of things—what a poem or a painting or a power formation like empire really, invariantly, is . . . allows us to better capture the specificity of a given case, which can be seen only against the backdrop of a comparative partner."

One could, of course, ask if claims about specificity were not plagued by the same problems as might haunt propositions about "what a poem or a painting or a power formation like empire really, invariantly, is." How would one select two elements from two different places and histories for comparison unless at least a vague shadow of some commonality was already visible? And how would one know if that vague shadow was not a ghost of the "invariant" one was trying to get away from? The essays here use genres and categories—such as history, poetry, or the state—to cobble together facts and observations about the two histories. But, of course, what we learn at the end of the exercise is how provisional and unstable the genres and the categories were to begin with: sometimes they help us to sift through differences, sometimes they are like sacks into which we pour diverse elements in all their heterogeneity. Perhaps we could, following Paul Veyne, push our distinctions further to see what may be specific (a particular illustration of the general) and singular (that which resists all general schemas—idiosyncrasies of language, for example) to Chinese and Indian history? The overall argument in this book does not consciously move in this direction, but it raises the possibility. For each of these histories carries the condensations and accretions of a multitude of individual events that come together in particular places and times to constitute what outsiders may see as the peculiarities of that history and the insiders see as simply "natural."

The popularity of biography in early modern China and that of hagiography in India, as pointed out by Brokaw and Busch in chapter 4, is a case in point, or the contrast that Guha and Pomeranz in chapter 1 draw between the very different futures that three common animals—horses, elephants, and pigs—enjoyed or suffered in the two countries; or the importance of haze in Chinese-Japanese traditions of painting in contrast to the preeminence of the clear line in the Indian tradition (see Aitken and Wang's chapter 8), or the very different relationship that poetry had to historical chronology in the two cultures (see Owen and Pollock, chapter 5). Comparison here serves to bring out the force of what is peculiar to a place and its time. This peculiarity, particularly in the realm of the aesthetic or the religious or even the political, cannot always be explained by sociological analysis, for we are in the end dealing with the accretion of meanings that represent complex and unpredictable developments over the passage of time in each place, something like what in another context would be called "the arbitrary nature of the sign." This arbitrariness itself belongs to the stuff of history. Or consider, to give yet another example, the use of the word "heaven" or the reference to a deity in Chinese political theology, as pointed out in chapter 2 by Crossley and Eaton:

An ideological tradition—by Qing times, based on the Four Books of Confucian scholarship—helped unify imperial officials (see also chapter 5). There was also a ritual structure, bringing together ancient themes of worship of Heaven, Earth, the ancestral spirits, and seasonal changes with specific veneration of Confucius (551–479 BCE). And there was a very strong rhetorical tradition allowing the emperor to express himself as a moral guardian and not as the head of a state based on extraction or coercion. Foremost among the rhetorical themes was the ideal of "benevolent government," in which the state acted to prevent predation upon the common people by elites, used its powers to protect the people and encourage agriculture, and maintained a harmonious relationship between humanity and Heaven.

Governments fulfilling these ideals were regarded as enjoying the "Mandate of Heaven"—the endorsement of a supreme deity that either sustained the current dynasty or led to its replacement by another.

Eaton and Crossley do not explain words like heaven (*tianzi*) or the nature of the "supreme deity" invoked here. But I am sure explaining these terms—a philological exercise—would take us only deeper into the "peculiarities" of the Chinese. This would not be an ahistorical project—think of E. P. Thompson's vigorously argued essay, "The Peculiarities of the English"—but would constitute an invitation to cease comparing and dwell instead in the history of the Chinese on "their own terms," as it were.

The strength of the comparative project involved in this kind of an exercise—studying China and India directly in comparison to each other—arises from the tension between two extreme positions that nuanced comparative analysis can both generate and inhabit. One extreme is presented by the invitation to be local—to go native, as the common expression has it—an invitation that is built into any interpretive exercise, if it is not held in check by the countervailing force of categories in the modern human sciences. The other extreme is presented by these categories themselves, for their assumed universal provenance often betrays particular and provincial origins. There is, of course, a process of hybridization—or translation, to switch metaphors—whenever an analytical category of very distinct cultural origins achieves universal or hegemonic status and comes to be embedded in our analytical common sense. Elman has elaborated this process in a masterful way in his book *On Their Own Terms,* discussing how the Chinese translated many of the modern categories of academic disciplines via the Japanese, who themselves followed German, Dutch, and other European models. But the translation or the hybrid ends up—more often than not—playing second fiddle to the dominant and universal terms by which we moderns classify disciplines or different systems of knowledge. There was clearly a time, as Elman and Minkowski show in chapter 6, when the subjects of medieval learning—grammar, logic, rhetoric, arithmetic, music, geometry, and astronomy—in Europe corresponded only "somewhat" to "the Six Arts of the Chinese scholars (rites, music, archery, charioteering, calligraphy, and mathematics), which had formed the Chinese basis of education and actions since ancient times" or when "conservative opinion about education" in Brahmanical India "converged on an ideal curriculum of fourteen sciences (*vidya*): the four Vedas (the sacred texts of the Brahmans) and their six limbs (*anga*)—language analysis (*vyakarana*), etymology (*nirukta*), phonetics (*shiksha*), ritual (*kalpa*), metrics (*chandas*), and astronomy (*jyotisha*)—along with their four subordinate limbs (*upanga*), law and moral philosophy (*dharma*), discourse analysis and scriptural hermeneutics (*mimamsa*), logic and epistemology (*nyaya*), and mythology (*purana*)."

But this plurality of medieval or early modern knowledge categories have not survived the onslaught of words that came to attain analytical status in Western/European social sciences in the nineteenth and twentieth centuries, whatever the particular politics of translation at particular places and times. This is not simply a result of imperialism; it is also a result of modernizing elites in different parts of the world desiring modern institutions, including European-style academies and universities. The politics of translation, as I have said before, could never overcome the power of these European categories that have provided the arsenal of weapons of criticism in modernity everywhere. The politics of translation, while real and deserving of a justifiable claim on our attention, cannot silence their rule. Instead, they still constitute the basic categories by which we classify knowledge and critique society. Note, for instance, how words that achieved analytical status in European human sciences in the nineteenth and twentieth centuries constitute the bedrock on which Crossley and Eaton's narrative in chapter 2 on statecraft stands: "By the fourteenth century, some Hindu rulers incorporated into their ruling ideologies rites and norms of Persian kingship." Granted, the word "rite" in its anthropological sense is older than the discipline of anthropology, but "ideology" and "norms" are clearly of nineteenth- and twentieth-century origins. After all, there is no denying that this volume is itself based on modern, universal categories of science, literature, history, art, gender, religion, and ecology (the last incorporating economy and demography).

This is why one particular claim made by the editors in their introduction gives me pause, even as I agree with the rebellious spirit of their prose: "It is hardly surprising, first of all," write Elman and Pollock in their introduction, "that cosmopolitan comparison [as undertaken in this volume] should explode our received conceptual categories for understanding the larger world, given that those categories originated in Western historical experience. But this occurred so frequently in the course of our project that it seems to have been intensified by the act of comparison itself." A good example is "religion" (see Benite and Davis's chapter 7). But if such "explosion" of the received and ruling analytical categories were all that there was to the larger narrative of this book, we would be hard put to explain why, even when he is treated as merely a misguided and forgettable adversary, Hegel's shadow, long and unmistakable, falls across the structures of many of the arguments presented here, especially in the chapters on history, literature, and gender. Why do Hegel's monumental errors have such a long life? Why are his mistakes so "durable" (as Saussy puts it)? Why do we still feel called upon to debate them?

In an essay he published late in life, in 1983, on "The Future of the European Humanities" (before anybody could imagine the fall of the Berlin Wall), Hans-Georg Gadamer broached the problem of "how the experience of thought which modern Europe has lived through can acquire some relevance on a planetary scale." Like many other thinkers of his time, he wondered if the spread of the capitalist market and technology would lead eventually to a world unity or its opposite: "will the continuation of the industrial revolution lead to the leveling of the cultural articulation of Europe and the spreading of a standardized world civilization, in which the history of the planet almost stands still in the ideal status of a rational world bureaucracy—or, to the contrary, will history remain history with all of its catastrophes, tensions, and its manifold differentiations, as has been the essential characteristic of humanity since the building of the Tower of Babel?"

There were undesirable aspects, of course, to both alternatives. A cold and purely rational bureaucracy could affect human dwelling on the planet as badly as technology. "The homelessness with which the modern industrial world threatens humans" would then only intensify the latter's drive "to search for home," a prospect that in turn could lead to unattractive options: a future history of "catastrophes and tensions," their effects only magnified by modern technology. Surely, "the authentic task" of a globalized world, argued Hans-Georg Gadamer (in his essay "The Future of the European Humanities" in *On Education, Poetry, and History: Applied Hermeneutics*), would "lie in the area of human coexistence." But the toleration needed for such coexistence would require each culture to feel strong in itself, for "only where strength is, is there tolerance." In Gadamer's thought, this was where European humanities or the "human sciences" achieved "a new relevance." "Many countries in this world," he wrote, "are in search of a form of civilization which would accomplish the trick of uniting their own traditions and the deeply rooted values of their forms of life with ideas of economic progress derived from Europe." Perceptive "minds in other countries" were not necessarily even seeking to adapt "the European Enlightenment and its form of civilization"; in Gadamer's view, they were more concerned with the question of "how people and society will be able to achieve a true development from the basis of their own tradition." But this was also where, he felt, European academic disciplines had a positive role to play. In privileging the European university and its knowledge forms, Gadamer was not denying what European thought owed to non-European thinkers. "One needs to remember what the Near East and Egypt bequeathed the developing European science in Greece," he wrote. "However," he added, "what one can say without reservation is that only in Europe did the pattern of science crystallize into an autonomous and ruling cultural structure . . . modern science and research, education and higher education everywhere follow the European model—or its American reproduction—this is all still a result of European science." Only in Europe, he would go on to argue, could one see the emergence of "the concepts of religion, philosophy, art, and science," and to "this differentiation, there is no original counterpart in other cultures." "It would be futile," to quote him further, "to search for such categories, for example, within other traditions and to burden, for example, the wise sayings of the great Chinese thinkers or the epic tradition of India with such differentiation." All those cultures, however, could be approached by "using our separating and differentiating concepts of today." And how would other cultures respond to this proposition? Gadamer did not directly address this question, but an answer is implicit in the statement that "modern science and research and higher education *everywhere* [emphasis added] follow the European model—or its American reproduction." The other nations would also come to use the same set of European differentiating categories in order to know themselves!

There is much to criticize today in Gadamer's statements. In locating the capacity for toleration in "one's own strength, in one's own existential certainty," he remains open to postcolonial criticisms of claims of cultural authenticity or autonomy. Nor is he sufficiently sensitive to late twentieth-century critiques of nationalism. But there was something to the proposition that if there were to be varieties of humanities in today's world—which was once Léopold Senghor's dream in Africa—they would have to be organized around the abstract and universal concepts supplied, ultimately, by the universities of Europe. However we might disagree with Gadamer, his basic proposition rings true, going not only by the global experience of universities but even by the categories that hold together the division of labor—the distribution of chapters and topics—in this book.

I am not denying the role that European institutions played in processing information and material, theoretical and objective, collected all over the world, but the fact is that only Europe in the early modern and modern periods, and later the United States, possessed the institutions that could perform such processing that resulted in the emergence of the modern disciplines in the human sciences. Indian travelers in the seventeenth and eighteenth centuries may have visited other parts of the world, but India did not possess institutions that could process their travelogues into the beginnings of the science of anthropology (think of the use that Kant made of such travel literature in teaching his course on anthropology). Besides, as I said in *Provincializing Europe* with reference to India, all the commentarial traditions available once in Sanskrit, Arabic, or Persian in particular Indian institutions underwent very significant transformations during British rule. The study of older texts now had to be organized into the abstract universal classificatory categories that European universities supplied. The European categories thus became valued gifts in our intellectual life. But they were also unworkable as such. A lot of translational doubt was expressed over every category that Gadamer mentions as foundational: was our *dharma* really what was meant by "religion"? Did we mean by "art" what Europeans meant by it? Was *darshana* the same as "philosophy"? In other words, the conversation with Europe could only proceed through a process that questioned and tweaked the received categories. This process did not produce alternatives as such but it did bring into these categories memories of other life practices, just as the categories themselves carry—even to this day—signs of their own parochial origins.

The creative energy of this book unleashes new battles on this frontier—battles that do not aim to dislodge completely European or Western categories from their positions of dominance but rather to produce enough cracks in them so that the richness of practices, institutions, and concepts not amenable to these categories can shine through. This intellectual effort is not the same as historians' frequent quest to find "the past in the present," for that exercise often turns out to be unhealthily dependent on the historian's reading of the present. For example, the very same historical characteristics of Chinese society and state that were once mobilized to explain why China was good at socialism are now mobilized to explain their success in global capitalism! Pollock, it seems to me, has articulated clearly the utopian vision that informs some of the most ambitious intellectual scuffles that this book wants to engage. At the heart of his position is what one might call a "truly global" vision of the university. As he put it in "Future Philology? The Fate of a Soft Science in a Hard World": "The decades-long critique of disciplines may finally be gaining traction, to the degree that recent attempts at reconstruction, reform, or renewal of the university made all over the world . . . actually aim to produce a new, truly global university." He names three conditions as the prerequisite for this development: "historical self-awareness . . . the humbling force of genealogy must be part and parcel of the every disciplinary practice," "non-provinciality," and "methodological and conceptual pluralism."

One cannot deny the powerful appeal of this utopian vision—but I think that for it to be realized, a fourth condition must be met. And this relates to the role of Chinese and Indian intellectuals themselves in creating new universities (the presently upcoming ones seem to be aiming to produce "global citizens" for the corporate sector). Let me briefly explain this point in bringing my section of this afterword to a close. There is no doubt that Europe and Europeans once dominated this planet. By the end of the nineteenth century, 80 percent of the surface of the earth was under the rule of one European power or another. Since 1945, however, we have seen a retreat of the colonial great powers of Europe and the rise (and then the fall) of superpowers like the United States and once the Soviet Union as well. China and India today aspire to similar status. China has already achieved a lot more of this status than India. A superpower that dominates us surely dominates us economically, militarily, and technologically. It also undoubtedly influences our imagination—the twentieth century, which became the American century, cannot be imagined, for example, without the global dominance of Hollywood or American television or technology. Yet a distinction remains to be made between European colonial domination of others and the sheer economic, military, and cultural weight of a superpower: when European powers became imperial-colonial "lords of humankind" from the period of the Renaissance to that of the Enlightenment and into the nineteenth century, they also gave their victims the terms and categories of thought with which to critique and challenge European domination. Two such great "weapons of criticism" forged in the European workshop of the nineteenth century—but with their intellectual genealogies stretching farther back into history—were Marxism and liberalism, both wielded with great effect by many decolonizing nations and thinkers who criticized European domination. No dominant power is ever totally benign. As someone who grew up in the Indian subcontinent, I understand Indian and Chinese desires to be superpowers. But I ask of them: If and when you do come to dominate the world truly and effectively, what terms of criticism will you provide to your victims—not just nations or peoples outside these countries but dissident groups in places like Tibet, Kashmir, or Nagaland—so that they can criticize your domination? Surely technology, economics, and the media alone cannot produce such terms. Which is why, even in the age of American domination, European thought has been critical to most imaginations of human freedom.

Will we move beyond the horizons of European thought as China and India become dominant, powerful countries of this century? Will India and China be able to search their traditions—as Gandhi did once—to produce new grounds for thinking on which humanity will meet as one? On one of my last visits to China, a few years ago, I was quite struck by discussions in English-language Chinese newspapers on the need to move from the "Made in China" phase to the "Created in China" one. I assume that these newspaper writers had material products in mind when they spoke of things being "created in China"—something like cars and gadgets of Chinese design. But European domination of the world went much further than that in creating concepts that framed some of the normative ideas for all of us. Can India and China aspire to the same role in the world to come? On that will depend the prospects of realizing the profoundest aspirations of the fundamental exercise undertaken in this fascinating collection of essays.

In Which Loose Ends Meet: A Conversation

Dipesh Chakrabarty: So let's try to pull some things together. What made you think of adding the subtitle "Both Sides, Now"? I suspect some humor in that choice. Maybe you could go into why humor comes to you at this point, because the book is not especially humorous.

Haun Saussy: You're right, there's a little joke. "Both Sides, Now" is the title of a song by Joni Mitchell, written in 1967, that has been popping up in my head every time I think about this book and its project. Every chapter in the book presents an issue from "both sides"—in relation to the border separating China and India. And our previous attempt at a conclusion took the book's insistence on symmetrical contrast as an attempt to cross another boundary and answer, also from "both sides," a traditional distinction between the East and the West. So there are really four sides here: China and India, and China-and-India as framed by a West that designates the Orient as other.

But maybe I should go into the song, if you don't remember it. As a child of the sixties, of course I do. In it the narrator reflects on clouds as seen first from the perspective of the ground, then from the perspective of an airplane passenger. From the ground they look like magical castles rising up into the sky; from the other perspective they look like piles of vapor. And the song extends this double perspective into human relations (a breakup, I think, and a feeling of distance from one's earlier passions and desires). The lyric of the song points to the sort of humor that comes up when the things you thought were important turn out to be a subset of the things that were really important. And that effect of distancing and maybe irony comes with the territory of intercultural comparison. At least, this is how I've benefited for thirty-odd years of my life from thinking about China: things that I was brought up to think were inevitable turn out to be, well, optional.

DC: Like my experience growing up in India, and then going back and looking at India from the outside and inside.

HS: And since the song is about air travel, and we do a bit of that in our line of work . . . The song's about the loss of illusions, but it's not a bitter song, and I think that fits the tone of the book generally. We're discussing some painful periods of human history, with conquest and enslavement and annihilation, so that bitterness and resentment would be justified; there's some of that here, but not only that. The willingness to think about how things could have been different keeps a kind of utopian hope alive.

DC: The book also reminds me a little bit of something Michel Foucault said in *The Birth of Biopolitics* when he was asked about the question of freedom and what he meant by it. Insofar as I remember it, he said that your sense of freedom is always formed in relationship to your sense of unfreedom in the immediate past. So there is no absolute freedom, and similarly, there is no absolute benefit to be reaped from directly comparing China and India. Because when you look at India and China interacting without the West being there, when they themselves put themselves side by side, it's not as if they don't misunderstand each other, and it's not as if their understanding of each other is outside of the realms of power and interests and ideology and kingdoms and their motives and wars, and so on. Even the story of the migration of Buddhism to China and the translation activity that followed is deeply influenced by these factors. So the utopian aspiration of this book makes sense only in the context of the immediate past of European domination and the absurdities, say, of certain formulations like the Hegelian ones discussed in this book. In other words, the desire to put these two entities side by side, the desire to circumvent the West, is somewhat of a utopian desire but makes perfect sense when you keep in mind the fact of the general intellectual domination of Western categories.

HS: I see another dimension of this fact in the time limits that the book sets itself. It really starts around 1500, which corresponds to the time frame of Immanuel Wallerstein's theory of the world system: the moment when the Europeans begin to get out and about, and set up the circuits of exchange and rapine that made them colonial powers. So it's an appropriate choice of period for foregrounding that set of power relations. But what would be good to think about too is what happens when we throw the backward limit of the investigation much farther in the past, so that we see the period of European dominance starting in 1500 or so as a parenthesis in a much longer human history, in most of which the Europeans were marginal players at best: the sort of economic history that people like André Gunder Frank were advocating. The necessity of that kind of perspective is brought home to me every time I encounter somebody, in life or in print, who's astonished to see that these Chinese and Indians are suddenly crawling out of their straw huts to become major economic powers and take over the world: "How is this possible?" and so forth. . . . But they weren't living in straw huts and they weren't helpless until the Europeans disembarked. In the long run of a three- or four-thousand-year time frame, India and China were always the places where the greatest amount of riches aggregated and where knowledge aggregated, along with other symptoms of being dominant cultures in their world. So it shouldn't surprise anybody that the long-term norm is being restored now. On the other end, the book doesn't deal with the period after 1800, when things changed dramatically for all of Asia.

DC: East Asia works out to be the economic laboratory for the region where the larger ambitions of Indian and Chinese states pose some threats to other countries' perception of themselves, not to speak of Sino-Indian conflicts. Think of Thailand, or the terms of Coedès's book, *The Indianized States of Southeast Asia*, which, if it were to be published today, couldn't possibly come out under the same title, because people resent being seen as a mixture of Sino-Indic elements. And the Thai nationalists' struggle for a long time has been to establish a sense of Thai uniqueness, which they call *ekkalak Thai*: they set up as the sign of being Thai the fact of being neither Indian nor Chinese. The Thai prime minister's office issued a monthly magazine in the 1970s called *Ekkalak Thai*.

HS: The corresponding invention in Japan, *kokusui* or "national essence," underwent transliteration into Chinese as *guocui* and stimulated an infinite industry of specifying and re-vindicating the national identity.

DC: As in India! Something I found interesting in reading through this book relates to what I think of as academic folklore, particularly when it comes to comparing China and India, such as Chinese centralization versus Indian fragmentation, the importance of diversity in India (which the Chinese seem to have been commenting on for a very long time), and so on. It raised a question for me: how does one think of such stereotypical themes ubiquitous in China-India comparisons? As elements in a common repertoire that could be put in different combinations at different times? This is the whole question of the presence of the past. In my part of our essay, I commented on Joseph Needham's use of Chinese characteristics in support of socialism—the very same characteristics that other scholars since have used as preconditions of Chinese capitalism, the two positions explaining Chinese success at building socialism or capitalism by reference to exactly the same bundle of traits. But beyond this obvious irony, it is also true that scholars actually *see* these traits. So do you think these academic-folkloric themes catch something of the long histories of these places?

HS: Yes. For example, a novelist I like very much, a tremendously perceptive person with the bilingual's matchless ear for implicit meanings, recently brought out a nonfiction book purporting to explain the difference between East and West [Gish Jen's *The Girl at the Baggage Claim: Explaining the East-West Culture Gap*], and it's a book I find myself in deep disagreement with. The thesis is, as so often, that Easterners are family-based collectivists and Westerners are individualists, and to achieve mutual understanding, we have to take this Deep Cultural Difference into account. And I ask myself, who's setting the standards for individualism and communitarianism? Where are the examples recruited from? For although this novelist is responding to actual, definite cultural clashes that she's observed and wants to resolve, my experience of China includes some of the most radical individualists who've ever existed, admittedly most of them people from centuries ago whom I know through their writings alone. So obviously this novelist and I are not going to agree on the East-West difference. Despite all the psychological surveys and American ethnic diversity theory you might bring into the present-day case, there are these counterexamples, and it's in the spirit of a counterexample to resist a collective average or generalization. But the generalization is plausible, shall we say real, and useful for my novelist friend and her audience, and I don't know where to lodge my protest on behalf of the antifamily, individualistic Chinese.

DC: Do you think this appeal to centralization, for example, happens because we often mistake the history of a place for the history of a state, as it were, with that fundamental Hegelian collusion at work?

HS: There's an inbuilt bias there, and to counteract it, in China you'd want to focus on the people who tried to escape from the state: the hermits, the bohemians, the alcoholics, the noncooperators who survived into the future by their reputation as writers, philosophers, and so on.

DC: So do you think people exaggerate this contrast between China and India, or do you think there's something to it? Is it all in the eye of the beholder, or is there something there that's peculiar but enduring?

HS: The nice thing about a consensus ideology is that when you pronounce it, you have the comfort that no one is going to say you're wrong. Some things that two generations ago would have been taken as a terrible critique of China ("their culture did not generate rebels and individualists!") today may seem like an advantage that compensates for flaws in the Western self model. There may be benefits to having this attitude, but once the discussion flips over from describing to prescribing what the proper way of being Chinese is, I want to look out for the lost souls, the ones who didn't fit in.

DC: Two other questions that I want to pursue are perhaps connected. One is the continuity of the class of victims. In the end, foot binding and *sati* are customs and practices that have been rejected. Criticized, rejected, internally and from the outside. But I often wonder what the past contributes, if it does at all, to the present state of the question of Tibet or the question of Kashmir: particularly the question of the Nagas, who never wanted to be part of India. They made that very clear. Historically, there's no dispute that they didn't want to belong to India after independence. The British had made them into a buffer zone, not quite part of India, and there's something in the imperiousness, at least of the state ideology of group formation, that tends to create this internal leaning toward megastate bigotry.

HS: I just recently learned about a similar example of border management. The booklet published by the Chinese about the visit of the first official delegation from India in the early 1950s contained, as these things will, a lot of transcriptions of after-dinner speeches, toasts to eternal friendship, and so on, in the spirit of Bandung. And there were also photographs of an excursion to the Yonghe Gong, the Tibetan Lamaist temple in Beijing. You could imagine the lead-up to this as being: "Of course you'll be interested to see how Buddhism became a part of Chinese culture: come see this grand historical monument of Buddhism located right in the center of Beijing, this touchstone for our present-day alliance, and maybe it will remind you of home." But the Yonghe Gong is also the site commemorating the Qing-dynasty emperors' patronage of Tibetan Buddhism, with inscriptions and artifacts that record the pledges of fealty that the previous Dalai and Panchen Lamas made to the Qing court (the rule of which ended in 1911), so that, through this visit, the Chinese Communist government was also saying, "Incidentally, we endorse and adhere to the former dynastic rulers' assertions of control over Tibet, so don't get any ideas about shaking things up on your northern border. Welcome to our temple, enjoy your visit!"

DC: And with Nagaland the question is quite similar, leaving room of course for differences. And so I also wonder: this book includes scholars, some of us of South Asian origin, including myself, but based in the West, in the U.S. academy. Does that lend the book a particular color, does that affect its vision? I was wondering, what would this book be like if it had included scholars working in China or India? Scholars, for example, from regions inside India and China where the imperious nature of the modern state has arguably been an issue?

HS: I don't know exactly. I'd hope that this book, though incomplete in that regard, might touch off that kind of conversation, as a kind of first ripple.

DC: I'll tell you why I ask the question. Sometimes, when I read early modernists—and I read them, whether in literature or in history, as a modernist, and as a modern person who has no desire to have been born in the Muhgal period—

HS: Nobody asked you!

DC: Nobody asked me, but even given reincarnation as part of my Hindu heritage . . .

HS: You must have brought it on yourself.

DC: Sure! But often, in reading history, you may think of a period and say, "Oh, wouldn't it have been nice if I had been there." And I've never wished to be a Mughal aristocrat, or wished to be born among them. What I'm really trying to point to is that modernity and its categories are never just an imposition by imperialists. The desire to be modern that we see among Chinese intellectuals, Japanese intellectuals, or Indian intellectuals often involved gestures of rejection of aspects of their own pasts. The critique of caste, for example, was given a completely new life by the context of Europe, by the abolition of slavery in America, the freeing of slaves, but also by Tom Paine and by reading about all sorts of rights theory, and the ultimate product of it all was somebody like Ambedkar whom you can't imagine without Europe's or the West's work in the background. Nor can you imagine a Gandhi without Europe. Maybe the same could be said of Mao or Sun Yat-sen?

HS: And let's not forget Tolstoy, who wasn't or didn't see himself as entirely European.

DC: All these people. The Theosophists, with their interpretation of the *Gita* that was very important for Indians. . . . So sometimes I wonder whether, in this desire to suspend the West, there is actually at work a desire to bracket the desire for modernization in these countries—that is to say, to bracket the versions of Europe that were to be embraced by people in China, India, and Japan (Japan, and to some extent China, always being cited as cases of modernization without direct colonization). Could there be a case made that the exercise of juxtaposing India and China, their intellectual heritages, would be significantly changed by shifting the time frame to the moment of 1800, say? To what degree do the peculiarities of the practice of "early modern studies" in the West (especially among U.S.-based academics) leave their imprint on this book?

HS: 1800 was a moment when people began to talk a lot about "humanity," thanks to the French revolutionaries' fondness for speaking not out of their own interest but in the name of the species. Political legitimacy at the highest level wasn't a matter of realizing the objectives of this or that group that had had enough of being dominated, but of presenting particular acts of liberation as steps on the way to liberating absolutely everybody, and that's how an idea can travel.

DC: Just as in Marxism and liberalism: that's their appeal.

HS: And the critique of the idea that Enlightenment spread like a series of dominos falling across the globe (a critique voiced, for example, in Samuel Moyn and Andrew Sartori's *Global Intellectual History* volume) marks valuable points for local appropriation, filtering, adaptation, but I don't think it has completely dispensed with the idea that Enlightenment ideas traveled and spoke to people who were not in their original intended audience. Being exported on the backs of colonialists, these ideas had a vehicle for breaking into new territory that they might not have had if they were simply topics of discussion.

DC: Or they would have carried over differently. I often say that for many Indians the message of colonial rule wasn't bad; the messenger was.

HS: A few years ago, a conference about Enlightenment or *Aufklärung* at the Goethe-Institut in Beijing broke down over just this issue, the message and the messenger. Some of the German eighteenth-century specialists were all too happy to tell the Chinese what they ought to do to bring their society in line with Enlightenment ideals, and this was exactly the wrong way to put across that message—if indeed there was a message separable from the messengers in that case. By blaming the Chinese *en bloc*, the self-designated apostles of Enlightenment backed the other party into a position from which they could not very well do anything but refuse to accept the advice, though this meant defending some rather indefensible practices in present-day China.

DC: On the other hand, without the history of the love for European ideas, at least on the part of some, how do you explain Nehru or Mao coming about and considering liberalism or Marxism, however Indianized or Sinified, to be their own? What I'm asking, I guess, is whether maybe if we had a similar volume for a later period, something of the non-Western investment in European ideas would have come through, whereas the representation of Western categories in this book, to me, seems to be mostly of domination and of something that blocks our view, as it were, so that we have to create this energy of friction by putting China and India side by side. And that's why I think the participation of scholars from China and India might have made for some interesting differences. Not that their methods would have been entirely different. But if you live in societies where some of the assumptions, say, of liberal democracy are taken for granted, then that context provides the ground for disputing different legacies of the past—of slavery, of immigration, industrialization, Obamacare—everything. Whereas if you are a scholar living in China, or in India, Pakistan, or Bangladesh, this is not a ground of the debate. The benefits of democracy or modernity are what many are still struggling for. And that changes their innate feelings about how they relate to the heritage of the Enlightenment intellectually. So maybe that's one way to understand both the significance and the limits of this book?

HS: Correlatively, I like to forget about the European origins of certain potent philosophical or political terms, and just watch their behavior within Chinese fields of discourse. What do they do, what do they stick closely to, what do they repel? You might find them doing things that you didn't think them capable of doing.

DC: Sometimes these obvious contrasts between, let's say, the Chinese tradition of dating poems and the Indian tradition of not dating them that Pollock and Owen talk about in chapter 5, or the Chinese tradition of recording history and the Hindu, at least, tradition of not recording it that Brokaw and Busch talk about in chapter 4, sounded to me like a human struggle that probably could be found in any civilization. The attitude toward time: what will defy the work of ruination that time performs? What will endure? And it seems to me that for peculiar reasons of history maybe the Hindus thought that poetry is that which endures. If a king patronizes poets of sufficient prowess, their poetry—and not some stone monument—will carry his name forward. And in a similar way you might think that time is what defies time: it's what doesn't die. Everything else that comes under the spell of time dies. Dating, then, is like putting a scratch on a monument that is not subject to the ravages of time because it's time itself. So I'm wondering whether one couldn't take a step back and see both of these civilizational ensembles as dealing with some very fundamental questions of human existence—answering them differently, and maybe those different answers are what we normally contrast; but clearly behind those contrasts lie the same questions you'd find in all human cultures, namely attempts to deal with the question of finitude.

HS: You're reminding me of the Pitt-Rivers Museum in Oxford, where you find a plethora of objects from different cultures but arranged according to functions. Hundreds of examples of spears, hundreds of types of boats. The same basic tasks (to kill a moving prey, to get across bodies of water) but solved by using different materials, under different latitudes, with different affordances. How people frame the step into the nontemporal through texts must vary. In China the example is the *Book of Changes* (*Yi jing*), where there is narrative, but always interrupted, disconnected, broken into fungible parts and subject to a logic of combination. It's like the vocabulary list of a historical record, minus the syntax that would enable us to parse it. Though historical texts in China are full of dates, individual lives, events, causes and effects, here those things are unspecified. And this must have been how some people in ancient China conceived of time, as the setting into sequence of invariant elements. So between the *Changes* and the *Twenty-Five Dynastic Histories* (*Ershiwu shi*), you have a pair of alternatives regarding how you narrate present time. From the little I know about India, I have the sense that narrative, what we imperfectly call in neo-Hellenic terms "mythology" and "epic," occupies a lot of the space that in China is demarcated by the *Changes* and *Histories*, but that space is shaped differently.

DC: In one of his essays Hayden White describes a chronology that includes dates when nothing happened. Whatever humans notice or don't notice, the flow of time never ceases, so it's more a statement about the nature of time. And it's on that question that this book has the potential of defying its self-imposed chronological limits, 1500 to 1800. It's taking a peek into questions that are really perennial ones of human civilization, to the extent that you can think of humans as civilized. Whether we're reading about history, literature, art, women, or the environment, the same question arises: of human finitude, and the resources available to human beings to deal with their problems.

HS: You're right. It's about the tasks, not about the monuments.

Chronology

1145–221 BCE	Zhou dynasty
	Confucius 551–479 BCE
544–483 BCE	Gautama Buddha
320–185 BCE	Mauryan Empire
	Ashoka r. 268–232 BCE
221–207 BCE	Qin dynasty
206 BCE–220	Han dynasties
320–550	Gupta Empire
618–907	Tang dynasty
960–1280	Song dynasties
c. 1192–1526	Delhi Sultanate
	Muhammad bin Tughluq r. 1325–51
1451–1526	Lodi dynasty
1215–1294	Khubilai Khan
1260/80–1368	Mongol Yuan dynasty
1350–1600	Vijayanagara Empire
1368–1644	Ming dynasty
	Ming Taizu r. 1368–98
	Yongle Emperor r. 1402–24
1526–1858	Mughal Empire
	Babur r. 1526–30
	Akbar r. 1565–1605

	Alamgir r. 1659–1707
1644–1911	Qing dynasty
	Kangxi emperor r. 1662–1721
	Yongzheng emperor r. 1722–35
	Qianlong emperor r. 1736–95
	The Opium War 1839–42
	The Taiping Rebellion 1851–64

Chinese and Indian Terms

AHAR-PAIN irrigation systems
BAIHUA vernacular Chinese language
BHAKTI devotion
BOWU "broad knowledge of things"
CAKRAVARTIN universal king; the Buddhist ruler extending enlightenment to all nations
CARITA biography
DIGVIJAYA actual or ritualized conquest of neighboring kings
FANGZHI local gazetteer
GEZHI (also GEWU ZHIZHI) "investigating things and extending knowledge"; also "modern science"
GHAZAL genre of Urdu couplet poetry
GUO state, empire
HUANGDI emperor
ITIHĀSA genre designator of India's two great epics
JHAROKHA DARSHAN small, elevated balcony that projected from palaces to enable the public to view royalty
JIA family, lineage
KEXUE science
KAVYA poem; literature in general
KHAGHAN the Mongol supreme ruler
KHARIF the autumn festival marking the first major harvest
LEISHU reference encyclopedias
LIEZHUAN exemplary biography

MANSABDARS holders of a *mansab'* (rank)
QI stuff of the universe
RASA mood (literature)
RASIKA "taster" (in conjunction with *rasa*)
TUDIGONG local earth gods
YAVANA the astronomy of Arabo-Persian astronomers
YESHI unofficial history
YI GU doubting antiquity
YUGA cosmic eon
VIDYA knowledge; ideal curriculum of fourteen sciences
WENYAN classical Chinese language
ZAMINDAR local chieftain
ZONGPU, ZUPU, JIAPU genealogy

Contributors

Representing China:

Zvi Ben-Dor Benite (New York University)
Beverly Bossler (University of California, Davis)
Cynthia Brokaw (Brown University)
Pamela Crossley (Dartmouth College)
Benjamin Elman (Princeton University)
Stephen Owen (Harvard University)
Kenneth Pomeranz (University of Chicago)
Haun Saussy (University of Chicago)
Eugene Wang (Harvard University)

Representing India:

Molly Aitken (The City College of New York and CUNY Graduate Center)
Allison Busch (Columbia University)
Dipesh Chakrabarty (University of Chicago)
Richard Davis (Bard College)
Richard Eaton (University of Arizona)
Sumit Guha (University of Texas, Austin)
Ruby Lal (Emory University)
Christopher Minkowski (University of Oxford)
Sheldon Pollock (Columbia University)

Index

Abdel-Malek, Anouar, 315
agriculture: and ecological decline, 58; fertilizer, 36, 37, 38, 49–50; and global exchanges, 31–32, 35, 39, 54, 55, 60; and migration, 49–50, 54–55, 57; and soil nutrients, 34, 36; and textiles, 48, 49–50; and water management, 28–31, 33
Aisin Khanate, 77–78, 79
Ajanta Caves, 290–94, *292*, *293*
Akbar (Mughal emperor): and astronomy/calendars, 220, 221; and gender systems, 71, 99, 106, 113–14; and historiography, 18, 146–47; and literature, 177; and marriage, 110–11; and Persianate culture, 10; and political power, 71, 85 86, 88; and religion, 241–42
Akbarnama (Account of Akbar) (Abu-l Fazl), 18, 99, 114, 145, 146, 152, 188
Akhlaq-i Nasiri (Nasirian Ethics) (Tusi), 104–5, 143
akhlaq, 143

'Alamgir (Mughal emperor), 75, 84–85, 90
Amanat, Agha Hasan, 191
animals: domesticated, 29, 35, 36–38; megafauna, 45–47. *See also* domesticated animals
Annals and Antiquities of Rajasthan (Tod), 158
architecture: and gender systems, 98, 99–101; and political power, 42–43
Ardastani, Maubad Zulfiqar, 233
Arithmetica Logarithmica (Briggs), 219
Arjan Das (Sikh Guru), 260
arranged marriage, 96, 112
art, 265–308; China-India comparison, 266, 268, 306–8; and estrangement, 19; and modernity, 10 11. *See also* Chinese art; Indian art
Arthashastra, 133
Ashk, Khalil Ali Khan, 190
Ashoka (Indian emperor), 78, 131–32, 133, 145, 161–62
Ashvaghosha, 137–38

Astronomical Tables (Tabulae Astronomicae) (de la Hire), 224
astronomy/calendars, 209–11, 212–27; British colonial India, 225; China-India comparison, 4, 225–27; and estrangement, 21–22; and Jesuit order, 210, 218, 219–20, 221, 223–24, 226; Ming dynasty, 217–20; Mughal empire, 220–24, 226; observatories, 213–17, 223, *223*
Auerbach, Erich, 320
Aurangzeb (Mughal emperor), 222, 242, 304
Autumn Melodies (Gao Jianfu), 285, *286*
Awliya, Nizam al-Din, 257

Baburnama (Account of Babur), 143–44
Babur, Zahir al-Din (Mughal emperor): and concubinage, 116; and ecological issues/energy use, 29, 40; and historiography, 143–44, 146; and homosexuality, 113; and marriage, 110; and political power, 70–71, 76, 85
Badauni, Abd al-Qadir, 113, 146–47
Bahmani sultanate, 69
Balban (sultan), 70
Bana, 138
Barani, Zia al-Din, 143
Bengal School, 287–90, 291, 294, 303, 304, 306
Bernal, Martin, 322
Bhagavad Gita, 177
bhakti poet-saints, 255
Bharat Mata (Tagore), *289*
Bhavabhuti, 177–78
Bhushan, 153
Bijapur sultanate, 69
Bilhana, 138
biography, 136–39, 143–44, 161, 179
Birbal, 147
The Birth of Biopolitics (Foucault), 333

Al-Biruni, 211, 227
Book of Changes (Yi jing), 340
Book in a Stone Casket (Shigui cangshu) (Zhang Dai), 154
Bose, Nandalal, 306
"Both Sides Now" (Mitchell), 332–33
Brahe, Tycho, 219
Brahmans: and astronomy/calendars, 221, 222; and historiography, 130, 150; and political power, 65, 69; and religion, 254–55; and sciences, 200, 202, 206, 207, 208, 209
Brahmendra Swami, 47
Briggs, Henry, 219
British imperialism. *See* British India; Western penetration
British India: and art, 287; astronomy/calendars, 225; and early modern period definitions, 7; ecological issues/energy use, 37, 42; and gender systems, 120; and historiography, 157–58; and language, 88; and literature, 191–92; and religion, 64
brush-and-ink painting, 269–70
Buck, J. L., 33
Buddha, Ajanta Caves, *293*
Buddhacarita (Ashvaghosha), 137–38
Buddhism: and art, 268–69, 290–94, *293*; and biography, 137–38; and China-India connections, 232, 236, 261; and Chinggisid ideology, 76; and diversity, 261–62; and divinity, 250; and estrangement, 17; expansion of, 235–36; and historiography, 131–32; Indian decline of, 235–36; and megafauna, 46; and Qing political power, 78, 79; religious specialists, 255, 257, 258; and sciences, 201, 202, 228; and scriptures, 259, 260; Tang suppression of, 17, 236, 243
Bundela, Bir Singh Deo, 152

Caitanya-carit-amrta (Nectar of the Life of Caitanya) (Kaviraj), 185
cakravartin, 78
calendars. *See* astronomy/calendars
caliphate, 66–67, 68
calligraphy, 19, 307
Cao Mei, 180, 181
caritas, 137–38, 146, 148, 150–51, 152, 159
caste, 3; and marriage, 110, 112–13
censorship, 18, 148, 154–55
Central Asia, and China-India comparisons, 12
Chakrabarty, Dipesh, 332–41
Chalukya dynasty, 69; and historiography, 133–34
Chand, Nihal, 304
Chen Duxiu, 282
Chen Shuren, 283
Chen Zilong, 280
child marriage, 95
China: definitions, 4–5, 12–13; essentialization of, 311, 312, 314; influence of, 2–3; modernity overview, 8–9. *See also* China-India comparisons; China-India connections; Qing dynasty
China-India comparisons, 11–23, 310–32; art, 266, 268, 306–8; astronomy/calendars, 4, 225–27; and border disputes, 336–37; Chinese use of, 317–19, 321; and commonalities, 322–23; and conceptual categories, 22–23, 324, 325–30, 333, 339; and connective history approach, 11–12; cosmopolitan approach, 12–13, 327; and essentialization, 12–13, 310–17, 320–21, 335–36; and estrangement, 17–22, 322, 323; historiography, 160–62; and human struggles, 339–41; and identity, 319–20, 334; literature, 192–94; and modernity, 337–39; political power, 84–89; scholarly deficits, 3–4, 11; and singularity, 323–25; standard approaches, 13–14; and structural determinants, 15–16; and superpower status, 330–32; time frame for, 333–34, 338; and Western standard, 4, 12, 14–15, 316, 321–22

China-India connections: and art, 265, 266; and Buddhism, 232, 236, 261; and China-India comparisons, 11–12

Chinese art, 268–86; and domestic spaces, 101; and estrangement, 19; Ming dynasty, 278–79; Mi-Ni opposition, 276, 278–80; Mi-style landscape painting, 274–76, *275,* 278, 279; Northern Song dynasty, 269–70, 271, *272,* 273–76; Qing dynasty, 278–85, *286;* Romantic-Stoic opposition, 280; and Shadow Cave, 268–69; Tang dynasty, 270–71, *271;* twentieth century, 282–85, *286;* and Western penetration, 281, 282; Yuan dynasty, 276, *277,* 278

Chinese astronomy/calendars, 213; and India compared, 4, 225–27; Ming dynasty, 217–20; and political power, 21, 210–11, 225–26; Yuan dynasty, 211, 215–16, 217

Chinese ecological issues/energy use: agriculture, 33, 34, 35, 38, 49–50, 58; and domesticated animals, 37–38; early modern period definitions, 7; ecological decline, 57–60; and forests, 31–32, 38–39, 43–44, 52, 59–60; and megafauna, 47; and migration, 44, 49–50, 53–56; and political power, 41, 43–45; and textiles, 49–51; and trade, 27–28, 33, 49, 51–53, 60; and water management, 31–34, 58; and Western penetration, 90, 225

INDEX [351]

Chinese gender systems: and
Confucianism, 96–97, 103, 108; cult
of fidelity, 118–19; and domestic
spaces, 98, 100, 101; and
essentialization, 95–96; and
extramarital relationships, 114–16;
and family, 107–9; and marriage,
111–12; People's Republic of China,
119–20; women's agency within,
102–4, 106
Chinese historiography: and biography,
136–37, 161, 179; and censorship, 18,
148, 154–55; classical, 134–36, 156–57;
and Confucianism, 130, 135, 136, 137,
143, 150, 154; and critical analysis,
155–57, 160; early, 129, 130–31; and
essentialization, 127–28; and
estrangement, 18; and India
compared, 160–62; and language,
128–29; and literature, 178–79; local
histories, 149–50; and Ming-Qing
transition, 153–54; and modernity,
159–60; and political power, 135,
140–42, 145; and Qing dynasty,
153–57; unofficial, 148–49
Chinese languages: and historiography,
128–29; and literature, 18, 166–67,
193; and Qing political power, 78, 81,
83–84, 88; and sciences, 204; and
social status, 173; vernacularization,
175
Chinese literature, 103–4; and
aficionados, 182–83; early modern,
181–85; and epic tradition, 178–81,
193; and estrangement, 18; and India
compared, 192–94; and Japan,
184–85; and language, 18, 166–67,
193; lyric poetry, 170–72; and print
culture, 181–83
Chinese Man in Moonlight (Chughtai),
304, *305*, 306

Chinese political power: and astronomy/
calendars, 21, 210–11, 225–26; and
ecological issues/energy use, 41,
43–45; and historiography, 135,
140–42, 145; and religion, 243–44,
251, 253; Yuan dynasty, 76–77.
See also Qing political power
Chinese religion: bureaucratized nature
of, 248–49; and China-India
connections, 232, 236, 261; and
cosmology, 251–53; diversity in, 235,
239, 243–44, 261–62; and divinity,
244–45, 248–50; and estrangement,
17; People's Republic of China, 263;
and political power, 243–44, 251, 253;
religious specialists, 257–59; and
scriptures, 260; Tang suppression of
Buddhism, 17, 236, 243
Chinese Rites Controversy, 240
Chinese sciences: and civil bureaucracy,
204–6; classical, 203; and political
power, 210–11; scope of, 200, 201,
202; Yuan dynasty, 203, 208–9, 213.
See also Chinese astronomy/
calendars
Chinggisid Khaghanate, 77, 78
Chinggisid ruling ideology, 76
Chinggis Khan, 9, 76, 79
Chisthi, Moinuddin, 257
Citra-sutra, 291
Chokha, 304
Christianity: and art, 292; and
astronomy/calendars, 210, 218, 219;
Chinese suppression of, 244; Jesuit
proselytization, 235; Syriac, 234–35.
See also Jesuit order; Western
penetration
Chughtai, Abdul Rahman, 304, *305*, 306
civil bureaucracy: and estrangement,
20–21; and gender systems, 103, 106;
and inequality, 3; and Qing political

power, 79–80, 83–84, 86–87; and sciences, 204–6
Cixi (Qing empress), 107
Classic of Poetry, 284
Clavius, 218–19
climate change, 2–3
Cloudy Mountains (Mi Youren), 275
Coats, Thomas, 30
Coedès, George, 334
Comprehensive Mirror to Aid in Government (Zizhi tongjian) (Sima Guang), 141–42, 155–56
conceptual categories, 22–23, 324, 325–30, 333, 339
conceptual change, 23
concubinage, 96, 114, 115–17
Confucianism: and art, 284; and astronomy/calendars, 217; and gender systems, 96–97, 103, 108; and historiography, 130, 135, 136, 137, 143, 150, 154; and political power, 79; and religion, 239–40; religious specialists, 258–59; and sciences, 201, 203, 213; and scriptures, 260
Confucius. See Confucianism
connective history. See China-India connections
conquest transitions, 81, 90; and estrangement, 19–20; and historiography, 129, 148, 152, 153–54; and language, 175–76; and political power, 19–20, 63, 77–79, 83–86; and sciences, 208–9
Coomaraswamy, Ananda, 304
Copernicus, 215, 218–19
Corot, Camille, 283
cosmology, 251–54
cosmopolitan comparison, 12–13, 327
cotton, 48, 49
courtesans. See prostitution
Court of Indra (Indersabha) (Amanat), 191

Crowing-Against-Haze Society, 284
Cultural Revolution, 263

Dabestan-e Madaheb (School of Religious Doctrines) (Ardastani), 233, 238
Daodejing, 239, 260
Daoism, 17, 202, 236, 239, 260
Dara Shikoh (Mughal prince), 242
da Silva, Pedro, 224
Dastan-e Amir Hamza (Ashk), 190
Da Tang xiyuji (Record of Western Realms) (Xuanzang), 232, 236
Deccan campaigns, 90
deforestation, 31–32, 39–40, 52, 55, 59–60
Dehlavi, Bedil, 188
de la Hire, Phillippe, 224
Delhi Sultanate: and gender systems, 100; and historiography, 142–43; languages, 88–89, 187; political power, 67, 68–69, 70, 71, 84–85; and sciences, 209, 227
Devi, Rashundari, 105
difangzhi (gazetteers), 149
differentiation. See estrangement
Dinwiddie, James, 225
disciplinary categories. See conceptual categories
di (sovereignty), 245
divination, 130
divinity, 244–51
domesticated animals, 29, 35, 36–38
domestic spaces, 71, 94–95, 98–101, 104
Dong Qichang, 278, 279
Dong Yuan, 270, 273
dowry, 108, 109, 111
Du Fu, 18, 165, 170–72
Dunhuang cave paintings, 269

early modern period definitions, 7–8
Early Spring (Guo Xi), 272

INDEX [353]

ecological issues/energy use, 27–60; and domesticated animals, 29, 35, 36–38; ecological decline, 57–60; and forests, 31–32, 35–36, 38–40, 43–44, 52, 55, 59–60; and megafauna, 45–47; and migration, 41, 44, 49–50, 53–57; and political power, 40–45, 65; and structural determinants, 16; and textiles, 48–53; and trade, 27–28, 33, 48–53, 56, 59, 60; and warfare, 34, 40–41, 45, 57–58; and water management, 28–34
education, 103, 104–6
Eight Banners system, 77, 78, 82–83, 86, 87
elephants, 46–47
Elman, Benjamin, 322, 326
Elvin, Mark, 50, 52
Emperor Minghuang's Journey to Shu, 271
energy use. *See* ecological issues/energy use
Enlightenment, 338–39
epic literature, 176–81, 193
essentialization, and China-India comparisons, 12–13, 310–17, 320–21, 335–36; and gender systems, 93, 94–97; and historiography, 127–28, 158
estrangement, 17–22, 322, 323
Evaluations of the Events of Our Dynasty (Guoque) (Tan Qian), 148
Experiencing the Times (Yueshi bian) (Ye Mengzhu), 149
exports. *See* trade

family: and gender systems, 107–13; and sciences, 205–6, 208
Fang Congyi, 276
Fan Kuan, 270
Fazl, Abu-l, 99, 111, 114, 145, 146, 188
Feng Kecan, 149

fertilizer, 36, 37, 38, 49–50
Figuereido, Manuel, 224
foot binding, 96, 97
forests, 35–36, 38–39, 43–44; deforestation, 31–32, 39–40, 52, 55, 59–60
fossil fuels, 27
Foucault, Michel, 333
Four Wangs, 282
Frank, André Gunder, 333
Fu Sinian, 160
"The Future of the European Humanities" (Gadamer), 327–29
"Future Philology? The Fate of a Soft Science in a Hard World" (Pollock), 330

Gadamer, Hans-Georg, 327–29
Galilei, Galileo, 219
Gandhi, Mohandas, 331
Gao Jianfu, 283, 284–85, *286*
Gao Kegong, 276
Gao Qifeng, 283, 284–85
A Garden Gathering with Two Princes and a Sleeping Cat (Govardhan), *298*
Gathered Outside the Wanli Court (Wanli yehuo bian) (Shen Defu), 149
Geertz, Clifford, 6
gender systems, 93–121; and Confucianism, 96–97, 103, 108; and domestic spaces, 71, 94–95, 98–101, 104; and essentialization, 93, 94–97; and extramarital relationships, 113–18; and family, 107–13; and love, 117–18; and political power, 71; and reform, 118–21; and structural determinants, 15–16; women's agency within, 94, 101–7, 119
genealogies, 150
Ghuri, Mu'izz al-Din (sultan), 68
Gil, Amrita Sher, 306

Girl at the Baggage Claim: Explaining the East-West Culture Gap (Jen), 335
Gita-govinda (Song of Govinda) (Jayadeva), 186
global exchanges: and agriculture, 31–32, 35, 39, 54, 55, 60; silver, 48–49, 51, 52, 60
Global Intellectual History (Moyn & Sartori), 338
gods. *See* divinity; religion
Golkonda sultanate, 69
Gommans, Jos, 41, 56
Gonds, 110
Gong Xian, 280–82, *281*
Govardhan, *298*
government. *See* political power
Grand Canal, 32
Gregorian calendar, 218–19
Guandi, 249
Guanyin, 249, 250
Guha, Sumit, 43
Guide to the Religious Status and Duties of Women (Stridharmapaddhati) (Tryambakayajvan), 97
Gu Jiegang, 160
Gulbadan Begum, 106, 146
Gulistan, The Rose Garden (Sadi), 104
Guo Shoujing, 216
Guo Xi, 270, *272*, 273
Guptas, 6
Guru Granth Saheb (Revered Book of the Teachers), 260
Gu Yanwu, 280

Hafez, 187
Han dynasty, 5, 79, 213, 251
Han Yu, 250
harems, 71, 94–95, 99
Harsa-carita (Bana), 138
Harshavardhana (Kanauj ruler), 138, 141, 241

Havell, E. B., 287
haze, 268, 284–85; and Bengal School, 287–90, *289*, 304, 306; and China-India comparisons, 307–8; and Mi-style landscape painting, 274–76, *275*, 278, *279*; and Nihonga, 266, *267*, 268; in Northern Song dynasty art, 269–70, 271, *272*, 273–74; and nostalgia, 306; and Shadow Cave, 268–69; in Southern Song dynasty art, 276; in twentieth-century Chinese art, 282–86, *286*
Heaven (*Tian*), 244, 252–53
Hegel, Georg Friedrich: on comparative approach, 12, 14; and conceptual categories, 327; and essentialization, 310–13, 317, 320–21; on historiography, 127–28, 160; on literature, 176, 178, 193; and Western standard, 12
Herbert, Thomas, 246
Herder, Johann Gottfried, 313–14, 317
Herodotus, 6
Hindi language: historiography, 150–51, 152–53, 158; literature, 189–90
Hinduism: and art, 301–2; and cosmology, 253–54; diversity within, 237–38; and divinity, 245–46, 247; and gender systems, 97, 98, 105, 109; and historiography, 146, 150; and love, 117–18; and megafauna, 46; and Mughal empire, 71–72, 241, 242; and political power, 65, 70, 71–72; religious specialists, 65, 255; and scriptures, 259
Hindu-Muslim enmity, 263; and Mughal empire, 242; overstatement of, 238–39; simplification of, 1; and Western colonialism/imperialism, 158
Hishida Shunso, 287

Historical Documents (Shangshu), 134–35, 136, 156
historiography, 127–64; and biography, 136–39, 143–44, 161; China-India comparison, 160–62; classical, 131–36, 156–57; and conquest transitions, 129, 148, 152, 153–54; and critical analysis, 155–57, 160; early, 129–31; and essentialization, 127–28, 158; and estrangement, 17–18; and language, 128–30, 150–51, 152–53, 158; and literature, 17–18, 127, 132, 139, 143, 151, 178–79; and modernity, 157–60; and political power, 135, 138–39, 140–42, 145
History of the Yuan Dynasty (Yuanshi), 148
hogs, 37–38
homosexuality, 113, 114–15
Hongren, 278
Hong Taiji (Jin emperor), 77, 78
horses, 41, 43
Huang Binhong, 282
Huang Gongwang, 276
Huiyuan, 269
Hulagu Khan (Ilkhanate ruler), 213–15
Humayun (Mughal emperor), 71, 110, 146
Humayunnama (Account of Humayun) (Gulbadan Begum), 146
Hundred Lyrics of Amaru (Amaru-sataka), 168
hunting, 43, 45, 46
Hu Shi, 318–19

Ideals of the East (Kakuzo), 265
Iliad, 177, 178
imperial succession, 87–88, 138, 140, 141
India: agriculture, 28–31, 35, 57; caste system, 3; definitions, 4–6, 12–13; ecological decline, 60; essentialization of, 94–95, 311–14; influence of, 2–3; modernity overview, 9–11; partition, 5–6, 158. *See also* China-India comparisons; China-India connections; Mughal empire; Mughal political power
India-China comparisons. *See* China-India comparisons
Indian art, 287–306; Ajanta Caves, 290–94, *292*, *293*; Bengal School, 287–90, 291, 294, 303, 304, 306; common themes in, 302–4; and estrangement, 19; and Hindu-Muslim differences, 301–2; Mughal, 10–11, 297, *298*, 299, 302–4; and nostalgia, 304, *305*, 306; Persian, 294–97, *298*, 299; and political power, 75; Rajput, 294, 299–301, *300*, 302–4
Indian astronomy/calendars: and China compared, 4, 225–27; Mughal empire, 220–24, 226; and observatories, 213–15, 216–17; and political power, 211; variety in, 21–22, 212–13
Indian ecological issues/energy use: and domesticated animals, 29, 36–37; and forests, 35–36, 43, 60; and megafauna, 45–47; and migration, 41, 56–57; and political power, 40–41, 42–43; and textiles, 48–49; and trade, 28, 56; and water management, 28–31, 42
Indian gender systems: and British India, 120–21; and domestic spaces, 98–101; and essentialization, 97; and extramarital relationships, 113–14; and family, 109–11; and marriage, 112–13; women's agency within, 102–3, 104–7
Indian historiography: and biography, 137–39, 143–44, 161; and British India, 157–59; and China compared, 160–62; classical, 131–34, 146; and

Delhi Sultanate, 142–43; and
essentialization, 128; and
estrangement, 17–18; and language,
128, 129–30, 150–51, 152–53, 158; and
literature, 17–18, 139, 143; local
histories, 150–52; and Mughal
empire, 143–48, 150–53, 158; and
political power, 138–39, 140, 145,
146–47

The Indianized States of Southeast Asia
(Coedès), 334

Indian languages: and Delhi Sultanate,
88–89, 187; and historiography, 128,
129–30, 150–51, 152–53, 158; and
literature, 18–19, 166, 173–75, 193;
and Mughal empire, 88, 174–76, 177,
187, 188; and political power, 64, 66,
68, 69; and religion, 255;
vernacularization, 64, 68, 88–89, 128,
166, 173–74

Indian literature, 104; and British
India, 191–92; and China compared,
192–94; epic traditions, 176–78, 193;
and estrangement, 18–19; and
historiography, 17–18, 139, 143; and
language, 18–19, 166, 173–75, 193;
lyric poetry, 168–70; Mughal
empire, 10, 185–92; and social
status, 173

Indian political power: and architecture,
42–43; and Delhi Sultanate, 67,
68–69, 70, 71, 84–85; and ecological
issues/energy use, 40–41, 42–43; and
historiography, 138–39, 140, 145,
146–47; hybridization in, 67–70; and
Persianate culture, 64, 66–68, 69, 71,
74–75, 209; and Rajputs, 68, 71–72,
76, 85–86, 110, 145; and religion, 237,
241–43, 254; and Sanskritic model of
kingship, 64, 65–66, 67–69, 73–74,
209. *See also* Mughal political power

Indian Rebellion (1857), 7, 188

Indian religion: and cosmology, 253–54;
decline of Buddhism, 235–36;
diversity in, 234–35, 237–38, 247,
261–62; and divinity, 245–47; and
estrangement, 17; and Hindu
regional kings, 242–43; and Mughal
empire, 71–72, 237, 241–42, 261; and
political power, 237, 241–43, 254; and
scriptures, 259–60; specialists, 65,
254–57. *See also* Hindu-Muslim
enmity

Indian sciences: and Delhi Sultanate,
209, 227; and institutions, 206–8;
scope of, 200, 201, 202–4

inequality, 3, 21, 43

inscriptions, 131–32, 133–34, 145

*Investigation Into Manchu Origins
(Manzhou yuanliu kao)*, 155

irrigation. *See* water management

Islam: and art, 294, 297, 299, 301–2; and
astronomy/calendars, 211, 214–15,
217; and divinity, 246–47, 250;
expansion of, 236–37; and gender
systems, 94–95, 98, 110; and harems,
94–95; and historiography, 142–43;
and marriage, 111; and Mughal
empire, 71, 237, 241–42; and
Persianate culture, 66, 142–43; and
political power, 66, 71, 237, 241–42,
244; religious specialists, 256–57; and
sciences, 209, 227; and scriptures,
259, 260. *See also* Sufism

itihasa, 132

itihasa-purana, 133, 146, 159

Jahanara (Mughal princess), 118

Jahangir (Mughal emperor), 10, 85, 107,
110, 116–17, 143–44

Jahangir-nama (Account of Jahangir),
143–44

Jainism, 150, 255
Jaisingh II (Maharaja of Amber), 222–24
Jamal al-Din, 216
Japan: and Chinese art, 266, 267, 268, 282–84, 308; and Chinese literature, 184–85; imperialism, 7; and Indian art, 287
Jayadeva, 186, 301
Jen, Gish, 335
Jesuit order: and art, 281; and astronomy/calendars, 210, 218, 219–20, 221, 223–24, 226; and Confucianism, 239, 240, 258–59; observation of South Asian religions, 15, 233, 239, 240, 246, 250–51, 258–59; proselytization, 235; Qing acceptance of, 244. See also Ricci, Matteo
jharokha darshan, 71–72, 85–86
Jin dynasty, 77, 78, 80
Jing Ke, 180–81
Jin Ping Mei, 184
Journey to the West, 178, 184, 236, 250
Judaism, 234, 235
Juran, 270, 273
jyotisha, 209, 211, 212, 221, 222, 227. See also astronomy/calendars

Kabir, 255
Kakatiya dynasty, 107
Kakuzo, Okakura, 265, 287
Kalapurnodayamu (The Sound of the Kiss) (Suranna), 190
Kalhana, 139, 142
Kalidasa, 190
Kamalakara, 222
Kangxi emperor, 18, 87, 154–55
Kang Youwei, 282, 317–18
Kant, Immanuel, 12, 14, 329
kanyadan, 109

al-Kashi, Jamshid Ghiyas ud Din, 217
Kaviraj, Krishnadasa, 185
Kepler, Johannes, 219
Keshavdas, 152, 189
Khaqani Zij (al-Kashi), 217
Khubilai Khan (Yuan emperor), 76, 215, 216
Khusrau, Amir, 187
kinship. See family
Kitab al Hind (Al-Biruni), 211
Krishnadeva Raya (Vijaynagara ruler), 100
Kushans, 6

Lach, Donald, 322
Lalitavistara, the Long Story of the Playful Deeds (of the Buddha), 201
landscape painting: colorist, 270–71, 271; and estrangement, 19; and haze, 269–70; Mi-style, 274–76, 275, 278, 279; Northern Song dynasty, 269–70, 271, 272, 273–74, 276; Xiao-Xiang, 274, 275
language, 166–67; and bhakti poet-saints, 255; and conquest transitions, 175–76; and estrangement, 18–19, 21; and historiography, 128–30, 150–51, 152–53, 158; and Indian political power, 64, 66, 68, 69; and literature, 18–19, 166–67, 173–76, 193; and Qing political power, 78, 81, 83–84, 88; and sciences, 21, 204, 207. See also specific languages
Laozi, 239, 260
Laws of Manu, 97
Levi-Strauss, Claude, 45
Liang Qichao, 317, 318
Li Cheng, 270
Lifanyuan, 79, 83, 86
life and energy use. See ecological issues/energy use

Li Liufang, 278
Ling Daxie, 38–39
Lingnan School, 283
literacy, 103, 104
literature, 165–94; and art, 273–74; China-India comparison, 192–94; epic tradition, 176–81, 193; and estrangement, 18–19; and extramarital relationships, 117; and gender systems, 103–4; and historiography, 17–18, 127, 132, 139, 143, 151, 178–79; and language, 18–19, 166–67, 173–76, 193; on love, 117–18; lyric poetry, 167–72; and marriage, 112; and political power, 75; and religion, 236; and social status, 173
Liu Shifu, 284
Liu Xi, 317–18
Liu Zhiji, 155
Li Ye, 213
Lone Tree in a Mountainous Lake (Gong Xian), *281*
Lotus Sutra (*Saddharma Pundarika Sutra* or *Fahuajing*), 260
love, 117–18
Lu Xun, 285

Macartney, George, 225
Madman's Diary (Lu Xun), 285
Mahabharata, 132–33, 134, 146, 165, 166, 176, 177
Malana, Ram Singh, 56
Malcolm, John, 56–57
Man-carita (Narottam), 150, 152
Manchus. See Qing dynasty
Mandate of Heaven: and astronomy/calendars, 210–11; and historiography, 135, 140, 145, 153; and political power, 79; and religion, 243, 252

Manichaeism, 239, 243
mansabdari system, 21, 72, 75, 85, 86
Man Singh Kacchwaha, Raja, 150
Mao Zedong, 119–20, 161
Maragha observatory, 214–15, 216, 217
Marathas, 43, 110
mardana, 100
Marks, Robert, 47
marriage: and essentialization, 96; and extramarital relationships, 113–14, 115, 116–17; and family systems, 109–13; and female agency, 103
Marshall, Thomas, 45–46
Maruyama Ōkyo, 283
Matsumura Goshun, 283
Mauryas, 6
Mazu, 249, 250
megafauna, 45–47
Mewar Kingdom, 100
Mi Fu, 274
migration, 41, 44, 49–50, 53–57
Ming dynasty: art, 278–79; astronomy/calendars, 217–20; and ecological decline, 57–58; gender systems, 116; and historiography, 137, 141, 148, 153–55; and Manichaeism, 239, 243; and migration, 44; political power, 79; sciences, 213. See also Ming-Qing transition
Ming-Qing transition: and architecture, 43; and art, 279; and historiography, 129, 153–55; and political power, 19, 63, 77–79, 83–84
Mira Bai, 117–18, 255
Mir, Mohammad Taqi, 188–89
missionaries. See Jesuit order; Western penetration
Mi-style landscape painting, 274–76, *275*, 278, 279
Mitchell, Joni, 332–33
Mi Youren, 274–75, *275*

modernity: and China-India comparisons, 337–39; and historiography, 157–60; overview, 8–11. *See also* early modern period; Western penetration

Mongols: and astronomy/calendars, 210; and Qing political power, 78–79, 81. *See also* Yuan dynasty

Monkey God Sunwukong, 249, 250, 260

monsoons, 28

Moonlight in the Woods (Yokoyama Taikan), 267

Moyn, Samuel, 338

Mughal empire: art, 10–11, 297, *298*, 299, 302–4; astronomy/calendars, 220–24, 226; and conquest transition, 19–20, 63, 84–86, 152, 175–76; and definitions of India, 6; gender systems, 94–95, 99, 102–3, 106–7, 116–17; and languages, 88, 174–76, 177, 187, 188; literature, 10, 185–92; and marriage, 110–11; modernity overview, 9–11; and religion, 71–72, 237, 241–42, 261; sciences, 207, 208; and silver, 49; water management, 30, 42. *See also* Mughal historiography; Mughal political power

Mughal historiography: Hindi, 150–51, 152–53, 158; and literature, 151; Persian, 143–47, 148, 150; and Rajputs, 151–52, 158; Sanskrit, 146, 148

Mughal political power, 70–75; and China compared, 84–89; decline of, 90–91; and estrangement, 20; and female agency, 106–7; and imperial succession, 87–88; and language, 88–89; and *mansabdari* system, 21, 72, 75, 85, 86; and marriage, 110–11, 116–17; and Persianate culture, 71, 74–75; and Rajputs, 71–72, 76, 85–86, 110, 145; and territorial expansionism, 21, 73–74, 84–85, 90

Muqi Fachang, 276

My Life (Devi), 105

Nainsi, Mumhata, 151–52, 159
Nainsukh, 304
Nanak (Sikh Guru), 255–56, 260
Nanga School, 283
Narottam, 150, 152
Needham Question, 229, 334–35
New American History, 160
New Culture Movement, 160
Nihonga, 265–66, *267*, 268, 287
Nityananda, 221–22
Ni Zan, 276, *277*
Northern Song dynasty art, 269–70, 271, *272*, 273–76
Northern Wei dynasty, 80
Northern Yuan dynasty, 76–77
Notes on the Twenty-Two Histories (Nianer shi zhaji) (Zhao Yi), 156
Nurgaci (Jurchen chieftain), 77, 78
Nur Jahan (Mughal queen), 106–7, 116–17

observatories, 213–17, 223, *223*
Odyssey, 176
On Their Own Terms (Elman), 326
Opium War (1839–42), 7, 9, 90, 184, 225
Orientalism (Said), 315
Outlines of a Philosophy of the History of Man (Herder), 313–14
oxen, 29, 36–37

paksha, 212
pandas, 47
Pangu, 252
paper, 23, 130, 147, 186–87, 193, 269
Parameshwara, 222

patrilineal family systems, 107–8, 111–12
People's Republic of China: gender systems, 119–20; and historiography, 161; and literature, 165; and religion, 263
Perkins, Dwight, 33, 37
Persianate culture: and art, 294–97, *298*, 299; and astronomy/calendars, 222; and political power, 64, 66–68, 69, 71, 74–75, 209
Persian language: changes in, 174–75, 188; and historiography, 66, 142–45, 148, 150; and literature, 187–88; and Mughal empire, 174–76, 177, 187, 188; and political power, 66
Philosophy of History (Hegel), 310–11
Plutarch, 179
poetry. *See* literature
political power, 63–91; and astronomy/calendars, 21, 210–11, 225–26; China-India comparison, 84–89; and concubinage, 116; and conquest transitions, 19–20, 63, 77–79, 83–86; and ecological issues/energy use, 40–45, 65; and estrangement, 19–20; and female agency, 106–7; and historiography, 135, 138–39, 140–42, 145; and imperial succession, 87–88, 138, 140, 141; Indian kingship models, 64–70, 73–74, 209; and marriage, 110–11, 116–17; and religion, 237, 240–44, 251, 253, 254, 262; and territorial expansionism, 21, 66, 73–74, 80, 82, 83, 84–85, 90. *See also* Mughal political power; Qing political power; state
Pollock, Sheldon, 330
Prakash, Om, 48
print culture, 181–83, 186, 203, 204
property rights, 108
prostitution, 113, 114, 117

puranas, 133, 253
purdah, 95

Qianlong emperor, 80, 155, 244
Qian Qianyi, 280
Qing dynasty: art, 278–85, *286*; astronomy/calendars, 211, 219, 220; and definitions of China, 5; and early modern period definitions, 7; and ecological decline, 57–58; and historiography, 153–57; Hundred Days of Reform, 156–57; ideological control, 21; and migration, 44, 54, 55–56; and religion, 244; Taiping Rebellion, 9, 90; and trade, 52–53; water management, 32, 33, 34. *See also* Ming-Qing transition; Qing political power
Qing political power, 77–84; and astronomy/calendars, 211; and civil bureaucracy, 79–80, 83–84, 86–87; decline of, 58–59, 90–91; and ecological issues/energy use, 43–45; Eight Banners system, 77, 78, 82–83, 86, 87; and estrangement, 20–21; and female agency, 107; and imperial succession, 87, 140, 141; and India compared, 84–89; and language, 78, 81, 83–84, 88; Lifanyuan, 79, 83, 86; and Ming-Qing transition, 19, 63, 77–79, 83–84; reception of, 81–82; and taxation, 44–45; and territorial expansionism, 21, 80, 82, 83, 84, 90; and Western penetration, 90–91
Qin Jiushao, 213
Quran, 259, 260
Qushji, Ali, 217
Qu Yuan, 274

rajas, 65. *See also* Sanskrit culture
Raja-tarangini (River of Kings) (Kalhana), 139, 142

Rajendra Chola I (Maharaja), 69
Rajputs: art, 294, 299–301, *300*, 302–4; and gender systems, 100, 110; and historiography, 151–52, 158; and political power, 68, 71–72, 76, 85–86, 110, 145
Ramayana, 132–33, 146, 176, 177–78, 184
Ram-carit-manas (The Sacred Lake of Rama's Deeds) (Tulsidas), 186
Ranke, Leopold von, 159, 160
rasa, 187
Rasa-manjari, 299–300, *300*
Ravidas, 255
Records of the Grand Historian (Shiji) (Sima Qian), 136–37, 140, 150, 155, 178–79, 180–81
religion, 232–63; classification of, 262–63; and cosmology, 251–54; diversity in, 234–35, 237–38, 239, 243–44, 247, 261–62; and divinity, 244–51; and estrangement, 17; and Indian political power, 64, 65, 67, 68–69, 71; and political power, 237, 240–44, 251, 253, 254, 262; and sciences, 201, 202, 209; and scriptures, 259–60; specialists, 65, 67, 254–59; Western observation, 15, 233, 239, 240, 246, 250–51, 258–59. *See also* Buddhism; Daoism; Hinduism; Islam; Sufism
religions, world religions defined, 234
Republican China, and historiography, 159, 160
Ricci, Matteo: and astronomy/calendars, 218, 219; observation of South Asian religions, 233, 239–40, 246, 258–59; proselytization, 235
Romance of the Three Kingdoms, 183, 184
rooftops, 100–101, 106
Roy, Jamini, 306

Rudramadevi (Kakatiya queen), 107
rulership. *See* political power

Saadi, 187
sabk-i hindi, 187
Sadi, 104
Safavid state, 87, 187
Said, Edward, 315
Sanskrit culture: kingship model, 64, 65–66, 67–69, 73–74, 209; and sciences, 209, 221–22. *See also* Brahmans
Sanskrit language: and Brahmans, 255; and gender systems, 105; and historiography, 128, 133, 137, 146, 148; literature, 18, 168, 173, 176–78, 187–88, 190–91; and sciences, 207. *See also* Sanskrit culture
Sarkar, Jadunath, 159
Sartori, Andrew, 338
sati, 95
Satya Pir, 247, 257
Saussy, Haun, 321, 327, 332–41
Schall, Adam, 219
sciences, 199–209, 227–29; and institutions, 204–8; and language, 21, 204, 207; scope of, 200–4. *See also* astronomy/calendars
Sea Mirror of Circle Measurements (Ceyuan haijing) (Li Ye), 213
Sen, Amartya, 3
Senghor, Léopold, 329
Shadow Cave, 268–69
Shah Jahan (Mughal emperor), 85, 221–22, 242
Shahryar (Mughal prince), 116
Shang dynasty, 129, 131
shaykhs, 257
Sheel, Kamal, 318–19
Shen Defu, 149
shen (divinity), 245

[362]   INDEX

Shen Gua, 273, 274
Shenzong emperor, 270
Shibata Zeshin, 285
Shijō School, 283–84
Shivaji (Maratha king), 153
Shuihu zhuan (Water Margin/Men of the Marsh), 183
Shun dynasty, 81
Shyamaldas, 158–59
Siddhanta-sarva-raja (Nityananda), 222
Siddhanta-sindhu (Nityananda), 221–22
Sikhism, 238, 255–56, 260, 261–62
silver, 48–49, 51, 52, 60
Sima Guang, 103, 141–42, 155–56
Sima Qian, 119, 136–37, 140, 150, 155, 178–79, 180–81
slavery, 56, 57
Smogulecki, Nikolaus, 219–20
Song Di, 274
Song dynasty: and historiography, 137, 141–42; Islam under, 237; and sciences, 213. *See also* Northern Song dynasty art; Southern Song dynasty
sources, 22–23
South Asia concept, 6
Southern Song dynasty: art, 276, 284; sciences, 203
Spring and Autumn Annals (Chunqiu), 134–35, 136, 137, 156–57
state: and astronomy/calendars, 212, 215–16, 225–26, 228; and ecological decline, 57–60; and historiography, 141, 142, 149, 154–55; and migration, 44, 53, 54, 55–56; and religion, 241–42, 243, 262; and sciences, 204, 206–7; and trade, 52–53; and warfare, 57–58; and water management, 32–33, 34, 42, 58. *See also* political power

Staunton, George, 49
"Staying Over at White Stands Station" (Du Fu), 170–72
stereotypes. *See* essentialization
The Story of the Stone, 102
The Study of History (Shitong) (Liu Zhiji), 155
Sufism: and divinity, 246, 247; and love, 118; and political power, 81, 85, 242; proselytization, 237; religious specialists, 67, 257
sultans, 66–67, 68. *See also* Persianate culture
Suranna, Pingali, 190
Surdas, 189–90
Syriac Christianity, 234–35

Tagore, Abanindranath, 287–88, *289*
Taiping Rebellion (1850–64), 9, 90
Taizu (Ming emperor), 243–44
Takeuchi Seihō, 283
Tang dynasty: art, 270–71, *271*; and historiography, 155–56; Islam under, 237; political power, 80, 107; print culture, 181; sciences, 202, 204, 213; suppression of Buddhism, 17, 236, 243
Tang Hou, 276
Tan Qian, 148
Tarikh-i firoz shahi (Barani), 143
tarikh, 143–44
taxation, 44
technology, 75
territorial expansionism: and ecological issues/energy use, 44, 57–58; and estrangement, 21; and political power, 21, 66, 73–74, 80, 82, 83, 84–85, 90
textiles, 48–53
Thompson, E. P., 325
Thoreau, Henry David, 173

INDEX [363]

Tian (Heaven), 243, 244, 252–53. *See also* Mandate of Heaven
Tianqi emperor, 154
Tibet, 80–81, 110, 186, 336
tigers, 46, 47
Timurid empire, 9, 70–71, 76, 85, 216–17
Tod, James, 158, 159
trade: and ecological issues/energy use, 27–28, 33, 48–53, 56, 59, 60; and global exchanges, 31–32, 35, 39, 60; and modernity, 10; silver, 48–49, 51, 52, 60; state role in, 52–53; and Western penetration, 90
Travels of Marco Polo, 95–96
Tryambakayajvan, 97
Tughlak, Firoz Shah (sultan), 143
Tughluq, Muhammad bin (sultan), 68–69
Tulsidas, 186, 189
Turco-Persianate culture. *See* Persianate culture
Turner, J.M.W., 283
Tusi, Nasir al-Din, 104–5, 143, 214–15, 223
Twenty-Five Dynastic Histories (Ershiwu shi), 340

ulama, 256
Ulugh Beg, 216–17, 222
Umrao Jaan Ada, 117
United Nations Climate Change Summit (2015), 2–3
Upanishads, 242
Urdu language, 174, 188–89, 190, 191
Uttara-rama-carita (Rama's Last Act) (Bhavabhuti), 177–78

Valmiki, 176
Varahamihira, 212
Vedas, 129–30, 173, 207, 242, 255, 259

Verbiest, Ferdinand, 219, *220*
vernacularization, 64, 68, 88–89, 128, 166, 173–74, 175, 177
Veyne, Paul, 324
Vijayanagara empire, 42, 100
Vikramanka-deva-carita (Bilhana), 138
Vinayaditya I (Chalukya king), 134
Virvinod (Shyamaldas), 158–59

Wakeman, Frederic, 280
Wallerstein, Immanuel, 333
Wang Duo, 279
Wang Fuzhi, 154
Wang Honghui, 218
Wang Hui, 282
Wang Jian, 282
Wang Shimin, 282
Wang Yuanqi, 282
Wanli emperor, 154
Wan Shouqi, 280
warfare: and ecological issues/energy use, 34, 40–41, 45, 57–58; and Indian kingship models, 65–66; and technology, 75. *See also* territorial expansionism
wash. *See* haze
water management, 28–34; and agriculture, 28–31, 33; and ecological decline, 58; and political power, 41–42, 65
Western colonialism/imperialism: and gender systems, 94–96, 97, 118; and Hindu-Muslim enmity, 158; and modernity, 338–39. *See also* British India; Western penetration
Western penetration: and art, 281, 282, 283, 287, 288, 297; and astronomy/calendars, 210, 218, 219–20, 221, 223–24, 226; and China-India comparisons, 12; China overview, 8–9; and Chinese religious attitudes,

244; and conceptual categories, 329–30; and Confucianism, 239, 240, 258–59; and gender systems, 95–96; and modernity, 337–39; observation of religions, 15, 233, 239, 240, 246, 250–51, 258–59; and Opium War, 7, 9, 90, 184, 225; and religious classification, 262–63; and sciences, 225, 228–29. *See also* British India

White, Hayden, 340

widow remarriage, 118–19, 120–21

Wind among the Trees on the Riverbank (Ni Zan), 277

wolves, 47

women: and agriculture, 38; homosexuality, 114–15; and textiles, 50; writers, 102–3, 182. *See also* gender systems

world food revolution. *See* global exchanges

writing: and gender systems, 104, 106; and historiography, 129, 130, 132, 147; and literature, 179–80. *See also* language; literature

Wu Han, 161

Wu Weiye, 280

Wu Zhao (Tang empress), 107

Wu Zhen, 276

xian (immortals), 245

Xiao-Xiang landscape painting, 274, 275

Xuanzang, 6, 202, 232, 236, 241, 242, 259, 260

Xue Fengzuo, 219

yavanas, 222, 228

Ye Mengzhu, 149

yeshi (unofficial histories), 148–49

yi gu ("doubt antiquity"), 160

yin/yang, 251–52

Yokoyama Taikan, 267, 287

Yongle emperor, 141, 148, 244

Yongzheng emperor, 155, 244

Yuan dynasty: art, 276, *277*, *278*; astronomy/calendars, 211, 215–16, 217; and conquest transition, 129, 148, 208–9; gender systems, 108; and historiography, 129, 148; and language, 175; political power, 76–77; sciences, 203, 208–9, 213

Yuan Zhen, 165, 166

Yujian Rofen, 276

Yun Shouping, 279

zenana, 94, 99–100

Zen Buddhism, 261–62

Zhang Dai, 153–54

Zhang Hua, 172

Zhang Xuecheng, 156

Zhang Zhidong, 157

Zhao Kuangyin (Song emperor), 141–42

Zhao Mengfu, 276

Zhao Yi, 156

Zhou dynasty, 130, 213, 252

Zhou Xin, 249–50, 253

Zhuangzi, 171

Zhu Xi, 201, 203

Zhu Yousong (prince of Fu), 154

Zij Il-Khani, 215, 216, 217

Zij Jadid Sultani, 217, 220

Zij Muhammad Shahi (Jaisingh), 223, 224

Zij Shah Jahan, 221

Zoroastrianism, 239

Zuo Commentary (*Zuozhuan*), 135, 136

GPSR Authorized Representative: Easy Access System Europe, Mustamäe tee
50, 10621 Tallinn, Estonia, gpsr.requests@easproject.com